S0-ATF-020

ROCKMONT COLLEGE LIBRARY

Men in Business

Men in Business

Essays on the

Historical Role of the Entrepreneur

With two additional essays on American
business leaders by William Miller,
not included in the original edition

GREENWOOD PRESS, PUBLISHERS
WESTPORT, CONNECTICUT

Library of Congress Cataloging in Publication Data

Miller, William, 1912-   ed.
    Men in business.

    Reprint of the 1962 ed. published by Harper &
Row, New York.
    Bibliography: p.
    1. Capitalists and financiers--United States--
Biography. 2. Entrepreneur--Biography. I. Title.
[HF3023.A2M5   1979]   338'.092'2 [B] 78-21159
ISBN 0-313-20867-0

Copyright 1952 by the President and Fellows of Harvard
College
"The Recruitment of the American Business Elite"
copyright 1950 by the President and Fellows of Harvard
College "American Historians and the Business Elite"
copyright 1949 by the Economic History Association

This book was originally published in 1952 by Harvard
University Press and is here reprinted by arrangement.
Two essays by William Miller have been added to the
TORCHBOOK edition: "American Historians and the
Business Elite" which appeared in *The Journal of
Economic History*, Vol. IX, No. 2, November 1949, and
"The Recruitment of the American Business Elite" which
appeared in *The Quarterly Journal of Economics*, Vol.
LXIV, No. 2, May 1950. These essays are reprinted by
arrangement.

First Harper Torchbook edition published 1962 by
Harper & Row, Publishers, Incorporated, New York
and Evanston.

Reprinted with the permission of Harvard University
Press.

Reprinted in 1979 by Greenwood Press, Inc.
51 Riverside Avenue, Westport, CT 06880

Printed in the United States of America

10 9 8 7 6 5 4 3 2 1

ROCKMONT COLLEGE LIBRARY

38155

Contents

Preface

To the Torchbook Edition

By William Miller

The Editor of this book welcomes the opportunity to write for a new and wider audience a new Preface to a volume that may have seemed a maverick when first published a decade or so ago, but which has since won solid respect in the fields of history, economics, and sociology. Its own particular field, which we once called "entrepreneurial history," undertook to bridge these different disciplines, and others, such as psychology and anthropology. By employing the best that social science had to offer, entrepreneurial history sought especially to further the understanding of one of the principal institutions of modern life, the free business system.

That entrepreneurial history succeeded in its mission is not for me to say. But I assert with full confidence that its approach to history remains undeniably sound; and if one added to its predilection for social science a preference, too, for those engaging unscientific features of history in general—I mean imagination, judgment, and art—one would have the full kit for understanding man in his universe, so far as he can be understood. This preference for imagination, judgment, and art was rarely acknowledged by the strict entrepreneurial historians with whom I was associated at Harvard University for a few years before the initial publication of this book. But I here take the liberty to acknowledge it for them, and to suggest to the reader that he will find these essays at once enlightening, intellectually stimulating, and a pleasure to read. I am aware that essays of my own appear in this volume. But I am speaking of *my* pleasure in the others.

It is also most pleasing for me to note (in the order of their authors' appearance in the Table of Contents) at least those books, all issued by Harvard University Press, which grew directly out of certain essays first published here, and which elaborate the themes and approach here developed:

David S. Landes, *Bankers and Pashas* (1958)
Hugh G. J. Aitken, *The Welland Canal Company* (1954)
Harold C. Passer, *The Electrical Manufacturers 1875–1900* (1953)
Alfred D. Chandler, Jr., *Henry Varnum Poor* (1956)

I am also obliged to record here the death, some years ago, of Robert K. Lamb, before he could bring to fruition his strikingly original work on New England entrepreneurs, which is referred to in the Introduction to the Original Edition as being under way. Death also cut short the brilliant career of a still younger man, R. Richard Wohl.

The Research Center in Entrepreneurial History at Harvard, the sponsor of the present work, had a ten-year life, from 1948 to 1958. Its organization was foreshadowed, most pertinently, in the presidential address to the Economic History Association in 1946,* by Arthur H. Cole, now Professor of Business Economics *Emeritus* at Harvard. From start to finish, Professor Cole was the leading spirit of the Center. That his work in furthering entrepreneurial history did not flag with the closing of the Center is suggested by the publication by Harvard University Press in 1959 of his book, *Business Enterprise in its Social Setting.* That the work of the Center itself continues, despite the end of its formal organization, is also attested by the continuing publication, in its spirit, of important new books and articles by the writers represented in this volume, and by such others as Fritz Redlich, Thomas C. Cochran, and Leland H. Jenks, once the Center's strength. Their articles in particular now grace numerous scholarly journals in appropriately widely distributed fields; and perhaps it is a good thing that they reach widely dispersed audiences. But for the ten years of the Center's life it also published a journal, *Explorations in Entrepreneurial History,* of which I need only say that those fortunate enough to possess it treasure it; while those who do not, offer a king's ransom for the set.

A few technical notes may be in order here:

(1) The "Foreword" to the original edition by Professor Cole, and the "Introduction" by the Editor remain as they first appeared.

(2) The "locations" of the different authors noted on the original Contents pages are also unchanged. Any updating would surely itself soon be out of date. And in any case it was deemed worthwhile to retain, as stated, the identification of the Research Center in Entrepreneurial His-

* Published in Supplement VI, 1946, of *The Journal of Economic History,* pp. 1–15.

tory at Harvard as the then principal home of a number of the contributors.

(3) Only the merest few mechanical changes have been made in the text itself, and these only the more smoothly to accommodate references to two essays of my own which, with the cooperation of the original publisher of *Men in Business*, the original publishers of the essays themselves, and Harper Torchbooks, I have been privileged to append here. These essays lay the essential foundations for my *Men in Business* essay on "the business elite," and I hope they will contribute to the value of the Torchbook edition. I hereby wish to acknowledge permission to reprint these essays, granted respectively by *The Journal of Economic History*, and *The Quarterly Journal of Economics*.

West Redding, Connecticut
February, 1962

Foreword

To the Original Edition

The Research Center in Entrepreneurial History has, I believe, served a distinctly useful purpose in helping to make the present volume possible. Other fields of scientific investigation have gone through stages or experiences similar to those of the Center: the blocking-out of an area by a few, often mature scholars; the drafting of tentative hypotheses — as in our *Change and the Entrepreneur*; and then the search for younger men who will improve on these hypotheses, who will supply empirical data that will substantiate the earlier or the improved theses, and who will continue over the years to advance research and teaching in the general subject. Such a novel and complicated field as entrepreneurial history would soon become sterile if it were constrained by the ideas or schema of its first advocates — even those of our late colleague, Professor Schumpeter, whose concepts gave the early impetus to our work. It must grow and change — and the senior members of the Center may look hopefully to the contributors to this volume to constitute leaders in the improvement of our commonly won territory.

As the editor explains in greater fullness, the volume possesses both a unity and a diversity. All the essays contribute to an illumination of the history of entrepreneurship — that important but often neglected element in economic change — but they bear upon several aspects of that history. A volume upon entrepreneurial history is a real contribution to scholarship, since so little scientific inquiry has occurred in this field. And a book presenting various facets of the subject is also desirable, inasmuch as students in economics and sociology may thereby be drawn to make common cause with historians in the exploitation of this (and cognate) fields of scientific inquiry. Diversity helps to suggest the fruitfulness of our approach in the analysis of varied historical facts and situations.

It is then with real pride that I commend this volume to our friends, and to all who are interested in the scientific examination of businessmen in their social milieu — or, to look at the theme the other way, of social beings in a business milieu, of "men in business."

ARTHUR H. COLE

Introduction

To the Original Edition

By William Miller

"Every economist knows — if he did not, he could not help learning it from conversation with businessmen. . ." So wrote the late Professor Schumpeter in introducing a point in his brilliant essay on Keynes. The professor's irony here was typical. Economists as a rule talk with businessmen about as often as theories of economic activity and economic development take account of actual business behavior — and, Schumpeter was saying, so much the worse for most theories.

In the present book, business and businessmen are kept continually in the foreground. Common to all of these essays is the assumption that in the making of the western world in modern times business has been a prodigious force. The purpose of these essays is to further our understanding of this world and these times by studying the history of business and, insofar as this may be said of men in relation to social forces, the history of businessmen who ruled it.

It follows, of course, that there are no panegyrics here. To write of individual entrepreneurs, as some of these writers do, and not at the same time of the actual societies that molded them and which they simultaneously helped to shape, is to treat unimaginatively of imaginary men. In this book will be found accounts of many kinds of men, but none in splendid isolation. Here will be found accounts of the relations of business to a number of different societies, but none on almost deserted islands.

If business has been a force making for great social change and material progress in the modern western world, it has been most potent in America. It is fitting, therefore, that this book be occupied preponderantly with men in business in the United States. Eight of these eleven essays are almost wholly concerned with this country. This major theme, however, is given perspective by the first three essays, which focus respectively upon business and businessmen in France, Egypt, and Canada.

Much of the intellectual climate of this book is felt in the opening essay, by John E. Sawyer, the thesis of which is that the forms and pace of French business life and the hopes of French businessmen even now reflect sanctions and structures derived from the predominant social organization of France in the distant past. Sawyer makes explicit just what these sanctions and structures are and with what consequences for business enterprise — mainly inhibiting ones — they continue to work. "Manorial-ism," "feudalism," and similar concepts, he says, while redolent of a way of life long since gone, remain relevant indeed to understanding France today. In a concluding section he points up his thesis by sketching the contrasting social environment that has so stimulated business activity in the United States.

Where Sawyer's emphasis is on the "total social situation," David Landes', in the second essay, is on a particular international coterie of financiers and their operations in Egypt in the third quarter of the nine-teenth century. By means of a remarkable series of business letters which he recently found abroad, Landes is able to juxtapose the modern aspira-tions of an ancient patrimonial court to the ambitions — conflicting ones since the businessmen involved each had his own distinct social inheritance — of European bankers and promoters. The result is an extraordinarily detailed mosaic of the complex and shifting motivations of modern entre-preneurs, disclosed in the writings of the entrepreneurs themselves.

From the Mediterranean we move, in the essay on Canada by Hugh G. J. Aitken, to the austere and primitive environment of Lake Ontario and the St. Lawrence River. Here, early in the nineteenth century, we find a small up-country grain merchant frustrated by the colonial status and frontier condition of his country. In order to free a whole generation of businessmen like himself from handicaps that had forced him, almost at the outset of his career, to an ignominious settlement with creditors, this merchant became canal builder, orator, promoter, lobbyist, and ultimately a notable statesman. In his society, these activities were all part of the role of businessman.

These three essays on entrepreneurship abroad, by suggesting the range of actual business behavior and the force of different cultures in channel-ing such behavior, serve admirably as a kaleidoscopic background for the American story. They do more than that. For each has a theme found also in the business history of the United States, and thus is of value for com-parisons and contrasts.

Among the essays on the United States, Robert K. Lamb's is the most general one and the one most explicitly concerned with method in entre-preneurial history, just as Sawyer's is the most general one, and the one most concerned with method, on entrepreneurship abroad. Lamb's theme is the persistent and intimate relationship of entire national, regional, and local communities to specific instances of entrepreneurial behavior. He discusses in detail certain aspects of this relationship as seen in the devel-opment of the American cotton textile industry starting soon after the Revolutionary War. The specific connections Lamb shows among the Hamiltonian nationalists, the New England regionalists, and the particular textile developments in local New England towns suggests a major rewriting of American history in the Constitutional and early national period, which he, in fact, has under way.

Lamb's Fall River, clearly, is not Lille; nor is his Providence Rouen; nor his Boston, Paris. Yet as in the older France described by Sawyer, so in the America described by Lamb, businessmen's dynastic aspirations (along with other motivations, of course) are seen as affecting the founding of new firms, the spread of technological innovations, the rate of expansion of family enterprises. Miss Dorothy Gregg's essay on Colonel John Stevens (he won this rank during the Revolutionary War) supplements Lamb's work on the dynastic theme in America and may also be compared with Landes' Egyptian study. The state and federal governments which Stevens, his partners, and his rivals in steamboating early in the nineteenth century all wooed assiduously for franchises and other favors were hardly prototypes of the Pasha's court of fifty years later. Yet both Landes and Miss Gregg are concerned with the intimate relation of government and private business enterprise, especially in the field of relatively costly internal improvements.

The experiences of William Hamilton Merritt, Aitken's Canadian merchant-statesman-zealot, and those of Henry Noble Day, the Connecticut cleric turned Ohio speculator (as related in R. Richard Wohl's essay), also had more in common than may at first appear. Wohl reports a business debacle that, in the name of Christian good works and under the direction of one so trained that only by religious precepts could he act, almost ruined the excellent Day family whose head had always branded business the devil's game. But more than zeal, what Day and Merritt shared was a host of problems raised by frontier business life, problems which eventually forced both at critical junctures to call upon seaboard family connections for aid. In Merritt's case this aid helped him to his future business and public career. In the case of Day, it furthered his return to the callings of churchman and educator, for which he had been trained. Though Wohl's narrative stresses Henry Noble Day's projects, underlying them all was Day's personality, and how this was formed in extremely conservative Connecticut and how it was preserved in its full integrity in Ohio is the real subject of Wohl's work.

The Bordens and Durfees, Slaters and Browns, Cabots and Lowells of Lamb's essay; the Stevenses, Alexanders, Coxes, and Livingstons of Miss Gregg's paper; the Days of Wohl's study, all were born into upper class families or favored their heirs with this useful endowment. This suggests that while upward mobility was greater in the United States than in most of the countries of Europe, social stratification here as abroad affected the recruitment of business leaders. This suggestion is strengthened by the findings reported by Miss Frances W. Gregory and Miss Irene D. Neu in their paper on the social origins of approximately three hundred of the topmost men in American industry in the 1870's. Discussion of social stratification and its relation to opportunity is not uncommon in writings about Europe. The paper by Miss Gregory and Miss Neu is a significant addition to the discussion of the subject in the United States. If too much has been written about the Robber Baron character of American business in their period, insufficient stress, it would appear, has been given to the baronial part of the epithet.

Comparisons and contrasts with the history of entrepreneurship abroad heighten the meaning of the American story. The ever more important place of the United States in the world in the past two centuries, and of business in the United States, however, gives a special value to the American essays mentioned and to those by Harold C. Passer, Douglass North, and Alfred D. Chandler, Jr., which follow them. The latter three differ from some of the earlier ones in focusing less on the general environment and the pervasive social consequences of entrepreneurship — though these subjects are inescapable here as elsewhere — and more on special aspects of it in technological, financial, and managerial matters.

Passer's subject, Frank Julian Sprague, was an entrepreneur who founded numerous firms but was altogether without dynastic ambitions. He made considerable money but was scarcely motivated by opportunities for profit. He was associated with big corporations but was unconcerned with the problems of bureaucratic administration. Yet Sprague was eminently practical. A genius in the adaptation of the latest technological innovations to the needs of rapidly growing cities late in the nineteenth century, he made possible extensive systems of electric surface transportation, electric elevated and subway lines, electric passenger elevators. These developments were on the way in any case; Sprague certainly speeded their adoption. As a factor in economic change, but especially in the timing of it, his career is worthy of intensive study.

The life insurance magnates who are the subjects of North's essay were as inventive in finance as Sprague was in technology. Life insurance was one way for the growing number of propertyless inhabitants of industrial societies to save their families from destitution on the demise of the working members. Traditionally, therefore, as North says, "the function of a life insurance company was limited simply to providing family protection at its mathematically ascertained cost." After the Civil War, however, the growth of life insurance coincided with the colossal growth in the capital requirements of American industry. To help supply these requirements, certain life insurance companies, with the aid and comfort of politicians, rewrote their policies and altered their selling practices. How they did this, at considerable cost to their policyholders and at the cost of ultimate scandal to themselves, is North's story.

The new technology and new finance in the latter part of the nineteenth century speeded the growth of vast new enterprises and of business bureaucracies to administer them. Chandler's essay on Henry Varnum Poor, however, shows how the manifold problems of bureaucratic business administration were apparent, to one with Poor's vision, as early as the 1850's, when the corporation first became popular as a business device and corporate ownership and management became severed. Poor was a Transcendentalist who saw in the building of the American railroad network the prospect of the perfection of man's life on earth. To help give direction to this momentous development, he acquired the *American Railway Journal* in 1849. After his Civil War activities and a short experience in actual railroad work, he began to publish his railroad *Manuals* in 1868. But more than these, Poor's early grasp of the problems of entrepreneurship in the bureaucratic firm, and his articulateness about them, as Chandler discloses it, are what make him of extraordinary interest today.

In my own essay on business bureaucracies in the twentieth century, some of the same problems are discussed in relation to developments of recent times. The organization and effective administration of huge business enterprises itself takes talent of the first magnitude. But this essay, like other writing on management problems today, raises the question as to whether the achievement of orderliness in the functioning of complex private business corporations does not itself act as a brake on private entrepreneurship. For entrepreneurship by its nature abhors channels. In the past, as these essays show, it has tended to be individualistic, innovative, venturesome.

Each of the essays in this book stands squarely by itself. Yet all are also part of the same story, that of men in business in the western world in modern times, and all share a similar frame of reference. Though each essay is a study in history, almost half are by writers who are practicing economists, if not economic theorists. In this group are Aitken, Lamb, Miss Gregg, Passer, and North. Wohl is an economic sociologist. Sawyer, Landes, Miss Gregory and Miss Neu, Chandler, and myself are historians. None, however, respects the sanctity of academic borders. The work of all reflects developments in psychology stemming especially from George Herbert Mead; in sociology from Max Weber; in economics from Schumpeter.

General theories of personality and of society, like general theories of economic activity and economic development, have contributed to all of these essays. Some writers have addressed themselves to new questions raised by such general theories. Others have been directed to new materials by them. Still others have borrowed techniques of analysis. Yet none is a slave to such theories. General theorists, David Hume pointed out long ago, often forget the "vast variety which nature has affected in her operations." Such theorists tend to reify a few abstractions. History tends to be as concrete and as varied as life itself. If it borrows from general theories, it also serves as a check upon them and as a starting point for new speculations. The variety of the essays in the present volume reflects the potential range of entrepreneurial history and its potential uses to theory. The concreteness of these essays reflects entrepreneurial history's freedom from dogma.

I

The Entrepreneur and the Social Order

France and the United States

By John E. Sawyer

For as long as "one of the oldest of the arts and youngest of the professions" [1] has been practiced, men have been struck by the contrasting ways in which business has been conducted in different parts of the world. Yet for all its interest the subject from the beginning has been left largely to chroniclers — in earlier times to the tellers of tales of Persia, Venice, and Cathay; in our day to the accounts of travelers, traders, or government administrators recording in awe or anguish the varying behavior of businessmen in Rome or Paris, Hong Kong, Rio, or even Kansas City.

Our world, however, can no longer afford to leave to anecdote the problem of why men in business behave so differently all over the globe. It cannot today be satisfied with the simpler evolutionary optimisms inherited from the Enlightenment. Nor can it accept a tendency to set the problem aside as reducible to deterministic explanations based on relatively stable "objective" factors such as climate, race, resources, or markets; or as unknowable, an inscrutable mystery forever to be left in a limbo of "cultural differences." The social disruptions of recent decades have produced a world newly concerned with the whole problem of economic development. This has confronted scholars, administrators, and men in business with the need to understand the operation of complex social and cultural factors affecting the dynamics of business behavior. [2]

The study of entrepreneurial behavior does not yet lend itself to precision. It involves questions and considerations beyond the limits of the restrictive assumptions within which the science of economics has focused its major efforts and achieved its greatest successes; it clearly requires a social theory that will incorporate socio-psychological categories into the analysis of economic processes. While as yet no analytical frame has satisfactorily resolved these problems, the newer social sciences offer helpful approaches. As aids to comparative analysis, these sciences can help us attain a better understanding of entrepreneurial recruitment, motivation, and behavior; of the entrepreneurial role itself; and of its relation to economic development in different situations.

II

No one can study entrepreneurship without becoming aware, in addition to the work of Sombart and Weber, of the major contribution of the late Joseph A. Schumpeter. The creative entrepreneurial function was indeed "the central tower of Schumpeter's structure, and the rest of the building [was] designed to emphasize its impressiveness." [3] Both in the thrust that he gave to the whole idea of the entrepreneur's place in modern economic history and in his emphasis on the social relationships involved in its exercise, he was himself the innovator, the entrepreneur of entrepreneurial theory. Few other economists have, in fact, more powerfully driven home the interaction of economic behavior and social institutions; and no other major body of economic theory has attempted so to focus the dynamics of economic development in a single category of economic agents.

It is not necessary, however, to accept *in toto* the Schumpeterian construct of the entrepreneurial function or his arbitrary definition of the entrepreneur. Empirically it proves extremely difficult, for all but polar instances, to separate the "creative" from the "adaptive" response; and the point at which managerial functions shade into innovation is a judgment better left to the artist.[4] For our purposes it is enough to get general agreement on the particular importance of entrepreneurial behavior in the growth of the kinds of economies we are talking about: market-oriented economies characterized by private ownership, in which decision-making is decentralized (as to production, marketing and investment) and in which the technology is notably dynamic.

Whatever the entrepreneur's significance in other times and places,[5] the historical and institutional situation classically represented by nineteenth-century England or by the United States well into this century, tended to give him a unique role in the working of the economy. It concentrated a critical range of economic functions in the hands of individual decision-makers under conditions unusually favorable as to social context and entrepreneurial opportunity. Changes and discontinuities in economic activity — new products, methods, markets, resources, and combinations — were overwhelmingly introduced by individual producers or merchants, as differentiated from the play of community, consumer initiative, or bureaucratic planning.[6] In greater or less degree this situation prevailed during the growth of industrial capitalism over the western world in the period between Adam Smith and the Great Depression, the period with which we are concerned.

Such an economic order gives special significance to the question of entrepreneurial motivation. Again it is not necessary to press to extreme the particular monetary rewards that Schumpeter sometimes held indispensable to the flowering of entrepreneurial effort, in order to agree with his emphasis on the importance of "bourgeois motivation in the explanation of the economic history of the last two or three centuries."[7] That the forces entering into this motivation were wider than mere monetary returns, Schumpeter well knew. Speaking "as an economic sociologist," he again and again invoked the influences of the drive to do, to win, to create, to found a dynasty, a private kingdom; "the will to conquer; the impulse to fight, to prove oneself superior to others, to succeed for the sake, not of the fruits of success but of success itself."[8]

These Schumpeterian insights point the way, and the developing sciences of social behavior are opening up possibilities of more systematic analysis. One of the most useful of these approaches for our purposes focuses attention on the extent to which the motivation and behavior associated with any particular role are functions of the total social structure. Observable national differences in entrepreneurial activity, for example, cannot be accounted for in terms of economic factors alone, or in terms of the hero in history, the distribution of genes, or any simple psychological reductionism.[9] These differences cannot be explained without reference to the system of goals and values, the scale of social rankings and the patterns of conduct that are "institutionalized" in the particular society.[10]

The individual entrepreneur, like all other social actors, is oriented to this total social situation. The range of decisions he will normally consider, and his evaluation of the alternatives thus defined are functions of it. In large measure he acts in terms of prevailing patterns of aspirations and conduct, the system of roles and statuses that from birth have been absorbed and inculcated, consciously and unconsciously. These established goals and the prescribed means of achieving them are supported both by positive social rewards and by negative sanctions ranging from ridicule to ostracism. In the process any particular society will necessarily select, develop, and reward (and, conversely, discourage) certain personality types and traits for certain roles — a selective operation that inevitably affects entrepreneurship.[11]

The entrepreneur probably is peculiarly sensitive to the *generalized* goals and status relationships of his society, in that he is almost by definition less bound by objective necessity or by specific skills or courses of action than are most other economic actors. To the extent that he has latitude to choose and act, in some measure to create his own economic situation, to the extent that he does "innovate" and break through the established framework (the Schumpeterian circular flow), his actions point up questions of motivation and behavior that cannot be answered without reference to the social order.

The focus of this paper, then, is on the ways in which different societies, with differing interests, attitudes, systems of stratification, and the like, operate to produce different kinds of businessmen and different patterns of entrepreneurial behavior. In these terms we will compare specific elements in the social structures and cultural traditions of France and the United States which are directly relevant to entrepreneurship.

To concentrate here on these influences of social structure is not to argue their autonomy or their adequacy as an explanation of economic behavior. So-called objective factors in large measure frame all economic activity. The entrepreneur must act within limits set by available resources, income levels, and so forth, and differences here are fundamental to the scope of entrepreneurial opportunities. But early in such a list social factors must appear. Any important change in the objective situation presses itself upon the social order, the more so if abrupt; and while some parts of the social structure show a high resistance to change — peasant attitudes, for example — others are relatively responsive to alterations in the economic situation.[12] Our interest is not to set one against the other, but rather to observe certain ways in which social and cultural factors operate in and on economic processes.

III

Studies involving obvious as well as subtle contrasts are needed in the effort to understand the effects of social structure on business behavior. Given the relatively primitive methods of analysis now at hand, examples from Europe and America offer certain advantages. They involve peoples who have belonged to a common Western Christian civilization and in large measure shared a common world view, a similar frame of rational-legal forms, and the basic institutional requisites of capitalist development (transferability of resources, free labor, et cetera). They fulfill the economic conditions described above as giving the entrepreneur a role of special significance. Yet they present contrasts of social structure and business behavior sufficiently conspicuous to allow of fairly rough abstraction and simplification without imperiling the main lines of evidence or argument. The differences are such that national terms of reference like "France" or "the American entrepreneur" can be used with some meaning for comparative purposes, though necessarily neglecting an infinite range of local and personal variations.[13]

In the New World the United States before the Great Depression provided an instance of something like a golden age of Schumpeterian entrepreneurship. In the Old World each country bears the special imprint of its geography and history and each has its special claim to speak for Europe. For our purposes France has the advantages of the very completeness of her adaptation to the earlier European social orders,[14] of standing near the middle of the European spread in the growth of industrial capitalism, and of remaining a country where entrepreneurial responses continue to be of critical economic importance.[15] Any European-American comparisons of course involve gross contrasts in physical terms — in the size and scope of a virgin continent, geographical isolation, lateness of development, and so forth — that are basic to any comprehensive analysis. But differences of a corresponding order exist in the social structures into which industrialism came.

The most fundamental of these differences derive from the existence in the Old World of a pre-industrial pre-commercial social order that shaped the lives of men for about a thousand years. The set of institutions loosely described by words like manorialism and feudalism has left its impress on Europe and Europeans to this day and it undoubtedly will for centuries to come. A relatively stabilized society historically rooted in seigniorial agriculture established a formally stratified hereditary class system, taking as fixed given horizons and a given hierarchical ranking of statuses based on birth, land, and localism.[16] The institutional system tied occupation and property to family units proudly conscious of their status and identity over successive generations; and emphasized traditional, personal, and communal relationships, as against the impersonality, universalism, individualism, and conscious rationality characteristic of a wide range of capitalist institutions.

The beliefs and values of the medieval world gave divine sanction to this hierarchical structure, fixing men in the status and income to which they were born as part of the Grand Plan. The system of ideas powerfully mobilized sentiments for traditionalism and continuity as against change, mobility, and innovation. The body of values was notably inhospitable to trade and the trader.[17] Lay society, dominated by a nobility geared to the values of land, rank, and family, arms, honor, and excellence, tended to be contemptuous of the kind of aggressive commercial behavior functionally inherent to an expanding capitalism. Catholic doctrine, to be sure, progressively modified its Augustinian view that "Business is in itself an evil, for it turns men from seeking true rest, which is God," and came to provide for a wide measure of capitalist activity. Yet, as Tawney has said, "finance and trade . . . never fitted harmoniously into the medieval synthesis."[18] However much a St. Thomas or a later St. Antoninus might reformulate the Christian code in recognition of developing economic practices, Catholicism never provided the emerging entrepreneur with that positive drive to achievement in this world, that fortifying ethic for systematic business activity, which Calvinism later supplied.[19] Enthusiasts may exaggerate the play of the Protestant ethic, but it appears to be increasingly evident that the non-empirical attitudes toward work and "advancement" that are deeply embedded in a culture have very far-reaching effects on economic behavior.[20]

To the extent that commerce and manufacture did become separated from the manorial system and develop in the medieval town, they were still profoundly shaped by this general social frame. Here too the institutions and ideas of traditionalism and community, and a web of personalized social and economic relationships long resisted the revolutionary changes implicit in the new activities. Ideally, and in large measure actually, merchant associations and craft guilds determined products and prices, controlled the number of producers, and protected them in the income, station, and function appropriate to their place in the Christian Commonwealth.

All the countries of the Old World have carried forward elements of this European past. New economic foundations subsequently have come into being and with them a range of new social institutions. But the new still lives with a mixed heritage of the old. The very force of the Marxist insight into the shattering impact of new modes of production on old institutions and relationships has obscured the extent to which the new is itself molded by the old. Outer forms have gone, but nowhere have the habits and attitudes associated with them been totally eradicated. The new has grown within what it only partially destroyed.

All over Western Europe commercial capitalism and bourgeois institutions broke through the forms of feudalism and in varying measure came to prevail. The accompanying corrosives of rationalism and secularism have not less deeply cut into traditional values, symbols, and relationships. Yet behind these changes in forms and attitudes there have lingered widely diffused elements of the "feudal" heritage. Everywhere these differential feudal survivals have influenced patterns of industrialization and entrepreneurship. The way in which European businessmen have conducted their daily activities and responded to new techniques, new economic forms, and new opportunities has been fundamentally conditioned by the presence of traditionalistic survivals in the social structure.[21]

Pronounced national and regional differences require separate treatment. The continuing English and German feudal and imperial traditions illustrate ways in which certain feudal survivals could be compatible and even favorable to industrial development — for example, in the association of industrialization and national military power, or in the effect of large estates on the labor supply, the disposition to accept discipline, bigness, concentrations of power, and the like.

The French case offers striking testimony to the tenacity of inherited patterns. Here the old institutional structure was most violently assaulted; here more than anywhere else in Europe new ideas and institutions emerged triumphant in the Revolution and Republic. France remained the center from which they radiated throughout nineteenth-century Europe. Yet France too carried forward elements of the European past that have remained widely diffused to this day. Over the centuries when commercial capitalism was enlarging its place in the national life, a series of historical turnings kept peculiarly alive aristocratic values and patterns: First by reversing developments pointing toward a coalescence of old status groups with new economic functions along lines of the English model;[22] and then by perpetuating an aristocracy, more numerous than most, that increasingly stressed the honors, privileges, and vanities of rank as its functions diminished.[23]

The traditional elite, further identifying itself during the *ancien régime* with national ideals and symbols — majesty, rank, military glory, individual distinction, culture, style — managed over the centuries to "feudalize" elements of the upper bourgeoisie. Important segments of the *haute bourgeoisie* took on parts of the code and in many cases the juridical status of nobility.[24] Thereby, large numbers in business as well as the professions — through inclusion or aspiration — acquired a vested interest in a whole set of traditional institutional patterns. Moreover there was relatively little of the reverse of this process. The nobility discouraged entrance of its sons into trade; and the French bourgeoisie never gained a control of government and the fisc, a position of social prestige, or a dominance of the national capital comparable to that of the merchants of London.[25]

Other institutional complexes have also clearly had their influence on French entrepreneurship and might be separately analyzed. Here we can mention only three of the most significant: (1) A strong centralized state, combining policies of protection focused on national power,[26] and a bureaucratic tradition elaborated by a variety of regimes from the time of Philip the Fair, with an arbitrary and often irresponsible fisc; (2) the artificial perpetuation of the institutions of petty-bourgeois capitalism and peasant agriculture, enshrined in the revolutionary settlement and the Republic — maintaining in agriculture a protected system of small proprietors that has held surplus labor on the land, and in manufacture and trade "the most individualistic economy in Europe," a system built around small units, small volume, and small horizons;[27] (3) the growth in modern times of Marxist and related movements and ideologies that have mobilized deep and pervasive anticapitalist sentiments against business and the businessman, in an increasingly unstable political frame.

While these and other institutional systems have had significant consequences for French businessmen, the thesis being developed here can perhaps best be illustrated by examining the impress on entrepreneurship of survivals from the preëxisting social structure reviewed earlier.

IV

The impact of this heritage may be seen in examining, even in a very generalized way, each of the problems posed at the outset — entrepreneurial recruitment, motivation, and behavior.[28]

1. *In terms of recruitment*, inherited institutional patterns have operated restrictively in two quite different ways. First they have discouraged the flow of Schumpeter's "strong wills and strong intellects" into business careers and especially into certain kinds of business. And second they have tended to close off economic positions at the top as the special preserve of selected kinship groups.

The persistence of diffused feudal values and goals has meant that business has not been the "natural" choice of those enjoying the greatest advantages, either of birth or of talent and training.[29] In so far as an occupation was in order at all, the ablest tended to follow the well born into careers in the elite services, diplomatic and military, the ranking civil service positions like finance, or the professions, politics, journalism, the arts. All these fields have drawn from those most gifted, those most motivated by "the joy of creating, of getting things done, or simply of exercising one's energy and ingenuity."[30]

These orientations have also led to the partial or complete withdrawal from business of successful entrepreneurs or their more talented sons. In these cases individuals have sought to lay the basis for future personal satisfactions and social rewards by diverting money and time to the chateau and its style of life, or by financing a son's career in the elite services or in professions offering possibilities of slow assimilation to hereditary prestige groups.[31] An example of the resistances to achieving this social acceptance more directly appears in the remark of the politician Gambetta to the future Edward VII, that if the French Republic were to make noblemen of successful businessmen, as Britain had done, "Le Duc de la Roche-Qui-Mousse would never mingle with the Duke of Industry."[32]

Traditional social values have also affected the distribution of entrepreneurial recruitment within business. In general the social standing of economic activity in France has varied inversely in proportion to its distance from land and military power and (arts and crafts apart) directly in proportion to its distance from the customer. Thus, after wealth based on land itself, those activities stood highest in the scale which drew directly on the land, like mining, iron-making and glass-making (both tied to the forests in their earlier technology), along with high finance and maritime and colonial trade. Though some crafts and craftsmen enjoyed high social standing, manufacturing in general did not win great esteem, and the retail trades and services came near the bottom of the prestige scale.[33] This pattern, while never as absolute or uniform as a brief statement may suggest, has unquestionably affected recruitment as between fields, and contributed to the conspicuous failure of French entrepreneurship in distribution, marketing, and trade in almost all its forms.[34]

Social structure has also significantly restricted entrepreneurial recruitment in a second way, by reserving higher levels of economic activity to certain family dynasties or interlocking social groups. The latter frequently have taken over these positions and interests much like hereditary fiefs. Few have engaged in the wine trade of Bordeaux or the silk industry of Lyons, for example, without belonging to certain kinship groups; and a whole range of important financial activities has been a special province of allied families forming what is familiarly known as the "H.S.P." (*haute société protestante*). Of the six bankers who were among the Regents of the Bank of France in 1936, five were descendants of the great financiers of the First Empire;[35] and many of the major firms and fields have been in the same families and sometimes have been run exclusively by members of a single family for more than a century.

At far lower and wider levels where local families have become rooted in given lines, succession has also tended to follow automatically within the kinship group. In a relatively stabilized society this principle of family control and continuity has served to limit recruitment and possibilities of entrance into the business role.

In the most general terms the social heritage has meant that French entrepreneurship has not been able to recruit almost automatically those who from interest and ability seek the channels of community leadership. The French business role has never become established between a declining aristocracy and a rising socialism as commanding this sort of prestige or respect. The business community has never caught the popular imagination or loyalty, never become accepted as a "legitimate" elite in and of itself. This has deeply affected not only recruitment, but motivation and behavior as well.

2. *In terms of motivation,* those who have occupied the business role

have reacted to inherited patterns in many ways. A society that has never consciously made increasing output or productivity or even higher standards of living a primary goal has naturally not generated that dedication to business activity that has marked American entrepreneurship. The French businessman has never been stimulated by an identification with national goals and ideals; and individual entrepreneurial aspirations have tended to be defined more in terms of differential class goals than of boundless economic achievement.

The inherited system of social stratification has tended to undercut the drive to unlimited entrepreneurial success. The middle- and upper-class world revealed in French fiction, in extreme form in Proust's *Swann's Way*, living within fairly fixed horizons and pegging each family in its place in an ordered hierarchy, offered considerable social resistance to the parvenu. New wealth and power might with proper aging benefit succeeding generations, but a code of "to each according to his station" offered the entrepreneurial "success" fairly limited immediate social rewards. The self-made man has not been a hero in France. And to have gained success at the expense of established interests and accepted social position was to invite widespread hostility from above and below. Such institutional patterns (whether judged good or bad) have operated against the motivation to bold and aggressive entrepreneurship, against pushing and the pusher.

Furthermore the purely economic rewards of entrepreneurial success have been less significant, socially and culturally, in France than in the United States. While property and assured income are extremely important in French society, inherited patterns of values tend to reduce the significance of earned money income either as a symbol of success or, beyond a certain point, as providing "the good life." Even where consumption patterns have departed from the tradition of the landed gentleman, they have continued to center more about personal services and recreation, leisure and cultivation, then about visible expenditure on the newest durables. The differential nature of class goals and symbols has also worked to prevent the establishment of money as a general measure of status. The social order in France has thus in some measure undervalued the very prizes and penalties that have urged on the capitalist process.

The drive to entrepreneurial innovation has also been less active in a society heavily weighted in economic fields towards tradition and continuity, a society slow to adapt to economic change, slow to receive many of the products of mass production (as against hand craftsmanship) and slower still to accept the new methods and relationships involved. Psychological and cultural resistances to mechanization, and the cheapness of labor and services have alike made for continuation of established means and forms. The motivation to remain within the circular flow has been notably stronger, the incentives to innovate correspondingly weaker.

The carry-over of inherited family patterns into the important part of French business that has become identified with particular families has also strikingly affected entrepreneurial motivation. Given the structure of the family as an enduring entity enjoying an established place, the motivation has typically been to run the business so as to assure the preservation over time of the family status and the family honor involved in it.[36] Variously combined with bourgeois patterns, this has motivated businessmen toward caution, thrift, security, tradition, avoidance of risk — toward running the business as an annuity, maximizing security rather than profits, growth, output, or any combination thereof. The direct influence of institutional patterns derived from the past, reinforced by peasant and bourgeois influences, has been evident in the fierce identification of property with the family, the clinging to inheritance, the horror of loss, the view of bankruptcy as a lasting stain on the family name.

In the most general terms French entrepreneurial motivation has been seriously compromised by the difficulty of identifying the entrepreneurial function with a broad range of national cultural goals and values. French society has disposed the entrepreneur to ask the corrosive question of *why* he should try to sell more or make more without providing answers that were very satisfactory to him in terms of his society's values. In a word, and with exceptions, the French businessman has *himself* been unable to slough off the anticapitalist sentiment in his social inheritance.

3. *In terms of behavior*, finally, the influence of the traditional social structure can be seen operating even more directly.

Most conspicuous, perhaps, has been the relative absence of the kind of aggressive entrepreneurship requisite to the process of "creative destruction" — the process that Schumpeter placed at the heart of capitalist development, whereby economic innovators working through an impersonal market successively eliminate marginal firms and outmoded processes by forcing ever more productive techniques and combinations. In France the entrepreneur has in good measure rejected this process and found refuge from its workings. The state has protected the home market for agriculture and industry; and other social and economic institutions have favored the preservation of the "community" of producers or sellers.

Social patterns have operated against pressing technological or competitive advantage "destructively." The rules of live and let live, of maintaining each in his place and function, of respect for status, class, and tradition, have sanctioned patterns opposed to the working of market forces. Quite apart from the subtler social pressures more generally operative, conspicuous rebels (of whom the Péreires are the best known example) have found themselves destroyed by the economic community for trying to break the system. A market, in turn, arranged to preserve the marginal operator in a restricted group of entrants has been extremely profitable to the low-cost producer. While businessmen almost everywhere have moved toward such patterns, the striking aspect of the French scene is the degree to which they were successfully achieved, long before trade associations formally embodied them.

The social inheritance has also operated against organizing economic resources toward mass production for mass consumption. It has fortified the concept of inelastic and class markets, markets defined in terms of social classes rather than present or potential income groups. It has operated against the dynamic drive to expand, resisting what industrialism has made possible — quantity, scale, size, standardization.[37] The Frenchman has often shown far greater interest than the American in the machine itself, but the French entrepreneur and even the engineer has much less understood its relation to a productive *process*, to the flow of work and goods in time and quantity.[38] Old customers, old products, old qualities, old methods, have had a social sanction that specialization and mass production have not had.

In the low-prestige field of trade and distribution the lack of aggressive entrepreneurship has been conspicuous. French commercial entrepreneurs have failed to organize the flow of retail trade in terms of volume and turnover, failed to exploit the potential of the economy as a manufacturing-trading system. The retailer has continued to act on principles of a high rate of profit from individual sales to individual customers. A sociocultural context that has made men look with some scorn on catering to the tastes and wants of the masses has made for resistance to advertising, promotion, salesmanship, and the developments of modern merchandizing.[39] (The outcry against American "coca-colonization" in 1950 was symptomatic of these deep-lying attitudes.)

In the range of family businesses, inherited social patterns, again reinforced by bourgeois institutions and anxieties, have made prudence the key word: caution, modest aspirations, limited scale and volume of business, slow and self-financed investment. These patterns have been typical both of big and powerful firms — industrial dynasties that today live as though besieged, walled up in their big-doored, Kafka-like fortresses — and of smaller establishments, reflecting the deep bourgeois preference for *rentes* as against risks.

There have been in France great entrepreneurs, great profits, and great innovations. The 1850's and 1860's saw an important quickening under Saint-Simonian doctrines. But neither the Péreires of that day nor the Citroëns since have ever been strong enough or numerous enough to break through the institutional order and establish new general patterns. They have never been followed by that army of imitators necessary to capitalist development. The exceptions have, to a striking extent, come from groups less directly subject to the dominant social impress, from among those whom the virulent French royalist and nationalist, Charles Maurras, listed as "Anti-France" — Protestants, Free Masons, Jews, and *métèques* (foreigners not completely gallicized).

French entrepreneurship has repeatedly failed to exploit the very great scientific and technological innovations that France has produced. To take two cases of importance, France led the world in the early decades of the commercial development of both the automobile and the heavy electrical industry (electric generators, electric motors, and arc lights).[40] Yet in their manufacture France has failed to exploit her early advantage; and in the electrical industry, for example, has lagged far behind Germany.

In sum French entrepreneurship has shown far more of the bourgeois half of Sombart's spirit of high-capitalism — thrift, industry, calculation — than of the other half, the dynamic, restless, driving spirit of enterprise. It might be argued, in other terms, that the full development of the potentialities of industrial capitalism really required the classic Schumpeterian entrepreneur — a risk-taking innovator operating on credit; in France, however, the business system remained largely in the hands of traditionalized bourgeois, engaged in a rational process of cautiously increasing wealth through compound interest, saving, and reinvesting.

Our review has not covered a range of exceptions and variations to the patterns here described, nor has it emphasized aspects of the institutional system favorable to certain kinds of economic development. It has also not measured these influences of social structure against the perspective of objective economic factors that have shaped entrepreneurial opportunities and the lag in French economic development (if the Ruhr valley had been 100 miles west, for example, French economic history might have been markedly different). Nor has it discussed the extent to which efforts to break out of traditional ways have been periodically interrupted in this century by war and depression and mounting social hostility to capitalism in general. But enough has been said, it is hoped, to show the impact of inherited social patterns on a critical economic actor, the entrepreneur, and to show something of the ways in which they have operated on his recruitment, motivation, and behavior. Some American contrasts may sharpen the point.

v

American comparisons have been implicit throughout. Here we will only note certain relative differences that cast in sharper relief the thesis being developed as to the influence of social structure on entrepreneurial behavior.[41]

In the classic era of the nineteenth and early twentieth centuries American entrepreneurship grew and prospered in a society whose institutions and goals were as uniquely favorable to the individual entrepreneur as were its physical conditions. By inheritance and diffusion America is, of course, part of a common Western civilization. But the historical timing of the American settlement and the extremely uneven weighting involved in the social and cultural transfer gave the United States a highly selective extraction of the European heritage. Combined with the conditions of the New World, this selective inheritance gave rise to a social structure conspicuously more favorable to the kind of entrepreneurship most conducive to private capitalist development. Of the many factors making for this difference four of the most important may here be noted and briefly discussed.

Most striking is the general absence of widespread feudal survivals. America has had its classes, and many specifically European institutions are to be found in varying measure in the United States — in some cases, particularly along the Eastern seaboard, almost intact; but industrial capitalism and the entrepreneur have not, in the main, had to break into any such rigidly elaborated hierarchical social structure as existed in Europe. Travelers from abroad, of whom Tocqueville is perhaps the most eloquent, have been struck by the *relative* absence of hardened and hallowed patterns of stratification and function, of hereditary privilege and prestige, and of traditional rigidities surrounding property, occupation, and business activity.

It is an error to assume, however, as has sometimes been done, that industrial capitalism in America grew up in a virgin land. Here too it came into a going social system. The striking fact for comparative entrepreneurial history is the extent to which prior institutions and ideas were in this case favorable to the subsequent development of aggressive entrepreneurship. This difference was in part a result of the fact that commercial capitalism was never absent from the colonies, that it grew up with the Union, so to speak; but it must be remembered that for more than two centuries independent agriculture and the frontier dominated major parts of American life (with important regional exceptions). While certain conflicts and adverse elements were involved in this heritage, it was so overwhelmingly favorable that to this day the American businessman can and does identify himself with historical traditions ranging from that of Ben Franklin, Leatherstocking and the independent farmer.[42] He has thus been able to root himself, to draw strength from institutions and symbols from the past that remain central to the national values and aspirations — a fundamental contrast with the relation of the European entrepreneur to the inherited institutions and values of his society.

The American offshoot, coming when it did and as it did, heavily emphasized certain special lines of thought within the European heritage — notably Puritanism, Lockian individualism, Newtonian ideas of the working of automatic harmonies, the late Enlightenment's faith in the inexorable relation of reason and individual effort to human progress. Given the new lands and opportunities, American society fused these elements into a new faith, into a new vision of the promise of American life. Oriented toward building an ever-expanding future spelled out in terms of increasing material welfare, confident of the inevitable progress of man therefrom, glorifying economic achievement, mobility, competition, change, boldness, bigness, it was a creed designed to fortify creative and aggressive entrepreneurship. It was, moreover, a creed that at a moment of unusual clarity and simplicity was crystallized and codified in the basic symbols and laws of the Republic. The thrust of national aspirations was therefore behind the entrepreneurial role.

Finally, any analysis must recognize the extent to which industrial capitalism and its entrepreneurs have themselves shaped the social order. Coming into a society still fluid and rapidly spilling over a new land, they have been able to mold institutional patterns in their interests and their image to a degree not possible in the relatively hardened social structures of Europe. This point can be easily exaggerated, however. The extensive impact of industrial capitalism and its entrepreneurs on American institutions has been largely since 1850; it cannot by itself explain the favorable basic institutional frame into which it came.

These social circumstances and physical opportunities created in the United States a society that has carried further those institutions that generally favored the growth of capitalism and the entrepreneur in the western world: Not only the more abstract patterns such as universalism, rationality, specialization, transferability of resources, worldly orientation, and the like; but also those most directly related to entrepreneurship — individualism; competitive economic activity within an impersonal market; mobility, social and geographical; achieved as against ascribed statuses, with economic achievement the main ladder of advancement; emphasis on "success" in a competitive occupational system as the almost universally prescribed goal; [43] money income as a primary reward and symbol of success; the institutionalization of innovation, risk-taking, change and growth.

Over the classic period the self-made American businessman has probably more than any other figure embodied the agreed-on success symbols of the society. While here too he has in practice often enough sought to reduce the area of competition and risk, to protect inefficiency, to resist change, he has conformed to American *ideal* patterns in proportion as he has been an *enterprising* entrepreneur, aggressive, innovating, expanding, seeking new methods and markets and worlds to conquer.[44]

The place and role of the businessman has accordingly been fundamentally different in European and American society. To an extraordinary degree in America he has not only been free of much of the negative drag of earlier European ideas and forms, but, positively, the successful businessman, along with the economic rewards of success and the social and symbolic recognition accompanying high status, has been able to feel himself a leader in the national epic, in the effort to improve the world by producing goods and wealth on an ever-expanding scale. All this has entered into that conviction of mission, that sense of being the carrier of a freer and better life that has so fortified the American businessman and that has to this day so baffled the European, businessman and others alike.[45]

Conflicting elements, European and indigenous, were present, of course, even in the classic American era, and business practice involved any number of departures from the model we have drawn. But on any relative scale the American institutional system was overwhelmingly favorable to entrepreneurship. In terms of recruitment it resulted in relatively open access to business careers, and a natural gravitation of talent and energy as well as status to them. In terms of motivation and behavior, it brought a drive to aggressiveness and innovation, to growth and unlimited success that repeatedly overrode the more cautious and restrictive dispositions entering into business behavior. It is no accident that this kind of entrepreneurship developed in the society which more than any other has made culture-heroes of its Carnegies, Edisons, and Fords.

Social structure does not by itself, of course, offer *the* explanation of the differences between European and American entrepreneurship. It constitutes a significant part of the explanation, however; and without reference to it the differing economic decisions and actions of businessmen in different societies cannot be understood. It rightly focuses attention on the *patterns* of economic activity that become habitual, on the kinds of motivation and behavior that are institutionalized in a given society. A range of comparative studies should help us to delimit more precisely the nature, scope, and mechanisms of its influence relative to other factors in the economic process. We *can* get closer to the problem than simply saying that businessmen are somehow "different."

II

Bankers and Pashas

International Finance in Egypt in the 1860's

By David S. Landes

The account which follows is based on an unusually large and intimate correspondence between two businessmen of the nineteenth century: one, Alfred André, a leading international financier; the other, Edouard Dervieu, the private banker of the Viceroy of Egypt. The letters, which cover the decade from 1858 to 1868, number over one hundred, something less than half of them from Alfred André, whose methodical precision led him to make carbons of his own letters long before the typewriter existed. They are long, often running to six and seven pages, and are exceptional in their frankness and articulateness. On the whole, they suggest more the plain, even blunt, words of confidential conversation than the studied exchange of ideas on paper.

The correspondence was found in the vaults of the Bank of France, where it lay with the old business records of the André bank, now De Neuflize, Schlumberger et Cie. The officers of this firm, giving proof of an open-mindedness all the more remarkable in that it meant a sharp break with French business tradition, were kind enough to open their archives to a stranger. I am especially indebted in this regard to Messrs. Costa de Beauregard and Christian Monnier, whose generosity and patient assistance went far beyond the requirements of hospitality.

So far as the writer is aware, the letters offer the economic historian his first explicit insight into the methods and motivations of international finance capitalism as seen through the eyes of two independent figures of the highest rank. To the political and diplomatic historian, they offer firsthand evidence on the role and objectives, hitherto only guessed at, of European businessmen in the rise of the Egyptian debt, and throw new light on the responsibility of the Viceroy for the ultimate debacle. Limitations of space make it necessary here to restrict the narrative to one aspect of the story: the contrast in business behavior between two men of radically different upbringing and temperament.

I

Scarcity is the greatest alchemist of all. In the seventh decade of the nineteenth century, a long anticipated yet wishfully unexpected civil war in America erased at one stroke most of the world's supply of cotton, decimated the greatest of manufacturing industries, and turned fuzzy white fibers into gold.[1]

To the great mills of Manchester and Rouen, of the Low Countries and Alsace, the famine came slowly. In 1860, the United States furnished five-sixths of the entire European supply of cotton. The crop that year was superb, and merchants in New Orleans and Mobile, sensing the approach of hostilities, hastened to ship to markets overseas. Haste became fever after Fort Sumter, and by the end of August 1861 over three million bales had arrived in Europe to swell what were already large stocks. In the fall of that year, only a few improvident industrialists had begun to feel the pinch, and the inefficiency of the Union blockade of Southern ports gave the manufacturing interests reason to feel that their fears had been exaggerated.

By Christmas, the situation was already changed. There was not yet a shortage, but new arrivals were few and far between, and the prospect of a long war in the United States gave little hope of immediate improvement. The price of cotton, which had hovered about 7½ pence per pound during the first half of 1861, went to 12 by October and, after some hesitation, jumped frantically during the summer of 1862. Lancashire was in agony. Mules and looms stopped; plants closed; thousands of men and women walked the streets. And while committees were organized to care for the hungry and royalty set the example in contributing to succor the unfortunate, crewmen were looting cargoes to sell what had once been a bulk staple at a black-market price of a shilling a pound. In France, where the prestige and stability of the Empire had been pledged for the less than popular commercial treaty of 1860 with England, the very idea of depression was subversive. As the cotton shortage became more acute, Napoleon was reported ready to intervene, if need be, to put an end to American fighting.

The cotton manufacturers, who were losing hard cash daily, exercised every ingenuity to circumvent utter paralysis. They made thinner fabrics —for the first time since Napoleon I, filmy muslins were again the height of fashion. They imagined marvelous combinations of cotton warp and woolen or linen weft to shift part of the burden to other textiles. Many producers found it easier and more profitable to eke out their cotton yarn with flour and other sizes which increased the weight of the fabric by as much as 50 per cent.[2] To no avail. There simply was not enough cotton, and if America could not furnish it, some other place would have to.

Few places in the world are adaptable to the cultivation of cotton on a commercial scale. In the 1860's the only practical possibilities were India and Egypt, although the great manufacturing powers tried everything, even Spain and Australia, in their desperation. Of the two, India was by far the more important for sheer quantity, shipping in 1860 almost six times as much cotton to England alone as the entire Egyptian crop. Unfortunately, the Indian product was so coarse that, in many cases, textile machinery had to be readjusted to work it, and so filthy that Surat was a byword for cheap, dirty work. Moreover, the agricultural techniques of the ryot were pathetically backward, and the burden of taxes and the separation of ownership from cultivation combined to depress them to a level commensurate with bare subsistence and remove every incentive to amelioration. With the Lancashire mill owners afraid to risk their money in the improvement and extension of the Eastern crop, and the British government resolved on principle not to interfere with the normal flow of investment capital, Indian cotton was forced to stand still and watch the opportunity of a millennium go by.

Like India, Egypt had a long tradition of cotton growing.[3] And if it is true that the output of the Nile valley was small by comparison with that of the subcontinent, this was balanced in part by the superb quality of the long Egyptian Jumel fiber, second only to the American Sea Island for the manufacture of fine yarn. On the other hand, the weaknesses that were to balk efforts to develop the Indian crop were no less a handicap in Egypt. In ignorance and poverty, in ineptness of method and persistence in ineptness, the fellah was every bit a match for the ryot. Even the presence in Egypt of an enlightened despotism to set the example of efficient cultivation and impose change on the unchanging mass was as often as not a liability. For, as in all despotisms, the short-range interests of state and the long-range interests of the economy did not always coincide, nor was power always tempered with understanding, or good intentions balanced with good judgment.

Thus, for Mohammed Ali, founder of the present Khedivial dynasty, father of modern Egypt, and promoter of Jumel cultivation, cotton was primarily a source of state revenue. It was the increment yielded by the new crop that enabled him to pay for an Egyptian army and navy and wrest by arms the hereditary pashalik from a reluctant Constantinople. With these pecuniary objectives in mind, Mohammed Ali pushed the new plant like a flower in a hothouse. Energetic direction from above worked wonders. In the three years after its introduction in 1820, the yield of Jumel went from 300 kilograms to 9 million, far surpassing anything which the older indigenous varieties had attained. European importers were delighted with the excellence of the new fiber, which won itself a privileged position on the markets of Liverpool and Le Havre.

At the same time, however, Mohammed Ali's efforts to increase his income by controlling every facet of the Egyptian economy gave rise to a system of monopolies, the most far-reaching of which was his sole ownership of all the land. Nor were his tenants free to pay rent and taxes and then dispose of the surplus as they saw fit. Taxes were so calculated as to absorb any visible surplus, and if, through trickery, ingenuity, economy, or otherwise, the peasant succeeded in setting aside some cotton for market, he was compelled to dispose of it through the agents of the Pasha. Under the circumstances, the Viceroy dictated his own terms to the fellahin, terms whose short-sighted cupidity crushed the incentive of those who had adopted the cultivation of Jumel with enthusiasm in the hope of greater income. With all possibility of profit gone, the peasant simply bowed to his masters and went through the motions.

As a result, the phenomenal spurt of the early years was followed by decades of hesitant, spasmodic, and, on the whole, limited increases in quantity, obtained only at the expense of quality. The price of Jumel fell sharply, and efforts of the Pasha to augment his income by enlarging the area devoted to cotton only produced a poorer crop. In 1860, the total crop was something over 22 million kilograms, and cotton accounted for only a third of all exports. In spite of the obvious possibilities of Jumel as a cash crop, in the face of an untapped European demand for a good, long-staple fiber, Egypt remained on the eve of the cotton famine a food-producing country, a granary as in Roman times.

On the other hand, a series of reforms in the 1850's had set the stage for a new jump in cotton production. The disintegration of Mohammed Ali's paralyzing monopolies in the closing years of his reign and the abandonment of most of his costly experiment in industrial autarchy and military imperialism during the rule of his grandson, Abbas (1849–1854), did much to clear the ground and ease the burden of the peasantry. This new trend toward laisser faire, in which the incentive of profit would replace the goad of authority, was consummated by the reforms of Saïd (1854–1863), uncle of Abbas, who instituted the payment of taxes in money and, as an indispensable corollary, permitted the fellah to grow, buy, and sell what, where, and as he pleased.[4] At the same time, he changed the system of property from an onerous usufruct to a regime of *de facto* private ownership, giving the peasant the right to acquire and alienate land at will. The curve of cotton output began a slow but steady rise that contrasted sharply with the jagged fluctuations of the preceding decades. When the cotton famine came in 1860, Egyptian agriculture was ready for it.

Seen in larger compass, this growth of Egypt as a center of cotton cultivation was only one aspect of a national renaissance, a great awakening from the sleep of centuries. When Napoleon landed at the mouth of the Nile in 1798, he found the husks of civilization, a people in weary bondage, the crumbling remnants of a long-forgotten past. So well forgotten, indeed, that when Napoleon brought his carriage ashore, he was, according to some sources, reintroducing the wheel to Egypt.[5]

The invasion of the French expeditionary force was the shock that finally waked the country from its torpor. For one thing, it decisively undermined the authority of the Mamelukes, setting the stage for Mohammed Ali and political independence. For another, it brought to the attention of a few Egyptians the advances that science and industry had made in Europe, the degree to which time had passed them by. And conversely, it brought Egypt to the attention of the Western world.[6]

In this, of course, Napoleon was only anticipating the inevitable. The absorption of Egypt into the arena of European political and economic rivalries was implicit in the aggressive, expanding character of Western technology and business. The long isolation that had followed on the Portuguese discovery of the sea route to India was impossible in an age of steam and finance capitalism.

Strangely enough, it was the weakness of the early steamboats which made Egypt the pivot of the trade routes of a new age. Steam could not compete with sails in the long haul around the Cape in those early days of low-pressure boilers and paddle wheels, but it was ideally suited to short voyages in the Mediterranean and Persian Gulf. To be sure, all this required transshipment at the Isthmus, but for articles of high value in proportion to weight, the time saved more than compensated. Besides, there was always the possibility of a railroad or canal to link the Red Sea and the Mediterranean.

As early as 1830, the East India Company planned a steam service between Bombay and Suez, to connect at Alexandria with other ships coming from England. By 1834, the two sections were in operation, joined by an organized system of overland transport. Within the next decade, four new steamship companies had entered the field, and the trip from England to Alexandria had been reduced from forty to fourteen days. Hotels were built at Alexandria, Cairo, and Suez; steam tugs were brought in to draw the passenger barges up the delta canal, and steamboats to ply the Nile from Afteh to Cairo. The road from Cairo to Suez was improved to allow the passage of wheeled vehicles. The overland stage, which had once required anywhere from five to eighteen days, was reduced to as low as three.

Much of this improvement was due to the active coöperation of Mohammed Ali, who, in his desire to make Egypt a powerful nation, stood ready to encourage every effort to introduce the material advantages of Western civilization. Sometimes, of course, his enthusiasm for the creations of European technology blinded him to the facts of economic life. Egypt was not suited then, or now, to the sort of industrialization he envisaged. Even before his death, the sugar mills, forges, and cotton factories he had built lay rusting in the fields and in the desert. Nevertheless, these abortive efforts did much to educate the population to new ways and, what is probably more important, to direct the attention of Europeans to a new field for business activity.

The xenophobic reaction of his successor, Abbas, did much to nullify the accomplishments of the preceding decades. The new ruler, whose beneficence toward the lower classes has done little to improve his viciously reactionary name in history, carried a justified resentment of the incursions of Westerners to unfortunate extremes. For Abbas, it was not enough to stop work on the Nile dam. He had to destroy what had already been built. The schools of Mohammed Ali were closed; the canals, permitted to silt up; the irrigation system, neglected. Only once did Abbas, bowing to the exigencies of foreign policy, deviate from his unrelenting assault on the innovations of European technology. In 1851, his autonomy endangered by the pretensions and threats of Constantinople, he bought the support of England by conceding to a British firm the construction of the long-awaited railroad from Alexandria to Cairo.

Saïd, the successor of Abbas, was in all respects the antithesis of his dour, surly nephew. Personable and cultivated, he had been educated by his tutors to appreciate and admire the accomplishments of Western civilization. He was like his father in his sincere desire to improve the condition of the population and raise Egypt to the status of a great power, and his reign definitively consecrated the program of modernization so nearly vitiated by Abbas.

In 1854, the electric telegraph replaced the semaphore towers along the road from Alexandria to Cairo. The railroad from Alexandria to Cairo, after some four years of work, was finished in 1856, and in 1856–57 another line from Cairo to Suez completed the trans-Isthmus link. Around the middle of the century, French interests introduced the first modern flour mills, and English capitalists organized a corporation to supply pure water to the burgeoning population of Alexandria. With agricultural output climbing, exports rose to match the increasing demand for the machines and other products of European industry. During the five years from 1850–51 to 1854–55, Egyptian exports averaged £2,329,600; during the next five, £2,954,200. Imports similarly rose from £2,000,000 to £2,700,000 per year.

At the same time, through traffic on the Mediterranean route to India boomed, and for the first time since Roman days Alexandria was again one of the world's great entrepôts. The ancient city, which possessed the only harbor in Egypt where the large seagoing vessels of Europe could moor, grew from a small, somnolent town of possibly 10,000 at the time of the French invasion to a city of some 150,000 by the decade of the 1850's.[7] The volume of traffic, especially during the rush season that followed the harvest, outstripped the physical facilities of the port and the capacities of even so fast-growing a population.

The harbor was a forest of masts and funnels, a confusion of long-nosed xebecs and swift feluccas from the inlets and archipelagoes of the Mediterranean, of proud schooners and brigs from Marseilles and Genoa and small lateen-rigged tartans from the ancient trade centers of the Levant, of the mighty paddle-wheelers and screw steamers of Liverpool and Le Havre and the humble harbor tenders and barges of Egypt.

The docks, such as they were, were crammed to overflowing, with bales of cotton heaped high pell-mell, crates of machinery and immigrants' trunks, cases of cloth and chests of tea, bags of spices, sacks of grain, all the products and impedimenta of East and West meeting and parting at this crossroads of world trade — the whole scattered in profusion on the lumpy cobbles and dusty earth, overwhelming the docksmen and drivers and carters, who tried vainly to make animal strength and human muscle do where cranes and freight cars were desperately needed.

In little over half a century, Egypt had come a long way. The quiet eddy, by-passed by centuries of history, had been caught up in the main stream and was rushing headlong to make up the lost time. When the cotton famine came in 1861, Egypt was already in the throes of an economic revolution.

Opportunities have rarely lacked for ambition, nor wealth for appetite, nor gold for greed. With the good and evil of Westernization came the best and worst elements of the European and Mediterranean world: bankers and usurers, merchants and thieves, staid English brokers and mercurial Levantine peddlers, proper clerks for the offices of the Peninsular and Oriental, painted harlots for the Square of the Consuls in Alexandria,[8] dedicated scholars for the temples of Abydos and Karnak, cut-throats and confidence men for the alleys of Cairo.

When Napoleon came to Egypt in 1798, probably less than one hundred Europeans lived in the entire country, most of them traders in centers like Alexandria and Rosetta. As late as 1821, the first year of Jumel, there was only one British cotton house in Alexandria, a city that would one day abound in them. The first big immigration came during the 1820's and 1830's, when Mohammed Ali imported businessmen and technicians of all sorts in his program of industrialization. After a slight interruption during the reign of Abbas, the stream of foreigners resumed under Saïd — from 1857 to 1861 over 30,000 newcomers entered Egypt on the average every year.

But it was the combination of Suez and the cotton boom that turned an influx into a gold rush. In 1862, 33,000 foreigners arrived; in 1863, 43,000; in 1864, 56,500; in 1865, 80,000. Not until cotton finally collapsed in 1866 did the steady crescendo pause and fall off to 50,000.

This rush of visitors and immigrants cannot be understood without reference to the privileged position of foreigners in the Egypt of the nineteenth century. For the citizens of the great powers across the seas, Egypt, if nominally independent, whether in its own right or as a province of the presumably independent Ottoman Empire, was in fact a colonial territory. In this poor shadow of a nation, the Englishman or Frenchman, Prussian or Austrian could tread heavily, secure in the knowledge that, whatever he did, might made it right.

In 1840–41, the same treaties that ended Mohammed Ali's attacks on his Turkish overlord and consecrated the hereditary character of his pashalik established a set of independent consular jurisdictions which effectively removed the foreigner from the control of the Egyptian state.[9] All actions, civil or criminal, brought by Egyptians against foreigners were tried by the latter's consul in accordance with the latter's law, and all actions brought by foreigners against Egyptians were backed by the overt pressure of their national governments. The outsider simply could not lose, unless caught *flagrante delicto*.

The gates of corruption were opened wide. An arrangement purportedly intended to protect the European in his unwitting difficulties with an alien law and civilization was almost immediately subverted into an aggressive encroachment on Egyptian sovereignty. As soon as it was apparent that the Egyptian government was incapable of resisting threats of force, one consul vied with another in pressing the most importunate, the most fantastic, claims against the harassed treasury. Moreover, not only was the representative of Austria prepared to defend the causes of all Austrians, or the representative of France those of all Frenchmen, whatever their intrinsic merit, but he was generally ready — for a reasonable sum, of course, or a percentage of the spoils — to plead the case of anybody, alien or even native. Worse yet, the consuls themselves were usually only businessmen with their own pecuniary interests, to which the duties of their office were inevitably subordinated.

The result was a spoiler's field day. Nothing was too far-fetched or unreasonable to serve as an excuse for a raid on the Viceroy's purse. If a man was robbed because of his own negligence, it was the fault of the government for not maintaining law and order. Indemnity. If a man sailed his boat poorly and caused it to founder, it was the fault of the government for leaving the sandbar there. Indemnity. The story is told that once, when Saïd was in conversation with a European businessman, he interrupted their talk to order a servant to close the window. "If this gentleman catches cold," he said, "it will cost me £10,000." [10]

In the last analysis, however, those foreigners who were content to plunder the treasury only when they had suffered real or imagined losses were playing for petty cash. The real stakes lay in concessions and contracts, for the construction of public works, the creation of public services, the purchase of supplies, and almost any other governmental function within the realm of imagination. For the fact was that for all his abusive presumption, the foreigner was indispensable. Only Europeans could supply the capital and know-how to build the tools and structures of modern civilization and perform the multitude of unfamiliar operations that had grown out of intimacy with the Western World. The Europeans knew it too, and they demanded and received every farthing that the traffic could bear.

This great rape of the Egyptian treasury was closely connected with the particularistic character of the society and economy. Government in the Egypt of the nineteenth century was personal, centering almost entirely in the Viceroy and his family, and authoritarian, with little if any concept of a continuing, sovereign body of law. Public offices were not the impersonal embodiment of public functions, but private properties exploited by their holders for whatever they would yield. Business was, in the sociological sense, irrational, resting on traditional practice and on subjective as against impartial market criteria. In general, position and prestige depended not on achievement or merit, but on relations and background, not on what you did, but on who you were.

As a consequence, success in the great Egyptian concession hunt was not to the fastest, or cheapest, or fairest, but to the canal builder who knew the Viceroy from childhood, or the merchant who dined with the Minister of Public Works, or the promoter who slept with the mistress of the nephew of the Minister. On the more exalted levels of the administrative hierarchy, friendship and influence could be bought with timely services, tactful kindnesses, tasteful gifts. With minor functionaries, crass bribes were at least as effective.

Much, of course, depended on the character of the ruling Pasha. Mohammed Ali, who accepted the principle of business based on friendship, was nevertheless far from an easy mark. Despite his affection for merchants like Briggs and Pastré, he tried with some determination to handle his sales of Jumel on an impersonal auction basis. Abbas, in his detestation of all things foreign, was even less susceptible to alien blandishments, although at the same time less resistant to alien pressure. It was really not until the accession of Saïd that the floodgates were opened. Good natured and debonair, Saïd lacked the unlettered shrewdness and canny judgment of his grandfather. He was anxious to please, too anxious, for he simply did not know how to say no. No proposal was too fanciful to be considered; no promoter too disreputable to be heard. Things reached the point where people sought concessions despite their inability to carry them out, indeed precisely on that account, for a canceled contract, whatever the justification, was certain to bring an indemnity. And what indemnities! One plaintiff, at once a merchant and Consul-General of Belgium, demanded the unconscionable sum of £3,000,000 because Saïd had reneged on a verbal promise, allegedly made by Mohammed Ali over a decade before, to concede him the handling of goods in transit across the Isthmus. Before the campaign of agitation, appeals, and pressure was over, Saïd was glad to buy the tardy claimant off for 3,000,000 francs. And this was a trifle by comparison with the burden that the concession of Suez would one day impose on Egypt.

When the cotton famine came, it was open season on the Nile, and one of the hunters was Edouard Dervieu.

II

Alexandria, 25 December 1858

My Dear André:

. . . Our dream is still to go and retire in our native land, as soon as a small fortune will permit it. Very fortunately, I have no complaint about having quit the Messageries. My little deals have done well, and I have begun to put something aside.

Edouard Dervieu was the descendant of one of those families of small businessmen which formed the backbone of the old French bourgeoisie. His ancestors of the seventeenth and eighteenth centuries had been tailors at Condrieu, a country town on the banks of the Rhone not far from Lyons. One branch of the family, prosperous and ambitious, had left the shop to purchase the dignities of office and noble rank. The ancestors of Edouard Dervieu had remained content with the less brilliant but more enduring rewards of slow, prudent mercantile accumulation. From tailors they became drapers; from drapers, *fabricants*; from *fabricants*, *négociants* and citizens of Lyons.

Robert Dervieu, the father of Edouard, was born in 1795 into an age of ferment and change. Perhaps it was the iconoclastic spirit of the times that led him to break with the bourgeois traditions of generations and strike out along new paths of business enterprise. Perhaps the family had suffered financial reverses during twenty-five years of revolution and war, and some new, exceptional effort was required to restore their fortune. The record does not say. In any event, Robert Dervieu, after serving in the army until well after the general demobilization of 1815, abandoned the dour, Jansenist industry of Lyons for the colorful, volatile commerce of Marseilles, where he became a partner with an uncle in the mercantile firm of Barry, Dervieu et Cie. But cargoes of wine and consignments of cloth did not suffice; from the start, Dervieu was interested in the possibilities of Algeria as a field for enterprise. He bought property in Algiers and became alderman of the city and a spokesman for Franco-Algerian business interests. He acquired lead mines, promoted under the Second Empire at least one corporation for their exploitation, and became the friend and business associate of some of the outstanding merchants of Marseilles.

Edouard Dervieu, his second son, was born in Marseilles in 1824. The boy grew up in a family in transition from one level of wealth and status to another. When he reached maturity, the new Dervieu patrimony had not yet crystallized in the solid, hereditary form suitable to the creation of business dynasties. Like his father, Edouard was to spend his life making his way up the social and economic scale, seeking his fortune and seizing the main chance in France and throughout the Mediterranean.

Thanks undoubtedly to family connections, he began as an office executive, an early example of the business bureaucrat so familiar today. In 1843, when only nineteen, he was director of the Oran agency of the Bazin steamship line. After an interlude as head of his father's mines from 1848 to 1851, he returned to the shipping business, directing a succession of agencies of the Messageries Maritimes in Greece, Syria, and finally in Egypt.

In this way he accumulated some means, enough to persuade him to strike out in business for himself. More than that, however, he had two important friends, his father-in-law, Koenig Bey, once the tutor and now the private secretary of the Viceroy Saïd, and Alfred André, the head of one of the leading private banks of Paris. The one gave him entrée into the court circles of Egypt; the other, into the money markets of Europe. It is hard to say which was the more valuable.[11]

Dervieu's first major venture, one that derived directly from his experience with the Messageries, was the Medjidjié, a steamship firm whose capital had been subscribed in 1856 by the Viceroy and other members of the royal family. Two years had not sufficed to collect on the unpaid shares. The company had nevertheless held its own and, with four ships, was preparing in 1858 to exploit the Red Sea traffic, always dependable thanks to the annual pilgrimages to Mecca.

Besides my direction of the Medjidjié, I have several other small commercial and industrial affairs which are doing well. I give you all these details because I know your interest in me and because I am convinced that you will be pleased to learn of my successes in the new path I have taken.

Dervieu's prosperity was all the more commendable in view of a certain stagnation of Egyptian trade in 1858.[12]

. . . so far as I am concerned, I want very much to see the Suez Canal put through. This enterprise would bring a lot of capital into Egypt and would certainly be the making of prosperity for the country. We need it. As I mentioned to you above, the last financial crisis has ruined our trade; the stagnation of business in Egyptian wheat and cotton has weighed heavily this year on our imports; and the overall total of transactions in Egypt in 1858 will not have amounted to a half of the average of the preceding years. Moreover, the Egyptian government is deep in debt. The Viceroy has wasted a pile of millions since he is in power. He owes almost ten months' salary to his employes and he has let himself be taken over by a few individuals, who have caused him in that way to hate Europeans.

Fortunately, Dervieu was not among those hated. Good times succeeded bad, and in the Egypt of 1860 it was hard for a friend of the royal family not to be successful. In December of that year, Dervieu set up his own banking firm. He dealt mostly in commercial paper, in cotton bills and Egyptian treasury notes. The latter, especially, were a profitable field of enterprise for the banker who could find his way in the maze of the Egyptian administration. Since the impecunious government of the Pasha was never in a position to pay its officials in cash, it was compelled to resort to paper promises of varying maturity and sincerity. These were eventually redeemed, but how and when depended on circumstances. Banking, under such conditions, was an art and a branch of politics. Dervieu apparently held his own at both.

Alexandria, 12 March 1862

My dear André:

. . . You will have noted from the relations of my firm with yours that I have been taking every opportunity to increase our dealings. We owe you this credit, that no one, either at Paris or Marseilles, treats us better than you. Your discounts are always ¼ percent less than those of your colleagues, the other bankers. Thus not only because of the good friendship which binds us, but also in our own interest, our relations with you are most precious.

Dervieu was a sincere, candid person. This remarkable, almost unbusinesslike frankness is evident throughout the correspondence. The tie with André was a precious one, and would have been so even at the regular discount rate. A European correspondent was indispensable — to collect the notes that Dervieu discounted, to pay the holders of Dervieu's paper, to dispose of Egyptian bills on the European market, and so on. All this was a small beginning to be sure, but Dervieu had already come a little way from the "small fortune" of 1858. He was beginning to think of credit.

You must have judged our way of working by the choice of paper which we send you. I told you in Paris that, before asking you for credit, we wanted to gain your confidence. Have we reached that point? I should be pleased to read it in your own hand.

He was also beginning to think of allies and syndicates.

I recently took the liberty of recommending Messrs. Oppenheim to you. I did it without fear because I knew that with these gentlemen there was nothing to fear.

This was the start of a long and checkered association. Hermann and Henri Oppenheim were financiers by birth and tradition. While they may or may not have been related to the great dynasty of that name in Cologne, the Oppenheims' business ties were with Frankfurt and the powerful house of Frühling and Goschen in London. The two had just founded the bank H. Oppenheim, Neveu et Cie at Alexandria with a capital of £150,000 as a companion to firms in London and Paris. Like Dervieu, the Oppenheims had useful connections at the Egyptian court.

You probably know that Messrs. Oppenheim had assumed the administration of the fortune and properties of the Prince El-Hami Pasha, son of Abbas. The Prince died last year after having squandered his fortune, and it was asserted at the time that the Oppenheims had contributed to this in no small way. The Viceroy named a commission to liquidate the estate of the Prince, and this commission recognized and affirmed that the administration of Messrs. Oppenheim had been most honest and upright. Another judicial commission was named to estimate the damage and indemnities due to M. Oppenheim for breach of contract, which the executors have not wanted to maintain, or rather have not maintained, since it was necessary to sell the properties to pay the debts. This commission has just rendered its verdict awarding an indemnity of £93,000 to M. Oppenheim.

Dervieu omits to mention that special commissions of this sort, composed in the majority of Europeans, were standard procedure in litigation between foreigners and the Egyptian government or its high officials. They lent an air of impartial justice to the most inequitable proceedings. Even in Egypt, however, such a verdict was hard to swallow. It was bad enough to mismanage the Prince's fortune and abet its dilapidation. But then to sue for breach of contract because the presumably unintentional death of the unfortunate client had precipitated the settlement of his debts! The breath of scandal was to stick to the Oppenheims throughout their career in Egypt.

To be sure, £93,000 was only a drop in the milking of the great, patient cow of the Nile. Henri Oppenheim, who was more or less in charge of the Egyptian firm, was interested in bigger things.

M. Oppenheim is leaving at the same time as this letter for Paris and Frankfurt; he is taking with him the contract of the loan which he has just signed with the Egyptian government and which he is going to present for ratification to a syndicate of German bankers, at the head of which is the Bank of . . . [Saxe-Meiningen]. This loan, which is for forty million francs, is an excellent affair.

An excellent affair indeed. The loan, originally for forty millions, was increased to sixty when the former sum was seen to be grossly insufficient. For its sixty millions, which it needed to consolidate its chaotic floating debt, the Egyptian government agreed to pay 198 million francs over thirty years. These annuities were secured by the state revenues, especially those derived from the most fertile provinces, those of the Delta.[13]

You can see, therefore, that from the standpoint of integrity and fortune, these gentlemen offer every guarantee, and my information must coincide with yours, since you have accorded them the credit of 500,000 fr. requested by telegram.

Dervieu was also prospering, though more discreetly. His new bank gave a dividend of 18¼ per cent on its one millon francs of paid-in capital for the first year of operations. His house represented in the new loan, for one-fifth the total amount, the Egyptian element, comprising the local business houses and that small group of native landholders and officials being initiated into the mysteries of international capitalism. He himself subscribed the modest amount of 300,000 francs, esteeming his nominative share of 20 per cent more than enough for purposes of prestige. This marked Dervieu's first important departure from the commercial banking on which he had built his fortune. It was a long stride on the high road to royal finance.

We have participated with M. Oppenheim in a fairly important operation with the Prince Mustapha Pasha.[14] We are lending him 4,500,000 francs, at ten percent, payable in nine years at the rate of 500,000 francs a year, with interest calculated semi-annually. We have taken the liberty of indicating in the contract that interest and amortization would be payable by your firm in Paris, and that the sums should be deposited by the Prince in our hands one month prior to maturity, so that we could get them to you in time. The Prince will carry as a result both our expenses and yours. . . The annual payments will be represented by letters of exchange signed by the Prince. We have as collateral the amount of his revenues and harvests in Egypt, all of which is to be deposited in our hands, and to that end we are opening for him a current account, bearing interest at 12 percent if the balance is in our favor. The affair is a good one, and offers all the security desirable.

This, again, was apparently Dervieu's first venture in personal loans on such a scale. It was a type of business that could prove extremely profitable at prevailing rates of interest, and besides, there was always the good will of the borrowers to consider. As for the latter, the improvident and prodigal grandees of the viceregal court, they found it so easy to affix their signatures to slips of paper that the whole process must have seemed an excellent way to get money for nothing. Egyptian notes began to circulate in increasing quantities on the markets of Europe.

André was pleased with the growing importance of his Alexandrian account, and only too glad to express his pleasure "in his own hand." His reply was the long-awaited promotion that raised Dervieu from cash-on-the-barrel into the debtor class.

Paris, 28 March 1862

My dear Dervieu:

. . . I can also tell you that I am pleased to see your good intentions to further our business relations, and we ask no better than to help you, by offering certain facilities, in giving them the extension we seek. Let me simply remind you that when it was a question between us of the amount of credit you would want to have at your disposal, I told you that our custom was to proportion the importance [of this figure] to that of the independent current transactions passing through our hands. Now, if we follow this ordinary rule of proportion in your case, we could not, considering the columns of your account, give you more than a relatively insignificant credit. But then, I understand that the transactions in which you are participating at this moment are a little exceptional and that they represent perhaps a vein which it is important for you to exploit. I have, therefore, just placed at your disposal a credit by acceptance of 100,000 francs, which you can mention in your next official letter to our house. Our commission will be the customary ½ percent on this part of your account.

The year 1862 was a busy one, and Dervieu went quietly on his way. Presumably, the credit offered by André sufficed for the moment. In any event, there are no more letters until eight months later.

Alexandria, 5 November 1862

My dear André:

. . . I hope that on your side, my dear friend, you will have been able to judge by our manner of working the full extent of our prudence and of our desire to earn for ourselves a good name and an unquestioned reputation for faithfulness and integrity. We could have thrown ourselves in, with our friends, the Oppenheims, on a vaster stage, but we have preferred to remain content with our regular train of affairs on the Alexandria market. We undertake less than they, but we work more surely.

Dervieu knew what he was saying. Such zealous prudence was ideally calculated to impress his colleague in Paris. The scion of seven generations of Huguenot bankers, Alfred André found himself in 1862, at the age of thirty-five, the effective head of Marcuard, André et Compagnie, the oldest private bank in France and perhaps on the continent. It dated from 1667, when David André, a religious refugee from Nîmes, founded a merchant house in Genoa. The new firm, which engaged particularly in the shipment of leather goods and textiles to and from France and central Europe, and in the importation of colonial products, prospered, and the merchants soon became merchant-bankers. Their financial activities grew directly out of their commercial relations: arbitrage and change, commodity loans and consignments, the discount and acceptance of short-term paper. Here the international fellowship of the Huguenot exiles was invaluable — no group was in a better position to deal with known and reliable correspondents in every European center. The bank in Genoa extended its operations, gave birth to offshoots in London and Geneva, even went so far as to underwrite on occasion large personal and industrial loans.[15]

At the end of the eighteenth century, the Revolution had made France once again a safe place for Protestants, while the campaigns of Napoleon left an Italy decidedly inhospitable to international business. In 1800, therefore, the bank of Genoa was liquidated and a new firm established in Paris. There the family continued its traditional operations, concentrating at first on Franco-Italian trade, but gradually widening the sphere of its relations.

It was after the fall of the Empire, however, that the house firmly established itself as one of the most influential in Paris. Extending its activities to include participation in French and foreign government loans and investments in industrial undertakings, André, Cottier et Compagnie, as it was then known, was a full-fledged member of the Haute Banque, that small group of houses, for the most part Protestant, which dominated the French money market. These private banks derived their power, not from their resources, which were almost always extremely limited, but from their impeccable reputation for solidity and prudence, a reputation generally based on generations of banking experience and generations of kinship solidarity. Names like Mallet, Hottinguer, and André meant more than wealth. They stood for tradition, international alliances, unimpeachable integrity. On a commercial bill, they implied more than the simple ability of the bank concerned to honor its signature. They meant — and this was far more important in the intensely personal business world of the day — that the house in question would never have given its signature if it had not had the means to honor it.

As a result, these banks formed a sort of aristocracy of their kind. There were to be wealthier firms, more enterprising financiers. But it was the Haute Banque which in the last analysis commanded the clientele and controlled the purses of France's capitalists. When a new loan was floated, a new corporation launched, their coöperation was indispensable. Their representatives throned over the Bank of France, the leading insurance firms, the big railroads. And when the great joint-stock banks of the Second Empire rose to push them from the center of the stage, they lost only in relative importance. These new, giant corporations fed on the previously untapped purses of the middle classes; the Haute Banque retained the portfolios of France's rich, who would trust their funds nowhere else. Even today, these dynasties — for ancient and powerful families like these are nothing less than dynasties — remain the trustees of France's great private fortunes.

Louis-Edouard-Alfred André fitted the traditional pattern perfectly. The son of Marie-Jean André, banker and *receveur des finances*, he received as a boy the usual education of his group, a strict grounding in Protestant schools and a practical commercial apprenticeship. These two influences set the tone of his character. Devout and righteous, ascetic and purposeful, André was at once the image of Weber's Calvinist and the epitome of the French private banker. Active in church and affectionate with family, he nevertheless dispensed charity with puritan severity and tempered personal sentiment with practical calculation. In business he was cautious and conservative, a firm believer in the antique virtues of arbitrage and exchange, of ¼ per cent and the 90-day note, profoundly convinced that good banking rests on unshakable liquidity and the proportioning of ends to means. Above all, he had faith in character first and money second; a risk was only as good as the man behind it. He had old-fashioned notions, the idea that a contract was a contract, that a man's word was as good as his signature, that debt was abhorrent and a sign of moral weakness, that slow and steady wins the race. Alfred André could never have made a cent in Egypt.[16]

In Alexandria Dervieu was making money hand over fist. The dividend to the partners in his bank was 15 per cent for the first half of 1862 alone. It rose to 19 per cent for the second half — this in spite of the fact that capital had been increased from one to three million francs. Most of these profits were still derived from what the merchant bankers of the period would have described as normal operations: arbitrage, exchange, the discount and acceptance of short-term paper. The commissions were small, but the volume was enormous and grew with the cotton boom, especially since actual transfers of funds were absurdly complicated and every intermediary took his slice.

But Dervieu was already well on his way to the higher sphere of royal banker. His letter of 5 November continued:

At the moment we are soliciting His Royal Highness the Viceroy to be charged with the payments which he still has to make to the Comptoir d'escompte. It involves 7 million francs a year for three years to come, at the rate of 1,750,000 fr. per quarter.[17] We have some hope of obtaining this operation, on conditions that are less than brilliant, to be sure, but still quite pretty relative to the importance of the sum concerned. We need in that case a banking firm in Paris to whom we could make our remittances in advance, so that it, in turn, might discount them and effect the payment to the Comptoir. We have naturally thought of you, and I should like to ask you, in case our plan is realized, if you would not consent, in view of the importance of the affair, to reduce your banking commission from $\frac{1}{4}$ to $\frac{1}{8}$ per cent. This reduction, you understand, would enable us to make several additional concessions to the Egyptian government, to make sure the deal does not get away from us. I should appreciate it very much if you would send me a few words in reply by return mail.

Dervieu was obviously still a neophyte, talking of concessions to the Egyptian government. André's answer was prompt and to the point.

Paris, 14 November 1862

My dear Dervieu:

. . . I only wanted to speak to you today of the major inconvenience from our point of view of handling for you, at the reduced commission which you suggest, the affair which you have in prospect and which I should be delighted to see pass through your and our hands. Up to now, we have always felt obliged to reject all requests of that nature, requests often made us by excellent houses in France and abroad who would like to work major transactions through us. Not more than a week ago, we had to reply negatively to a similar request from your neighbors, the Oppenheims, with a view to facilitating the shipments of gold which we have been making to them for some time on an important scale. Now if there is any business where concessions are called for, it is the operations of arbitrage and exchange rather than those necessitated by the unreasonable demands of a government which can and must pay. I hope, my dear friend, that this small difference (whose importance is multiplied for us by a question of principle) will not prevent you from obtaining and working the transaction in question through us and will not prove an obstacle to the success of your negotiation.

Alfred André was nobody's fool. If Dervieu was ready to accept the Viceroy's notes and enable the latter to pay old debts with new, he had no objection to handling Dervieu's payments at the Paris end for a commission. But he could not see why he should pay for Dervieu's eagerness to do the Egyptian government a favor.

The letters give no indication of the result of this negotiation, but we may feel sure that if Dervieu did eventually make the payments through André, he did so on André's terms. After all, it was a question of principle.

There were to be other clashes between Dervieu's opportunism and André's principles. On January 26, 1863, the latter addressed his friend in aggrieved tones:

My dear Dervieu:

. . . One word more, however, before ending, a word which I should prefer not to have to write to you.

Why, may I ask, do we have the misfortune to see in circulation notes drawn by your firm on a young man who is starting out with all the ardor of his youth and his fortune still to be made? What do Messrs. E. D. and Cie [Edouard Dervieu] need with a third correspondent in Paris, and especially a correspondent like M. de B. [Blonay]? In view of relations like ours and our eagerness to place ourselves entirely at your disposal, I confess to you that I have been very pained and that I prefer to tell it to you frankly and hope that you will answer me likewise . . .

André had good reason to be disturbed. He could hardly feel secure about his advances to Dervieu if the latter was going about accumulating liabilities to other bankers without his knowledge. Besides, Blonay was not just another banker. He was a newcomer whose fortune was "still to be made," an interloper whose ambition obviously conflicted with professional ethics. No member of the Haute Banque would have dealt with one of André's clients without his consent and coöperation.

Alexandria, 9 February 1863

My dear André:

. . . I was pleased to hear your reproaches concerning our drafts on M. de B., and should be delighted not to deserve them any more. But with our business expanding every day, we need credit on Europe more than ever. We have only three credits at the moment, 100,000 fr. with you, the same with Roulaud, and 150,000 with Blonay. We give our ninety-day notes only when people want them and when the difference of the exchange with commercial paper leaves us 1 to 1½ per cent profit. Without flattering ourselves, our paper is very much sought after, and we are very sober about giving it. But now that we are almost certain of sharing half-and-half with Oppenheim all the transactions of the Egyptian government, we must necessarily figure on credit requirements and we must place ourselves in a position to satisfy them. Oppenheim, who owes to us his new place with the Viceroy, has offered to get us credit with Homberg.[18] We answered that we did not think that would be necessary, counting thus on you. I have made a special effort with your firm to prove that we deserved your confidence; with Roulaud and de Blonay, I have simply used the credit I had, when I had to. . . In a word, we deal with you in everything that we have to do with Paris, but when we have reached the limit of the credit which you have extended us, we draw on other correspondents. There is the key to the riddle, my dear friend, it is simply up to you not to have to guess at others of the same sort. . . we ask nothing better than to work with you, but in that case, increase the blank credit which you make available and rest assured that you have nothing to fear.

You must have remarked from the choice of paper which we remit to you as security how prudent we are; we act that way in all our transactions. Today we can say, without flattering ourselves, that we stand with Oppenheim at the head of Egyptian banking, and a still brighter future lies before us under the reign of H. R. H. Ismaïl Pasha, with whom we were very close before his accession to the throne.

Edouard Dervieu could afford to adopt this high and mighty air. As we have seen, 1862 had been a banner year. The hesitations, the inevitable delays in switching to cotton from traditional crops were quickly overcome as the magnitude of the world cotton crisis became apparent and prices soared. By the end of 1862, Egyptian "good-fair" was selling for twice as much as it had at any time in 1861. Cotton exports jumped from 596,200 quintals worth 37 million francs in 1861 to 820,110 quintals valued at 126 million francs in the succeeding year. Total exports more than doubled in value; imports followed suit. Trade and exchange with England and France boomed, and Edouard Dervieu et Cie boomed with them.

Moreover, as Dervieu was careful to point out, all this was but a piddling indication of what the future would bring. On January 18, 1863, Mohammed Saïd Pasha, Viceroy of Egypt, died in Alexandria. That same day, his nephew Ismaïl was proclaimed Viceroy in Cairo. And where under Saïd, Dervieu had been dealing with the former pupil of his father-in-law, under Ismaïl he was dealing with an old friend. In an absolute monarchy where everything depended on the good will of the ruler, where market competition was subordinated to privilege and political favor, such a tie was without price. The quiet hopes of yesterday were forgotten; the sky was the limit.

Paris, 24 February 1863

My dear friend:

. . . In effect, I should be delighted to give you a large proof of confidence as further evidence of the price we attach to our relations [with you] and our desire to see them gain in intimacy and importance. But you are too much a businessman not to understand that for banking relations to be intimate, they must be exclusive or nearly so, and when we see ourselves competing with two other houses, and perhaps soon with a third, with all of whom you enjoy extended facilities, we find ourselves compelled necessarily to adopt a certain reserve which is implicit in the situation itself and which we would very much prefer not to see exist between us. And then again, as I have already told you, we are not the sort to try and corner business. I find it very natural that our young friend Blonay should want to gain for himself a good connection like yours, and very natural as well that you should accept offers like his which are not the kind to be refused. If I have any regret, it is only that I was not informed by you of the increasing importance of your operations and the higher credit which you wanted made available. For if you had let me know, I should have been glad to confirm what I told M. Gallo [Dervieu's partner] in Paris one day, that we would have no objection to raising to 200 or 250,000 francs the amount of the credit previously agreed on between us.

It seems to me that your legitimate ambition and the requirements of your business will in that way be largely satisfied. In the position in which you find yourself today, disposing of an important capital and distinguished patronage, your success seems assured, and you are continuing, I am sure, to seek much less after speculative undertakings and vast combinations than after limited negotiations and sure transactions.

André's hand was forced. Dervieu had become too promising a client to lose, yet it was unthinkable to share him with an unknown number of other banks, each extending credit independently. In such a situation, it would be next to impossible to proportion the overdraft to the assets and possibilities of the borrower. And for all Dervieu's promise, André was reluctant to give him *carte blanche*. The pride and optimism of the Alexandrian's letter were encouraging, but to the practiced eye of André there was a certain elation, even inebriation, about it that gave him pause. To the cold, calculating Puritan, enthusiasm and banking simply did not mix. Two hundred or 250,000 francs. André hoped that his friend would stick to the lower figure.

III

The character of Ismaïl, first of the Khedives, is one of those moot questions that are the spice of history. In the thirteen years following his accession, the Egyptian national debt rose from £3,300,000 to £91,000,000; in 1876 Egypt was bankrupt, an easy prey to foreign domination. So much is fact. The rest, the reasons and responsibilities, is conjecture and controversy.[19]

For many historians, he has always been Ismaïl the Profligate, a man who found his country rich and thriving and left it poor and in bondage, a man of overweening ambition and reckless prodigality, a wastrel and voluptuary, spendthrift and fool. For others, he is Ismaïl the Magnificent, pathfinder and statesman, a man of vision and sincerity whose only desire was the happiness and greatness of his people. If he borrowed, it was for the worthiest of reasons: to help his subjects in their misfortunes, to build public works, to bind his nation with railroads and steamboats, to convert Alexandria and Cairo into healthful, comfortable cities. And if he borrowed too much, it was only because he was at the mercy of as unscrupulous a band of knaves as ever plucked a bird.

Actually, the tangled, contradictory facts of Ismaïl's life furnish evidence for both points of view. As a young man, he was a highly successful landowner. By progressive, efficient farming, he increased his holdings threefold; his cotton was the best to be found; his fortune was untouched by debt. At the same time, he was active in politics and was thoroughly versed in the techniques and problems of government well before he became ruler. Under Abbas, he led an informal family opposition, a *parti des princes*, and almost paid for his temerity with his life. His uncle Saïd was more receptive to his talents. Ismaïl was given a "ministerial" portfolio and sent to Paris and Rome on special diplomatic missions. When, in 1861, Saïd left Egypt to visit Mecca and Europe, it was the young heir apparent who acted as regent. And when, the following year, revolt broke out in Upper Nubia, Ismaïl led an expedition which, through tact and energy, suppressed the uprising with a minimum of bloodshed.[20] In 1863, therefore, the new Viceroy gave every promise of ruling sagely and with moderation.

On January 20, Ismaïl, in accepting the congratulations of the consular representatives of the foreign powers, explicitly confirmed these impressions.

"I am firmly decided [he declared], to devote to the prosperity of the country which I am called upon to govern, all the perseverance and all the energy of which I am capable. The basis of all good administration is order and economy in finance; I shall seek this order and this economy by every means possible, and to give an example to all, at the same time as a proof of my firm intentions, I have decided as of now to abandon the system followed by my predecessors and to set myself a civil list which I shall never exceed.[21]

No one could have put it better. The consensus of observers was that Ismaïl, if not brilliant and imaginative, possessed just those qualities of sobriety and judgment that Egypt needed. And yet, almost from the very start, the character of Ismaïl proved to be far less straightforward and far less obvious than his career and frequent professions of policy had given to believe.

Essentially, he was a benevolent despot, with all the merits and faults generally associated with so paradoxical a position. Solid and methodical in everyday life, Ismaïl was nevertheless a visionary. He had big plans for Egypt. Unfortunately, this sincere interest in the welfare and greatness of his people was not allied with the practicality so indispensable to effective statesmanship. He lacked a sense of proportion. His plans were more than big; they were grandiose: huge public works, an empire in Africa, a position of international eminence — all the paraphernalia and creature comforts of Western civilization, all the prestige and trappings of Western power, the accomplishment of centuries in a matter of years.

Nor was he capable of the day-to-day decision and maneuver that such a program implied. Not that he was lazy. Ismaïl was a conscientious manager. Those who knew him were unfailingly impressed by his assiduity in accomplishing the painstaking paper work and tiresome formalities of government. But diligence is not skill or tenacity. In the continual skirmishing for advantage, in his struggles with Lesseps over Suez, with European bankers over loans, concessions, and contracts, with England, France, and Turkey over the status of Egypt, Ismaïl seemed to lack the ability to assess the possibilities of his own position or the doggedness to stand and fight when a little resistance or persistence would have made all the difference. He was at bottom an opportunist who preferred to skirt obstacles rather than overcome them — a fatal mistake. For not only did it prove costly in specific negotiations with diplomats and financiers who never forgot the business at hand, but each redoubt turned rather than stormed remained a threat to his rear, sapping his strength and eventually dragging him down.

This tendency to dodge issues derived in part from a certain tender concern for the dignity of his station. Ismaïl wanted to govern as well as rule, but he was not ready to demean himself, before Westerners especially, by rolling up his sleeves and grappling with the mundane trivia and sordid bickering of business and politics. When it was important enough, in the case of Suez, for example, he did condescend to argue and bargain, usually with considerable shrewdness. But even then, he did so half-heartedly, almost apologetically — one can almost feel his relief at turning his litigation with Lesseps over to Napoleon III for arbitration. The exalted stature of kings can be a serious handicap. Constitutional monarchies have solved the problem by interposing a government between the ruler and the nation. Despots must reconcile the contradiction alone.

In Ismaïl, the conflict was especially acute in that, personally, he was not above worrying about petty things. The reputation for thrift of Ismaïl, the man, was not unearned; to the end of his days he was almost miserly about the expenses of his household. He could fight with his gardener over trifles or refuse a tip to his bellboy in a Paris hotel. Unfortunately, Ismaïl, the Viceroy, could not see the pounds for the farthings, and demonstrated before long an appalling talent for spending unconscionable sums of money. Not that he was a sybarite. Even when he spent on palaces and entertainment, it was for the palaces and entertainment of the Viceroy, not of Ismaïl. But he felt keenly the dignity and duties of office, and in the oriental tradition placed great emphasis on the efficacy of pomp and circumstance as instruments of policy.

He had one real talent. Though far from prepossessing in appearance — one observer has described him as "undoubtedly ugly," with "large, thick, and broad" ears, eyebrows projecting in a "ragged, red tangle," and one eyelid drooping more than the other — he was a fascinating personality, a superb conversationalist with a genuine feel for human beings. Unlike most absolute monarchs, Ismaïl was always ready to receive visitors, important and unimportant, with courtesy and kindness. Swift in his observations and acutely adaptable, he was never the same thing to different people. As the same observer expressed it: "I have heard him praised by different people for precisely opposite and contradictory qualities. To one man he would be all suavity and mannerism, and you would hear him praised for his polished manner and knowledge of *savoir-faire*. Another man would laud him because he was businesslike and went straight to the point." [22]

Under the circumstances, one must credit Dervieu with sincerity if not perspicacity in his optimistic assessment of the prospects of Egypt during the coming reign. On March 27, 1863, he wrote André:

With Ismaïl Pacha as Viceroy of Egypt, we are going to see the country prosper more than ever. He has a serious, thrifty disposition. We shall no longer see those government contracts yielding an incredible profit, those monstrous lawsuits, those rapid fortunes which characterized the reign of Saïd Pacha. We shall see business done regularly, coherently; we shall see the credit of Egypt establish and fortify itself. . .

Of course, there was more to it than good administration and the anticipation of "regular, coherent" business. Where, after all, would the Dervieus have been if the Viceroy had really been thrifty? The same letter of March 27 continued:

My relations with Ismaïl Pacha continue to be excellent, even intimate. They have not yet produced results, to be sure, in a material way, but that will come. I am certain that no big financial operation will be organized without my participation; we have a lot of plans on the fire with Oppenheim. There is no need to tell you that the first ones we shall think of to work with us in Europe will be you.

Three weeks more had still not produced anything when Dervieu wrote on April 18:

They have announced the arrival in the near future of Prince Napoleon — that makes still another visit to prevent our Viceroy from setting in motion the reorganization of the country, as he has planned to do since his accession. We have not yet been able to do anything with him in the way of business, and we are anxious to see our excellent relationship with him translated into results.[23]

Dervieu was clearly disappointed. He found himself in the position of the man who sat down hungrily to dinner only to find that the table had not yet been set. Worse yet, there might not be any dinner at all. His fears proved groundless. On May 8 he wrote André in barely contained triumph:

To you who have always given evidence of so much interest in me, I owe a confidence, and you are one of the first with whom I must share it. I should thus like to announce to you that the Viceroy, as evidence of his benevolence and confidence in me, has just urged me to increase the capital of our firm to ten million francs, so that I may be able to take over the first place in the country and undertake all the affairs to which the desire of His Highness to develop the agriculture, commerce, and industry of Egypt will give rise. The Viceroy has been kind enough further to declare to me that he would inscribe himself at the head of my silent partners for a sum of two millions at least, and that he would engage all his high officials to follow him. You must understand, my good friend, you who understand the Orient, what possibilities the participation of His Highness opens to me. He could have done nothing which would be more agreeable to me, which could bring more honor to me, and it puts me in a position to preserve my individuality and make a fortune in a few years. I immediately communicated this good news to my silent partners, who have all agreed and have even subscribed an additional two million francs, which, added to my present capital of three million and the viceregal subscription, gives me a total already of seven millions. I have no doubt about finding the other three here on the spot; nevertheless, as soon as I reach eight million, I shall organize a new firm to start the first of July. We shall give 16 per cent to our shareholders this year and we have not had any privileged affair with the government; we ought thus to do better in the future.

If, among your friends, there were some desirous of participating in an Egyptian affair, I should be pleased to accept some partners from Paris, but in that case, let me know by telegraph since, without flattering myself, I think I can reach the figure of ten millions easily and promptly. I should make you aware of the conditions of our association: limited partnership; four years' duration (I hope to get along after that without silent partners and even to retire in Europe); profits: first 6 per cent to capital, the rest shared 60 per cent to capital and 40 per cent to the active partners; prior deduction of 25,000 francs for the active partners.

This was spectacular progress, even for the Egypt of the cotton boom. Barely two years before, in December 1860, Dervieu had started with a piddling 400,000 francs, some good contacts, and a healthy dose of optimism. Now he had ten million francs, even better contacts, and the prospect of taking over "the first place in the country." The future could not have looked brighter.

Nevertheless, this was not quite the sort of thing André envisaged. On May 10, even before he received Dervieu's letter of the eighth, he wrote:

. . . I should have liked to speak to you of the Bank of Egypt. That which exists today is really not one, and it would be necessary, while preserving the title of the establishment, to transform it by obtaining for it privileges analogous to those which we have obtained at Constantinople for the Ottoman Bank. The public looks favorably on the organization of concerns of this nature, and a firm like that which I am thinking of with solid support in London and Paris would soon get the best of the Société financière d'Egypte. If we could organize something along these lines, we could then build up intimate relations with the Ottoman Bank.

Here lay André's real interest, and the magnitude of the project gave something of the measure of his thinking. The original Ottoman Bank had been founded in 1856 by a syndicate of English businessmen to engage in ordinary commercial and financial operations. Over the years, it had built up close relations with the Turkish government — the directors had proved most helpful and understanding in tiding the prodigal and inefficient sultanate over repeated financial difficulties. This sympathetic policy was amply justified by subsequent events. The failure of the Ottoman loan of 1860, which precipitated a disastrous crisis among the Levantine merchant houses that had invested or speculated in Turkish treasury notes, convinced the Porte of the need for a house-cleaning. The keystone of the new financial structure was to be a semiofficial national bank along the lines already laid down in England and France, and despite considerable competition from rival groups, the Ottoman Bank was chosen for the role. In 1862–63, the original firm was accordingly reorganized as the Imperial Ottoman Bank, this time under the auspices of some of the outstanding figures of Anglo-French finance. Under the terms of the concession, the new firm was to issue notes, administer the Turkish debt, and act as the sole financial agent of the imperial government. As might be expected, the flotation of such a promising enterprise was a profitable operation. British investors paid premiums of up to 13 and 14 pounds during the weeks preceding issue on shares whose paid-in value was to be only 10 pounds.[24] Their expectations of future profits were not disappointed.[25]

This was the sort of possibility Alfred André envisioned for Egypt. The stakes were tremendous; the field, wide open. As regards possible competition, there were only two conceivable candidates, neither of which was really a threat. The Bank of Egypt, founded in 1855–56, had the right name, but the substance was lacking. Engaged in enterprises of a limited character, it was already turning from the Egyptian scene by merging with an Indian bank.[26] The other, the Société financière d'Egypte, was a more ambitious firm, brash to the point of offending even the tenuous dignity of Alexandrian finance, and presumptuous in its efforts to arrogate to itself privileges that clashed sharply with the intentions and policy of the Viceregal government.[27] Under the circumstances, André was more than justified in building plans on Dervieu.

The latter's letter of the eighth, with its announcement of an expansion of the existing partnership, may therefore have been something of a disappointment. The change was nevertheless a step in the right direction and in no way precluded the later creation of a national bank. On May 17, André wrote in haste to congratulate his friend and to accept a share in the new firm. This was followed by two telegrams setting his participation at 300,000 francs on his own account and 100,000 francs on behalf of an unnamed friend. The whole was confirmed at length by letter of the twenty-sixth, with one stipulation that throws light on the prudence and discretion of the Haute Banque:

On the other hand, there could be some inconvenience for us were our firm to figure in its own name in your act of formation; we shall have to see, then, under whose name and in what way our participation is to be expressed.

André was chary about the effect his participation might have on the other Egyptian firms with whom he did business. On the other hand, the proposition was too promising to pass up and Dervieu too good a client to antagonize, whatever awkward adjustments might have to be made. The letter continued:

I wish now that everything works out for you as the patronage of your powerful protector leads you to hope: that he really turns over to you the sum promised and that afterwards he sees that the sums on which you are counting pass through your hands. Those are prospects which our friends naturally had in mind in associating themselves with our resolution, and it is essential, it goes without saying, that your royal partner carry out his promises at once, especially insofar as his participation is concerned.

On the basis of his knowledge of previous Egyptian financial transactions, André had good cause to worry. The viceregal government had a habit of paying with promises and paper. André was simply reminding Dervieu to collect his two million francs — in cash.

Dervieu hastened to reassure his friend by return mail.

Alexandria, 3 June 1863

My dear friend:

I do not have the time to have you a copy made of my *acte de société*, but here is the first proof from the printer. You will see therein the bases of our establishment; I think you will approve them. Our affair is rather an affair of confidence, done among friends, than a firm whose foundation is a public matter. In effect, without any sort of publicity, our subscriptions are up to 9,200,000 francs today, and if we have not brought them up to ten millions here, it is simply that we are waiting to learn how much some of our old partners, now in Europe, desire to increase their share in the firm. Among our subscribers are all the Egyptian princes and all the high officials, the ministers at their head, several of the first houses of Alexandria, among others Briggs and Co. for 500,000 francs,[28] Ruyssenaers for 600,000,[29] Dumreicher for 325,000. Our friend Hermann Oppenheim insisted on subscribing for 250,000 francs in his wife's name; we could not refuse him. . .

You can put away your fears. We are no longer under the regime of Saïd Pacha; the Viceroy will pay up his share to the last cent. He said it to us quite explicitly, even though we thought on our own initiative that we ought to offer him some time. He thanked us, but told us that his children would do their part just like all the other shareholders. We have no privileged subscriptions. They have all been requested, in several cases solicited. There was a great to-do hereabouts; certain consuls wanted to protest to the Viceroy; our colleagues were terrified, except for good old Oppenheim, who rubbed his hands with us. The Viceroy stood up to it and signed our statutes four days ago before going to Cairo. Everything is now perfectly in order. You will see in the preamble to the statutes that mention is made of the viceregal subscription.

This made all the difference. If André's other Egyptian clients were participating in the new firm, they obviously could not object to his doing the same. He wrote Dervieu a brief note to this effect:

I only want to tell you at this time that the information contained in your letter of June 3 eliminates the principal objection that we could have had to being mentioned by name in your *acte de société*, that is, the inconvenience that might have resulted to our relations with other firms of your city. Now everybody will understand, I think, that the figure placed against our name is

of relatively little importance, because it is a question less of an affair for us
than of a sign of friendship and confidence. You will receive, then, our official
letter of adherence for

		150,000 francs
with those of	M. Armand Heine	75,000
our friends:	M. Michel Heine	75,000
	M. J. Denion Du Pin	100,000
		400,000 francs

Dervieu had definitely arrived. Heretofore, his only tie with the powers
of international finance had been with André and, friendship aside, their
relationship had been essentially one of banker and client. Now they were
partners. More than that, other members of the French financial aristocracy had joined André in this gesture of "friendship and confidence." In
Denion Du Pin — the name was orthographically if not phonetically impressive — Dervieu was consorting with one of the leading capitalists of
the day, a director in such powerful firms as the Société générale,[30] the
Messageries maritimes,[31] the Forges et chantiers de la Méditerranée,[32]
and the Ottoman Bank. The brothers Heine, if less prominent at the
moment, were to play an even more important role in the long run. Like
André, they were bankers by profession and tradition, members of the
same family of which Heinrich Heine was at once the most exceptional
and most remarkable progeny. It was a family which, like the other great
Swiss and German financial clans, had sent forth its children to the four
corners of the globe, wherever there were bills to be discounted and money
changed. Armand and Michel had made their fortune in New Orleans,
where they had long been in close relations with Marcuard, André et Cie.
Now established in Paris, they were starting on a new career which was
to make them in one generation one of the most important houses of the
Haute Banque and bring Michel to the Board of Regents of the Bank
of France.

In the meantime, Dervieu's letters made it clear that, for the moment
at least, André's idea of a national bank would have to be abandoned.
Apparently Oppenheim and Dervieu had anticipated their friend by suggesting such a project to Ismaïl who, after consultation with his ministers,
had categorically rejected it. Both by inclination and from hard experience,
the Viceroy found it more convenient to deal with men whom he trusted
personally than with the impersonality of a corporation. As Dervieu told
the story in a letter of May 20, 1863:

. . . one evening the Viceroy tells me: Dervieu, I have turned down all your
projects because, with my plans to put my finances in order, I do not need to
create resources for myself, but I do need near me none the less a strong credit
establishment on which I can count and which has all my confidence. You know

the esteem I have for you. I am quite certain that you will never create difficulties for me, that you will never pursue me with litigation. It would not
perhaps be the same with a corporation. Today you would set up a firm in
which you, Oppenheim, and several others who are devoted to me would hold
seats on the Board of Directors, but who is to guarantee me that those who
succeed you in a few years will act in the same way. I should thus prefer to
see your capital increased, and since you have been able, working alone, to win
your present position, I have no doubt that you will do even better, especially
when people know that I am one of your partners to the extent of £100,000
sterling.[33]

You can imagine, my good friend, whether I rejected such proposals. I
thanked His Highness and we immediately agreed on all the conditions.

That is the exact story of what happened. That will prove to you, my good
friend, that there is nothing to be done for the moment along the lines you
indicate, but that will come, you may be sure, and we are placed in such a way,
Oppenheim and I, that no affair in Egypt can escape us. We have always
counted on you first in Paris. Your collaboration will be precious to us.

In all this, the contrast between André and Dervieu was evident. To
begin with, there was an important difference in objectives. The Paris
banker was thinking in terms of big international operations, of the
organization of corporations whose flotation would yield sizable profits
and the service of whose stocks and bonds would mean commissions in
the future. To be sure, Dervieu, by his own admission, had gone along
with Oppenheim to suggest an establishment of this sort to the Viceroy.
But we may feel certain that the whole thing was Oppenheim's idea. For
Dervieu, such creations had competitive implications of the most distasteful nature — he had everything to lose and little to gain in these combinations of high finance.

Moreover, this disagreement derived not only from a momentary
divergence of material interests but, more important, from a deep-seated
conflict between the philosophies of banking of the two men. André was
a financier by calling — what else would an André do? He saw his house
as a permanent institution filling a well-defined niche in the business
world. Indeed, for André, the very permanence of his bank resided in its
performance of a definite role, the transaction of financial matters for a
small, intimate circle of businessmen and investors, one of many such
circles built around similar banks. The private bank was of its essence particularistic: its clientele was restricted to friends and friends of friends; its
operations were secret; its whole procedure, as confidential as possible.
Among such firms there reigned a certain understanding, a sort of gentlemen's agreement that restricted uncouth competition and made high
finance a quiet, well-bred game. Note, in this regard, André's readiness to
share his participation in Dervieu's new company — despite the prospect

of substantial dividends. The important thing was not to maximize immediate profit, but to strengthen the network of relationships on which the ultimate prosperity of his house rested.

Beyond this dignified sphere lay the impersonal, universalistic corporation, the Ottoman Banks, dealing with anything and anybody so long as the risk was good, publicizing its operations, even advertising for clients. To be sure, it was often the small private banks which promoted and controlled the joint-stock companies, but, for one thing, the firms involved in such enterprises were always careful to maintain the distinction between the two spheres of activity, and for another, the houses concerned took great pains, in accordance with tradition and for the sake of security, to share the venture, however profitable, with their colleagues.

Dervieu was aware of these fine points of banking behavior, but tended to forget them. Unlike André, he was thinking in terms of a very limited future — he had already expressed his hope of retiring in four years. His objective was simply to make as much money as possible as quickly as possible. The favor shown by Ismaïl in preferring Dervieu's personal house to a powerful, impressive national bank, in asking him to expand to accommodate the projected development of Egyptian agriculture and commerce and, even more, offering his moral and financial support, represented a fabulous opportunity. The question never entered Dervieu's mind of the possible incompatibility of the character of his firm and the task imposed on it. He was ready to tackle the whole of Egyptian finance and trade if need be. As for the discontent of his Alexandrian colleagues, it only redoubled his enthusiasm. It was too bad they did not know the Viceroy too.

IV

Being royal banker in the Egypt of the cotton boom had its advantages. Pecuniary, to begin with. As the Viceroy's preferred financial agents, Dervieu and Oppenheim naturally handled a large proportion of the purchases, contracts, and other transactions of Ismaïl and his government. And when one considers that in 1862–63 the Viceroy's income in his own right was over ten million francs, that official revenues came to more than 150 millions in 1863, and that expenditures were well over twice this amount, one gets some idea of the sort of clients Dervieu was dealing with.

Much of this, naturally, never passed through Dervieu's hands, but even after deduction for administrative salaries, direct transactions, Oppenheim's share, and so on, there was more than enough left over. There were payments to be made to European creditors like the Comptoir d'Escompte in Paris. There were supplies to be bought for the public services, steam engines and cotton gins for Ismaïl's estates, cement and iron for dams and factories. There were hundreds of thousands of head of cattle and livestock to be replaced following the worst murrain in Egypt since the days of Moses.[34] Dervieu was ready to order all of these, not directly, of course, but through specialized merchant houses, always adding his own sizable commission to the already oversized price.

At the same time, Dervieu's intimacy with the Viceroy was a tremendous stimulus to his regular banking business. He was now a marked man, the target of all manner of blandishment, flattery, solicitation and exhortation. In all of Egypt, who better to do business with, who better to have as a friend, than Edouard Dervieu? He began to branch out. If a new corporation was formed, Dervieu was sure to be on the Board of Directors. He bought into manufacturing enterprises, built ginning mills, helped create the new industry of cottonseed oil.

But at least as satisfying as the crinkle of bank notes and the jingle of coins was the psychic income yielded by Dervieu's new, exalted role. For as royal banker he was in effect a man of state, a minister without portfolio, an intimate adviser on problems of national and international import: budgets, loans, the Suez Canal, the foreign relations of Egypt. How much real influence Dervieu exercised in these fields, it is impossible to say. In any event, these new concerns made a heady brew. Bursting with pride, thoroughly impressed with his own importance, the Alexandrian never tired of impressing it on his colleague in Paris. His letters were spiced with remarks like:

His Highness has great plans and he is persevering enough to push them to their conclusion. He has charged me to have a plan prepared for the construction of the port of Alexandria. (June 19, 1863.)

I have just passed a week with the Viceroy in Cairo. . . Yesterday evening I remained alone in *tête-à-tête* with the Viceroy. . . (October 20, 1863.)

I spend my life between Alexandria and Cairo. I have in a way replaced Nubar Pacha for the Viceroy,[35] and you can well understand the intimacy created between His Highness and myself by this job of interim private secretary. Although it doubles my work and does not leave me a moment's rest, I am very happy about it since it builds up my credit and my reputation. (October 26, 1863.)

Unfortunately, these advantages and perquisites were more impressive in appearance than in substance. True, the rate of profit was high and the volume of business large, but much of the profit existed only on paper, and much of the business depended on an extraordinary combination of viceregal favor and cotton boom, neither, of its nature, eternal.

Dervieu's books were filled with bills outstanding and accounts receivable, for there was no country where accommodation paper was so popular as in Egypt. Any business firm in need of money would simply draw on some friendly concern willing in turn to accept the bill, which then looked like any other piece of commercial paper except that it had no basis whatever in a real commercial transaction. This was, in effect, a disguised form of unsecured loan. Dervieu discounted and marketed masses of these notes, which many of his clients found an ideal means of meeting their obligations.

The greatest exponent of paying old debts with new, of course, was His Highness, Ismaïl Pasha. And while, as a nonbusinessman the Viceroy could hardly create accommodation paper he did not need to. Since his own signature was considered ample security, he found it a simple matter to issue all kinds of bills, notes, bonds, and similar promises, which fed the fires of Egyptian speculation and floated through the markets of Europe. From Dervieu's point of view, of course, this technique of deferred payment was dangerous only insofar as his bank held on to the Viceroy's paper and listed it among receivables. More often, however, he disposed of it, through André and other intermediaries, to European bankers and investors.

More serious was Ismaïl's penchant for borrowing on account. One of his prime motives in investing two million francs in Dervieu's bank to begin with had been to open a drawing account big enough to accommodate his appetite for money. For Ismaïl, borrowing by overdraft had it all over the issuance of notes and other types of formal indebtedness. It was private — there could be no unpleasant publicity that might adversely affect his credit on the open market. It was flexible in a way that regular loans could never be. And it was a personal matter that by-passed even the moral strictures of his ministers and evaded any efforts of Constantinople to control Egyptian finances.

Nor were his calculations disappointed. For the two millions invested, Ismaïl had already drawn some seven millions by the end of 1863. Dervieu was badly squeezed. Half his capital was tied up in an unsecured account, with little prospect of release. For one thing, Ismaïl's financial difficulties had a certain perdurable quality. For another, there was little Dervieu could do about it. His prestige and profits depended on the favor of the Viceroy, which was contingent in turn on the facilities extended by Dervieu, which facilities in turn weighed ever more heavily on his business operations — a vicious spiral that could well lead to ruin.

To André, this was madness. He was a pessimist, by inclination and conviction, and the ebullient optimism of Dervieu made little impression — and that unfavorable — on his skeptical temperament. For the prudent scion of generations of prudent Calvinist bankers, all this apparatus of accommodation paper, of debts piled on debts, all this mess of notes and bills and bonds and overdrafts, was just an invitation to disaster. From his office in Paris he saw the distant gyrations of Egyptian commerce, the gay dance of paper prosperity, with the jaundiced eye of a defender of the faith confronted with the distasteful twitchings of some heretical sect of Shakers.

The problem was to communicate his reservations to Dervieu as tactfully as possible. Almost from the start, the letters from Paris were dashes of cold water on the warmth of Dervieu's enthusiasm. When, on October 20, 1863, Dervieu wrote to inquire about the feasibility of a loan of some six or seven hundred thousand pounds to Ismaïl on current account, André hastened to express his doubts about the Viceroy's intentions:

let us speak of *His Highness the Viceroy*.

Honor to whom honor is due! He is evidently a man of perseverance and a great intellect. I understand how pleasant it is to submit to his influence and further his vast projects. You find yourself marvelously placed for your business thanks to the confidence you have been able to inspire in him, and you are probably directing all your efforts toward maintaining your position intact. But this type of permanent absorption of your capital, which he makes use of and which he could abuse, this excessive sensitivity with which he is animated so far as his credit is concerned, this calculating and bargaining mind which he gives evidence of in all circumstances, prove to me that you are dealing with a strong party. Thus, in your negotiations with him, whatever they may be, you have to fear above all allowing yourself to be drawn into something, justified perhaps by your friendly relations and your desire to serve him faithfully and well, which, however, I think he would be very clever in taking advantage of, even to your detriment, if it were to his interest. You are evidently placed in a difficult position so far as he is concerned. You have to give him all the assistance possible and, in view of the increasing needs which are manifesting themselves, you have to exert all your efforts to keep up with your task. But at the same time, you must keep yourself on the defensive, for the tendency of all governments, in Egypt as in France, is and will always be to take over for their own profit the credit of the establishments or houses around them. In this struggle with the powers on which you depend, you are helpless as it were, and you must always be on guard; if not, you will come to see at a given moment — at a moment of opportunity — your resources paralyzed in your hands.

And then a short lesson in the technique of banking:

To make a loan on account is for the lender to place himself absolutely at the discretion of the borrower, is to risk not being reimbursed at a fixed date, to submit to extensions, to find oneself disputed perhaps by a successor to the throne — all things one cannot expose oneself to when it is a question of millions to be ventured far from one's personal control.

.   .   .   .

[Our line of conduct] is clearly indicated. It must have as its keynote this double idea: to give you the most extensive coöperation possible without deviating from the rules of prudence. In the state of our relations, there is no need for us to debate questions of confidence. A simple retrospective glance at your account would show you that we can on occasion do more than our share in holding the fort with our friends. But what I want to convince you of is the utility, both for *you* as well as *for us*, of handling one's credit with extreme care, of never opening oneself to criticism in any way, and of not taking the chance of attracting, I shan't say the blame, but only the attention of the public by serving as intermediary in operations which are too vast, so that the accumulation of current risks during a prolonged period does not constitute, in the event of certain possibilities, a real peril. These possibilities are a political revolution here at home, or a crisis in cotton. God protect us, my dear Dervieu, from another 1848! In any case, let us know how to conduct our operations with enough prudence so that, if we should see such days, we could get through them again without accident. As for a crisis in cotton, I do not see one for the moment, quite the contrary. Even if there were peace tomorrow between the belligerents in America, what a long time there would be before you would see production return to its former figure. But after all, we have to count on the follies that speculation is capable of. . . The current prices of cotton are excessive, you must not forget that. You must thus be on your guard against all speculative paper, that is, drafts of one house on another house; for the same reason, you should wisely proportion to circumstances and to the worth of your clients the advances which you are asked to make on cotton prior to the shipment of the merchandise or the acceptance of the drafts. . . And to clean up the subject, I should only like to add once more that we are counting on you, on your prudence, on your care in going along with us, as you have in the past, on the basis of this principle: that you are to try as much as possible to keep your account leveled off. I have no doubt that that will be the case in the future as it has been in the past, if you know how to keep your resources liquid and to resist at times royal demands. (November 5, 1863.)

And when, despite remonstrances, Dervieu's generosity to the Viceroy left him far behind in his account with André, the latter took the occasion to preach once again the principles of sound banking:

Finally, my dear Dervieu, then as now, . . . I believe that you would have better served your true interests had you, instead of involving yourself more and more every day with the government, simply refused the Viceroy facilities which the resources at your disposal do not permit you to make available now. I am sorry that I do not have a good hour before me to develop my ideas, for I feel that you have an interest, from the point of view of the large credit which one must enjoy in the business world, in not losing sight of the ideas and principles of France and in guarding yourself against the dangerous traditions of the Levant, all the more dangerous because they are more tempting in their immediate results. (January 26, 1864.)

André's normal reservations, his almost instinctive suspicions of an alien way of business, were aggravated by the shakiness of the European money market. The fall of 1863 was one of liquidation and retrenchment for European finance. It had been a boom year in company formation: in England alone, security issues had absorbed 145 million pounds; in France, 800 million francs. At the same time, millions were being siphoned away to the Orient, especially to India and Egypt, where the farmers had a penchant for hard coin. By June 1863, the drain was apparent in the bullion reserves of the Banks of England and France. Before the end of the year, the former was discounting at 8 per cent; the Bank of France held to 6 and 7 only under pressure from the government, which feared the effect of a crisis on its Mexican War loan.

In Egypt, prosperity went on unabated. In spite of a record harvest, the price of Jumel at Liverpool rose from 21 pence a pound in July to 29¾ in October of 1863. From the Viceroy, who with some eight or nine million pounds of cotton was looking forward to almost one million pounds in income for this source alone, to long destitute fellahs who were now able to eat white bread and meat and buy slave girls for domestic work and distraction, everyone connected with the cultivation or trade of the new white gold was reaping a bonanza.

Everything in the Nile Valley was sacrificed to cotton. From a country which had always shipped its grain and beans throughout the Mediterranean, Egypt was now near the point where imports of food would be necessary to stave off famine. Prices rose precipitately. Eggs were three or four times as high as in 1862, oil and vegetables had tripled, grain and fowl were up 400 per cent. In this euphoric atmosphere of inflation, the bearish fears of André seemed far away. On October 26, 1863, Dervieu wrote:

If we are helped this year by credit from Europe, we can handle an enormous volume of transactions. We have the good will of all; it is known that we do not take advantage of our clientele, that we work faithfully, that we have the support of the Viceroy. Hence everybody in business, big and small, comes to us, and even if our capital were three times the size, we could use every bit of it.

At the same time, Dervieu vigorously defended his royal partner against André's criticism. Replying to a particularly severe letter from Paris, he wrote, with some indignation:

Before going with you into the details likely to interest you concerning our business and Egypt, allow me to correct an opinion which you express in your latest letter, namely, that the Viceroy is tight-fisted. That is an error, a very great error. If Ismaïl Pacha has been, and is still, very embarrassed in his finances, it is because he has wanted to break with all the traditions of his predecessor and that he has insisted that all sums due by the government be paid on the dot. He found the finances in a deplorable state, the taxes collected eight months in advance, the pay of employees eighteen months in arrears, and numerous engagements undertaken. The purchases made by Saïd Pacha during his last trip to Europe alone amounted to more than 15 million francs. The greater part consisted of useless objects, greenhouses, silver fireplaces, jewels, a yacht making twenty miles an hour, two 600-horsepower marine engines without hulls, etc., etc. The Viceroy has had the greenhouses turned into railroad stations, has sold the yacht at a loss and has taken in exchange tugboats for the Nile; he has exchanged the big machines for freight cars to transport cotton, etc., etc. All that cost money. The arrears of the employees have been made up; today, they are paid on the dot, month by month. The same goes for the army, which had to be reconstituted; today there are twenty thousand men. The arsenals and the storehouses were empty; Saïd Pacha had sold everything. Do you think that all that has been accomplished without enormous expenses? The Viceroy was counting on the income from cotton; there came the disastrous murrain, which has just absorbed everything the cotton crop will provide. But trade profits thereby, since the imports of cattle will amount to at least as much as the exports of cotton. The Viceroy alone has been obliged to order 120 steam plows, coming to no less than a sum of 6 million francs. Add to that the steam pumps, the cotton gins, etc., etc., and you arrive at an enormous figure of useful expenses which have been imposed on the Viceroy by circumstances and by his practical knowledge as an administrator.

In such a situation, our path was all traced out, for Oppenheim and for us. We had to help him with all our resources, and profit at the same time from all the needs the Viceroy had. For my part, I have not been ahead with him for more than five million francs. It was a lot, I admit, by comparison with my capital, but how much business have I not had, precisely because of this outlay? Today this figure is down to about three millions, and it is going to go down even more in a little while. The same sum is also owed to Oppenheim, who has had much less in the way of orders than I. I have had a large share in the importation of horses, 2,000 from Marseilles, 1,500 from Syria, 1,000 mules from France. I have not been forgotten in the case of steam engines; I am going to supply from two to two and a half million francs' worth. All of these, my good friend, are good deals bringing handsome profits, but necessitating a large outlay as well, and you must not be surprised that we have made full use of the credit by acceptance which you opened to us. (February 2, 1864.)

Dervieu was indignant about André's captious timidity. In Egypt, people were throwing money around, and in Paris and London, the most powerful international bankers were trimming sail and groping their way through decidedly uncertain weather. Surrounded by prosperity, he felt that he was being unjustly penalized for the perverse afflictions of the European market. He ceded reluctantly to André's exhortations to liquidity, insisting nevertheless on the solidity of his firm and the reasonableness of his policy.

Although we have to meet very large outlays at the moment, outlays which have earned us and are still earning us very handsome profits, I have none the less determined to reduce as much as possible our account with your house. I have no doubt that you have noted it, my good friend, but I shall not hide from you that the most frightening thing in the position of a banking house in Egypt is the thought of being exposed to a diminution or suspension of credit with one's European friends as a result of political events which have nothing to do with our country and when we are not handling a single affair which can end in a loss, that is to say, when our outlays derive only from supplies furnished the government and when all the paper we take is the product of merchandise shipped abroad. There are few places in the world which can match us in that. (March 5, 1864.)

Reading this, André could only shake his head. He was convinced that Dervieu was overextended, that Egyptian prosperity was artificially swollen, that sound banking is the same anywhere at any time and that infractions of the rules are sooner or later fatal. All the same, with conditions in Europe improving, there was no point in antagonizing his correspondent, who was beginning to be somewhat restive under the steady scolding. Besides, there did seem to be something different about Egypt . . . André pulled in his horns.

Paris, 18 March 1864

My dear Dervieu:

Gallo and Oppenheim confirm what you say about the relative abundance of money in Egypt. Here we have not reached that point. . . You are going to accuse me perhaps of always seeing the dark side of things, but I prefer to see the future from that side than from the other. It is more prudent. All the better if I am wrong. Thus I consider that we must count here, for many months yet, on money being dear, very dear even in autumn if our harvest is mediocre, as certain symptoms would indicate, and if this cause of the export of bullion should come to be added to the other causes still operative at present.

Now, unless there is a European war, which, for my part, I do not fear, I calculate that our business will remain active, healthy, and profitable. I am counting, in particular, that nothing will come up to hinder or diminish our relations. That should indicate to you that, while desiring, as I have previously explained, not to find ourselves in a state of permanent overdraft in your regard, we are not — far from it — the kind to suspend over your head a sort of Damocles' sword. I do not think that anything in what I have written to you on this subject previously is of a nature to justify on your part any anxiety of this kind, or I have expressed myself quite poorly. I have only tried to get you to share our idea, to the effect that in all business, however good it may be, one has to know to remain faithful to the principles of moderation. I have

no doubt, moreover, that that is your rule, just as ours. The only thing that
may cause us to differ from time to time is that, for judging things, we are
placed at poles a little apart. The essential thing, then, is that we enlighten
each other's judgment by an exchange of friendly information.

v

André was right. So long as Dervieu's position, however impressive,
depended on the good will of the Viceroy, he was building on quicksand.
Moreover, it was at least in part a quicksand of his own making, since
Ismaïl, for all his appetite for money, could never have consumed it so
quickly without the aid, indeed the encouragement, of his bankers. The
Viceroy, his expenditures running well beyond even the unprecedented
revenues of these years of unprecedented prosperity, passed from one pecuniary crisis to another, resorting each time to new and ever more complicated devices to fill his empty pockets. And each time, Dervieu bore part
of the cost.

Under the circumstances, the alleviation offered by the diminution of
Ismaïl's overdraft at the beginning of 1864 could only have been temporary. With more and more of his funds frozen in big, profitable operations,
Dervieu found himself more cramped than ever. The time was rapidly approaching when he would have either to stop giving money away and
start collecting, or take some radical steps to secure additional capital to
maintain the mad pace.

As is so often the case, the former alternative was at once the more
sensible and the more disagreeable. A return to sound, liquid banking
would free Dervieu for the normal business operations on which he had
built his early, modest fortune; it would also mean, however, his abdication
of the proud and privileged situation he had won for himself at the side of
Ismaïl.

There was, perhaps, one way in which accounts could be settled without
squeezing and alienating the Viceroy. If the latter could float a national
loan big enough to pay his existing debts and meet his expenses for some
time to come, he might be ready to satisfy his creditors without begrudging
them their due. Such a loan had, in fact, been under consideration for
some time. As early as the fall of 1863, Oppenheim, whose firm had negotiated the first Egyptian loan for Saïd Pasha in 1862, was urging Ismaïl
to issue another. Dervieu, who was naturally consulted, had been cool at
first. In an international flotation of this kind, he could at best be an enthusiastic supporter. He was eventually converted, however, by the urgings
of André, who had every reason to favor such an operation, and by the continued pressure of Ismaïl's demands. On February 2, 1864, he wrote André
a confident report on the progress of the project:

we are pressing the Viceroy to make a loan as soon as the conditions of the European markets improve. He has a thousand legitimate motives for offering it to the financial public. . . For us there would be the advantage, first of all, of being charged with the operation, then, of not being obliged to pull teeth so far as money is concerned, as we shall still be obliged to do for some time. The Viceroy is resisting, but he will come around.

For Ismaïl, of course, the reasons which had long deterred him from such a step, despite its effectiveness as a means of raising a large sum, were still valid. He preferred, therefore, Dervieu's second alternative, an infusion of capital to enable the banker to catch up with his royal master. And in his heart, Dervieu agreed with him, for that, after all, was the only way he could meet future opportunities without sacrificing present gains. The difficulty was that, on the one hand, no one — and André was the only real possibility — would want to furnish the funds on account or as a credit, and that, on the other, no one was likely to look with favor on the expansion of a firm which only eight months before had increased its capital from three to ten millions. André, especially, would hardly be pleased by new construction on the old paper foundations. Dervieu broached the subject cautiously, even deprecatingly:

I have also to ask your opinion on a step toward which the Viceroy is push-ing me and which I am resisting. It is a new increase in my capital. His High-ness, with a view to what he is planning to undertake, would like to see my firm have a still larger capital. He would double his investment, and all his high officials would follow suit. Others, who now have nothing, would like to place some funds with me. In short, I am certain that, without having recourse to Europe, I shall find another ten to twelve million francs here. (February 2, 1864.)

André rejected the idea out of hand.

The months went by, Egyptian spring turned to hot Egyptian summer, and Dervieu's financial position deteriorated with the weather. Pinch was rapidly becoming paralysis. At this juncture, André received a letter. It was a typical Dervieu missive, bubbling with excitement and enthusiasm. Apparently some interlopers had appeared on the Egyptian scene, tres-passers on ground sacred to Dervieu and Oppenheim. The Viceroy had let it slip and immediately sworn his bankers to secrecy. These intrud-ers planned to organize a 100-million-franc corporation, an Egyptian Crédit mobilier, to supply the capital requirements of the Nile Valley.

Dervieu, Oppenheim, and the other financial interests of the country were frantic at the very idea. That sort of competition would be ruinous. Confronted with this threat, a representative of one of these other interests offered to reorganize Dervieu's bank as a corporation and throw in a bonus

of £200,000 for Dervieu's good will and three years of his services as director of the new firm. The idea appealed to Dervieu, who immediately
thought it would be even better to arrange the deal through his own
friends — on the same conditions, of course. Moreover, the Viceroy was
sympathetic and promised an increase in his own investment if necessary.
So Dervieu wrote to André, offering him a position as a founding member
and debating the pros and cons of his own position with a decided leaning
toward the former:

This project has its pros and cons so far as I am concerned.

Its realization would diminish, I think, my personality. I shall be no more
than the director of a concern, a big one to be sure. I would be placed under
the supervision of a Board, whereas today I am perfectly free. Besides, my
present partnership will be over in three years. At that time, I shall probably
be able to part company with a large number of my partners, to have my firm
almost to myself, and to leave it later on to my children and those of Gallo. I
would quite certainly have realized the profit offered me in the three years
which remain, and perhaps sooner. I hope to give 20 per cent to my shareholders for the year which is concluding. On the other hand, the realization of
this project frees my name of all eventualities, assures me of a handsome
fortune right away, places me at the head of an affair which will dominate the
country, and prevents any other firm of similar nature from coming and establishing itself here. My capital of ten millions is no longer sufficient to handle
the development of my business. The government is absorbing the greater
part of it, and I still have at the present moment over seven million francs in
orders to be carried out. And I will obtain a lot more the day when I shall be
able to get along without pestering the Viceroy for money any more. . .

Anyway, my good friend, look the project over and give me your opinion,
even by telegraph, so that I may promptly know where I stand and can give
an answer to Oppenheim. (June 4, 1864.)

For the first and only time, a proposal of Dervieu's met with André's
unqualified approval. Here, after a long hibernation, was his old plan for
a national Egyptian bank, somewhat modified, to be sure, but with its
essential features of international flotation and operation intact. André
could savor already the breadth of the conception, the financial ramifications, the prestige that such an operation would confer. Perhaps — and
this is only conjecture — he pictured himself as an emulator, if not of the
Péreires, then of Goschen and the other more conservative financial capitalists of this golden era of company promotion. André hastened to wire
his endorsement: "Full approval in principle of projected combination.
Accept position offered. Count on large participation and agency." This
was followed by a more detailed encomium:

I told you in my wire: I approve the principle in every respect, and what I see you inclined to do is only the execution of a scheme long ripened in my mind. We considered it a year ago with Hermann Oppenheim, and I see further evidence of the favor shown you by Him who directs for us all things, in the fact that a combination which is desirable and advantageous to all interests has captured here, on various occasions, the attention of eminent men, has given rise to conferences, projects, etc. which, after all, seemed certain to result against you rather than for you, and that nothing of the sort has happened.

You have profited by the delay. Stronger and more firmly established in the country, you take the matter in hand once again: well done. How many advantages there are to this sort of abdication, more apparent than real, the idea of which troubles you and gives you pause! You are mobilizing your capital; you are discounting fortune. In governing a business of the first order, your importance as a businessman increases rather than shrinks. You necessarily keep a hand in everything of advantage and importance done in Egypt, and if, as I foresee and hope, you steer your handsome bark well through the reefs and currents, you will not be making a mediocre contribution to the development of the public prosperity and civilization of the country to which you are henceforth attached. It seems to me that, however vast your ambition may be, there is much satisfaction in these perspectives.

Among your partners, there will no doubt be some who show themselves less satisfied, who will miss no longer being *en famille*, as it were, in your firm and who would have preferred to continue being partners with you in affairs which, while less vast, are relatively more certain and lucrative. Some — I think that they will be a minority, but there will be some — will feel that one could or should proceed otherwise in the division of the sum which the new company would pay for your contribution. But on the whole, the transformation will be understood as being in the common interest and, if the circumstances are in the least favorable and the statutes satisfying, your affair will appear before the public assured of success. That is what I said yesterday to M. Du Pin, who is writing you by this mail, and what he will repeat to you on my behalf.

. . . .

As for us in Paris, you have our active and devoted coöperation, and we shall be most happy to collaborate both in the preparation of your statutes and the flotation of your affair. I am therefore confirming here what I wired you the other day, that is to say, that we accept with pleasure the place of founding member which you plan to reserve for our firm.

. . . .

As regards [the] eventual participation of French firms, I should be very embarrassed to try and fix a figure, even offhand. But it seems to me that if, of the 140,000 shares remaining (after your partners are taken care of), Messrs. Oppenheim take 60,000 with the evident intention of drawing on this large quantity for enough to satisfy their personal friends in England; if there are in addition 50,000 shares offered to the public, which is just about the minimum to set up a market, nothing will prevent you from reserving 20,000 shares for the Paris market, whose placement through us in solid hands seems to me assured if the circumstances are in the least favorable.

But we shall come back to this when things are more advanced. For the moment, I want to repeat to you again *that it is advisable to hurry.* Circumstances compel you to take prompt action. At the opening of the coming [cotton] season, you must be there, all ready to serve the interests of your country. (June 17, 1864.)

The one time that André abandoned his characteristic reserve and pessimism he was wrong. Not that the operation was a bad one or the time ill chosen. Subsequent letters, to be sure, were to point to the traditional summer stagnation, to an alleged surfeit of Egyptian securities, to the unallayed threat of renewed hostilities between Prussia and Denmark over Schleswig-Holstein as divers factors precluding the proposed flotation. The fact remained, however, that 1864 was a record year of company formation. During the first third alone, a period dominated in part by high rates of discount and disturbing diplomatic tension, the English investor had paid out over 75 million pounds, more than half as much as for the whole of 1863, itself a boom year. Perhaps financial circles were becoming just a bit finical about new promotions. It was one of those moments when the businessman, pleasantly tired by a long bull market, begins to wonder how long it can last. But André was well aware of this, and felt justifiably that the qualms of prudence would hardly rule out a solid venture of this kind.

The real difficulty would seem to have been his colleagues' unwillingness to swallow Dervieu's price: £200,000 or 5,000,000 francs — in whatever currency expressed, it remained a tremendous sum. To international financiers, accustomed to split such windfalls among themselves, this must have seemed an unwarranted prodigality to an outsider who had little more to contribute than good will. And while Dervieu's good will and banking experience could be expected to yield big profits in the future, such distant rewards cannot have had too much attraction for capitalists who were primarily interested in putting across a remunerative flotation and assuring themselves useful positions of control. Potential dividends could well be left to the investor, who would hardly look with favor on a venture burdened from the start by so great an outlay. To the prospective stockholder, Dervieu and his £200,000 would be not a guarantee of prosperity, but an augury of ruin.

There was resistance from the start. Frühling and Goschen were lukewarm. The French houses which André had hoped to associate with the enterprise, the Mallets and Pillet-Wills, were not accustomed to Egyptian investments, and wary. Even Oppenheim, who had helped Dervieu prepare the project, seized the occasion to aim a few barbs at his colleague in a letter to André of July 1, 1864:

Dervieu has communicated to me the contents of your letter regarding the scheme which we had thought up for his firm. I was pleased to see that you approved our project in principle. But since opinions in England differ somewhat from yours and since they feel above all that the present moment would be impossible, I should very much like to have your opinion on the sum which we have fixed as compensation for Dervieu and his shareholders. I have felt this sum to be too big from the very beginning, and I have looked for a combination which would make it possible for us to give Dervieu's partners simply an interest in the new operation, the success of which would assure them a premium, but here that meets with little understanding. Do you think that one could justify in such an affair a sum of £200,000 paid to a firm which has been in existence only two years and whose prosperity has thus far rested on the favor of the Viceroy? As for me, I should be willing to go along, first, to carry out an idea which is mine in principle, and second, for Dervieu himself, but we have to think of the public. The 60,000 shares which we have reserved for ourselves are not for us alone, you understand; they should serve to procure that financial support in Europe which is necessary. I believe that we must absolutely find a way to carry out, to give effect to, this combination.

Time was running out. The summer is a hot, uncomfortable season in Egypt, especially for cultivators like Ismaïl who have spent the proceeds of the preceding harvest and are awaiting the autumn with impecunious impatience. But debtors, particularly habitual borrowers, are rarely as miserable as their creditors. Dervieu, rich in promises and poor in cash, cringed at the very thought of the approaching cotton season. On June 30, he wrote André, reviewing the obstacles encountered and calling on the latter's help, with or without the coöperation of others.

There is no one, then, but you, my good friend, who can take the affair in hand and bring it to port. If, as Du Pin has told me, you can find in Paris, among first-class sources, a demand for 25,000 shares, that is, £500,000, I can take it on myself to find 50,000 shares here, that is, one million pounds, including my present capital and the £200,000 which would be alloted us. We could limit ourselves for the moment to a capital of £2,000,000, and offer only 25,000 shares to the public in Paris and London. I am even convinced that Oppenheim would take 25,000 shares for his private account, and if that were the case, you would have to decide if it would not be advisable to fix the capital immediately at £4,000,000, while offering half to the public. The unreasonable demands which Frühling-Goschen have made in the projected merger and in the flotation of the Agricole et industrielle have got as far as you,[36] and since you offer me your collaboration in London in case that of Goschen should be wanting, I accept it whole-heartedly. I feel, like you, that the London market is necessary to our affair, but do not lose sight of the fact that, while desirous that our shares enjoy a handsome premium, I do not want to make our affair a speculation. I am certain that with a paid-in capital of £2,000,000, I shall still be able to give a very handsome dividend to our stockholders. I am reduced at this moment to turning away business; I have almost ten million francs in orders from the Viceroy which I am dragging along and not carrying out, since it would be that much capital immobilized for several months, until the Suez affair is finished and the Viceroy can definitely conclude a big loan. This loan, or at least a large participation in it, is promised to me. The advances I have made the government are so considerable and I have so little idea of the time of their reimbursement, that I am obliged to reduce all my credits on the local market. There is no great harm done at this time of the dead season, but in October, when the cotton season begins, it would be unfortunate to lose the first-class clientele which I have built up in Egyptian trade. I am thus very much interested in being assured of an increase in capital or the realization of a big loan. If I cannot be certain of either of these by the end of July, I must give up the execution of the orders which I have got, trim sails, or find other resources.

It was a good letter: just enough frankness — Dervieu implicitly admitted that all the warnings of André about the immobilization of his capital had come true; plenty of confidence — Dervieu was ready to take on everybody; a touch of virtue — the flotation might encounter difficulties, but after all, this was not meant to be a speculation; and the faintest suspicion of presumption — André had never really promised to handle the flotation in London in the absence of British coöperation. Dervieu followed it a few days later with a hasty note indicating that Ismaïl, too, was becoming impatient:

I wrote to you on the 29th of last month and told you that it would be very difficult for me to go to France to follow up the project of cnverting my firm into a banking corporation. In the course of a conversation with the Viceroy, he was the first to urge me to leave, so well does he understand the importance for his country of the creation of such an institution. . . I decided, therefore, the day before yesterday, to leave for Paris and London, and I shall be right on the heels of this letter, since I plan to embark on the 9th with our friend Du Pin. (July 5, 1864.)

July was not June. If Dervieu thought that all this confidence and hopefulness could persuade a man like André to ignore the real stagnation of the summer market and, even worse, to fight the whole of international finance singlehanded, he was in for a bitter disappointment. André wired at once that "if his trip was motivated by the combination in question, . . . it was preferable to put it off until September."

This at least was only postponement. On August 26, André wrote to tell Oppenheim that not only had the matter been definitely shelved, but that a reconsideration of the question might well indicate the advisability of some other arrangement.

We are letting M. Alberti [37] leave today for Constantinople without having succeeded in finding a combination which seemed capable of assuring the transformation of the Dervieu firm. There are real difficulties, and I must give our friend Dervieu the credit that, although upholding, as he should, the position of his present partners, and taking into reasonable account the more or less firm propositions which he has received from London, he is quite disposed to modify his ideas and his plans along the lines best suited to conciliate all interests. The main thing is that the affair be good for everybody. The difficult thing is to find now a serious public to whom we can present an affair which is not too burdened at the start and to find at the same time some firms with enough insight into the future of the operation to take over the risk. I fear that we shall lack both the one and the other when we see the whole thing boil down to the two following questions:

(1) Does the public want to go into an affair loaded at the start with an outlay of five to six millions without any other guarantee than the guidance and influence of a man who announces his intention of retiring in three years? [38]

(2) Do capitalist banks want, except at a considerable remuneration, to run the risk of a large operation and to guarantee its success to Messrs. Dervieu et Cie with the perspective of a doubtful or limited profit?

I fear that for the moment and in view of the general state of affairs, both questions must be answered in the negative. In that case, the best thing for everybody would be either to make a large increase in the capital of the firm in its present form, or to leave it as it is and to establish in Egypt between you and the public a new institution with special attributions and privileges.

André had gone back to his idea of a national bank.

In Egypt, things were moving rapidly. For both Dervieu and Oppenheim, money had become a matter of life and death. The Viceroy, his funds from the cotton harvest of 1863 long exhausted, continued to draw on his running accounts at an ever faster pace. By September he owed 40 million francs to his unfortunate "private bankers." With the treasury empty, the privy purses submerged by debts, and even the willingness of creditors worn out by their sheer inability to lend any further, the oft-discussed loan could no longer be postponed. Whatever the condition of the European market — and it was in an extremely discouraging state — Egypt simply had to borrow.

Not that she lacked for prospective lenders. If anything, the depression of the European exchanges gave credibility to the most exaggerated demands. Like a maiden heiress, the Viceroy was courted by a small crowd of unctuous suitors, all only too eager to help. In the end, Oppenheim won out. On September 10, he wrote André to announce agreement on the major points: £5,000,000, 15 years, 9 per cent. There still remained the details, which were to require months of negotiation.

For Dervieu, the loan came none too soon. On October 8, he announced to André: "There we are, then, saved financially speaking."

VI

Dervieu was saved. He was also ruined. On the one hand, he could now collect at least part of his due from the Viceroy and the Egyptian firms which had been paralyzed by the penury of the treasury. On the other, he had lost his situation with Ismaïl, who preferred creditors who did not expect their money back. Dervieu did his best. He dunned his master tactfully, humbly, apologetically. To no avail. He had simply lost his usefulness. Once the current was reversed, once the Viceroy had to pay Dervieu more than he was getting, he lost interest in cultivating the banker's friendship and favoring his business activities.

Of course, the change was gradual. Dervieu was not ready to cede his advantages without a fight, nor was Ismaïl so foolish as to abandon outright a connection which might still prove worth while. There were periodic renewals of the old intimacy. Dervieu collected, lent, collected again. He tried repeatedly to reorganize and expand his firm or to promote a new loan. He never quite succeeded. André's happy letter of June 1864 had been the high-water mark. Dervieu was never to get any closer to the fulfillment of his dream.

There is no space here to tell the ups and downs of Dervieu's slow decline in subsequent years. This was a period of deflation for the entire Egyptian economy. On May 4, 1864, General Grant crossed the Rapidan to begin the campaign that was to end at Appomattox. By June 15, the Union army had driven to the breastworks of Petersburg, and the steady attrition of Lee's forces had made the outcome only a question of time. That winter, cotton broke and the boom was over.

With his privileged position gone and his regular business crippled by the end of cotton prosperity, Dervieu had come full circle. In 1867 he liquidated his bank and began again as he had some seven years before. His effacement was embittered by the final realization that he had been wrong all along and André right, that he had been a credulous fool. It was a tired, disillusioned man, worn out by years of bickering over claims and counterclaims, who wrote André in the spring of 1868 to express his "great sadness at seeing the Viceroy maneuver so wickedly, continuing to be so faithless, so false."

The lesson was driven home by the sight of Oppenheim who, less scrupulous and tactful than Dervieu, had retained his influence by maintaining his usefulness as a provider of capital. In 1865–66, Oppenheim mortally offended the Viceroy by first attempting to trick him in negotiations for one loan, and then walking out on another just at the moment when the parties to the contract were affixing their signatures. Three years later, Ismaïl found it easy to swallow his pride and let the same man arrange a loan of twelve million pounds. It yielded only seven.

The fact was that Dervieu had been too trusting. An honest man at heart, he had reconciled within himself the contradiction between selfish and guileful motives of profit and a sincere desire to see Egypt prosper. The former were always paramount in fact; the latter was always paramount in principle. Dervieu was an optimist in the true sense of the word. He believed in his own honorableness; he also believed in that of others.

Moreover, like most Europeans in Egypt, Dervieu had a double code of behavior: the same rules did not apply in dealing with the in-group of Westerners and the out-group of natives. Unfortunately, he did not appreciate the double-edged implications of such a relationship. It was all right to milk Ismaïl for all he was worth; it was unthinkable that Ismaïl might want to return the favor.

III

A New Way to Pay Old Debts

A Canadian Experience

By Hugh G. J. Aitken

This is the story of how a young businessman got into debt, and how he got out again. It has some of the elements of a melodrama, and more than a little which might have been taken from a romance. It involves a rich uncle, a young wife, and a mortgage on the family homestead; secret negotiations, intrigue, and a voyage to a far country; hurried letters, suspense, disappointment, and final good fortune. It is a story which might be fiction, but happens to be history. And, as often happens in history, although it is the story of one specific individual, its importance goes well beyond his particular case.

One day in March 1815 at the conclusion of the War of 1812 a young man of twenty-two, William Hamilton Merritt by name, returned to Upper Canada from the prisoner-of-war camp in Massachusetts where he had been detained since his capture at the battle of Lundy's Lane eight months before. Merritt had been born in the United States in 1793, but had come to Canada at the age of three when his father decided to settle in British territory.[1] Before the Revolution the Merritts had been a closely knit clan of freehold farmers in Westchester County, New York. The events of 1776 had dispersed them, and now in 1815 there were two main Loyalist branches of the family in the British provinces — one in Upper Canada, the other in New Brunswick. That in Upper Canada was headed by Thomas Merritt, our young man's father; that in the maritime province by his grandfather, also named Thomas Merritt, and after the latter's death in 1821, by his uncle, Nehemiah Merritt. A merchant and shipowner of St. John, described by Sabine, historian of the Loyalists, as "a gentle-man of great wealth," [2] Nehemiah Merritt will play a major role in the events we are about to describe, and it is unfortunate that, very well off though he undoubtedly was, very little more appears to have been recorded about him.

Apart from infrequent letters, the only link at this time between the two branches of the family was provided by W. H. Merritt himself. He was the only member of Thomas Merritt's family who had visited and stayed with the Merritts of St. John since the two branches had separated in 1784, and none of Nehemiah Merritt's household, it seems, ever visited Upper Canada.

How W. H. Merritt came to occupy this role of intermediary, so important for his future career, may be briefly told. He was intended from an early age for a career in the army or navy,[3] but unless his service in the militia between 1812 and 1814 can be taken as a partial fulfillment, this aspiration was never realized. Instead, when his schooling at Niagara ended at the age of fifteen, he was sent off to sea under the care of his uncle, Nehemiah, whose ship, the *Lord Sheffield*, was engaged in the Quebec–Nova Scotia–West Indies trade.[4] His maritime career embraced only this one rather disastrous voyage, late in 1808, but apparently it was enough to win him Nehemiah's respect and confidence. His uncle sent him back to school at Windsor College, in St. John, and, when he returned to Upper Canada, was always ready with advice and on more than one occasion with financial assistance.

Merritt took up civilian life once again in 1815 with very little experience of commercial affairs. For a short time before 1812 he had acted as junior partner in a local store at St. Catharines in the Niagara district, but, as he later confessed in the privacy of his journal, "[I] understood no branch of business in which I was engaged, having been brought up without any fixed object in view of earning a livelihood." [5] Nevertheless, immediately the war was over, he plunged energetically into business, impressed, it may be, with the newly acquired responsibility of supporting a wife who was the daughter of a New York senator.[6]

Merritt began by arranging for the construction of a large house and store building in St. Catharines. Shortly thereafter he bought a farm and mill site on Twelve Mile Creek, adjoining his father's property, and there built a mill dam, a sawmill, a flour mill with three run of stones, a distillery, a potashery, a cooper shop, and a smithy, not to mention five dwelling houses for the accommodation of his employees.[7] At the same time he began drilling for salt, sinking two shafts to tap a spring under his property.[8] In September 1816, when his sister married a certain Charles Ingersoll, who had been Merritt's subordinate officer in the militia during the war, Merritt took his brother-in-law into partnership and moved the store into his partner's house.[9]

By the end of 1816 the firm of Merritt and Ingersoll could boast extensive property and an unusually well-integrated range of business activities. For this achievement the entire credit was due to Merritt, who in these two years displayed for the first time the driving energy, impatience, and enthusiasm which were to be the most striking characteristics of his subsequent career.

II

Securely founded as the new partnership might appear, it had its weak points. Merritt and Ingersoll had discounted the future very heavily, and the evidence of their optimism hung over them in the form of debts and liabilities. For the house and store building in St. Catharines — now unnecessarily large since the business had been transferred to Ingersoll's establishment — Merritt had incurred a debt of $1250. The farm and mill site had originally been part of the estate of Robert Hamilton, first and most influential of the Niagara merchants, and it was still encumbered by a debt to Hamilton's executors. In purchasing the property, Merritt gave bond that he would pay up to $1000 in satisfaction of the debt, the whole transaction ultimately costing him $4000.[10] In addition, the mills, distillery, and other ventures, while valuable ancillaries to the store business, were all built on borrowed money. In taking his brother-in-law into partnership Merritt was following the pattern of family relationships in business usual at the time. He also gained the assistance of a wartime comrade whom he could trust and whose capacity he knew. But it does not appear that Ingersoll contributed any financial resources beyond the use of his house. Only highly optimistic forecasts of their future earning power could justify their heavy liabilities.

Apart from these long-term encumbrances, Merritt required working capital to buy stock for his store. During 1815 he traveled to Montreal, Quebec, New York, Albany, and Utica, making arrangements for credit and ordering consignments of goods. His purchases were extensive for the time, amounting in all to just under $6640. A little over half the credit was provided by one Montreal firm, Gerrard, Yeward, Gillespie, and Company.[11] Since his house was not yet completed, Merritt divided his consignments into small parcels, and opened them for sale at St. Catharines, Queenston, and the naval station on Grand River — all in the Niagara peninsula — and this first venture, coming as it did in time to reap the full benefit of high prices and inflated postwar demand, appears to have been successful.[12]

There was nothing novel or original about the store business, although the scale on which Merritt planned to operate was perhaps exceptional for the time. He was merely following the example of many other up-country merchants in Canada and throughout North America, Montreal being for him what Boston, Albany, New York, Philadelphia, New Orleans, and similar seaports were for others.[13] It was a system which, so far as Upper Canada was concerned, had not altered materially since 1797, when Richard Cartwright of Kingston had written to Davison and Company of London to explain why he could not deal with them directly:

Not having a seaport in our Province, it would be impossible or extremely inconvenient for any person here to import goods except through the medium of a Montreal house. Goods must be there received, the damages they have sustained at sea (as this sometimes happens) looked into and authenticated; from thence they must be carted to Lachine, where boats and men are to be procured to transport them this far. On the other hand, payments can be made there in bills or money when it would be very difficult to convert them into remittances for England. . . The mode usually practised is this: the merchant sends his order for English goods to his correspondent at Montreal, who imports them from London, guarantees the payment of them there, and receives and forwards them to this country for a commission of five per cent on the amount of the English invoice. The payments are all made by the Upper Canada merchant in Montreal, and there is no direct communication whatever between him and the shipper in London. . . This mode of business seems necessarily to be imposed upon us by our inland situation. . .[14]

The strength of Merritt's position, however, lay in the integration of the store with the manufacturing establishments which he was erecting on Twelve Mile Creek. It was on the proceeds of these enterprises — the mills, distillery, and the rest — that he was mainly relying to meet his notes as they fell due, to maintain his credit standing in Montreal, and to pay off the local debts incurred at St. Catharines. Especially important was the gristmill, which would enable him to send consignments of flour, less bulky and more valuable than wheat, down the St. Lawrence to the Montreal market. There it would be disposed of by the commission agents with whom he had established regular correspondence, Messrs. Armour and Davies. The proceeds of these consignments, supplemented to be sure by such Government bills as he might receive at the store from half-pay officers, pensioners, and the like, would, assuming remunerative prices, suffice to pay his debts as they fell due and maintain amicable relations with his wholesalers. Such, at least, was the system on which Merritt proposed to operate, and which gave point to the closely interrelated enterprises he was building around the water power of Twelve Mile Creek.

III

Store-keeping was a not inappropriate choice of occupation for a young man like Merritt — not much inclined to farming, without sufficient influence to obtain lucrative employment in the colonial bureaucracy, and without the education to equip him for a profession. It was generally regarded as highly profitable. As late as 1844 John Langton asserted that he knew of no money-making business in Upper Canada other than the law, store-keeping, tavern-keeping, and horse-dealing. "Store-keeping," he wrote, "is decidedly the most money-making and is carried on with very little capital, but it appears to me that those who make it pay are invariably those who have started with next to nothing and have gradually crept up in the world, increasing their business as their capital, custom, and experience increased." [15] A knowledge of simple bookkeeping and a healthy fear of the consequences of over-trading were more important qualifications than formal education, political influence, or high social position.

Merritt had, however, entered upon his business career at a time when the effects of inflationary war finance between 1812 and 1815 were still being felt. War expenditures for the supply of troops in Upper Canada had created a situation which was highly abnormal, and which dissipated itself by 1818. What was an effective response to the short-lived prosperity of the three postwar years was not effective in the long-term situation. His heavy investments and the extended scale on which he planned to do business were not to prove justified outside of the immediate economic context which had inspired them.

The slump in agricultural prices which followed the brief postwar prosperity in 1818 subjected the economy of Upper Canada to severe strain. By 1821 a well-informed observer could write:

most of the merchants have very large outstanding debts, which, if collected by means of suits, would ruin two-thirds of the farmers in the Province; and should the Montreal wholesale dealers have recourse to similar measures, many of their correspondents would become insolvent likewise.[16]

Merritt fared no better than most. Between 1817 and 1820 his business affairs deteriorated steadily, along with those of the economy as a whole. By the end of 1816 the firm of Merritt and Ingersoll had local debts to the amount of $8400, most of them incurred for the purchase of property in the neighborhood of St. Catharines.[17] By 1819 Messrs. Armour and Davies of Montreal had obtained judgment against them for a debt of $1307, and the house and mills, as well as Ingersoll's property in Orford, were mortgaged as security for payment.[18] The salt works, moreover, proved difficult to exploit; rock drilling was necessary, and the lining of the shaft to prevent the entry of fresh water was an unlooked-for expense.

Not till January 1818 was brine obtained in strength and volume sufficient to make boiling commercially practical.[19]

By the end of 1819 the firm of Merritt and Ingersoll was insolvent. Ingersoll took himself off to Orford in the western part of the province, leaving Merritt at St. Catharines to handle all negotiations with the Montreal creditors. The story of these negotiations is told in the letters which Merritt received from George Davies in Montreal during 1821, 1822, and 1823, and, with a little interpolation and inference, it is possible to reconstruct the whole incident.[20]

Early in 1821 Merritt arranged with Davies, himself an important creditor, that the latter should, for a commission, act as his agent in dealing with the Montreal houses to whom he was indebted. Merritt himself was too busy with the mills and store to be able to stay in Montreal for the weeks, perhaps months, that would be necessary before a settlement was negotiated. But there was more to it than this. Davies, who was a Montrealer, probably knew the parties concerned better than did Merritt; he was a familiar and respected member of the Montreal mercantile community, whereas Merritt was an Upper Canada man, resident in a different province and subject to a different legal jurisdiction. Davies could talk to the Montreal merchants as one of themselves; Merritt would have to play the suppliant, the man in severe, perhaps inextricable, financial difficulties. Further, although Davies would thereafter be acting in a triple capacity — as commission merchant for the sale of Merritt's flour, as his representative in negotiating for the best settlement possible with the creditors, and as agent for the trustees of the estate of Armour and Davies (the partnership having been wound up on Armour's death) — Merritt could with some assurance count on their interests coinciding. The only *continuing* relationship which could exist between them was that of commission merchant and forwarder. If Merritt went into bankruptcy, Davies would lose his business. Apart therefore from any bonds of friendship between them, it was in Davies' interest to see the negotiations completed as quickly and conveniently as possible. Neither of the two appear to have entertained any doubts as to the other's honesty and good faith.

This multiplicity of roles did, however, occasionally prove embarrassing, particularly in connection with the disposal of the receipts from the sale of wheat and flour shipments. Were they to go to satisfy the mortgage held by Davies, or to pacify the creditors, or could these receipts be expended on the purchase of imported goods? On the one occasion when this question did arise in acute form, it was in connection with Ingersoll's remittances, not Merritt's, and Davies was quick to define his position in unambiguous terms. Ingersoll had expressed a desire that part of the proceeds of a remittance he was sending down should be applied toward furnishing him with a small stock of imported goods, as none of the wholesale houses would give him credit. Davies wrote to Merritt in reply:

you are of course aware that I act in two distinct capacities, one that of a General Commission Merchant, the other that of agent for the trustees to the estate of R. Armour & Davies, and tho' these occupations are center'd in the one person, it must be considered as tho' it were in the hands of two people entirely unconnected with each other as well as ignorant of each other's movements, and therefore whatever he sends me down with instructions to apply it towards the liquidation of his old debt shall be so applied, and whatever he sends down with other instructions, they shall be faithfully complied with.

The negotiations involved in Merritt's failure were both complicated and delicate. He was fortunate in having such a man to act as his deputy.

IV

On March 22, 1821, Merritt sent to Davies a full statement of his own and Ingersoll's personal and business debts. As security for payment he had very little to offer, as most of his property was already mortgaged to Armour and Davies. He therefore made two proposals: firstly, that Armour and Davies relinquish their mortgage on his house, which he valued at $4000; and secondly, that his various creditors agree to accept an assignment of his own and Ingersoll's remaining property in proportion to the amount of debts owed them.

Neither of these proposals was well received nor at first accepted. The first in itself was no trifling request, and on April 5 Davies wrote to Merritt that the trustees would have none of it. He added, however, that he had represented to the creditors that it made little difference whether the mortgage was relinquished or not, as there was little doubt that Ingersoll's property in Orford would be sufficient to secure the sum mortgaged. Davies continued:

I represented also in as strong colours as I well could the propriety and handsomeness of your conduct in not bringing forward your private debts, to a very large amount, to your own and Mrs. Merritt's relatives, all of which might without the smallest impropriety have been brought in along with the rest. Irritated however beyond measure (as every one at first is on hearing of a fresh loss being sustained) they one and all of them are obstinate in declaring that they would rather give up the whole than take their proportion of the debts and property exhibited in your statement.

In spite of this double refusal Davies was not discouraged, being of opinion that "many of them will, on exercising a little cool reflection, materially change their determination." He had, indeed, good grounds for hoping that a compromise settlement could finally be arranged, and this in spite of the fact that Merritt had practically nothing to bargain with. If they persisted in their refusal, what would the consequence be? Merritt would lose his property, and whichever of the several importing houses managed to get execution first would find itself burdened with the task of disposing of a highly illiquid and unattractive investment in another province. The prospect of appointing an agent to operate Merritt's enterprises on their behalf was not pleasant. This was not the kind of business Montreal importing firms liked to handle. They were interested in self-liquidating credit, not investment in real estate. They sent their profits home to Britain to be invested, not to the upper province.[21]

And yet, what were the alternatives in this case? Either they could attempt a forced sale in the midst of an agricultural depression, which would certainly entail a severe loss, or they could agree to some assignment of property which would give them security for the debts owed and would hold out some prospect of repayment over a period of years. It was in their interest, whether they would admit it to Davies or not, that Merritt should be enabled to retain possession of his mills and to continue forwarding consignments to Montreal. In no other way was there any prospect of obtaining relief from the pressure which they themselves had to support from their creditors in England.

The situation was complicated by the fact that Merritt was in debt, not to one firm, but to several. The list of his business creditors includes some of the largest importing houses in Montreal at the time:

Forsyth, Richardson & Co.	£ 472.	17.	4
Zabdiel Thayer & Co.	67.	0.	0
Shuter & Wilkins	40.	0.	0
George Platt & Co.	400.	0.	0
Horatio Gates & Co.	400.	0.	0
Bridge & Penn	180.	0.	0
Hart & Ley	40.	0.	0
	£1599.	17.	4

Besides this, he owed money to the firm of J. Wragg and Company, but the amount of the debt is nowhere specified in the correspondence. The multiplicity of creditors, however, made things easier for Davies by enabling him to play off one against the other, representing to each that unless they agreed to a speedy settlement, one of the other firms would institute legal proceedings and obtain early judgment and preferential treatment in the division of the spoils.

What Davies hoped to do was to persuade the eight creditors to act in concert, appoint a single agent to represent all of them in Upper Canada, and come to a common agreement for the settlement of their claims in proportion to the debts owed them. This was not easy: there was always the danger that one or the other would break ranks. Davies' primary task was to keep the matter out of the law courts and see that Merritt stayed in business. Everything depended on his skill in handling men who had been caught napping, who felt aggrieved, and who were under financial pressure themselves.

Within one month this first objective had been partly accomplished. By May 1821 a Mr. John Breakenridge, an Upper Canada lawyer, was appointed trustee for the seven firms listed above, Wragg and Company refusing to enter the agreement at that time as they had already instituted suit. Merritt was to assign to Breakenridge the following assets:

Securities for lands in Zone	£ 800.	0.	0
Farm in New Purchase	250.	0.	0
House Lot in St. Catharines mortgaged to assignees			
of Armour & Davies	400.	0.	0
Outstanding debts due to Merritt	1191.	12.	7
	£2641.	12.	7

The lands in Zone had been granted to Merritt after the war as compensation for his services in the militia, while the "outstanding debts" were, of course, accounts receivable from the store business.

The agreement went on to state that, having assigned these assets to Breakenridge, Merritt would remain unmolested for four years, and on a dividend of 15s. in the pound being realized from the property assigned, would be granted an immediate discharge. This assignment, however, was not to vitiate their claim to a dividend of 20s. in the pound if the property should realize that amount. If, on the other hand, it realized less than 15s. Merritt was to have the option of making up the dividend to 15s. within four years from the date of the assignment.

This settlement was by no means harsh, particularly with reference to the assignment of property already mortgaged to Armour and Davies. This concession was made, not because Merritt had been released from the mortgage, but because Davies, after "considerable pains, explanations and entreaties," had finally managed to persuade Merritt's creditors that the mortgage was almost certain to be satisfied by Ingersoll's property in Orford. Even apart from this feature, however, the settlement was a mild one. Merritt was granted a four years' breathing-space, and he retained possession, if not outright ownership, of the mills which were his basic source of income. A few minor details remained to be cleared up, but Davies did not anticipate serious trouble:

Shuter & Wilkins will not agree to come into any agreement short of principal and interest for the last debt contracted by Mr. Ingersoll, concerning

wh[ich] Shuter seems unusually bitter considering the smallness of the amount
. . . J. Wragg & Co. would not agree to sign the inclosed letter . . . [but]
I doubt not when they find they cannot derive any preference (the property
being once out of your hands) over the other creditors from having obtained
judgement, they will not hesitate to come into the measure.

In this particular Davies was too optimistic, as will later appear.

For the time being, however, the agreement held good, and for the
rest of the summer Merritt from St. Catharines and Ingersoll from Orford
continued to send down consignments, flour and wheat from the former,
potash and "high wines" from the latter. Davies applied the proceeds to
the original mortgage, for "our trustees begin to cry out a good deal," but
poor wheat and flour prices prevented any real improvement in Merritt's
affairs. On June 7 Davies wrote: "There is no sale whatever for flour; but
I am in hopes now that it is fairly decided that U.S. flour shipped from
this country to the W. Indies cannot obtain a drawback on the return produce, it will give a stimulus to the U.C. flour." By the second of August
the situation was even less cheerful: "Flour (fine) is nominally 18/6 p.
barl. & superfine 22/—but it is a folly to quote the price as it is actually
unsaleable. Yours is all on hand, but I am in hopes of bartering it for
West India produce so as to be able with some trouble to realize the above
prices in the end." At the end of the month the story was the same: "Flour
is almost nominal as to price, as every one is afraid of shipping while it is
more than probable the ports are shut against it in Britain." Commercial
intelligence in this vein must have made gloomy reading for Merritt.

Meanwhile Wragg and Company were proving by no means as ac-
commodating as Davies had hoped. In spite of promises to the contrary,
they made no effort to postpone execution of the judgment they had obtained, excuse after excuse being given to Davies to explain their course.
By the middle of September it was becoming urgent that they should be
brought into line, but Davies could do nothing with them. On September
13 he reported: "They have . . . put me off from day to day untill [sic]
another post has elapsed, and as it is pretty evident their wish is to let the
suit proceed whilst at [the] same time they do not absolutely like the
odium of refusing a short delay, I am by no means sure I shall succeed in
getting their answer today." Shuter and Wilkins also were obdurate in their
insistence on full payment for Ingersoll's last debt, but they at least made
their position clear. Wragg and Company represented the real danger;
they had obtained judgment and execution was, if the urgent tone of
Davies' letter is any guide, a matter of days.

At this juncture, on the twelfth of September, while Davies' letter was
still in the mail, Merritt played his ace. What happened seems at first a

little bewildering, especially in view of the fact that the crucial letter has not been preserved. But it is quite clear that a completely new twist was given to the whole affair. When Davies wrote to Merritt on the nineteenth, it was not to advise or console, but to report that certain precise instructions had been carried out:

I represented [to your creditors] having received a letter from a near relative of yours resident in another country, who (without having received information from you of an arrangement having already taken place with most of your creditors), wished me to sound each individual to whom you are indebted and to ascertain whether, provided he placed the means in my hands within three months from this of paying every one of them 10/– in the pound on the amount of their claims, they would grant you a discharge in full.

So far there was nothing very unusual — merely a rather flimsy attempt to re-negotiate an agreement. But the promise of payment within three months and the reference to an unidentified benefactor were new elements. Further complications followed:

I at the same time stated that this proposal of your relation was by no means to be made known to you, neither was I at liberty to mention his name, as however anxious he might be to assist you if by so doing he could actually extricate you from all difficulties, still he was decided not to advance one penny for you, to be swallowed up in the mass[?] of your estate, or in fact on any other terms than those of seeing you completely free of debt. . . I would by no means let anyone know that this proposal has come from yourself, as if you do you may rest assured the whole business will be knocked in the head.

Here deception entered. Davies was obviously acting under Merritt's instructions; yet he maintained the pretense of deep secrecy. What purpose was this intended to serve? Perhaps the eagerness with which the proposition, in this guise, was snapped up by the creditors will give us some inkling of its significance:

Forsyth, Richardson & Co., Gates & Co., and Bridge & Penn immediately agreed to grant you a discharge in full provided *your relation* pays them within three months from this 10/– in the pound on their debts . . . and I have every reason to believe that Wragg & Co. and Shuter & Wilkins will likewise accede to it before I close this, in which case I shall get from Wragg & Co. a letter to Breakenridge to delay the execution until the business can be accomplished.

At the same time, the assurances demanded were significant:

All those that have agreed to your present proposal, were very anxious indeed to know in what shape the money or means of paying them was to be sent

down, as produce being now so very unsaleable, they would by no means agree
to wait until sales could be effected. . . You have not a moment to lose either
in placing funds in my hands to make good the proposal, and the instant I
receive these I will grant my own acceptances to each and get their receipts
in full, as I dread them retracting.

Payment had to be in money, or at least negotiable paper, and it
had to be made soon. This was the crux of the matter.

v

Here indeed was a revolution of fortune. Instead of a Merritt waiting
in daily expectation of bankruptcy and painfully scraping together enough
property to satisfy suspicious creditors, we find him offering ready cash
and a quick settlement. What had happened to put this new complexion
on affairs? How much of what Davies told the Montreal creditors was
true, and how much false? Was there really a "near relative . . . resident
in another country," and if so, who was he and why should he pay Merritt's debts? Why was it so important that the Montreal houses should
believe the offer was being made behind Merritt's back and without his
consent? Where was the money to come from? And what was the point
of the elaborate deception?

Not all of these pertinent questions admit of a definite answer. The
new terms which Davies was offering are a major clue. Merritt's creditors
were asked whether they would be prepared to accept, in full settlement
of their claims, 10s. in the pound, payable in negotiable drafts within three
months, instead of a minimum of 15s. in the pound, payable in four years.
Not surprisingly, they jumped at the offer, favorable alike to Merritt and
themselves. Liquid resources which could be remitted to England in the
near future were what they really wanted, rather than the doubtful prospect of a somewhat larger return within several years. The prospect of
receiving cash or its equivalent was the bait, as is confirmed by their
anxiety to know whether the remittance was to be in the form of produce
or drafts. Furthermore, 10s. in the pound, or 50 per cent of the principal,
though less than the previous compromise, was more than they could expect
from most bankrupt country merchants.

As regards the need for seeming to keep the negotiations secret from
Merritt, the motives are less easy to uncover. There is the obvious point,
made by Davies himself, that it enabled the funds to be channeled directly
to the creditors, without the remotest possibility that they might be misdirected by Merritt into further extravagances. This pretense made the
offer appear more definite and therefore more attractive. Further, if the
money came directly from Merritt, it would be a ticklish matter to keep
the discharge separate from the previous arrangement, by which they were

entitled to at least 15s. in the pound. Perhaps it could be arranged, perhaps not; in any event, if Davies could now be taken as acting on behalf of a person not previously concerned in the negotiations, the whole matter would be much simpler to manage. If it could be regarded as a separate transaction, it was that much easier for all concerned to change their minds and play different roles.

There seems, however, to have been more than this involved. Davies was not dealing with simpletons who could be gulled by a tale of a mythical fairy godfather. It was in the interests of the parties concerned to believe him, and it was in his interest to make the suspension of disbelief as painless as possible. If the offer had come openly from Merritt, the Montreal houses would have had to refuse it. If they had dealt directly with Merritt, typical as he was of many Upper Canada merchants with whom they did business and who owed them money, they would never have scaled down their demands to the same extent as they were prepared to do in this slightly clandestine negotiation involving an anonymous somebody with whom they were never again to have business dealings. Davies no longer represented Merritt, the debtor; he represented instead a person whom nobody knew, an X whose role in the transaction was simply that of providing money and clearing up uncertainty — nothing more. In dealing with Merritt, softness would set a precedent; in dealing with this mysterious X, it would not. The offer, to be acceptable, had to come from somebody they did not know, and it had to be on a "this or nothing" basis.

Believed or disbelieved, the story fulfilled its function. The really interesting thing about it, however, is that like all good lies it contained a strong element of truth. Merritt really did have a near relative in a distant country, and it really was this relative who was offering to pay his debts. The key person in the plot, the man who made it possible and who, in all probability, thought up its ingenious ramifications, was his old uncle, Nehemiah. Nehemiah Merritt had been rich even before the war, when his nephew, as we have seen, had won his friendship and confidence, and by this time he seems to have become rather more than wealthy. Apparently the commercial opportunities of the war, both legitimate and contraband, had not passed him by. In any event, he had command of ready cash in New York and Boston. But he had to remain anonymous; had the Montreal firms known who was financing the transaction, they would have held out for better terms.

Fortunately for the historian, the progress of the settlement can be traced practically from week to week in Davies' letters between September 1821 and January 1822. On September 29 he received from W. H. Merritt drafts drawn by Nehemiah Merritt on New York and Boston to the amount of $3200, or enough to cover 50 per cent of the capital sum owed in Montreal. In acknowledging receipt, Davies reminded Merritt of the need for continued secrecy:

> I fear I shall have to lose 1 p. cent. on the drafts, but rest assured I shall do for you as well as if it were my own. . . Meantime I would have you keep the affair perfectly still and quiet as the smallest hint to the creditors that there was a probability of doing better would effectually quash every chance of success. . . Even after this business has been all finally arranged, it would be extremely hurtful to me, should it be known you were acquainted with the negociations [*sic*] pending, until all was settled.

By November 15 the negotiations had reached the stage of detailed bargaining. Forsyth, Richardson and Company insisted on charging compound interest on their debt, and Davies thought it best to concede the claim, remarking that "they seemed so perfectly satisfied . . . to get off their agreement if I gave them an opportunity of doing so handsomely." One of Nehemiah Merritt's drafts on Rice and Thaxter of Boston was not accepted, Davies having to meet the difference — some $200 — until the acceptance was made in January 1822. Finally, as if to accentuate the difficulty of the negotiation, Mrs. Platt, executrix of her husband's estate, turned skittish, "refusing to sanction the agreement made by me with John Wragg, in consequence of a *sudden squall* between the parties."

The crisis, however, was past, and by the sixth of December Davies had the receipts in his hands, was giving vent to conventional grumbles over the size of the lawyer's bill, and with the buoyancy which was typical of him was congratulating Merritt "most sincerely on having thus favourably closed your old concerns and that at a period, too, when I feel pretty well convinced business of every kind is going to revive materially." The negotiation had been carried through with discreet efficiency, and we may be permitted to hope that Merritt did not strongly protest when Davies announced that he proposed "to charge you 1 p. Ct. on the amount of debts settled which [I] hope you will not think too much, as I assure you I have had more trouble with the business than you can well be aware of." By August 1822 Merritt had regained title to his mills, his father having sold his homestead for $6000 thus enabling him to cancel his remaining obligations.[22]

VI

If this story appears slender, it nevertheless illustrates, as such stories often do, patterns of human behavior and personality which are far from trivial. In this instance Merritt failed. But why did he fail? What role did he and businessmen like him, failures though they sometimes were, play in the St. Lawrence economy? What factors in that economy could Merritt, as an entrepreneur, control and regulate, alter and otherwise affect, and what did he have to take as given, as inexorably limiting and restricting his choice of action — factors to which he had to adjust as best he could? Pose such questions as these to the historian, and he will answer by using abstractions — by stating general propositions about human behavior and environment. But these general propositions are, or ought to be, based on just such apparently trivial human narratives as this.

The year 1815, when young Merritt returned to Canada, saw the conclusion of the war between Great Britain and the United States which for three years of sporadic campaigning had threatened the existence of Upper Canada as a British province. Like most wars, it had brought prosperity of a sort to those parts of the colony not directly exposed to the opposing fleets and armies. Flour, Upper Canada's staple product, brought eight dollars a barrel in Montreal in June 1812, rose to twelve dollars in September, and to thirteen in November.[23] Throughout the war, prices remained extravagantly high. The military commissariat spent freely, for the regular troops and the militia had to be fed, and thanks to the open-handed issue of Army Bills by government agents at Montreal and Niagara there was no shortage of currency. By February 1815, there was a total of £1,300,000 of these Bills in circulation.[24] Extensively used by Upper Canada merchants for their remittances to Montreal, Army Bills supplanted the system of long credits typical of the years before the war.

But this was only one of the changes brought about by war. Take an undeveloped colony, still only a little removed from subsistence agriculture, as Upper Canada was at this time, and plant in the middle of it a hungry army which can pay cash and which must be supplied, no matter what the expense: it is easy to see that the economic development of that colony will receive a rude and profoundly disturbing shock. Not that the shock in Upper Canada was depressive; on the contrary, the short-run effect was highly stimulating. Suddenly it became easy to make money. So far as an agrarian economy, only one stage removed from barter, can experience an inflation, Upper Canada did. Whether or not the farmer reaped any advantage is hard to say, but certainly the millers and merchants prospered.

But such salutary effects of the war inflation lasted only a little longer than the war itself; and its long-run consequences for Upper Canada were unhealthy and retrogressive. The normal commercial orientation of the colony, for geographical as for economic reasons, was toward Montreal, the source of its commercial credit and the market, by way of the St. Lawrence, for its slowly expanding agricultural exports. But the high wartime prices in Upper Canada itself between 1812 and 1815 put a complete stop to the movement of produce down the river. Cash expenditures by the military commissariat, moreover, erased the prewar system of debts and credits between the hinterland and the metropolis. When peace returned, therefore, the businessmen of Upper Canada, rich though they may have been, were faced with the critical task of re-creating a commercial system which war had destroyed.

This task forced them to deal with two sets of business problems. The first were those involved in recovering from the war inflation. The price level was certain to fall rapidly. A businessman gifted with unusual foresight — enough to see four or five years ahead — would therefore have restricted his inventories to a minimum, avoided long-term indebtedness, and waited until near the trough of the price fall before committing himself to heavy investments. The second set of problems were those involved in reëstablishing credit relationships with Montreal. In the immediate postwar period the demand for imports in Upper Canada was heavy and, thanks to the inflation, effective. A businessman concerned with this problem, and forgetful of the first, would lose no time in arranging for credit in Montreal and anywhere else he could get it, with a view to ordering large consignments of goods for sale in the interior. In other words, a smart businessman would utilize his credit to the utmost as soon after the end of the war as he could. He would get into debt; but, if he was aware of the first problem — that of the falling price level — he would make sure his debts were short-term and that he paid them off by remittances as quickly as possible.

Nevertheless, there was a certain conflict involved in responding to both sets of problems at the same time. What the Upper Canada merchant actually decided to do depended on several factors: whether he foresaw the fall in the price level; whether he thought he could liquidate his obligations quickly enough; and — since he had to make a living — whether he could afford to wait. With credit freely available in Montreal and Upper Canada starved of imported goods, optimism and the short-run view went hand in hand. It was easy to get into difficulties.

The difficulties of the postwar readjustment were aggravated by developments over which the individual merchant had no control and which he could hardly have foreseen. Army Bill currency was rapidly called in and converted into bills on London which were remitted in payment for imports, thus exercising a highly deflationary influence.[25] This was accentuated further by the heavy imports of livestock from the United States for the restocking of Canadian farms which resulted between 1815 and 1818 in an unfavorable balance of trade with that country, apparent in numerous complaints that precious specie was disappearing across the border and not returning.

Meanwhile in Britain the Corn Law of 1815 closed the ports to colonial wheat until the British price rose above 67s. a quarter.[26] An excellent British harvest in 1820 brought the price well below this level. With the demobilization of the militia agricultural labor was released for employment, and increased Canadian production, when the British ports were closed, glutted the Montreal market and brought catastrophic price falls. Deep depression in the United States after 1819 completed the picture. Between 1819 and 1822 the Upper Canada price of wheat declined from about one dollar to fifty cents a bushel. Livestock values were reduced by one-half and real estate values by a greater percentage.[27] The downward trend of agriculture prices accentuated the burden of the farmer's indebtedness to the local merchant and of the latter's debts to Montreal.

Beneath all the price falls, bankruptcies, and mortgages lay one intractable and persisting problem — the failure of Upper Canada agricultural surpluses to find a market virtually at any price, as Davies had pointed out to Merritt.[28]

But superimposed on and contributing to the ruinously low prices which this failure occasioned was the heavy expense and risk which Upper Canada produce had to bear on its journey to the sea. Until the late 1830's the St. Lawrence was, for all practical purposes, an unimproved waterway.[29] Between Kingston on Lake Ontario and Montreal there were in 1820 only the tiny Haldimand canals, built between 1779 and 1783, to indicate an awareness of its imperfections. Not until the completion of the Erie Canal in 1825 had exploded the comfortable belief that the St. Lawrence was the "natural outlet" for the produce of the interior was the improvement of the river seriously taken in hand. High costs for freight, transshipment, storage, and insurance meant that, even in favorable times, the Upper Canada merchant operated on a slim margin and was highly vulnerable to fluctuations in export prices.

The economic historian can identify these factors — the Montreal debt structure, the St. Lawrence transportation system, and the movement of export prices — and discuss in broad terms their combined influence on Canadian economic development. What they meant as intractable realities to the businessman of the time is strikingly illustrated in a series of shipments which Merritt, already insolvent, made to Davies during the late summer and fall of 1821.

Between August 15 and September 19 of that hectic year Davies received from Merritt for sale on commission a total of 94 barrels of flour of various grades, which sold at prices between 10s. and 10/9 a barrel and brought total gross receipts of £77.5.6. From this total Davies was obliged to deduct the following charges:

Freight from Niagara, 94 bbls. at 5s.	£23.	10.	0
Cartage to store		15.	0
Inspection		15.	8
Preparing for inspection, receiving, and delivery		8.	9
Cooperage, hoops, and nails		8.	4
Proportion of advertising		6.	4
Storage	2.	16.	4
Commission at 2½ per cent.	1.	18.	8
	£30.	19.	1

Leaving out of account, therefore, all costs incurred by Merritt himself at St. Catharines, charges from shipment at Niagara to sale at Montreal made up approximately 40 per cent of gross receipts. These charges (except the commission) were fixed and not proportional to the price received for the shipment. Flour and wheat prices might fluctuate, but not the cost of sending them to Montreal. From this always slim and never certain margin between prices received and costs incurred, Merritt made his living.

Not only was the St. Lawrence route expensive; it was risky as well. It will be noticed that in the invoice reproduced above there is no charge for insurance. Merritt normally sent his produce down through a forwarding company at his own risk. On this occasion the shipments arrived intact, but he was not always so lucky. Between December 1822 and April 1823 he shipped 122½ minots [30] of wheat and 43 barrels of flour. The wheat shipment was badly damaged. On December 9 Davies reported:

What has been received since my last is 30 Bars. and 4 tierces of wheat, part of which has I am sorry to say received damage, the boat having struck on the St. Louis Rapids, and it must therefore be sold immediately, and there is little chance of getting it fairly dry, unless I had a room with a stove, to shoot it in, which unfortunately I have not.

By the 23rd of the month he was even more gloomy:

The 34 barrels and tierces of wheat has turned out infinitely worse than I had any idea of, being so completely frozen together that not a single grain would start on opening out the heads of the casks, so that many of them have been broke [sic] up to get the wheat out. I was quite at a loss to dispose of it, but judged it best, if profitable, to get rid of it immediately, and therefore tried to prevail on some of our distillers to buy it, but the price offered was so very trifling that I could not think of letting them have it and then as a derniere resource sent it to a kiln near town where it is now pretty well dried and I am in hopes of getting something like a reasonable price for it from the distillers when they see I am not entirely at their mercy.

The accounts for these shipments which reached Merritt in April 1823 told the story even more graphically. The spoiled wheat brought a poor

4/2 per minot, while the flour sold at quite good prices ranging between
23/9 and 25*s.* a barrel. The total shipment of 122½ minots of wheat and
43 barrels of flour resulted in total gross receipts of £84. 14. 2. Deducted
from this figure were the following charges:

Drying 122½ minots wheat at 9*d*	£ 4.	1.	11
Freight down of 43 bbls. flour at 5/3	11.	5.	9
Ditto, 30 barrels wheat at 5/6	8.	5.	0
Ditto, 4 tierces wheat at 8/3	1.	13.	0
Coopering 43 bbls. flour to ascertain damage . . .		12.	11
Cartage to store, to and from mill		15.	10
Labor, inspector, preparing for inspector		15.	5
Storage on 43 barrels flour, 1 month at 4*d* p. bbl. .		14.	4
Ditto, on 43 barrels flour, 4 months at 2*d* p. bbl. . .	1.	8.	8
Ditto, on 30 barrels and 4 tierces wheat		11.	4
Commission at 2½%	2.	1.	10
	£32.	6.	0

Thus on this occasion, excluding all costs of purchasing and processing at
St. Catharines, charges after shipment amounted to 38.6 per cent of gross
receipts. From such margins as these Merritt had to pay the interest on his
debts and finance new purchases.

VII

This, however, is not the whole story. Certainly Merritt's behavior as
a man in business was limited and channeled by the environment in
which he lived. But to stop there is to take a one-sided view of a two-way
relationship. In the short run, there was little or nothing Merritt could do
about the dangers and expense of the St. Lawrence waterway, or the state
of the British market, or the rigidities of commercial credit. They were
part of the environment to which he had to adapt as best he could. But
this was not always to be so. The story of the remainder of Merritt's life
is a story of one attempt after another to change that environment, to
answer its challenges at precisely those points where he had felt its restrictions and limitations most keenly. It is not Merritt the miller and storekeeper who has become familiar to Canadian historians; it is Merritt the
canal builder, the railroad promoter, the financier, the statesman. Yet the
Merritt to whom Davies wrote in January 1822, "your statement of the
loss on flour is certainly sufficiently discouraging, and almost enough to
tempt a man never to send down a barrel again" was the same Merritt who
in newspaper, pamphlet, and departmental minute was to weary a generation of Canadians with his reiterated preaching of canals, low tolls, and
free trade, who as Commissioner of Public Works and President of the

Executive Council was to supervise the completion of the St. Lawrence canal system and attempt to make those canals the basis of Canadian public finance, and who in 1854 was to receive full credit from those who knew for the part he had played in the Reciprocity negotiations.

Merritt's career was, in fact, one unusual for its devotion to a single principle and a single set of problems. With uncanny accuracy, it reflected the problems of pre-industrial Canada — its simplicity of structure, its concentration on staple production, its dependence on foreign markets and sources of capital, its reliance on the commercial potentialities of the St. Lawrence river. When we seek an explanation for Merritt's lifelong obsession with these problems, it is to his early experiences as a miller and merchant that we must turn. The philosophy which he preached was not that of an industrialist, banker, or manufacturer; it was the philosophy, on a grand scale, of a country storekeeper. The difference between Merritt and other country merchants was that Merritt could articulate that philosophy, preach it, and realize its directives in action.

IV

The Entrepreneur and the Community

By Robert K. Lamb

Entrepreneurial studies need to advance simultaneously from two ends, taking the development of the whole community — in its time and space dimensions — as the largest unit, and an individual decision as the smallest unit. From these two starting points we can surround our problem.

Within this framework I suggest these two statements as hypotheses: first, the detailed workings of entrepreneurship are best studied in the setting of a single (local or regional) community, and among its entrepreneurial group or groups; and, second, the assumptions within which entrepreneurs in such groups operate need to be understood in the setting of a national economy.

Using these statements as hypotheses, I propose to discuss the role of entrepreneurship in a particular nation and period, the United States between 1787 and 1816. By three related examples of communities, national, regional, and local, taken from American economic history, I shall show some of the evidence on which I base these hypotheses.

Entrepreneurship is that form of social decision-making performed by economic innovators. Social decision-makers draw their sanction from the political, legal, economic, and social assumptions around which the people of the community organize their lives. It is the entrepreneur's reciprocal function as an economic innovator to help change these assumptions. He does so by the effect of his decision-making upon the structure and functions of the community (especially its economic structure and functions).

Throughout this paper I shall use the terms "structure," "function," and "change" for my own general purposes, and not with specific content drawn from any particular theorists. As I go along, I propose to put social content into these concepts; meanwhile, by reference to their biological analogies I shall indicate in a footnote something of the workings of these concepts in society.[1] This essay will examine one facet of the emerging American national economy: the launching of the cotton textile industry in the years between 1787 and 1816 (with some reference to the later development of the experiment). It will discuss this development in its national setting, in the regions centering on Boston and Providence, and in the locality of Fall River.

The questions we shall undertake to answer are: How were the organizers of the structures and functions of our national economic system related to the entrepreneurs of the textile industry? How did certain communities, mercantile centers before the Revolution, become regional textile-industry capitals after the ratification of the Constitution? What entrepreneurs were responsible for these developments, and how much did they depend on other groups in their local or regional communities, or in the national community?

To answer these questions we must consider the emergence of the American national economy in its historical setting, and this requires a reëxamination of the events leading up to our independence. The American Revolution, seen as one of a series of related movements occurring within western culture, appears as an economic, political, and social rebellion against the effort to consolidate a world-wide London metropolitan economy and a British Empire, following the global victory of Britain over France in the Seven Years' War.

By stating in a few words how the economist, the political scientist, and the social anthropologist would each approach this period of consolidation of the London economy within the British Empire, we can see why a model is needed to describe comprehensively the structure and function of a national and international community. For the economist these developments may be summarized in the phrase "growth of a market economy," if we include the growth of a *world-wide* money market based upon London, and the expansion of world-wide commodity markets similarly focused upon London and Liverpool. For the political scientist the phrase "rise of constitutional government" parallels that of the market economy. For the social anthropologist this historical movement may be summed up in such phrases as the shift from "status" to "contract"; within this we see "increasing social mobility" as illustrated by the marriage of self-made men into local, regional, or national family groups of social leaders.

To bring these several approaches together into one systematic whole, we need models descriptive of the structures and functions of national and international communities at moments of time, and of their changes through time. These models should be made by students of entrepreneurship, working with political, social, and economic historians. To build such models we need, for example, to trace the pattern of a given social structure, such as an extended-kinship family at a moment of time, study its connections with the surrounding community, and follow its changes over time.

By relating the major groupings from which the structure of a given community is formed to the functions performed at strategic points within its structure, we shall have a general description of those interrelationships which organize the economic, social, and political life of that community. For instance, if the chief political institution is a parliament or a congress, membership in that congress is a key to the political structure of the community. If we find a correlation between its membership and the social leadership of the communities politically represented in the national assembly, we are on the way to a broader understanding of the social structure and functioning of the community. If we are then able to trace a further connection between these points of social and political decision-making and the strategic points where economic decisions are made, we begin to see how leadership is provided for the individual communities, and for the regional and national communities of which they are parts. By watching these structures and functions as they change over time, we shall begin to be able to describe the processes by which certain decision-makers at strategic points in the social structure contribute to economic, political, and social change.

Since we lack experience of such model-building, descriptions of total community developments tend to elude us. This model-building should include a description of the workings of that interdependent system we call in economics the London "world metropolitan economy," and in politics the British Empire operating in a concert of nations. Such a model will enable us, for instance, to see that whereas the American Revolution brought into being a new national economy, and the War of 1812 opened the way to its expansion into an economic system of continental proportions, Americans continued to operate within the orbit of London as a world economic and political capital right down to the outbreak of the First World War.

Within this "universal" model we need smaller-scale models showing the role played by the United States and other nation-states as political containers for the development of increasingly integrated national economies and national social systems. Once we have found adequate devices for describing these national models at a moment of time, and for watching these changes over time, we shall begin to see the extent to which man-made systems of interpersonal relationships tend to differentiate into separate sets of institutions to carry on the functions of society: into economic forms such as banks and industrial corporations; government bureaus and political parties; social organizations and clubs of all kinds, religious, educational, recreational. These institutions tend in turn to channel the oncoming generations into their individual posts within the increasingly hierarchical structure. It is within this framework of institutions, national, regional, and local, that decision-makers must operate at strategic points in the social structure. The entrepreneur whom we are studying is here regarded as that *economic* decision-maker concerned with the problems of change in such a system.

II

Turn, now, to the London metropolitan economy as the matrix within which Britain and America developed in the eighteenth and nineteenth centuries. While the final establishment of London as metropolitan center of a world-wide economy developed after Britain's removal of France as a major opponent after 1750, London emerged as the *potential* hub of such a world-wide economy after the Revolution of 1689; it became the economic center of a consolidated British Empire by formation of the Bank of England in 1694, by reform of the British currency in 1695, reëstablishment of the Board of Trade and Plantations in 1696, and reorganization of the East India Company in 1702.

Sixty years later, the little American metropolitan centers of Boston, Providence, New York, Philadelphia, and Charleston were growing stronger and more self-conscious at just that moment when the problems of empire seemed to their British rulers to call for tightening up the system governing colonial trade. Prior to 1760 these various provincial city-states tended to conduct their affairs with little intercommunication among themselves, and with direct reliance on London as the economic and political capital city. Only for Indian affairs and speculation in frontier lands did they look to a focal point on the American continent: Albany; hence, the Albany Congress of 1754 which brought together American land speculators from colonies north of Virginia, and ratified Franklin's Plan of Union.

When the new restrictive policies began to bear heavily on colonial shipowners and land speculators after 1763, merchants and mechanics joined the gentry in resisting Britain. Their first great intercolonial protest resulted in the Stamp Act Congress at New York in 1765; they next succeeded in calling the first Continental Congress in 1774, where a new nation came into being, an American national economy centering upon the political and economic metropolis of Philadelphia.

We need to remind ourselves that the events of this formation of our new national economy have few parallels in history. They provide in foreshortened form a process requiring decades and centuries to unfold elsewhere: creation of the objective conditions wherein a group of able men can organize a continental economic system within a new nation-state.

A group of leaders of provincial city-states within the orbit of a world metropolitan community broke with their mother country by a revolution, waged as a civil war in the colonies, and overthrew that group of American families whose members continued to serve the King and his royal governors. Between the removal of the French in 1763 and the outbreak of the Revolution in 1775, forces at work in the colonies since their foundation came to a head. By combining political and military attack against the Crown and Parliament with a social upheaval against the local ruling class, the indigenous Patriot aristocracy cleared the way for their own social, political, and economic control of each colony. The assembling of a continental congress in 1774 composed of spokesmen for the leading groups in each colony carried them the next step towards a continental merger of their provincial vested-interests, and speeded up social change. When these representatives formed congressional committees to defend their interests against Britain they recognized their mutual interdependence: their need to stand together at home, and to seek alliances abroad. War contracts and authority to privateer multiplied chances for entrepreneurial activity.

The entrepreneurs of the new national economy used their membership on (or family connections with members of) congressional committees to lay the foundations of a nation-state. Successful war economies are of necessity centralized and closely integrated in their operation: the American Revolutionary war economy proved hard to integrate, but not for lack of effort by many of these men. They had great obstacles to overcome: the absence of a continental system prior to the war, due to economic and political gravitation of the separate colonies around London; the poor communications of the times; the heavy emphasis upon the family system as the means for achieving economic security in the absence of well-developed business organizations.

When the Confederation was established in 1781, the balance of power shifted to the conservative bloc centered in New York and Pennsylvania, who had congressional allies in Boston, Providence, Charleston, and other towns. This group, acting as the chief war contractors and privateers, had learned to work together within a continental pattern. With the defeat of Britain, they sought a stronger political union and, even before the negotiation of a peace treaty, began projecting new economic ventures: banks, land companies, and the funding of foreign debts. These undertakings called for new and more impersonal, more widespread, corporate institutions.

The deep-seated contest between centralizers and decentralizers continued to divide Americans down to the Civil War, and beyond. It was rooted in differences between them as to whether the individual state seemed to provide a sufficient base (legal, political, and economic) to protect the social system favored by each of these two groups. The continentalists (as Hamilton called them) wanted the benefits of a funded national debt, a national money market, the protection of a national navy for their merchant marine, and of a national army to defend their expanding land-speculations against Indian attacks. They were very confident that they could secure and maintain control of such a national government. The states-rights group, many of them landlords, thought they could retain control of state legislatures, but would find it harder to dominate the Federal executive, legislative, and judicial departments.

The continentalists became Federalists; the states-rights supporters became anti-Federalists, after the signing of the Constitution. Through the contract clause and other parts of the new Constitution, the Federalists were able to give national legal protection and executive and legislative encouragement to their new corporate institutions. For a generation after the Constitution was ratified, the leading Federalist families dominated the new corporate structure.

These Federalist families and their anti-Federalist opponents united in attacks on Parliament and the Crown on the eve of the Revolution, whereas they split during and after the Revolution over questions of centralization *versus* decentralization of the economic and political systems of the states and nation. To relate the growth of these families and their development of colonial metropolitan centers before the Revolution to the postwar rise of the textile industry, we focus on the life of Boston and Providence, and their satellite towns. Both centers were active in smuggling, defying the Sugar Act; both depended heavily on contraband trade with foreign ports in violation of the Navigation Acts; both resisted imperial restraints.

III

In Providence, the leading family on the eve of the Revolution was that of the Browns, whose ancestors had been among its first settlers. By the 1760's four Brown brothers, Nicholas, Joseph, John, and Moses, were trading in rum, slaves, and other West India goods through the firm their father James Brown and his brother Obadiah had formed thirty years earlier.[2] By 1763 the four brothers were at the center of a "trust," the Spermaceti Candle Manufacturers, operating in Providence, Newport,

Boston, and Philadelphia. Moses' three brothers became active Patriots, and his brother John was widely believed to have been the ringleader in the *Gaspee* affair. But in 1773, after his wife (Obadiah's daughter) died, Moses Brown withdrew from the family firm and turned Quaker, objecting to slave trading and war profiteering.

When war broke out, and the Secret Committee of the Continental Congress gave out Rhode Island war contracts through his brother Nicholas, Moses did not share in them. Instead he turned his attention to manufacturing experiments. The Browns were ready, when the federated American states achieved a national union, to make Providence a center for commercial activity at home and abroad comparable to its rival Newport before the Revolution. Among the four Brown brothers, Moses was prepared to go even further, and to lay foundations for Providence as a manufacturing center.

The Lowells of Boston [3] show a family system like that of the Browns in Providence, their founding entrepreneur being John Lowell, son of the Reverend John Lowell of Newburyport. After graduating from Harvard in 1760, and studying law in Boston, young John Lowell returned to Newburyport to practice and quickly became attorney for the town's leading merchants, Patrick Tracy and Tristram Dalton. In January 1767, he married Sarah Higginson, daughter of Stephen Higginson and Elizabeth Cabot of Salem. Sarah Higginson Lowell died in 1772, and John Lowell married her cousin Susan Cabot. In 1775, John and Susan had a son, Francis Cabot Lowell, whose mother died within two years; in 1778 John Lowell took Mrs. Rebecca Russell Tyng, a widow, as his third wife.

By his father's three marriages to a Higginson, a Cabot, and a Russell, Francis Cabot Lowell grew up in an extended-kinship group second to none in Boston and its satellite towns on the North Shore, a family connection based upon several generations of merchant-shipowning. The marriages of Francis and the other sons and daughters of the Judge were to enlarge that family circle. Families like the Higginsons of Salem, the Cabots of Beverly, the Russells of Charlestown, were active in the same trade on which the Browns of Providence founded their fortunes. They were not all among the earliest to defy the Crown, but were handsomely rewarded for their American patriotism through war contracts and privateering.

During the war Judge Lowell served as attorney for various Loyalist estates, including that of former Governor Hutchinson — chief target of the rebels Sam Adams and James Otis. Lowell also found time to act as counsel for his privateering relatives by marriage, the Higginsons, Cabots, and Russells, and personally filed seven hundred of the eleven hundred libels against prize vessels in the Boston court, being concerned as assistant counsel in nearly half the rest. We can understand why he was one of the first to move up from the North Shore to Boston when the Tories sailed away to Halifax; they left opportunities in the legal and mercantile life of Boston for able men with financial backing.

Lowell served in the Continental Congress in 1782, where he became familiar with John Brown of Providence, Alexander Hamilton and other New Yorkers, and the Philadelphia group around Robert Morris and his partner Thomas Willing, who a year earlier founded the Bank of North America hoping to make it a national central bank patterned after the Bank of England. Late in 1782 Lowell was given a congressional appointment as judge of appeals in admiralty cases; on returning to Boston he joined with his family connection in organizing the Massachusetts Bank, the first bank in Boston. It was opened in 1784. His cousin, also named John Lowell, was made its teller, and the "judge" served for a while as cashier.

Judge Lowell, according to his son and partner John Lowell, accumulated during the war upwards of $200,000, but held much of it in continental paper money. He and his relatives by marriage became, after peace was signed, leaders of the group seeking a constitutional convention and a new national union to replace the Confederation. His relatives, and especially his brother-in-law George Cabot, were spokesmen for the Essex Junto which elected James Bowdoin as the first Federalist Governor of Massachusetts in 1785, and went on to put down Shays's rebellion the next year.

The Judge died on May 6, 1802. Four years earlier his son Francis had married Hannah Jackson, daughter of the Judge's old friend and neighbor Jonathan Jackson, and granddaughter of Lowell's wealthy client, Patrick Tracy. Francis had already assumed responsibility for investing the Judge's fortune, chiefly in "Adventures at Sea," and was established as a Boston merchant-shipowner operating eight vessels; his brother-in-law Patrick Tracy Jackson was his partner.[4]

Beginning with the first Continental Congress in 1774, a national economy was formed by the efforts of provincial leaders like the Browns in Providence and John Lowell and his family connection in Boston. After these local entrepreneurs became active in the national war effort, by a series of gradual changes they created a new economy to fill the vacuum left by separation of the American colonies from London's metropolitan economy. During the war this new economy enabled Americans to trade with France and other continental nations, and their island possessions; once war ended, the problem became: how to compete in trade abroad in the face of the growing industrial revolution in Great Britain, and how to restore the disrupted peacetime economies of the individual American states.

By 1789, when President Washington was inaugurated, the aristocratic family groups consolidated by the American Revolution had tacitly agreed on one chief economic spokesman: young Alexander Hamilton who in 1780 had married General Philip Schuyler's daughter Betsey. From 1772, when Hamilton arrived in New Jersey as a boy, he was the protégé of the Livingston-Schuyler-Van Rensselaer connection, chief manorial families of New York and New Jersey. During the war he served as Washington's military secretary, forming a more extensive acquaintance among leading Americans than did any other young man of his generation.

Building on these connections, Hamilton became at a remarkably early age one of the three or four chief exponents of a constitutional convention, and one of its youngest delegates. He had been proposed for the Superintendency of Finance in 1781, at the age of twenty-four, when Robert Morris was chosen. Once the new nation was formed, Hamilton was a logical candidate for the Secretaryship of the Treasury in the first Washington Administration, as head of an alliance between the leading mercantile and landed families of New York and Pennsylvania. Included in this alliance were mercantile families in other cities; for example, the Browns of Providence and the Lowell family connection in Boston.

Hamilton was now in a position to become the great entrepreneur of the new American national economy. With the aid of William Duer (the first Assistant Secretary of the Treasury), Tench Coxe (Duer's successor, a protégé of Morris, Willing, and Benjamin Franklin), and other representatives of his alliance, Hamilton established the original financial patterns for the new nation, and in a series of famous reports laid down its original economic programs and principles. Working together they defined the structure and function of the Federal Treasury, the first Bank of the United States, the New York and Philadelphia money markets, a national currency, and the outlines for a protective tariff. Within this national structure, the regional groups centered in the chief towns could organize their own new patterns of entrepreneurial activity. We exaggerate if we argue that this was a singlehanded performance of one financial genius. What Hamilton and his friends were able to do was to complete by their initiative the work of a generation.

IV

One of the chief problems of the group around Hamilton was how to restore economic connections with London, without sacrificing political independence. The struggle between the Federalist party led by Hamilton and the Democratic-Republican party led by Jefferson revolved around the terms on which the United States would come back into the orbit of the London economy. As author of the *Report on Manufactures*, Hamilton was a strong advocate of the need for tariff protection for "infant industries," like the textile industry of which his Society for Useful Manufactures at Paterson, New Jersey, and his New York Manufacturing Society were early (but financially unsuccessful) promoters. Hamilton's efforts to restore good trade relations between the United States and Britain were hampered by Britain's practice of forbidding her mechanics to emigrate, and by her prevention of the export of textile machines, models, or blueprints.

It was paradoxical, but true, that Hamilton, Tench Coxe, and others who worked successfully within the Federal government and the New York and Philadelphia money markets to create a new national economy failed to launch a manufacturing industry. Nevertheless, they provided the national setting wherein Moses Brown of Providence, by employing Samuel Slater, became the first great entrepreneur of the American cotton textile industry.

Alexander Hamilton was appointed Secretary of the Treasury on September 11, 1789. Two days later a young Englishman, Samuel Slater, boarded a vessel bound for America, where he was first employed by the New York Manufacturing Society. Quickly disappointed by its incompetent management, Slater wrote in the first week of December to Moses Brown in Providence, Rhode Island (a state not yet admitted to the federal union), saying:

A few days ago I was informed that you wanted a manager of *cotton spinning*, etc., in which business I flatter myself that I can give the greatest satisfaction, in making machinery, making good yarn, either for *stockings* or *twist*, as any that is made in England; as I have had opportunity, and an oversight, of Sir Richard Arkwright's works, and in Mr. Strutt's mill upwards of eight years. If you are not provided for, should be glad to serve you. . .

Brown and Slater with the aid of the Wilkinsons, a Pawtucket family of ingenious mechanics, were able within a year to start 72 spindles on a water-frame, driven by an old fulling-mill wheel. This success depended on the knowledge Slater had smuggled out of England in his head, defying the British regulation against emigration of skilled mechanics. He had first been drawn to emigrate by an English reprint from a Philadelphia paper saying that a society there was aiding the growth of cotton textile manufacturing in the United States by offering bounties to native and foreign mechanics trained in the methods of that industry. This was probably the Pennsylvania Society for the Encouragement of Manufactures and Useful Arts, which had been founded in Philadelphia in 1787 while the

Constitutional Convention was sitting there and which had the blessing of Benjamin Franklin and the support of Tench Coxe, later Hamilton's Assistant Secretary of the Treasury. Coxe used the Slater mill as one of his chief examples in drafting Hamilton's Report on Manufactures.

By 1793 the firm of Almy, Brown and Slater had built a small factory of their own in Pawtucket (and Slater had become a son-in-law of Ozias Wilkinson). Their operations were pitifully small compared to those Slater had left behind in England, where Arkwright throughout a generation had operated a dozen or more mills, some of them with 600 workmen. Nevertheless, thanks to Slater, America was launched on the cotton textile industry as a young rival of the British. The infant industry flourished in the small-scale operations of the Blackstone Valley where it could rely on skillful mechanics, small water powers, and a close indentity between capital and management. The United States was not ready for large-scale corporate manufacturing experiments, such as those of Hamilton and his friends.

The other Browns were more immediately influenced by Hamilton's national experiments than by those of Slater and their brother Moses in Pawtucket. In 1791 the Browns helped found the Providence Bank (modeled on those in Philadelphia, New York, and Boston); in 1794 they built the *John Jay*, and launched her in the trade to India. It was not until 1804 that Nicholas Brown, Jr. considered his uncle's manufacturing venture sufficiently successful to justify the firm of Brown and Ives in buying its first water rights on the Blackstone River, above Providence.

v

This Blackstone Manufacturing Company quickened the interest of small merchants and mechanics as far away as Fall River, Massachusetts, on the Rhode Island border. By the time of Jefferson's embargo, the mills built at Pawtucket and elsewhere by Almy, Brown and Slater had become "schools" for machinists from the region twenty or thirty miles around Providence. The men they trained harnessed small streams to turn mill wheels and drive cotton-spinning water-frames; small textile villages grew up about these mills.

In 1808 a twenty-two-year-old named David Anthony, who hailed from near Fall River, went to work for Slater and the Wilkinsons. In 1813 Anthony and his cousin Dexter Wheeler, the mechanic, started the Fall River Manufactory, first cotton mill on the Quequechan River in the village of Fall River, on land belonging to Thomas Borden — later to be Anthony's father-in-law. That same year the blacksmith Nathaniel Wheeler, Dexter's brother, helped organize the Troy Cotton and Woollen Manufactory at the head of the stream, on land owned by the family of Simeon Borden.

The chief family structure in the village of Fall River at this time was an extended-kinship group centering around a series of intermarriages over several generations between members of the Borden and Durfee family connection whose ancestors were among the original settlers of Freetown after the Freeman's Purchase in 1658. By 1803, when the township of Fall River was carved out of adjoining Freetown and Tiverton by the legislature, there were eighteen dwelling-houses near the sites of the first two mills on the stream, and nine of the family heads had the name of Borden, while one was a Durfee.

The two Fall River mills founded in 1813, and a neighboring mill set up in 1811 in Tiverton, were all organized by members of this family connection. They had operated grist and sawmills on the Quequechan for generations, and traded with the Browns and other Providence merchants by sloop; through Anthony and others they established close relations with the Pawtucket experiment; and in the years to come maintained them. Thus the Fall River mills and families grew from the seed-bed of the American textile industry, and through Slater and the Providence-Pawtucket system derived their skills directly from the original British cotton textile industry founded by Arkwright and the Strutts.

Studies of entrepreneurship which place heavy emphasis upon the "creative personality" of the *individual* entrepreneur are apt to underestimate the importance of the *group* from which these entrepreneurs derive so much of their strength. The key group in the establishment and development of Fall River was the already described extended-kinship family system joining together its early entrepreneurs. For fifty years after the founding of the first mills, or until the panic of 1873 struck the city, this family structure founded in the seventeenth and eighteenth centuries was still close-knit. Its individual members usually exerted personal control over the major institutions formed there during that half century. The bad times in the 1870's forced a period we may call "trusteeship" when a few local members of the family modernized the institutional structure by which they held control. Then the group directing the family's affairs accepted the leadership of an outstanding member of their oncoming generation who had earlier been sent to represent them in New York, and he thereafter dominated the life of the town until the outbreak of the First World War, exercising final control from New York through his family connections in Fall River.

This process of growth goes through a number of stages, marked by an increasing impersonalization and institutionalization of the family as a social control group. The Fall River Iron Works was the chief local institution through which this control was exercised until after the Civil War. This company founded by the Borden-Durfee group in 1825 included, until the economic crisis of 1829, two of the Wilkinson brothers from Pawtucket: Abraham and Isaac. They brought to the company their knowledge of textile machine manufacture (notably that of the Scotch loom, long produced by their brother David), their skill in iron-making, and especially their father's nail-making machine.

The year of the formation of the Iron Works marked also a period of transition when the family generation of the founders, who had grown up in the shadow of Samuel Slater, Ozias Wilkinson, and Moses Brown, began to move into strategic positions in the newly formed local bank and savings bank founded by the family, or to concentrate on side lines like the running of a steamboat line to Providence (and later to New York). Thus the family was extending its influence within and outside the local community.

Prior to 1825 it would be difficult to point to any single member of the family group as the leader in local developments. Thereafter, right down to 1914, there was usually one member of the family whom we can designate as the prime mover in community affairs; frequently this was by no means the eldest member of the active group, but usually that one whose capacities and working experience best fitted him to give the kind of leadership needed at a given stage of community growth. This pattern of family control, rooted in the customary ways of the group on the land or in shipping ventures, was reinforced by their use of the joint-stock, limited liability corporation.

When the founding generation of entrepreneurs turned over control of manufacturing after formation of the Iron Works in 1825, a new generation of the family led by Holder Borden took charge. He had two claims to a central role in the family: first, though he was a bachelor, his three sisters had married Durfee cousins, while his mother's second husband was Major Bradford Durfee, another cousin; second, he was in 1825, at the age of 26, a success in the eyes of the Borden-Durfee family connection because of his responsible position in Providence with Brown and Ives. He continued this connection for over a decade, while dominating the Fall River scene. He made his major contribution to the growth of the community by extending the family interest to textile printing.

Known in Fall River and Providence as a great "driver" he appears to have hastened his death from consumption by "commuting" behind a fast horse, changed halfway between the two cities (it is said he chain-smoked cigars). Holder left his estate (apparently in equal shares; there is no will) to his three Durfee brothers-in-law and his Durfee stepfather, no doubt because of the restrictions on married women as estate-holders. By these legacies he helped to concentrate control of the family enterprises in the Borden-Durfee connection. This was compounded by his great-uncle William Valentine, a few years later, who left his estate including his Iron Works shares in trust, and made Jefferson Borden (Holder's uncle) his principal trustee.

Bradford Durfee followed Holder in the family leadership and provided a new impetus towards practical engineering; he made his chief contribution on the mechanical side of the cotton industry, by importing and helping perfect the English "mule" for the fine-spinning of cotton thread. By the time he died in 1845 after overexertion at a major fire in Fall River, he had begun the connection of the town with the Old Colony Railroad. Leadership of the Iron Works group passed with his death to his brothers-in-law, Richard and Jefferson Borden. Richard was the dominant one, but they worked out a division of labor, with Jefferson specializing in the "finishing" end of the cotton industry (he founded the bleachery and ran the American Print Works), and expanding the family's banking role.

By the 1850's, most of the nephews and nieces of Richard and Jefferson Borden had married cousins, keeping their Iron Works shares within the family connection of the Bordens and Durfees. There were in 1856 only 32 Iron Works shares outstanding, with a book value of $960,000 as against the original investment of $24,000; each *share* now had an individual value of $30,000. Nephews and nieces who held fractions of a share (e.g., ¾ of 1/32) wanted to use these as security for bank loans; they also wanted to be represented at the Iron Works when decisions were made about their shares. The family created a board of directors, and arranged a stock split-up, issuing 300 shares of a par value of $100 each in exchange for every one of the 32 shares outstanding, or 9600 shares in all. These changes shifted the company from close-knit family control to a more impersonal basis of financing and control, more subject to outside pressure from banks, and other creditors. The full effect of this was not felt until after the panic of 1873.

During the thirty-year regime of Richard and Jefferson Borden, the Borden-Durfee connection maintained its leadership in Fall River, in spite of the financial crash in 1857, and the textile boom of the Civil War with its mushroom growth of rival mills. Richard's death in 1874 and that of his younger brother Jefferson in 1879 revealed, however, the failure of the family to provide adequate local successors to their leadership. The crash also disclosed the financial weakness and overextension of some of the lesser members of the family group, especially the incompetent business operations of their nephew, Dr. Nathan Durfee, founder of the first steam-driven cotton mill in the city. He and his sons-in-law proved to have used the family connection as a basis for speculative financial dealings which nearly brought down the whole structure of family investments during the panic's aftermath. Only the creation of a family "trusteeship" enabled the Iron Works group to survive the financial storm.

After 1845 a generation of Yankees from rocky farms surrounding Fall River founded their own commercial banks and savings banks and during and after the Civil War built new textile mills. Until the war, more than two-thirds of the local mill operatives and their families were Yankee, largely drawn from these neighboring farm areas. The managerial group in mills, banks, and stores was also composed overwhelmingly of Yankees, tied by blood or marriage to the first or second generation of bank clerks, store owners, mechanics, and superintendents who ran local enterprises for the Borden-Durfee family connection. Their sons became the backbone of the new group of entrepreneurs of the Civil War generation, rapidly enlarged Fall River's mill-working population, and changed the sources from which the town drew its workers. The manufacturers continued to rely on rural family groups, but began sending agents to Canada and overseas. In less than twenty years the town grew from 15,000 to 45,000 residents, largely drawn from French Canada and the British Isles but increasingly from the European continent.

After the crisis of the 1870's struck, Fall River's recovery was slow; it waited for the appearance of a new entrepreneur, who could provide a wider horizon for its textile industry. The driving force to set the town back on its rapid upward expansion of mill-building was supplied by Matthew Chaloner Durfee Borden, who represented the Borden-Durfee family interests in New York. He realigned the family businesses in Fall River so as to make that city an industrial satellite of New York. Through association with Low, Harriman and Company, the large New York firm merchandizing cotton goods, he had a thorough knowledge of the marketing system growing up in that metropolis. Through his wider outlook the Bordens, rather than the newer men, held top leadership in Fall River.

M. C. D. Borden's allies back home included the Brayton brothers, whose sister Mary had been the second wife of Bradford Durfee. The Brayton's nephew, Bradford Matthew Chaloner Durfee, was due to come of age in 1864; in 1863 his Brayton uncles, as trustees for his estate (based on Iron Works shares), founded the B. M. C. Durfee Trust Company; they used its financial backing to build the Durfee mill, first of a series of their family holdings. M. C. D. Borden made the B. M. C. Durfee Trust Company his chief financial agency in Fall River, and relied heavily on the advice of the Braytons in his local operations. He converted the Fall River Iron Works, no longer able to compete in iron manufacture, into a cotton manufactory, and built the largest textile corporation in the United States, operating before the First World War about a million spindles.

We can conclude our Fall River example with a few statistics showing the extraordinary growth fostered by the Borden-Durfee connection. A community of less than 100 in 1815 became a city of over 100,000 by 1915, primarily devoted to the manufacture of cotton-textiles. When the textile depression set in after 1923, the town went through the financial wringer. Such cotton textile manufacturing as survived did so in plants tied to large nation-wide companies operating chains of mills, North and South; their product was marketed through close connections with the head offices of wholesalers and department-store chains in New York City.

VI

We turn from the Fall River example of the growth of a textile community out of the extended-kinship system of the surrounding countryside to that of Boston as a different type of community growth, one based directly on the family system operating in shipping and overseas trade. Comparison of Fall River with Boston shows a fundamental difference in the structure and function of these communities, and a comparable difference between the contributions made by their entrepreneurs to the growth of the American textile industry. Fall River's first mills were founded while Francis Cabot Lowell of Boston and Paul Moody were experimenting with their power loom in Waltham. Chronologically, the two experiments started together; their patterns of development, however, were decades apart.

The Bordens' influence on the growth of the textile industry was confined to Fall River until after 1880; the Lowells, operating from their Boston base, had a regional influence from the start. If we contrast the Boston region after 1814 with Boston and Providence after 1789 we shall see the stimulus to American manufactures of Jefferson's embargo and of the Louisiana Purchase. The treaty with Britain after the War of 1812, by reducing economic dependence of the United States upon London and removing restraints on westward expansion, changed the pace of American economic development and expanded national markets for cotton textiles. This was the period when the Fall River and Waltham mills got their start. In these years, also, after the Hartford Convention (chaired by Lowell's uncle George Cabot) the New England Federalists abandoned their close alliance with the British economy, and many Federalist families shifted into manufacturing, under Lowell's leadership.

The Fall River process of converting the extended-kinship family rooted in the soil into an economic institution dominating a whole community had certain inherent limitations not present when a family of merchant-shipowners undertook to give comparable leadership. Francis Cabot Lowell in 1814 started shifting the whole direction of Boston's entrepreneurial activities from overseas trade to manufacturing, and channeled them into a series of ventures modeled on his "Waltham plan."

Abroad in 1811, with some such plan in mind, he studied intensively the operations of the British textile industry, especially the new power looms then just in the final stages of experiment. His mathematical skill and remarkable memory enabled him to imitate Slater by evading British restrictions on export of machinery or models and, after his return to Boston, to invent a loom of his own. He set it going in an old paper mill in Waltham with the aid of Paul Moody's mechanical abilities. Lowell enlisted his brother-in-law Patrick Tracy Jackson, and secured some financial support from Nathan Appleton, a Boston merchant with whom he had discussed his plans while both were abroad.

When Lowell's power loom enabled his Boston associates to organize the production of cotton cloth at Waltham within one factory (instead of putting out the yarn to weavers, or letting yarn-buyers weave their own cloth), Jackson, Appleton, and Lowell were already experienced in the merchandising of cotton cloth, British and Indian. Available Boston capital derived from overseas commerce started the Boston Manufacturing Company with a capitalization larger than that of Brown and Ives' venture in 1804, and far larger than that in Fall River. By 1816 the Waltham experiment was acknowledged by members of the Lowell family connection to have succeeded. That year Francis Lowell lobbied the tariff on cotton cloth through Congress, a few months before his death at forty-two.

With his death, Lowell's associates Patrick Jackson [5] and Nathan Appleton faced new problems in carrying the experiment forward. By 1821 Paul Moody, under their direction, had harnessed all the available falls at Waltham, and they sought a new water-power site. Capital for the expansion was not a major consideration: by 1822 the Boston Manufacturing Company had paid dividends of 102.5 per cent on the original investment of $400,000. This large initial capital was in itself a demonstration of the difference between the new textile industry projected from Boston and that growing up simultaneously in Fall River. The Borden-Durfee group was forced to accumulate most of its capital locally, and to use members of its extended-kinship group as workers in its cotton mills.

Appleton, Jackson, and Moody found the new water power at Chelmsford, where a thirty-foot fall was owned by "The Proprietors of the Locks and Canals on Merrimack River." When on February 27, 1822, the first meeting of stockholders of the Merrimack Manufacturing Company [6] elected a board of directors, the Lowell connection was well represented: it included Francis Lowell's brothers-in-law Patrick Tracy Jackson, Benjamin Gorham, and Warren Dutton, who was named president.

ROCKMONT COLLEGE LIBRARY

In memory of Francis Cabot Lowell the company town, incorporated by the legislature in 1826, was named Lowell. It established a new pattern of industrial community life in the United States. Around Providence and Pawtucket had grown up a regional congeries of mill villages, each dependent on a small water power, and each drawing its workers from the near-by farm families. These villages were in no sense "plantations," but stemmed directly out of the existing rural structure. At Lowell, the Boston proprietors built dormitories for workers, and recruited their "help" from rural areas as far away as New Hampshire. They preferred young farm girls who wanted to supplement the family income. A much more rootless community was thus created, controlled by the superintendents of the companies' mills.

The foundation of Lowell in 1822 marked a turning point for Boston: a general movement began, spreading the manufacturing interests of Boston to the larger water powers of New England. Later in 1822 some of the stockholders of the Merrimack Company started a similar development at Chicopee, with some capitalists from the Connecticut River Valley. Both at Lowell and at Chicopee new mills rose in rapid succession, as the Boston associates saw markets expand in pace with their output. Within the next fifteen years the Boston group developed other water powers at Taunton, Massachusetts; Manchester and Somersworth, New Hampshire; Saco and Biddeford, Maine; and elsewhere. As steamboating on the Mississippi, grain traffic on the Great Lakes, and the building of the Erie Canal boomed western lands, the population of the country grew rapidly and the textile industry boomed also. This boom collapsed in 1837, but was soon revived by the railway expansion of the two decades before the Civil War.

The group of entrepreneurs who create a new community provide the most spectacular example of the role of the entrepreneur in relation to the community. Once the site was chosen and the town launched, these entrepreneurs among the Boston associates carried through their age-old entrepreneurial functions of organizing new institutions such as local banks, savings banks, real estate companies, manufacturing corporations, branch railroads, and the like. Meanwhile, these economic and social institutions within the local communities were being duplicated in Boston to tie the new industrial towns to their regional metropolitan capital. The growth of the region, stimulated by the "plantation" of these new towns, was accelerated after the development of the railroad and the importation of new working populations from abroad. New England differed from areas further west, however, by reason of the close-knit relationships between these long-established mercantile families and the newcomers whom they associated with their group. Town building assumed one pattern in the more settled regions of the east and another along the lines of railway expansion in the west; the resulting communities show to this day important differences in their patterns of entrepreneurship.

Years before the expansionist effects of the coming railway age could be felt in New England, the Boston associates turned to the federal government for tariff protection following the panic of 1829. In the Providence-Pawtucket center of the industry, the panic bankrupted Abraham and Isaac Wilkinson (and forced them to sell to Bordens and Durfees their shares in the Fall River Iron Works); Samuel Slater and many others were threatened. Fears of similar troubles undoubtedly strengthened the protectionist forces in Boston and elsewhere. The national political significance of the pattern of absentee ownership and the founding of company towns by the Boston associates was demonstrated to the people of Massachusetts in 1830. In that election the free traders supported Henry Lee for election to Congress from the Boston seat against Nathan Appleton, candidate of the protectionists. This campaign shook the old-family structure of Boston to its foundations: Henry Lee, for example, was the brother-in-law of Appleton's associate Patrick Tracy Jackson; Appleton's victory marked the permanent ascendancy of the protectionist interest in the city.

To consolidate the position of the Lowell associates as leaders of the textile industry, and the position of Boston as the metropolis of the growing region, many new entrepreneurial advances had to be made. New banking methods were needed, so Nathan Appleton, John Amory Lowell, and their friends originated the Suffolk Banking System to stabilize banknote currency throughout New England. Appleton had a long career as exponent of "sound money." [7] He was an original subscriber to the Suffolk Bank, along with his brother William; the list included John W. Boott, Patrick Tracy Jackson, and Amos and Abbott Lawrence.

Abbott Lawrence and Nathan Appleton, self-made men, were interlopers on the Boston scene by comparison with the Lowell family connection. Their personal histories show many parallels with those of the Bordens and Durfees in Fall River, but within the Boston setting they entered the charmed economic circle of the merchant-shipowner group by their careers as overseas merchants. They were accepted as social near-equals of the ruling group, however, by reason of the marriages of their children.[8] By their manufacturing careers, Appleton and Lawrence gave a driving force to the expansion of Boston's entrepreneurial role which would probably otherwise have been lacking to the operations of the Lowell family group after the death of Francis Cabot Lowell.

Nathan Appleton and Abbott Lawrence showed many parallels in their careers, but Lawrence started his in Boston fourteen years after Appleton arrived in 1794. Like Appleton, Lawrence as a boy entered his older brother's Boston commercial house, bringing a bundle of clothes under his arm and a fortune of three dollars in his pocket.[9] The children of two rural deacons became the founders of the two greatest textile centers spawned by Boston; unlike Fall River, however, the cities created by Appleton and Lawrence were company towns, controlled by the methods of absentee ownership fostered by the Lowell family connection at Waltham. Neither Appleton nor Lawrence used his ancestral acres, as did the Bordens, to raise up a community with which they mingled the lives of their family connection, except remotely as mill treasurers and corporate directors.

After the panic of 1829, Nathan Appleton felt that the time had come to enlist the support of new capital and persuaded Abbott Lawrence and his brothers, who had acted as merchandizers of textiles for the mills of Lowell, to join "The Proprietors of the Locks and Canals on Merrimack River," and build their own mills to take advantage of the remaining water power. From this moment Lawrence moved up to take his place beside Appleton and John Amory Lowell as a leading cotton manufacturer. Fifteen years passed, however, before the Lawrences were ready to found a textile city bearing their name.

On March 20, 1845, fourteen leading Bostonians,[10] including Nathan Appleton, Patrick Jackson, and Abbott Lawrence, set out on an "excursion" by rail to inspect a new power site on the Merrimack River, some distance short of the city of Lowell. The new industrial city of Lawrence was built at a time when the characteristics of the mill workers of Massachusetts were changing, and Lawrence became at the start a more heterogeneous community than Lowell. Mill girls, a majority of the workers at Lowell in the 1830's, were drawn chiefly from the farms of New England; they worked to supplement the declining income of their farm families, and to save money for their own dowries. By the 1840's their places were being taken by English and Irish immigrants whose families joined them as mill workers. With the decline of working and living conditions after the panic of 1837, strikes commenced to plague the proprietors.

That there were other troubles we can see from a letter written in July 1842 by Henry Lee, Sr. (whom Nathan Appleton had defeated for Congress in 1830) to his son Henry Lee, Jr., then in Paris. The senior Henry Lee had begun in 1841 converting a fortune made in commerce into active investments in manufacturing and railroad stocks, continuing for at least the next ten years. He writes:

A *reforming party* has been at work with Wm. Appleton — at its head & sustained by Geo. Lyman, Col. Perkins, the Brooks, E. Francis, H. Cabot, Geo. How(e) — and nearly all the independent men who don't get salaries & are not influenced by those who do — They have been resisted by the combined power of Lawrence, N. Appleton, the Lowells & the Jacksons & their allies — but it was *ineffectual*. Salaries are reduced (operatives were 6 mo ago) more work done at the factories.[11]

This letter shows how the insiders who dominated the operations of the Boston associates in Lowell, Lawrence, Chicopee, and elsewhere struggled against the outsiders drawn from the ranks of the overseas merchants, who like Lee had become investors in mill stocks. On the wave of recovery after the panic of 1837, new stockholders like Henry Lee helped found the city of Lawrence in 1845. Thereafter until the Civil War the growth of industry in New England continued within the pattern laid down by the Boston associates.

After the start of the railway age, the Boston associates linked their metropolitan center to its regional hinterland; they planted textile cities at available water powers and tied them together by a railroad network. The proprietors of Lowell led this movement in 1830 by projecting the Boston and Lowell road, and Patrick Tracy Jackson climbed back into harness to direct its construction. With the completion of its links to its neighboring cities, and especially its span across the Berkshires to the Hudson River, Boston had laid the foundations for its position as "The Hub" city.[12]

Thomas Handasyd Perkins, who deserves much of the credit for joining Boston and Albany by rail, kept himself in the background of most of the ventures in which he was interested.[13] He was outstanding among the merchant-shipowners who became investors in textile manufacturing on the second wave (he was probably the "Col. Perkins" of Henry Lee's letter). A leading Boston merchant, long prominent in the China trade, he appears in 1828 as an incorporator of the new mills of the Lowell and Appleton companies in the town of Lowell.

The most important result of Perkins' interest in railways was its effect on his nephew John Murray Forbes, who while a boy had followed his uncle as a China merchant, returning by the age of twenty-four with a comfortable fortune. Through Forbes the entrepreneurs of Boston leapt over the Hudson with their railway investments, before they spanned it by a railway bridge. The career of John Forbes, promoter of the Michigan Central, and the Chicago, Burlington and Quincy Railroads, directed the attention of Bostonians to the expanding West at a time when they would probably otherwise have devoted their major energies to further industrializing of New England. The result was to launch Boston as a national source of investment funds, although the city did not mature in that role until after the Civil War, when several old-family firms (among whom Lee, Higginson was foremost) became active traders in the securities of Western railroads, mines, real estate, and lumber companies outside of New England.

By the end of the Civil War the original "Boston associates" who established their city as textile capital of the United States were dead: Patrick Tracy Jackson died in 1847, followed in 1855 by Abbott Lawrence. In July 1861, three months after the firing on Fort Sumter, the Boston Merchants' Exchange held a memorial meeting for Nathan Appleton, dead at eighty-one. John Amory Lowell, presiding, said:

> [The name of Nathan Appleton] is too intimately connected with finance, with commerce, with all the great industrial pursuits of New England, to need eulogium from any one; but it is a privilege which we, his fellow citizens, could not willingly forego, to bear our ready testimony to those qualities which have done more than those of perhaps any other one man to enhance the estimation and promote the prosperity, not of this city only, not of this State, nor of New England, but of the whole of our common country, North, East, West, ay, and South.

John Amory Lowell had already assumed the responsibilities previously carried by Nathan Appleton and Abbott Lawrence for directing the widespread concerns of the Boston associates of the Lowell family connection. Enterprises he directed included the whole gamut of operations from manufacturing textile machinery and steam engines in the Lowell Machine Shops, distributing water power through the Locks and Canals, railroading on the Boston and Lowell Railroad, cotton manufacturing in the Boott, Massachusetts, and other mills, banking in the Suffolk Bank, insurance in the Massachusetts Mutual, and the Massachusetts Hospital Life Insurance Companies, to cotton goods merchandizing through J. K. Mills and Company and other firms. Meanwhile he found time to oversee the affairs of the Boston associates through his son, Augustus, his cousins and other members of the Lowell family group. He remained active as the acknowledged head of the family throughout the Civil War and the panic of 1873, retiring in 1877 in favor of his son Augustus, then forty-seven.[14]

Boston, the political and economic capital city for much of colonial America, was stimulated by post-Revolutionary trade to the Far East and by the expanding textile industries. It ranked in the first four cities of our country right down to the Civil War but, after 1845 and the growth of western railroads, steadily lost headway to its more westerly rivals. It retained, and retains, its character as the metropolitan capital of a regional economy. While Fall River has continued throughout its career to be a satellite, first to Providence, and then to New York, Boston maintained a large measure of economic independence until quite recently. Much of the credit for this must go to the close-knit system of old-family leadership established before the Civil War.

Prior to the Civil War, in Boston as in Fall River, a new generation of self-made men founded banks and business corporations, and spread their influence throughout the region centered upon Boston, enlarging its structure and functions. It was not, however, until after the Civil War that this group began effectively to challenge the group we have called the Boston associates.[15] The Lowell family connection met this challenge and, while its absolute importance declined, successfully maintained a central position in Boston through collateral branches such as those of the Lees, Higginsons, Cabots, Jacksons, and Storrows. (See Appendix, p. 118.)

VII

After this examination of the development of the pre-Civil War generations of entrepreneurs who created the American textile industry, and our glimpse at some of the communities they helped expand, we are ready to return to the questions we asked at the start of this essay: How was the organizing of the structures and functions of our national economic system related to the development of the textile industry? How did certain communities, mercantile centers before the Revolution, become regional textile-industry capitals after the ratification of the Constitution? What entrepreneurs were responsible for these developments, and how much did they depend on other groups in their local or regional communities, or in the national community?

The development of the American textile industry between 1789 and 1815 was directly related to the formation of the national economic system. Providence began its shift from mercantile to manufacturing activity as a regional capital for the textile industry because of the entrepreneurial skills of Moses Brown; however, Brown needed not only the genius of Samuel Slater and the Wilkinsons but also the commercial capital and experience accumulated by the Brown family, and their connections with the new national economy. Fall River was only the most outstanding of a number of textile communities which grew from the Providence-Pawtucket experiment, but its entrepreneurs were rooted in a rural extended-kinship system which channeled the growth of a whole community. Boston's history, like that of Providence, depended upon the regional development of a mercantile capital city but especially upon the leadership provided by one group of merchant-shipowners who combined the extended-kinship system with the wider horizon of a family group engaged in overseas trade. The success of the Lowells as entrepreneurs of the textile industry began twenty-five years after the Browns, because it depended upon the arrival of a new stage in manufacturing: the operation of an integrated factory and the plantation of company towns. It depended also on the reorganization of the national economy which followed the War of 1812 (a reorganization marked by the tariff of 1816 and the formation of the Second Bank of the United States).

Let us turn now from this review of economic history to a discussion of its implications for studies of entrepreneurship.[16] When the economic history of communities like those of Fall River and Boston is dissected so as to lay bare their differentiation of function, their subdivision of labor, their channeling of growth, studies of individual entrepreneurs will reveal more than a limited, and distorted picture of entrepreneurial activity. By the same token, questions directed at students of entrepreneurship by economists can secure more adequate answers from a rounded picture of the context in which decisions are made within the community and its individual firms. One of the great shortcomings of the economists has been their failure to show clearly how community-building contributes to the incomes of this central group of decision-makers, and enables them to continue to channel the economic life of the community into the institutions they control.

Economists will urge, and rightly so, that the units in which entrepreneurs operate, whether family firms, banks, industrial corporations, or of whatever form, are dependent upon the economic rules of that society. As a corollary, economists will say that, insofar as we are studying that group of decision-makers we call *entrepreneurs*, we are or should be primarily concerned with their economic decisions. The economists must remember, however, that these decisions are most meaningful, and often *only* meaningful, within their social context.

If students of entrepreneurship have erred by overemphasizing biographies of individual entrepreneurs, as their critics charge, economists have erred by depersonalizing the functions of decision-making. More recently, economists emphasizing price fluctuations as the chief data of economic theory have sought to give these fleeting facts about economic life an appearance of substantial reality, and to build systematic models around them. While abstractions are necessary to theory, both groups prefer the data of biography or price theory to the substance of social institutions set up by flesh-and-blood decision-makers who shape or respond to events, build new economic, political, and social structures among interrelated human beings, and organize them to perform new functions. We are a long way from creating a science of society, and many students of society doubt that such a general social science can be attained, but certainly the orderly methods of the physical sciences can help students of society. For students of the economic aspects of society, social institutions are the basic data.

Here "model building" is relevant, provided that model-builders are as aware as are the physical scientists of how abstractions can generate errors in reasoning. The family or other small groups, the association, the corporate or institutional entity, and communities of various sizes and kinds provide the basic models for students of society, who need to remember the risks of building models on insufficient evidence. They need constantly to realize, also, that participants in a given situation are the best (although by no means the only reliable) witnesses as to the structure and function of such groups, associations, corporate and institutional entities.

With these precepts in mind, we can say that Fall River and Boston provide "models" of the middle group of communities: the local industrial city, and the metropolitan city at the center of a sizable region. The United States in 1789 provides a model of the new national economy, within the new nation-state. Our "models" as described above give a chronological account of certain contributions made by a few of their economic decision-makers towards the development of those communities, and show whence these men derived much of their strength. These models indicate only part of the structure and functions of social and economic institutions in the communities we are studying. They emphasize the processes involved in the creation and extension of such institutions: they show their dependence on family connections during this period of community development; and the social, economic, and political relationships of individuals and groups within the communities in which these entrepreneurs operate.

By studying the processes of decision-making as they developed in their time and space dimensions within the local "model" of Fall River, the regional "model" of Boston, and the "model" of the American nation-state in 1789, we can understand the changing character of the problems confronting their decision-makers. We see their decisions as dependent upon the point in time when each arrived upon the scene, and upon whether he was located in a local, regional, or national community setting. For example, interlocking models of such communities show the pattern of decision-making as it is woven between local and regional, or regional and national, centers: new structure is formed when state incorporation laws initiated in Boston permit the transformation of family firms in Fall River into corporations; new function is developed when the national protective tariff after 1816 encourages the Boston overseas merchant to become an industrial entrepreneur; change is achieved when Hamilton and his friends tie local and regional business groups together around the United States Treasury and the first Bank of the United States.

We can now, I think, venture some hypotheses as to what studies of entrepreneurship may gain by reëxamining the economic decision-maker within his community setting: the entrepreneur, active in economic life at points of strategic importance for decision-making, influences changes in the organization of society so as to increase economic efficiency, to raise profits, to create new economic and social institutions, and to transform and connect old ones by his innovations. Our examples drawn from Fall River, Providence-Pawtucket, and Boston show a direct relationship between the social setting of individual entrepreneurs like Holder Borden, Moses Brown, and Samuel Slater, or Francis Cabot Lowell (and, on the national scene, Alexander Hamilton and Tench Coxe), and the degree and kind of economic and social success they achieved within it, hardly attainable outside that setting.

For students of entrepreneurship, the individual *must* be considered as the basic unit around which each social system revolves. As we have seen, however, the individual entrepreneur (or any other decision-maker taken out of a given social setting) is a mere figment of the theorist's imagination; he becomes a reality only when he is studied as a member of his society. The social groupings or institutions of that social system wherein he operates prove, on investigation, to have their own value systems and goals of activity, within the larger set of assumptions which organize that society. Entrepreneurs, like other decision-makers, depend for their success on the measure of acceptance their values and goals of activity command from that society. As we have seen, they tend to act in small groups, and to work out their value systems in such groups as family or clique. Studies of these smaller groupings lead in turn to a series of more comprehensive social studies of communities in their time and space dimensions.

Our examination of certain communities and our study of some of their outstanding economic decision-makers indicates that, whereas decision-making is necessary in all societies regardless of their form of economic organization, ours has been the era and the civilization of economic men. The dominance of *economic* decision-makers achieved its maximum spread during the nineteenth century. The entrepreneur is the economic man in his outstanding role: as guide of economic change. It is necessary but not sufficient to say that individual entrepreneurs made great contributions to the building of individual firms, and the formation of economic institutions such as stock exchanges, commodity markets, and the like. All such accomplishments must be viewed as part of the larger process of building local, regional, national, and international communities.

Studies of economic innovation require a comprehensive understanding of the relationship of all forms of decision-making, from the individual entrepreneurial decision to the development of entire communities. A reëxamination of entrepreneurship within this context will show the critics of entrepreneurial studies how necessary it is for these studies to cast their net wide. In analyzing economic decision-making as one aspect of social decision-making, students are bound to consider the structure, functions, and processes of change of the societies in which entrepreneurs operated, to see in what ways the entrepreneur effects political and social as well as economic changes.

APPENDIX

The family relationships of Lowells-Higginsons-Cabots-Jacksons-Lees go far to explain the accumulation of Massachusetts mercantile fortunes invested in the Waltham-Lowell cotton textile industry experiment launched by Francis Cabot Lowell's power loom. The leading members of this family group developed the textile cities of Lowell, Lawrence, Chicopee, etc. As the genealogical chart shows, intermarriages of Higginsons and Cabots in Salem and other North Shore shipping towns started building this extended-kinship system before the Revolutionary War. In 1767 the young attorney, John Lowell of Newburyport, married Sarah Higginson, and after her death married her cousin Susannah Cabot in 1774; the following year their son Francis Cabot Lowell was born. George Cabot married his double-first-cousin Elizabeth Higginson in 1774, becoming John Lowell's brother-in-law. Cabot in 1788 founded the Beverly cotton factory, first power-driven (horse-driven) mill in the United States.

From this intimate family connection came the nucleus of the Essex Junto around which clustered the leadership of the Federalist Party of Massachusetts from 1784 to 1814. John Lowell moved to Boston ten days after the Loyalists sailed away in March 1776 with General Howe; there he became the chief admiralty lawyer, acting for his relatives by marriage, the Higginsons, Cabots, and Russells, leading Revolutionary privateers, and after the return of peace led them to form the Massachusetts Bank in 1784. His son Francis married Hannah Jackson in 1798, thus gaining new mercantile family ties for the Lowell-Higginson-Cabot group. Patrick Tracy Jackson, Francis Lowell's brother-in-law, became his partner.

In 1814, when Lowell and Paul Moody perfected the power loom, Lowell and Jackson persuaded Nathan Appleton to join them in the Waltham experiment. In 1830 Appleton succeeded Henry Lee in Congress on the issue of protection *vs.* free trade. Lee's mother was George Cabot's sister, and Lee married Patrick Tracy Jackson's sister Mary. Lee's first cousin Lydia Cabot married Patrick Jackson, and their daughter Anna Cabot Jackson married Charles Russell Lowell, grandson of Judge John Lowell by his third wife Rebecca Russell.

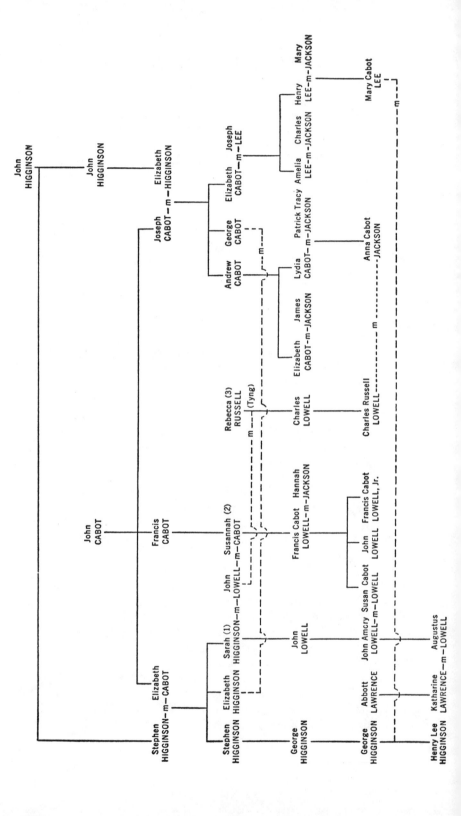

Among this family connection was George Higginson, Jr., founder of the Boston investment banking house of Lee, Higginson and Company; Judge John Lowell was George's great-uncle by marriage; George Higginson married the daughter of Henry Lee, and became a partner of Henry Lee, Jr. The leading representative of the Lowell family connection in the generation succeeding the founders of Boston's textile industry was the old Judge's grandson, John Amory Lowell, who married his first cousin Susan Cabot Lowell, daughter of Francis Cabot Lowell. John Amory Lowell was the father of Augustus Lowell who joined the Lowell and Lawrence fortunes by his marriage to Katharine Lawrence, daughter of Abbott Lawrence; John Amory Lowell and Abbott Lawrence founded the city of Lawrence. Augustus and Katharine Lowell were the parents of the famous Lowell trio: Percival, the astronomer; Amy, the poet; and Abbott Lawrence Lowell, President of Harvard University.

V

John Stevens

General Entrepreneur

1749–1838

By Dorothy Gregg

The period of flux which marked the American Revolution and the formation of a political nation produced a number of colorful, dramatic figures such as George Washington, Alexander Hamilton, Benjamin Franklin, and Robert Fulton, whose names are known to every high-school graduate, and a host of other entrepreneurs of lesser fame, such as Robert Livingston, Robert Morris, William Duer, and John Stevens, Jr., whose names are known to the historian. All of these men were products of the eighteenth century which marked the flowering of commercial capitalism and bourgeois culture. They were cultivated, imaginative, acquisitive individuals, who as gentlemen of commerce moved easily across international borders in their social and business pursuits. America from 1770 through the early part of the nineteenth century was characterized by rapidly changing economic and political conditions which offered singularly wide and varied opportunities to such men of enterprise and they were not slow to grasp them.

The source and exercise of authority in this society was not by the criterion of hereditary position but rather by the criteria of wealth and learning. Money is a flexible criterion of power: it, at least, is anonymous in its origins and almost infinite in its expansibility. For this reason American society on the eastern seaboard was less rigid than the older

European societies. Moreover, changing economic and political conditions, as well as the usual recourse to a good marriage, accounted for continuing additions to the wealthy class. But even money over a period of time has a tendency to establish its own institutionalized elite. Thus in every state a handful of families, usually closely interrelated by blood and marital ties, dominated economic, political, and social life. Their alliances and counter-alliances largely dictated the political history of the period.

Books, journals, travel, a proper education, and good manners were expensive to acquire and yet were the indispensable accouterments of the true gentleman. Learning was cosmopolitan and based upon common-sense ideas of natural law and natural philosophy. The leaders in the urban centers of the seaboard were frequently a combination of lawyer, politician, businessman, and moral philosopher. Many of them dabbled in the science of the day and aspired to the title and glory of scientist and inventor. The Industrial Revolution had fully revealed the incredible profits of "tinkering."

Continuous rivalry among such entrepreneurs led to the shifting of political ideals and allegiances, but at bottom most of these men were followers in varying degrees of the economic and political doctrines set forth in Harrington's *Oceania*. They believed that political power should follow economic power and not some kind of scheme arbitrarily propounded by a despot. By "representative government" they meant a government truly representative of the responsible, property-holding citizens. They varied in opinion as to the degree of power the federal government should exercise in order to enforce this truly representative government. Some believed in a strong, centralized government for this purpose; others believed in a loose, decentralized one. But all agreed that it was the duty of government to increase individual and national wealth. In challenging the authority of the Crown's judicial representatives they called for trial by jury, the members to be drawn from the responsible citizenry. All justified their beliefs and frequently contradictory actions in the name first of the common welfare and second of individual fortune and gain. They were adept at manipulating concepts and the utilitarian logic. They were patriotic, but a few traded military inventions across national borders and considered war to be partly a private business enterprise. They were essentially citizens of the western world.

As a group they were opportunistic and flexible, shifting their interests with the changing tides of fortune, but guided always by calculations as to fame and gain. The main wheel of chance which could quickly confer such rewards was trade. The entire urban economy was focused upon foreign trade. The man of commerce was active, aggressive, ingenious. He was typically interested in a number of commercial ventures and moved from one to another with consummate ease, without a permanent vested interest in a single enterprise. The commercial mind was preoccupied with pecuniary calculations, with trading for a quick profit, and thus was supple, shrewd, and venturesome. It is difficult to set up opposing personality types for businessman and landowner because there was such an intermingling of these two occupations. Businessmen often held large land tracts, for land was not only a source of profit but of prestige. But in the South where the distinction between landowners and entrepreneurs was more clear-cut, one observer remarked that the major difficulty in persuading the planter to invest in the steamboat was that the only way the planter knew "of adding to his Estate" was by buying more land and slaves and that he was not like persons "whose property is generally employed in various speculations."[1]

II

Among this select assembly moved Colonel John Stevens of Hoboken, New Jersey, a man who played a significant role in the development of transportation in the United States. The Colonel was a member of a wealthy and politically powerful New Jersey family. His grandfather had arrived in the New World in 1699 as an indentured servant, but one with an ingratiating personality, a keen, quick mind, and great ambition. His possession of a smattering of learning, particularly figuring, resulted in his being bound as a clerk to the Crown attorney for the province of New York. Through assiduous cultivation of the proper contacts among members of colonial officialdom and the gentry he soon gained a large land grant from the Crown. This started him on his path to fame and fortune — the bumpy road of real estate speculation. His marriage to the daughter of one of the great proprietors brought additions to his material holdings and access to the ranks of the colonial elite which carried with it its own intangible rewards. His widely scattered landholdings led him into active politics in order to secure favorable taxation measures, various improvements such as roads and ports for his real estate holdings, additional land, and, of course, prestige in being known to be seeking the general welfare.[2]

When old Stevens died in 1737 he left large landholdings to his several children, one of whom was Colonel John Stevens' father, John Stevens, Sr., who was born on October 21, 1716. With his brother Richard, he entered the field of foreign trade, while both continued the family's real estate activities. Richard and John Stevens operated a small but profitable fleet of merchant ships in the triangular trade between New Jersey, the West Indies, and the coast of Northern Africa, in which the chief commodities were molasses, rum, and slaves.

John Stevens, Sr., following his father's precedent of marrying into the landed elite, took as his wife the daughter of James Alexander, Surveyor-General of New Jersey. Her brother was William Alexander, the American General of the Revolutionary War who was known as Lord Stirling, and whose influence was to prove so advantageous to that hopeful band of future entrepreneurs which had gathered in and around the Quartermaster's Corps during the war. In the thick of hostilities Lord Stirling and John Stevens, Jr., along with a group of their officer friends, participated in several speculative schemes which were hatched in the Corps quarters.[3]

Like every important businessman during the mercantilist-colonial period, John Stevens, Sr. engaged actively in politics not only in Jersey but in the surrounding provinces of New York and Pennsylvania. He became a member of the New Jersey Assembly and was one of the men appointed to negotiate treaties with the Indians. This was a valuable appointment, for it offered many opportunities for the exercise of speculative ingenuity with respect to Indian landholdings. In 1776 he was appointed Treasurer of the Province of New Jersey, but despite such honors he sided with the Revolutionists, for he was much disturbed over the Crown's policies of discrimination against certain colonial trading interests and the incidence of increasing taxation upon the American landholding and merchant class. But on the other hand he greatly feared popular unrest in the Colonies themselves. In 1778 and 1781 he was Vice-President of the Council of New Jersey and in 1783 President of the Council of East Jersey Properties. Throughout the war he held high executive positions in the Revolutionary government. He was a member of the Continental Congress and a delegate to present New Jersey's ratification to Congress. The Honorable John strongly favored the adoption of the federal constitution because he feared the disorders beginning to break out in the various newly constituted states.[4] Under his father-in-law, James Alexander, he was appointed one of the commissioners to mark the northern boundary line between New York and New Jersey. In all of these political capacities he worked faithfully for the adoption of improved transportation facilities, low real estate taxation, and favorable policies for trade. Consistently, he added to his real estate holdings.[5]

John Stevens, Jr. was born in 1749 and his career was already well mapped out for him. His was a many faceted personality. Stubborn and revengeful, he could also be pliable and conciliatory and given to compromising in the face of insurmountable obstacles. At once courageous and imaginative, with his attention concentrated upon gain wherever it could be secured — the risk-taking entrepreneur — he was also cautious and calculating, with a singular passion for petty details. The complexity of his business activities forced him to delegate various powers to his sons, yet he was incapable of really relinquishing authority and could not refrain from "advising" them on even the smallest business matters. Grandiose schemes which spanned international boundaries occupied his mind but rarely materialized. He was not above giving military advice to the Tsar himself, and certainly to the President of the United States. In a late portrait of him we see a proudly held head, slightly too large for the body. A long, thin face is dominated by a great forehead and an imposing Roman nose, with cold, small eyes set beneath beetling eyebrows. Above the large, stubborn chin is a thin, tight mouth. The expression is haughty and appraising, with a trace of petulance around the eyes and mouth. He reminds us of those imperious, gout-ridden English aristocrats so faithfully delineated by eighteenth-century portrait painters.

Like all of the gentlemen of the time, John Stevens, Jr. was extremely class conscious, insisting upon the designation "Esquire" at the local post office and proudly using until his death the title "Colonel," which he had acquired in the Revolutionary War. He loved luxury and fine living. His large wardrobe of elegant clothes was imported from abroad, as was that of his wife. His elaborate Hoboken mansion, fitted with European furniture and overstaffed with Negro slaves, was one of the show places of America. To it, to be entertained with imported wines and delicacies, dignitaries from abroad and home were brought in his carriages which were among the most ostentatious in the land. He was a true pleasure-loving connoisseur and epicurean, a fit member of the leisure class; and this heritage he passed on to his sons, one of whom established the New York Yacht Club. Over his stormy brood of seven children he reigned as unquestioned patriarch, proud and unforgiving of any slight upon the family honor. He was a rigid disciplinarian and refused for years to speak to one of his favorite daughters because she eloped with a common seaman. Yet he complained when two of his daughters became old maids. His wife, a shrewd, competent, inquiring woman, addressed him as "Mr. Stevens" all her life.

Colonel Stevens' passionate hobbies were horticulture and books, and later "inventing." His gardens were famous, for he continually imported rare flowers and shrubs from distant places. In knowledge of metaphysics, the classics, natural philosophy, natural science, and political economy, he easily kept up with the standards of his station. He eagerly perused all of the foreign publications he could find. A devotee of the eighteenth-century concepts of natural reason and natural law, he was a foe of doctrinaire religious beliefs. Yet he was capable of eloquent appeals to the Divine Deity in the face of what he considered to be injustices inflicted upon him by business adversaries. He laid claim to the titles of author, politician, philosopher, lawyer, scientist, and inventor, as well as business-man.

As an aristocrat, Colonel Stevens had a concept of *noblesse-oblige*, along with the utilitarian ideals of general welfare and community service, which led him to take a leading part in community activities and politics. He helped to found societies for the promotion of useful arts and manufactures in New Jersey, New York, and Pennsylvania. Here he could keep a sensitive finger on the pulse of new inventions and ideas. He was one of the founders of the Pennsylvania Society for Internal Improvements, which in its early days operated as a propaganda agency for railroads.[6]

During and after the Revolution in the debates over the form of state and national government to be adopted, Stevens was as conservative and aristocratic as Hamilton. So traditionalistic was he that he opposed Adams' "balance of power" principle as dangerous because it allowed too much power to the legislative body. He believed that "The people ever have been, and ever will be, unfit to retain the exercise of power in their own hands; they must, of necessity, delegate it somewhere. Hence the immense importance of a *representative* Legislature and a Tryal by Jury."[7] He made quite clear what his concept of "representative" government was:

It is not enough that our representatives are wise men, they should be also men of such property, integrity and standing in life as would insure to them an extensive influence over the public councils, and at the same time place them above the reach of temptation. I feel myself deeply interested in this business, not from patriotic motives only, but from considerations too of a more private nature. What little property I have is altogether within this state, and as the latter prospers the former of course be advanced. . .[8]

By trial by jury, he meant a trial by a jury of his peers, all landholding gentry, and not a trial by a judicial representative of the Crown. He accepted the precept that the wealthy should rule and advised his fellow citizens to protect themselves against the corruption of authority by instituting the utilitarian principle "to connect the interest of those in power with the interest of the community at large, so as to make the promotion of the public good, and their own private advantage inseparable."[9] And, of course, he believed that he was one of those qualified to rule. That he had personal ambitions in this direction he candidly admitted to his father when he wrote that it would "be very convenient to me to be representative to Congress,"[10] a wish not fulfilled primarily because his father-in-law decided to run for Congress himself.

Stevens believed that individual and national welfare depended upon wealth and that it was the duty of government to aid and encourage its accumulation. He viewed agriculture as the basis for a thriving economy, and held that commerce and manufacturing were the means of converting this basis into a surplus of national wealth. He argued that improved transportation facilities were most essential for the expansion of commerce and the market. In this service the government should help but not control. In his recommendations for revising the federal constitution, Stevens emphasized that the president should be able to make appointments without first securing the advice and consent of the Senate, and the chief justice should appoint his own associates, but he should hold office only during good behavior. Stevens also advocated the creation of a new office, the superintendent of finance, which would control all collection and disbursement of revenues. This would constitute an economic ministry. The superintendent of finance, the president, and the chief justice were to constitute a board of review for all bills passed by Congress. He visualized a highly centralized government tightly controlled by this oligarchy of three; to the legislative body he would leave only the right of discussion and the power either to pass or to reject bills presented to it, but not the power to formulate them.[11] At a later time, aggrieved by his failure to secure patronage for some of his pet projects from an administration somewhat different from his design, Stevens commented caustically upon "that spirit of indecision and procrastination which naturally pervades and benumbs all the movements of a Republican Government."[12]

Stevens looked upon law as a necessary adjunct of business, and for him as for contemporary entrepreneurs natural law was the law of the commercial world. Trained in it, he was skilled in the art of turning legal and constitutional concepts to serve his changing business interests. At one time, when opposing the New York grant to Fulton and Livingston, he argued valiantly for federal rights; but when trying to secure for himself an exclusive steamboat grant from North Carolina in 1812, he vigorously defended states rights against federal encroachment. When opposing a rival's monopoly he argued that he detested monopolies and considered them "uncongenial and incompatible with the nature and genius of our free government";[13] yet he spent his life in building up a monopoly position in transportation.

Closely related to his attitude towards politics and government was Stevens' belief that war was to some extent a private business enterprise, and his attitude towards it, as to law, fluctuated with his business needs. In 1807 he urged the New Jersey delegation in Congress to intervene in his behalf in the matter of government contracts for military gunboats. In 1811, when he learned from his friends in Congress that the House of Representatives had just received an appropriation bill for establishing a dockyard for repairing naval vessels, the site to be selected by the President, Stevens wrote a letter to President Madison arguing the natural superiority of Hoboken over Wallabout, where a navy yard was already situated. He labored long to have Hoboken declared a navy yard; yet in the War of 1812, when the Navy really needed a base at Hoboken, Stevens suddenly began to worry about the effects of such naval construction on his real estate values.

Stevens had learned from long experience that national defense and preparedness were the most convincing arguments to set before legislative bodies in order to secure appropriations for various projects. During the crisis with Britain before the War of 1812 he had suggested that the government have constructed many steam engines, to be held in readiness to be placed aboard all suitable boats in the event of war, he, of course, to receive the contracts for them.[14] During the War of 1812, he petitioned the Vice-President and Commissioners on Harbor Defense for New York Harbor for a "small appropriation" of $50,000 to build floating batteries in the harbor to protect it against enemy ships. He also petitioned the United States military departments for an appropriation of $50,000 to build an experimental steam frigate, with machinery below the water line and armed and made seaworthy. In 1812, further, he and his son Robert designed an iron-clad vessel on the *Monitor* principle, and tried to promote that. Many of these propositions, however, were deemed impractical by military and naval engineers of the time, and all were turned down. The only direct appropriation for military purposes which the Stevens family received during the early part of the nineteenth century came for the invention of elongated shells by Robert, and later for the construction of an iron-clad warship.

Stevens and his sons had been working at least since 1814 to secure military appropriations to exploit the elongated shells as well as the iron-clad war vessel. The results of experiments with the shells in 1815 and 1816 were very satisfactory, both the Navy and the War Department were interested, and Robert proposed to the government that upon a contract being entered into with him for not less than 5000 shells at a specific price, he would promise not to communicate his secret to any other person or government without the consent of the President of the United States.[15] But the military departments moved very slowly and Colonel Stevens began to suspect intrigue and procrastination. Therefore, in 1817 and 1818 he secretly offered Robert's invention, along with his own steamboat and railroad plans, to Tsar Alexander of Russia. At the same time he strongly advised Robert against receding an inch from his original offer, even though he felt there was little hope that the American government would meet Robert's terms:

Upon the whole I think from the present aspect of the political state of Europe it is highly improbable that peace among them can be of long continuance, and on a war breaking out you will be able to make a much more advantageous bargain as *we* have very little chance of being involved in their squabbles, government will feel very averse to incur additional expenditures to a large amount unnecessarily. This consideration combined with the hostile complication of the Committee of the Navy and the heads of the ordinance department will defeat you at the *present* moment. Had you not better then let matters rest, and take your chance of a European war between this and the next sessions of Congress.[16]

When Stevens discovered that Robert was considering closing a contract for 3200 shells with the government he quickly wrote Robert an admonishing letter:

I think you ought not to bind yourself absolutely so as to deprive yourself altogether of reaping any further advantage from an improvement of such immense importance . . . to give to Government an absolute monopoly for so slender a compensation, would be to make a bargain most miserably lopsided. But I have already proved that such exclusive use must in the nature of things, be very temporaneous. To insure to Government then this transitory superiority, you are to loose perhaps $1 or $200,000. When too it cannot be denied that the use of these shells in the defence of harbours against ships of war is intrinsically worth millions. . . I would never consent to a contract so glaringly unequal. Although no consideration should tempt me to communicate the secret either to Great Britain or to France without the approbation of Government, still should an advantageous offer be made by Russia, I would never suffer myself to be debarred from accepting it. . . I will pledge myself either to make Government adhere to your first terms, or to consent to a negociation with Russia.[17]

In haste Stevens wrote to the Tsar offering him the shells and promising to prevent Robert from giving exclusive use of them to the United States unless the United States agreed to take 10,000 shells at a set price. Stevens assured the Tsar that since there was no prospect of war Congress would not appropriate funds for such a purpose. He justified this attempted international business transaction on the grounds that he had first offered such inventions to his own country which had stupidly failed to accept them and that he had no alternative but to approach foreign governments. The progress of the world would be retarded unless his inventions were developed. He pointed out that there was no possibility of war between Russia and the United States. In addition, Russia would be doing a service to mankind by using his inventions to conquer the Turks and thus bring Christianity to such murderous heathens. But the Tsar did not even deign to reply to Stevens' proposals.

Stevens never relinquished his dream of becoming a naval architect and military engineer and he continued to bombard presidents and members of Congress with his various petitions. He became convinced that his plans had been rejected by the Navy Board — that "heterogeneous motly crew of sailors" — because, if put into operation, naval warfare would be destroyed.[18] He believed, therefore, that all naval officers had been alarmed, apprehensive, and jealous. He charged that the Federalist Party supported the demands and unseemly conduct of the military in order to build up an oligarchy in this country. He tried to persuade Andrew Jackson to reorganize the Navy Board out of existence by promoting its officers to the rank of admirals with a $10,000 per year annuity for the rest of their lives. Stevens hoped this would remove the chief block to his ambitions, for he had come to look upon the professional military mind as essentially backward and opposed to all change.[19]

On the grounds of military advisability, Stevens lobbied in Congress for a subsidy to establish a steamboat line from Rhode Island to Georgia. Actually, this would relieve him of the financial obligations of an old commitment which he had never fulfilled — the 1812 North Carolina exclusive steamboat grant to him. Stevens never achieved any success in the national Congress. He was more fortunate on the state level.

Motivated by the powerful desire for fame and wealth, Stevens pushed forward relentlessly toward his chosen goals despite reverses and defeats. To follow his career is to watch the evolution under stress of a great business empire.

III

Stevens was familiar with his father's trading business, but this was not an occupation which he himself chose to follow. Rather, he trained for the law at King's College (now Columbia University) and graduated in 1768. In 1772 he obtained an attorney's license, but instead of practicing law he entered politics in New Jersey. Upon several different occasions he served as special aide to Governor William Franklin, Benjamin Franklin's son. The innumerable political contacts he made were soon supplemented by military and family ones and all were utilized later in the service of his business interests.

With his father, he remained loyal to the colonies, although neither had been an ardent advocate of the immediate separation of the colonies from the mother country.[20] When hostilities actually broke out, John, Jr. entered the colonial army, and rapidly rose in it, through his father's arrangements with Lord Stirling. Washington, who was acquainted with his family, friends, and relatives, made him a captain and later appointed him loan commissioner for Hunterdon County, New Jersey, to collect money, food, and supplies for the Continental Army. From 1777 to 1782, during which period he attained his title of Colonel, young Stevens held the office of Treasurer of New Jersey and was so careless in his book-keeping in this capacity that it required years to unravel the finances of the state. It is true that the War complicated the duties of the Treasurer and made his a "roving office," but New Jersey's finances seem to have been unduly confused by Stevens' numerous activities. This, however, despite numerous public complaints, did not interrupt his political career, for in 1782 his uncle, William Alexander, the former Lord Stirling and now Surveyor-General of the Eastern Division of New Jersey, appointed the Colonel Deputy-Surveyor-General of this Division.

This was the kind of political position which offered opportunities for the land-speculative bent, and the use Stevens made of it probably was further enhanced by matrimony. Continuing the family tradition of excellent marriages, Stevens, in 1782, wed one of the daughters of John R. Cox, a member of a prominent and wealthy landholding and profes-sional family which had long been part of the New Jersey elite. Cox himself was at this time Assistant Quartermaster-General of the American Army under General Greene.

Stevens' political contacts, family ties, and record of patriotic services must have placed him in a favorable bargaining position when it came to the acquisition of Tory estates, for in 1784 the Colonel bought at auction the whole island of Hoboken (564 acres) for 18,340 pounds.[21] Hoboken formerly had been the estate of a prominent Tory merchant, William Bayard. The title to Bayard's ferrying monopoly from New York City to Hoboken also passed to Stevens. This was a grant conferred by the City of New York. The ferry service provided the vital transportation link between Hoboken and the thriving metropolitan port. Later, the Colonel bought the adjoining tract known as Weehawken for 1250 pounds and continued to add to his holdings and to deal in land for the rest of his life.

Because specie was so scarce, Stevens' land was the main source of capital accumulation for his various business activities. Land possessed the disadvantage of being difficult to convert quickly into cash, but through rentals, sales, mortgages, and increasing real estate values, Stevens obtained money and credit for his multiple ventures.[22] It is interesting to note that in the case of the steamboat in the northeast the primary source of capital accumulation was not commerce and trade but land, two of the great landed families of the day — the Livingstons and the Stevens' — becom-ing leaders in the development of this mode of transportation.

For everyday business dealings Stevens was dependent upon short-term promissory notes carrying small interest charges which often cir-culated as a medium of exchange during this period. For larger sums he depended upon bank loans carrying the endorsements of such powerful figures as Livingston, or on some other form of security. Stevens' monetary speculations also afforded him a small surplus for investment. For earlier transportation ventures, such as bridges and turnpikes, Stevens' grandfather and father had relied upon communal lotteries as a means of raising sufficient funds. But quite early in the nineteenth century in New Jersey lotteries were replaced in transportation undertakings by the joint-stock company as the chief agency for collecting and centralizing large sums and for creating credit through issuances of stocks and bonds.[23] The typical arrangement was for the Colonel to form a joint-stock company to build a steamboat and to keep one-half of the stock (or at least enough to give him a controlling voice) as a payment for his services and the patent rights and to sell the rest to subscribers.[24] Stevens sometimes used his stockholdings as security for large borrowings. As the nineteenth century wore on there was an elaboration of credit devices, such as bank loans, upon which businessmen came increasingly to rely.

The acquisition of such large tracts as Hoboken and Weehawken confirmed the Colonel's main interest as real estate speculation and development. When his father died in 1792, to Stevens' own land was added his father's extensive holdings, and he was forced to hire Samuel Stockton, real estate agent, to help him in the management of his enlarged interests. Stevens' efforts to build up Hoboken as a suburb of New York and as a pleasure resort depended largely upon quick and cheap transportation facilities, and it was to get these that he enlarged his political relations. He kept lists of the members of the national congress and various state legislatures where his interests were involved. These constituted master working-lists for his politico-economic activities.

On the local scene the Colonel labored to secure the coöperation of New York City's businessmen and politicians. He lobbied with the members of the New York City Council to extend exclusive ferrying rights to him and not to his Paulus Hook (or Powles Hook) rivals. He tried to persuade the Council of New York City to take over the shore line of Hoboken where the ferries landed and to beautify it. Some of the expenses he offered to bear, for such beautification made Hoboken and the ferry service more attractive. He urged that wharves be built at the various places where his boats touched, and he opposed high landing fees and harbor fees. He lobbied for low real estate taxes and for measures to encourage trade.

On the state level the Colonel was also unceasingly active. He was directly interested in keeping the level of land taxation low. Also, he needed state aid in the competition which existed between rival land-speculating interests. His eagerness to promote the growth of Hoboken and to prevent the expansion of competing neighboring localities, for example, prompted him to seek an incorporation charter for the town of Hoboken and to block the granting of such charters to rival towns. He also lobbied to have main state roads run through his holdings, rather than take other routes. In addition, from the state he needed business incorporation charters, appropriations for roads, rivers, and harbors, exclusive grants, protective legislation, permits to hold lotteries. As the state controlled toll rates on bridges, ferries, and roads, Stevens also required political influence to manipulate these charges.

On the national scene the Colonel was one of the first to secure a patent for a steamboat and to use this right as a business expedient. He also had visions of Hoboken becoming an important national seaport and commercial depot. From 1804 to 1807 he was busily lobbying among members of Congress to have Hoboken declared a port of delivery, but the opposition from rival New Jersey towns was too powerful. He also worked for mail subsidies and internal improvements appropriations.

Every rumor and scheme which reached his sharp ears found fertile ground for future cultivation, for he was always on the lookout for the main chance. From all technical and scientific literature which came his way and which he read voraciously, he selected principles and ideas, some of which he patented. At the various societies for the encouragement of the useful arts and manufactures in New Jersey, New York, and Pennsylvania, he picked up additional information. He had a widespread circle of correspondents who passed on to him useful data about new inventions. As his interest in the mechanical arts was well-known, he was often approached by inventors eager to secure financial backing. Sometimes he purchased their patent rights, but at other times the mechanic-inventor did not fare so well. The patent law was so loose and the criteria of "originality" and what constituted an "invention" so vague, that the law served mainly to protect those who could withstand long infringement suits. The exclusive state grants afforded much stronger monopoly protection.

Like his fellow-entrepreneurs, Stevens simply assumed that the innovations of his own mechanics belonged to him. His practices often brought him into conflict with rival entrepreneurs and mechanics. Floating bridges, underwater tubes, horse-drawn carriages on rails, steam-drawn carriages on rails, high-pressure steam engines, horseboats, fireboats, hospital boats, iron-plated steam warships, as well as indoor toilets, non-smoking fireplaces, indoor gas lights, sprinkling the streets of New York City with ocean water — all of these ideas and more he appropriated and tried to capitalize, after having first sought political monopoly-grants. His projections of these ideas were crude, meager, and often unworkable, for he was no mechanic. However, this did not prevent the continued exercise of his entrepreneurial bent in such directions. In his pride Stevens insisted upon being known as an inventor and scientist, but there was practical pecuniary value in this too, for exclusive rights were conferred upon the "original inventor" by state grants and federal patent law.[25]

IV

As a great landowner and as a self-conscious member of the ruling class, the Colonel was convinced that his own prosperity and that of the locality and the nation depended upon the rapid growth of transportation facilities. As the son of a merchant and a member of the business elite of the seaboard communities oriented towards foreign trade, it was natural, moreover, that he think of transportation primarily in terms of water routes. The backwardness of road-building technology also acted to rivet attention on rivers and the sea. The Colonel's local experience and keen pecuniary imagination, however, soon permitted him to visualize the inherent possibilities of such innovations as the steamboat for direct exploitation and for the development of the new country, and his business acumen dictated the strategy of exclusive appropriation. Eventually he was to coördinate land and water routes and to extend his transportation activities far beyond the borders of New Jersey and far beyond his interests in land.

Stevens' curiosity about the steamboat had been aroused when he saw John Fitch's vessel going up the Delaware River near Burlington, New Jersey. He examined the engines and paddles of Fitch's crude device with the greatest care. Compared with the capital funds required to start a textile mill or a mining enterprise, those needed for the building of a steamboat were small. Estimates ran from $900 to $1200 for the small early boats, to $8000 for a medium-sized ferryboat, to $15,000 to $25,000 for the larger steamboats, to $50,000 for the later luxury ships. In the early days such capital requirements made it comparatively easy for newcomers to enter the industry and thus one of the economic requirements for a basically competitive industry existed. This meant that business security and the assurance of stable, high profits could come only through political aids such as state grants and federal patents. The latter were fairly easy to get but were effective only in combination with the financial resources to develop the patented device and to intimidate competitors by the threat of expensive patent litigation suits. As Stevens once bitterly remarked, it was a competition "not of merit but of purse."[26] Financial resources for such development or such litigation, in turn, as Fitch himself learned early, could be had only after the more secure state grant was obtained.

The state grant was the most significant monopoly device utilized in the early steamboat industry in the northeastern part of the United States, for it conferred an outright monopoly protected by the legal and police powers of the commonwealth. Although it was easy to secure a patent, it was difficult to obtain a state grant which typically went to those business-men who exercised considerable political power. In the struggle over exclusive rights bitter fighting broke out between rival business groups which cut across family ties.

State grants and patents eliminated freedom of entry to the market place and created a noncompetitive condition. Since in transportation (turnpikes, canals, bridges) the pattern of exclusive rights under state grants was early established, a clear precedent was laid out for the steam-boat entrepreneurs. But the steamboat owners fared even better than their predecessors for whereas the states had set traffic rates for chartered turn-pikes, canals, and bridges, there were no rates set for steamboat companies. Through the licensing system the state grant and patent right thus be-came the cherished medium of monopoly control over the steamboat in the northeast. Under licensing agreements territory was allocated and the number of steamboats agreed upon.

On March 18, 1786, the New Jersey legislature had passed a law giving Fitch the sole right to build and operate steamboats in that state for fourteen years. Any person interfering with this right was liable to a fine of 100 pounds, plus lawsuit costs, for each offense and also had to forfeit his boat and machinery. Backed by this grant, Fitch succeeded in forming a joint-stock company to exploit his steamboat. Fitch possessed little wealth or political power but had succeeded in obtaining state grants because very few, if any, of the larger entrepreneurs were interested at that very early date in exploiting such an untried invention. When the steamboat proved mechanically feasible, richer entrepreneurs such as Stevens and Livingston became interested, quickly appropriated the in-novation, and succeeded in securing state grants which invalidated Fitch's prior claims.

Needing additional backing in 1787, Fitch had secured exclusive grants from Delaware on February 3, New York on March 18, Pennsylvania on March 28, and Virginia on November 7, that year. The New York grant was passed over the contentions of Stevens and James Rumsey. However, on February 11, 1789, the New York Assembly reversed itself in favor of Rumsey alone. This was but a month after the same Assembly had rejected another petition by Stevens. The New York grant was so eagerly sought because it carried with it a monopoly of the Hudson, the main artery of water travel in the northeast. After his defeat in New York, Stevens felt that the federal government, not the states, should grant exclusive rights, and he was soon to act on this idea; but he also persisted in his efforts to secure state patronage.

On August 6, 1791, Stevens received a patent on his steamboat boiler and engine.[27] In 1797, he entered into an informal partnership arrangement with Nicholas Roosevelt and Chancellor Robert R. Livingston to exploit the steamboat. Livingston, by then, had married Stevens' sister and the two landed families were closely bound together. No sooner had the actual experiments started than Livingston busied himself on the political front to get the invaluable exclusive New York State grant. With his great political influence, he easily secured the passage of an act by the New York Legislature on March 27, 1798, repealing the law which had given Fitch exclusive rights to the steamboat on the grounds that for more than ten years Fitch had not attempted to put his right into execution. Under the new act Livingston was given exclusive rights for twenty years, provided that within a year he had on the Hudson a twenty-ton steamboat with a minimum speed of four miles per hour. The *Polacca*, which was built for this purpose, proved to be deficient in speed and the grant expired. However, on March 29, 1799 they secured an extension for a two-year period.

In 1800 Stevens, Roosevelt, and Livingston entered into a new formal twenty-year partnership agreement to build steamboats. However, Livingston was appointed United States Minister to France the next year and departed for Paris where he met the persuasive, charming Fulton. After various steamboat experiments in Paris, the Chancellor and Fulton entered into a contract on October 10, 1802, whereby the former agreed to provide the funds and necessary legislation for exploiting the steamboat in the United States and the latter agreed to provide the mechanical knowledge, technical guidance, and assistance in fund-raising. On April 5, 1803, Livingston succeeded in getting the New York Legislature to extend the rights in the act repealing Fitch's rights to Fulton and himself for twenty years, provided that within two years they had in operation a twenty-ton steamboat with a minimum speed of four miles per hour. Later, Fulton married one of Livingston's daughters and thus further solidified his alliance with this wealthy and politically powerful family. It was this alliance, rather than inventive genius, which accounts for Fulton's place in American history books.

As early as their first Paris experiments, Livingston and Fulton had offered to take Stevens into their steamboat project as a partner provided he would agree to work under Fulton's plans. This offer they repeated in 1806, but Stevens insisted upon proceeding independently with his own experiments. In order to develop an integrated system of transportation in New Jersey he had to devote some attention to turnpikes and stagecoaching. In 1802 he became the president of the Bergen Turnpike Company, which became a fairly profitable enterprise, and he invested in the stocks of various other turnpike companies in New Jersey. In May 1802, Stevens tested a tiny steamboat propelled by a single screw in the stern. The hull was built by local shipwrights and the parts for the engine were constructed by the famed British mechanics at Soho, New Jersey. Some parts of the engine had to be retooled in Stevens' small Hoboken machine shop, where the engine was assembled by local mechanics. This boat was a mechanical failure.

In America the major difficulty in building steam engines and steamboats was the lack of standard equipment, standard precision work, tested materials, tested principles, and skilled workers. Everything proceeded along trial-and-error lines and every new engine or boiler offered the most unpredictable results. For machinery and know-how America was dependent upon Europe. But even with machines imported directly from England as models, American mechanics could not produce adequate engines. Although steam-engine building as a trade had long existed in England, it did not exist in the United States until the beginning of the nineteenth century. The prohibitions of the exportation of machinery from England were not lifted until 1820 and this, despite evasions, retarded the rate of introduction of technological innovations into America. The invention of interchangeable parts and precision machinery was a necessary step in the establishment of the new machine age.

In the case of steamboating the division of labor between businessman and mechanic occurred from the beginning in America. By the nineteenth century the complexities of business traffic already had advanced to a point where most of the energies of the businessman were required for administration. And on the other hand as the technological arts became more intricate, the full time and skill of the mechanic also was employed. It was cumulative trial-and-error experience which was significant in the technological process for there was no reliable body of engineering science in existence. The skilled mechanic then occupied a role similar to that of the mechanical engineer at the present time. Actually, the mechanics were the ghost-inventors for many of the patentees. As John Fitch recognized about the steamboat, "nothing but able Mechanicks is required to make the prize sure." [28] The most amusing bit of evidence along this line is Fulton's angry letter to Stevens, in which the sobriety of their respective mechanics emerged as the chief factor in determining the victory of Fulton or Stevens in their competitive struggle for exclusive rights to steamboat technology.[29] It has been due to the scarcity of historical data about the mechanic and the tendency to glorify the entrepreneur that the latter has been assigned an "inventive" role in transportation technology.[30]

The evolution of techniques of credit and accumulation of money-funds made it impossible usually for the mechanic to capitalize his own innovations. Thus, the aid of the businessman was necessary if the innovation were to be commercialized.

On April 11, 1803 Stevens obtained a patent for a multitubular boiler, despite Oliver Evans' contention that Stevens had stolen the idea from him. Actually, both Evans' and Stevens' boilers bore a strange resemblance to a multitubular boiler patented in 1791 by Nathan Read, a Massachusetts mechanic, whom both Evans and Stevens knew.

In May 1804 Stevens used a twin-screw propeller and multitubular boiler on the *Little Juliana,* which attained a speed of about three and one-half miles per hour. The parts of the machinery for this boat were built by the Soho mechanics and retooled and assembled in Stevens' workshops by local mechanics. The hull was built by local shipwrights. Though by no means the inventor of either the single or double-screw propeller, Stevens was one of the first to use both the single and double screw in America. But twin screws required high-pressure boilers for their successful operation, which necessitated a revolution in the design of the steam engine. Also, a new body of engine-drivers had to be trained, because such engines required an unprecedented amount of attention and skill. The *Little Juliana* was not a mechanical success. Thus, Stevens was forced to abandon his attempts to use the twin-screw principle because of his failure to produce a successful high-pressure steam engine.

On May 31, 1805 Stevens' son, John Cox Stevens, obtained English patents for Stevens' boiler and steam engine, but he failed in his effort to persuade Watt and Boulton to build a high-pressure steam engine according to Stevens' specifications. Neither was he able to secure English financial backing.

In 1806 Fulton, accompanied by an English mechanic, returned to the United States with a Watt-Boulton steam engine, which he had obtained only with great difficulty. Immediately, under Livingston's auspices Fulton started to work supervising the construction of a steamboat. The 1803 legislative extension to Livingston and Fulton had expired, but on April 6, 1807 Livingston secured an act to revive the 1803 act for two years. And on September 7, 1807 the first trial run of the *Clermont* was made in the midst of much fanfare and publicity.

The success of the *Clermont* prompted Stevens to approach Livingston and Fulton to find out on what terms they could work together. They offered him the lines from New York to Brunswick and from Trenton to Philadelphia if he would agree to acknowledge Fulton's patents and work under them. Fulton and Livingston wished to avert an open legal battle and usually attempted to induce potential competitors to enter into contracts to work under their state grant. But because the title of "inventor" meant so much to Stevens and also because he doubted the legality of their exclusive grant, he refused their terms and proceeded independently with plans for his own boat, the *Phoenix*. This was launched the next year and the warfare between the competing business interests started. This struggle, which cut across family relationships, largely dictated the course of steamboat history on the Hudson until at least 1824.

Alarmed by the persistence of competition from such a source as Stevens even in the face of their state grant, Livingston and Fulton succeeded in securing further legislation from New York State. On April 11, 1808 the New York Legislature passed an act which reaffirmed the right of the state to give exclusive grants for the use of the steamboat within its boundaries, and the Hudson was claimed as New York territory. Anyone infringing the state grant had to forfeit his boat and machinery and pay the lawsuit costs. In addition, penalities were provided for injuring or destroying any boat. Finally, in order to encourage further the building of steamboats, the act provided that for every steamboat built in addition to the one already running, Fulton and Livingston were to be entitled to a five-year extension of their grant, provided the whole term of the grant should not exceed thirty years after the passage of the act. On January 24–25, 1811 the New Jersey Legislature passed a retaliatory act which asserted that the Hudson belonged as much to New Jersey as to New York, and set forth the same claims and penalties as the 1808 New York act. These state grants formed a basis for much of the continuing conflict and rivalry between the states and established barriers which hampered internal commerce.

Although Fulton and Livingston had for years threatened Stevens with Fulton's patent rights, Stevens finally discovered much to his amazement that Fulton had not obtained his first patent until February 11, 1809, and his second on February 9, 1811. Fulton and Livingston had heretofore relied upon their state grant. They now agreed that the patents were to be taken out in Fulton's name only, but "one moiety" of the patent and all profits arising therefrom belonged to Livingston. For this purpose they both had to swear that the inventions and improvements were solely Fulton's. Fulton made two basic claims to originality in his patents: (1) an accurate table of proportions for building steamboats in which Fulton claimed to have discovered the laws of ship-resistance and the proportioning of vessel and machinery in accordance with the work to be done by them, and (2) the vertical paddle wheels. The validity of patenting a table of principles was questionable even then, the table itself was grossly inaccurate in the light of contemporary experience, and Fulton was by no means the discoverer of the laws of ship-resistance. Finally, the invention of vertical paddle wheels predated Fulton by at least seventy-five years, if not longer.[31] But on such flimsy claims Fulton was granted federal patents which he used to intimidate potential competitors.

Actually there had been at least sixteen steamboats constructed by about eight different men in operation on American waters before the *Clermont*'s appearance. The steamboat itself was a'complicated machine which was the result of many unknown men's work over several centuries. As the social nature of inventions becomes better understood, the claims of Fulton and other early American entrepreneurs to inventive originality in the case of the steamboat seem fantastically exaggerated; but it must be recalled that at that time it was a common practice to secure patents without having to prove originality. As Cochran and Miller have pointed out,

> Before 1836 America allowed every "inventor" a patent without requiring any proof of originality — he had but to convince the Patent Office his device was not harmful to the community. In such circumstances early American racketeers received monopolies on devices already in use and fleeced their credulous countrymen by demanding money under threat of suit for infringement.[32]

In order to discourage potential competitors Fulton and Livingston decided to preëmpt strategic areas by granting contracts to individuals who would agree to work under their exclusive grant and patents in those places. John R. Livingston, the chancellor's brother, had been granted an exclusive right to operate steamboats between New York City and Brunswick under a contract with Fulton and Livingston. Stevens disregarded John R. Livingston's warnings and in May 1809 started running the *Phoenix* between New York and Brunswick. Immediately, Livingston informed Stevens that he would run his boat, the *Raritan*, on the same route at the same hour and day at one-third the passage money. In a dramatic dash to escape legal seizure by the New York courts, the *Phoenix* was taken on a coastwise trip from Hoboken to Philadelphia. There she undertook the Philadelphia-Trenton run on the Delaware, which proved to be a profitable route.

Despite their differences Stevens and John R. Livingston concluded joint preparations to connect New York and Philadelphia by stages and steamboats. The entire journey required from one and a half to two days. Livingston's *Raritan* was to run between New York and Brunswick, touching Elizabeth-Town Point and Perth Amboy. Stevens' *Phoenix* was to run between Philadelphia and Bordertown on the Delaware. Because the *Raritan* could not make a round trip each day, Livingston was forced to share his route with the packets. The *Raritan* lost money at first, but later returned a modest profit. The most lucrative part of the stage-packet-steamboat line was Stevens' water route on the Delaware.

v

It is difficult to ascertain with any satisfaction the expenditures and receipts of any given steamboat business. The bookkeeping of the period was crude and the records which have been preserved are fragmentary and often inaccurate. Louis Hunter's statement about Mississippi steamboating to the effect that "It is doubtful that the typical steamboat operator had a clear idea of the financial condition of his enterprise," [33] applies with equal validity to steamboating in the northeast. The operating expenses of steamboats on the Mississippi were greater than the operating expenses of those in the northeast, due primarily to heavier depreciation and insurance charges on the Mississippi. The Mississippi steamboats were more flimsily constructed and subject to greater navigation hazards, such as low water, snags, and floods; [34] typically, moreover, they relied upon high-pressure steam, which resulted in more accidents and explosions than in the case of the northeastern steamboats which utilized low-pressure steam. As compared with the average life span of from three to four years on the Mississippi, steamboats of the northeast lasted about seven years. On the Mississippi, annual operating expenses were as high as one and a quarter to two times the original value of the boat, whereas Fulton estimated the annual operating expenses of a steamboat on the Hudson at only 28 per cent of the original value.[35] On the Mississippi operating expenses could be broken down as follows: wages, 36 per cent; fuel, 30 per cent; depreciation, 25 per cent. On the Hudson, Fulton broke down his operating expenses thus: wages, 32 per cent; fuel, 54 per cent; depreciation, 14 per cent.[36] To these expenses must be added state taxes on the steamboat, payments to cities for exclusive ferry rights, wharfage fees, harbor fees, and advertising expenses.

The primary sources of income of the steamboat industry were passengers and freight. On the Mississippi, freight was more important than passengers, whereas the reverse was true on the Hudson in the early years. Minor sources of income were provided by mail contracts and barroom concessions. Estimates of profits varied on the Mississippi, with some boats reporting as much as $25,000 for a single trip, but this was exceptional. On the Mississippi where patents and state grants were ignored competition was keener and profits less consistently high than on the protected rivers of the northeast. On the Mississippi after 1817 there was a growing volume of complaints from steamboat entrepreneurs about the low profit rate. By 1833 it was estimated that steamboats on the Mississippi made a net profit of only 6 per cent per year.[37]

In the northeast where state grants and patents provided a monopolistic condition, Fulton and Livingston made a clear profit of $50,000 per year on two steamboats operating between Albany and New York City.[38] Stevens estimated that the net revenue of a steamboat line operating from New York to New Brunswick and from Trenton to Philadelphia would amount to 33½ per cent per year.[39] He calculated that he would clear at least 61 per cent per year on the capital advanced for a line of three steamboats on the Delaware.[40] On a line of three steamboats in North Carolina he estimated that the gross receipts would amount to $6000 per week.[41] Stevens cleared $1000 per week during the first year of the *Phoenix*'s operation. Indeed, the Delaware run of the *Phoenix* proved so profitable from the start that Stevens used it to set up a minor dynasty. First his son Robert was placed in charge of the boat itself; later to the management staff for his Delaware business he added his son Edwin and his nephews, Richard and Francis B. Stockton.

In steamboating, this early period in the northeast was characterized by business strategies which resembled more the tactics of warring armies than the peaceful pursuit of trade. The chief techniques were first to secure the advantage of a state grant or patent right, or both, through political pressure, and then to defend this advantage by threats, intimidation, coercion, cutthroat competition, seizures, and reprisals. In New York State, the exclusive grant was the primary weapon of Fulton and Livingston, but outside of that state they had to rely upon their patents as protection against potential competitors. Laws were pushed through state legislatures to reinforce these positions. Under such circumstances, potential competitors usually saw the advantage of coöperating by agreeing to work under a licensing system. Fulton summarized the business procedure of the time when he wrote to Stevens:

> It is important to get as many persons as possible to work under the patent, they will then defend it instead of attacking it. I have told Mr. Bayard that my plan for building boats by subscription is that on each year the accounts shall be settled and for the year all expences being paid and a fixed sum allowed for wear and repair . . . then should the net profits exceed 10 per cent the patentee and subscribers to divide the surplus. . . He says these terms are liberal and the company would prefer them to risque an experiment to be had with a stranger or a suit with us under the patent.[42]

The contestants usually preferred to keep the battle out of the courts. As Fulton put it to Stevens, "In this business my dear Sir let us meet and investigate like friends, more good is to be done by reason than by law."[43] But when agreements could not be reached privately, the courts became the scene of bitter suits and mighty constitutional arguments. The main advantages to be secured by recourse to the courts was the use of the injunction and the assessment of damages. This use of government power as an offensive and defensive weapon by rival business groups in their struggles remained as more than a vestige of the mercantilist mentality, despite frequent allusions to private competition and individualism by entrepreneurs.

Envious of Stevens' success on the Delaware, Livingston and Fulton decided to bring him to terms in a way consistent with this business milieu, by theatening cutthroat competition and patent infringement suits. Although Stevens was determined to resist, the state of his financial affairs plus Livingston's political power forced him towards an agreement with his rivals which was entered into on December 1, 1809 only a few months after the *Phoenix* had begun its lucrative operations.[44] Under the terms of this agreement the originality of Fulton's inventions and improvements and the validity of his patent were acknowledged. He and Livingston granted to Stevens the exclusive right to use their patent rights and any improvements which they might make on the Delaware, Chesapeake, Santee, Savannah, and Connecticut rivers, and in Rhode Island. In the event that Stevens within seven years failed to have at least one steamboat running on each of these routes, the unused ones would revert to Livingston and Fulton. In return Stevens agreed to relinquish all claims to steam navigation on the waters of New York, including Lake Champlain, and any point between New York and Brunswick in New Jersey, and on the Ohio and Mississippi and the waters running into them. Livingston and Fulton reserved the right to use Stevens' improvements on all of the waters included in their exclusive territory, except in the case of establishing steam ferryboats to run between New York and New Jersey. If Fulton and Livingston used Stevens' inventions on any waters of the United States other than those already specified they agreed to pay him a reasonable compensation.

Like many similar "gentlemen's agreements" of dubious legal sanction, however, this contract did not end the rivalry between the two factions. Both Stevens and Fulton continued to press their respective claims for originality until their deaths. Each one passionately desired to go down in the annals of posterity as *the* inventor of the steamboat, and neither could forgive the other for his "pretensions."

The rivalry was resumed in 1810 over New York City ferryboats. On February 5 that year the Corporation of New York City granted Stevens a twenty-four-year ferry lease, on the condition that he have a steam ferry running between Hoboken and New York City within two years. Shortly after, New York City granted the Paulus Hook Ferry Company a lease for ferry services from Cortlandt Street to Jersey City despite Stevens' protests. Fulton and Livingston held stock in the Paulus Hook Company, which operated under a license from them, using Fulton's patent and state grant. Thus, there began a new race to see which party — Stevens or the Paulus Hook interests — would build the first steam ferryboat. Despite many difficulties and delays Stevens won in this competition by completing the *Juliana*, in 1811. This was the first steam ferry in the world and it made sixteen round trips per day, averaging 100 passengers per trip.

At this time, however, Stevens' main interest lay not in New York City ferryboats, however successful, but in expanding his more southerly operations by establishing a joint-stock company to operate a line of steamboats on the Delaware between Philadelphia and Wilmington, and on the Chesapeake between Baltimore and the head of the Elk. Thus by 1811 he agreed to settle for the moment his disputes with his New York rivals by allowing a paragraph to be added to his 1809 agreement with them whereby Livingston and Fulton reasserted their right to grant exclusive privilege for a ferry from New York City across the East River, and agreed not to grant to anyone but Stevens permission to run steam ferryboats between New York and New Jersey within the distance of three miles above and three miles below the slip at the foot of Cortlandt Street.

Meanwhile, however, the Paulus Hook company construed their grant from New York City as meaning the elimination of competition from the Colonel's Hoboken ferry. This soon developed a new row and Stevens' wife, who was by now on friendlier terms than her husband with the Livingston family, appealed to the chancellor. He stated that he would consent to any agreement which Stevens and Fulton might reach. But Fulton's terms were unacceptable to the Colonel, who continued to operate his ferry, relying upon Fulton's reluctance to precipitate an open legal conflict with him. As one phase of the controversy at this time, Fulton and Livingston had secured the passage of an act by the New York legislature on April 9, 1811, for the more effectual enforcement of the act passed on April 11, 1808 which had given Livingston and Fulton exclusive New York State grants. Now, any boat against which action was taken by Fulton and Livingston could not be removed from New York waters, nor could the machinery be moved other than to the place which the court ordered. In addition, the courts were directed to bring speedy injunctions and suits.

To buttress his own claims, and thus to check threats of competition on the Delaware, Stevens, in turn, secured another patent on his steamboat "improvements" on April 10, 1811. The new threats of competition, Stevens felt, were due primarily to the recent decision of the Judge of the United States Circuit Court in the Albany case, plus the profitability of the steamboats already in operation. Livingston and Fulton had applied to the Circuit Court of the United States for an injunction to restrain the Albany vessels. The application was denied on the ground that the court lacked jurisdiction, and this was taken by astute speculators to constitute an opening in the legal armor of the Fulton-Livingston monopoly. Stevens threatened enthusiastic steamboat aspirants with patents owned by Fulton and himself. Under the terms of his 1809 agreement with Fulton and Livingston, he held the right to use Fulton's patents on the Delaware and he used this right to force potential competitors to work under licenses issued by him. However, Stevens wished to avoid actual court cases for he feared the validity of Fulton's and his patent claims. Stevens counted upon the technical inexperience of his rivals as a factor in his favor. But projects for building steamboats multiplied and Stevens then thought of extending his territory to Long Island Sound. However, most people believed the Sound to be unsafe for navigation and this project did not materialize.

In order to discourage competitors further Stevens decided to build another boat of his own for the Delaware and thus preëmpt all of the business. During July 1812 he therefore entered into a joint agreement with James and Maria Stevens, his son and daughter-in-law, through their legal representative, Theodosius Fowler, who was Maria's father, to build a steamboat to run from Philadelphia to Trenton. By 1813, this new boat, the *Philadelphia*, started its schedule, while the *Phoenix* took over the Philadelphia to Bordertown route. Both boats proved to be profitable.

Technical difficulties, in addition to Stevens' threats of patent litigation, finally led his most important potential competitor on the Delaware — the famous old Union Line of Philadelphia, New Castle, and Baltimore packets — to open negotiations with him. On January 18, 1812 a notice was published to the effect that Stevens and the proprietors of the Union Line had arranged for the latter to run steamboats on the Delaware and Chesapeake under the exclusive right of the patents of Stevens and Fulton. The Union Line was recapitalized and 1000 shares were issued at $100 par value, with the Stevens family acquiring a large interest. The Union Line was to become one of the most powerful and profitable transportation monopolies in the northeast. Protected by patents, as well as by ample financial resources, it was able to vanquish all rivals by the use of intimidation and cutthroat competition.

As his steamboat interests expanded, Stevens more eagerly approached the legislatures of New Jersey and Pennsylvania to secure appropriations for dredging the Delaware at certain points in order to render the river more navigable. He argued that this would increase commerce and add to the general welfare. However, in such petitions Stevens typically inserted a clause to the effect that in return for his services in dredging the river the state should grant him exclusive steamboat rights for twenty years on that part of the river dredged by him, plus five years for each additional steamboat he built. This would give him, in fact, an effective monopoly of the entire river.

At the same time, Stevens was looking for territory to exploit which would be outside the long arm of the Fulton-Livingston monopoly. In December 1812 he turned to North Carolina where he attended the sessions of the state legislature. As a result of his attendance and of the services of such legislators as A. D. Murphey, who was a fervent supporter of internal improvements in his state, an act was passed giving Stevens an exclusive steamboat grant for twenty years if within two years he had one steamboat in operation. For every steamboat constructed over two, Stevens was to receive a five-year prolongation of his grant, provided the whole term of the grant should not exceed thirty years after the pasage of the act.

Fulton, and Oliver Evans now, immediately filed independent counterclaims with the North Carolina legislature. Each claimed that Stevens had received his grant under false pretenses and that he, not Stevens, should be entitled to exclusive privileges. But on December 20, 1813 the Legislature upheld its original grant to Stevens. The Colonel had powerful friends in that state.

Although Fulton was angered by the Colonel's unilateral action, both he and the Colonel needed each other's coöperation to some degree. Fulton needed the Colonel's coöperation against Fulton's Albany competitors and against Colonel Aaron Ogden. Ogden had refused to operate his steam ferry service between Elizabeth-Town Point and New York City under a contract with Fulton and Livingston because he maintained their terms were extortionate. Ogden was instrumental in having the 1811 retaliatory New Jersey law passed, and under its rule he prevented J. R. Livingston's boat, the *Raritan*, from touching the Jersey shores. In 1813 the New Jersey Legislature had passed a bill giving Ogden exclusive steamboat rights on New Jersey waters. On the other hand, Stevens needed Fulton's coöperation against his Delaware competitors and against the Paulus Hook Company. But their mutual distrust was so great that neither could furnish the other with whole-hearted coöperation, although this woud have been to their mutual financial benefit.

Stevens was so anxious to secure Fulton's permission to operate steam ferryboats on the Hudson that he offered Fulton one-half of his North Carolina grant. But Fulton drove a hard bargain and on May 27, 1813 an agreement was reached by Stevens, Fulton, and R. L. Livingston, whereby Stevens conveyed to Fulton and Livingston and their heirs two-thirds of his North Carolina grant plus the right of management of the grant, reserving for himself only the right to invest up to one-fourth of the capital of any steamboat built for North Carolina waters. In return Stevens received the right to run two steamboats from New York City to Hoboken for thirteen years under agreement with the Paulus Hook Company. A patent-pooling clause was included. Each party bound himself to the agreement in the penal sum of $20,000 fixed damages. Fulton later added a clause as to his originality in steamboat invention, but this Stevens refused to accept.

When Stevens failed to coöperate with Fulton in his fight against Ogden, Fulton moved to get revenge. Ogden held great political power in New Jersey and Stevens, who frequently needed political favors, feared to antagonize him. Also, Stevens secretly hoped that Ogden would be able to defy the Fulton and Livingston monopoly and thus weaken their strangle hold. In July 1813 Fulton obtained an injunction to prevent Stevens' ferry, the *Juliana*, from running on the Hudson River. Stevens had to transfer the boat quickly to the Connecticut River in order to avoid its seizure by the New York courts.

Thereupon, Stevens switched his interest in ferries from steamboats to the alternative of horseboats — on which horsepower was used to turn the paddles — and he tirelessly proclaimed the superior efficiency of horseboats over steamboats. The horseboats which he built actually proved quite profitable. The steamboats of this period were so slow, awkward, and top-heavy with machinery that the horseboat could compare favorably in terms of speed, comfort, and carrying space.

VI

In January 1815 in the Legislature of New Jersey the whole controversy between Ogden and Livingston-Fulton was aired, with much contradictory testimony. Robert L. Livingston was an old hand at the game of power politics, and he took advantage of the political situation in New Jersey to defeat Ogden. The Republicans were in the majority in the state legislature, and Ogden, as a Federalist governor, had made himself extremely unpopular with the Republican party. The greatest pressure was brought to bear upon Republican party members to repeal Ogden's grant and finally it was repealed by a small majority in each house. Enraged, Ogden went to Albany and attacked the Fulton-Livingston monopoly on constitutional grounds and lost his case by only a single vote. Ogden's near-success prompted the Fulton-Livingston interests to reach some kind of agreement with him to avoid further clashes. They finally agreed to sell Ogden the right to operate a steamboat between Elizabeth-Town and New York City for a reasonable price.

Stevens now became alarmed by this coalition between Ogden and the Fulton-Livingston axis, and his thoughts turned even more to the question of alternatives to the steamboat. But growing threats of competition on the Delaware required his special attention. By 1815 there were three rival steamboat companies on the Delaware. In 1817 Stevens decided to bring suit for patent infringements against his competitors. The more easily intimidated agreed to settle out of court. The recalcitrant were to be brought to court. But in 1818 Stevens' lawyer, Horace Binney of Philadelphia, advised the Colonel to drop his patent suits against his remaining Delaware competitors because it was his candid opinion that Fulton's patent claims, under which the Colonel operated, were unenforceable.[45]

Stevens then decided to attack by more direct business means. In 1820 the Union Line, in which Stevens and his sons some years before had acquired a considerable interest, was reorganized. It consisted of the steamboats on the Raritan and Delaware and of the coaches on the turnpike between Trenton and Brunswick. It ran about six steamboats on the Delaware alone.[46] Its major competition was from the Citizen's Line which operated three rival steamboats on the Delaware. In 1825, Edwin Stevens took charge of the Union Line, which by then carried nearly all of the passengers and freight between New York and Philadelphia and therefore proved to be quite profitable. In 1829 the Union Line purchased two-thirds of the stock of the Citizen's Line and thus ended the competition between the two companies. Against the Citizen's Line, the Union Line had used its usual weapons of threats of patent-litigation and cut-throat competition to bring its rival to terms. Edwin Stevens remained the business manager of the Union Line until it merged with the Camden and Amboy Railroad in 1832.

The Stevens brothers continued to expand their steamboating operations, particularly the ferry service between New York and Hoboken which had proved increasingly lucrative. In 1821 the Colonel incorporated the Hoboken Steamboat Ferry Company and the Stevens family maintained control of this company until around the close of the nineteenth century, at which time control passed to the Delaware, Lackawanna, and Western Railroad. In 1823 Stevens' sons launched the first steam-driven, double-ended ferryboat on the Hudson, the *Hoboken*. This boat traveled faster than nine miles an hour. The establishment of this fast and commercially successful ferry service insured Stevens' lifelong project of building up Hoboken as a pleasure resort. Hoboken came to be known as the "Elysian Fields" of New York City. There were merry-go-rounds, barkers, and hawkers to entertain and lure the public. The great influx of weekend visitors brought profitable trade to Stevens. But the city in terms of permanent population grew slowly.

Stevens continued his efforts to secure legislative appropriations, with exclusive steamboat grant provisions, for clearing the Delaware, Susquehanna, and Raritan rivers. On June 8, 1824 he secured a patent for an improvement which rendered rapid and shallow rivers navigable by steamboats at the head of and above tidewater. Stevens had adopted the method of making canals and rivers navigable which had long been known and practiced in Europe — a system of slides, wing locks, and dams. On February 12, 1824 the Pennsylvania and New Jersey legislatures passed contingent acts permitting Stevens to clear bars and build wing dams on the Delaware River and keep these in repair at his own cost, in return for which Stevens was given exclusive steamboat rights on that part of the river. Stevens, by inducing the states to accept part of the tolls, actually made the states partners in his monopoly with a vested interest in its security and profitability. This business strategy was later adapted and used to much advantage by the Joint Companies to insure their monopoly power. Stevens planned to form joint-stock companies to dredge the Delaware, thus removing much of the risk-bearing from his own shoulders.

In 1824 an event occurred which overshadowed all others in importance. It was in this year that Chief Justice Marshall rendered his famous decision in Gibbons *versus* Ogden. Thomas Gibbons was engaged in stagecoaching with the Stevens' brothers and thus his interests were allied with the Union Line. For personal and business reasons, Gibbons had become the chief opponent of Ogden, who by then operated under the Livingston-Fulton exclusive grant. Gibbons' determination to vanquish Ogden led him to question the constitutionality of the Fulton-Livingston monopoly in the Supreme Court. There, Chief Justice Marshall decided that the Hudson River was an arm of the Atlantic Ocean and therefore subject to the power of the national congress under the commerce clause of the Constitution. Consequently, he pronounced the Livingston-Fulton grant unconstitutional insofar as it attempted to regulate vessels engaged in coasting trade under the act of Congress. This decision made the Hudson a free river and the port of New York City easily accessible to all river traffic. The immediate consequence was a multiplication of the number of steamboats on the Hudson and an improvement in service, as well as a reduction in fees, due to the intense competition. The larger significance of this decision was that it marked one of the most vital steps towards freeing the internal market from hampering restrictions imposed by rival states.

After the Marshall decision, the Stevens family became all-important on the Bay run, with steamers on both the Raritan and Delaware, plus the connecting stage lines. In 1825 the New York Court of Errors ended the monopoly of state waters also. The North River Steamboat Company had tried to evade the Supreme Court decision by insisting that the Hudson River was not an arm of interstate traffic, but the New York court declared firmly against this position. With the ending of its monopoly power the overcapitalized North River Steamboat Company, with its antiquated equipment, proved unable to withstand competition and went out of business in 1826. The unscrupulous competition after 1824 led the states to enact regulatory legislation and the private steamboat companies to undertake self-regulatory measures. Out of this situation arose the Hudson River Association in which the Stevens family was prominently involved. This association regulated steamboat traffic on the Hudson by private agreements and it was rumored that its profits were huge. The more firmly established lines with strong financial backing managed to maintain themselves in the face of increased competition by means of rate wars which vanquished those weak of purse, and when this did not succeed, by buying out their competitors. In this fierce school of business warfare Vanderbilt and Drew learned the lessons of strategy which were later to cary them to the highest positions in the American business world. Vanderbilt, as captain for Gibbons, had a chance to observe closely the latter's ceaseless maneuverings against Ogden and he soon perfected his master's techniques.

VII

At various points in his career when faced by overwhelming obstacles Stevens turned to various alternatives to the steamboat as a mode of transportation, such as floating bridges, subfluvial tubes, and horseboats. Very early in this search he had fastened upon the railroad. The Colonel had petitioned the Commissioners of Inland Navigation. in 1812 to abandon the Erie Canal project and to build a railroad instead.[47] Livingston and Fulton, however, enthusiastically promoted the Erie Canal as they felt the canal would increase the general welfare and prosperity of New York State and they appealed to the chauvinistic pride of New Yorkers. Livingston and his two intimate friends, DeWitt Clinton and Gouverneur Morris, were appointed by the New York Legislature as Commissioners of Inland Navigation. Under these circumstances the Commissioners could hardly be expected to approve of Stevens' railroad proposals. But Stevens continued to propagandize for railroads at this early date in state legislatures and in Congress.

On February 6, 1815 the New Jersey Legislature gave him a charter to incorporate a company to build a railroad from the Delaware River near Trenton to the Raritan River at or near Brunswick. This was the earliest railroad charter granted in the United States. But the railroad was so new and untried that it attracted no investors. However, Stevens was not discouraged.

In his attempts to secure state appropriations for the railroad, Stevens

was opposed by a formidable coalition of lobbies composed of canal-dredg-
ing companies, canal companies, steamboat lines, stage lines, packet lines,
turnpike companies, as well as a few rival railroad enthusiasts.[48] Stevens
also complained that the farmers selling feed to stagecoach horses and the
innkeepers along the stagecoach routes lobbied at the state legislatures
against the railroad.

But in 1823, through Stevens' unrelenting efforts, the Pennsylvania
Legislature passed acts for incorporating the Pennsylvania Railroad Company to build a railroad from Philadelphia to Columbia in Lancaster
County. Stevens was given rights similar to a patentee, in that all profits
above 12 per cent were to go to him. He approached various prominent
people, such as Mathew Carey who agreed to serve on the board of directors of the new company. However, the company was unable to raise the
necessary capital.

Stevens was then convinced that the only way he could save a desper-
ate situation was to risk his own money in proving railroads practicable
and himself the man to undertake such ventures. In 1825 he had constructed a locomotive with a multitubular boiler which he operated on a
circular track on the grounds of Hoboken as a pleasure vehicle. The train
carried half a dozen people at a speed of about seven miles per hour. This
constitutes the first reliable record of a steam locomotive operating on
tracks in the United States. But Stevens' little train was still considered by
most to be a mere toy and he could not arouse the enthusiasm of investors.

Despite Stevens' efforts the Pennsylvania Railroad Company did not
materialize. Therefore, on April 7, 1826 the Pennsylvania Legislature repealed Stevens' grant and Stevens had no place in the considerably broad-
ened charter for a railroad which was then passed. On March 24, 1828 the
Legislature appropriated $2,000,000 towards the construction of a railroad.

Stevens devoted more and more of his energies to propagandizing for
railroads. In 1828 he spent most of his time lobbying among the members
of the New Jersey Legislature for support of the Camden and Amboy
Railroad. The real object of the incorporation of the Camden and Amboy
Railroad Company was to take over the large stagecoach traffic built up
by the Union Line. Here again Stevens was frustrated by a struggle between rival business interests which cut across family connections. The
People's Line, dominated by the Stockton, Potter, and Neilson families,
lobbied for the Delaware-Raritan Canal project and vigorously opposed
the granting of a charter to the Camden and Amboy Railroad. The Stockton family was related to the Stevens family by marriage. In the winter of
1829–30 the fight between the two groups grew so bitter that the partisans
of each thought it necessary to go about the streets of Trenton armed at
night. The issue seemed deadlocked. However, at an informal meeting

the Stevens brothers and Commodore Robert F. Stockton came to an oral agreement. As a consequence, the New Jersey Legislature on February 4, 1830 issued two charters — one to the Camden and Amboy Railroad and Transportation Company and the other to the Delaware and Raritan Canal Company. Most of the legislators believed that water travel would be much more popular, but exactly the reverse proved to be true.

Robert Stevens was made President and Engineer of the Camden and Amboy Railroad, and his brother, Edwin, was made Treasurer and Manager. A steam locomotive and rails were imported from the famed Stephenson works in England and by 1833 the road was completed.

The Delaware and Raritan Canal Company and the Camden and Amboy Railroad and Transportation Company had combined by permission of the Legislature. In 1832 the Joint Companies received from the New Jersey Legislature a guarantee of the monopoly of the New York-Philadelphia traffic. The Camden and Amboy Railroad already had given the state 1000 shares of stock on the condition of an exclusive grant in New Jersey. In lieu of taxes the company had agreed to pay a transit duty of ten cents for each passenger and fifteen cents for each ton of freight carried over its line. In return for the 1832 state guarantee of absolute monopoly the Joint Companies gave the state an additional 1000 shares of stock and it was agreed that if the sum of the transit duties and the dividends on the 2000 shares did not amount to $30,000 annually, the difference would be paid by the Joint Companies. The state now had a vested interest in maintaining the monopoly of the Joint Companies. The Joint Companies were successful from the beginning and, backed by special political privileges, they constituted a vested interest which controlled New Jersey politics throughout the middle of the nineteenth century. By threats of cutthroat competition the Joint Companies drove rival steamboat and stagecoach lines out of business. Protected by the state monopoly grant, the Camden and Amboy Railroad was slow to introduce technological improvements, and public criticism grew in volume. But not until after the Civil War was the railroad double-tracked although the single-track line was long acknowledged to be inadequate and probably the cause of some of the serious railroad accidents of the day.

VIII

On March 6, 1838 Colonel John Stevens died. He had possessed a restless ambition, enormous energy, and a fertile imagination. Although faced by many failures he remained undaunted and optimistic. Until his death he pioneered in the realm of transportation. His primary psychological motivations were prestige, fame, and status — not wealth alone. Here was no abstract economic man to be fitted into the Benthamite strait jacket of the rational motivation of self-interest or gain. At times he was willing to sacrifice financial gain for prestige and fame. His family had become a member of the business elite, and he did not intend to relinquish this position but rather to enlarge it. The first prerequisite was, of course, financial. Prestige he attained in various ways — as community-builder, transportation pioneer, "inventor," businessman, author, cultured citizen of the western world. To the instincts of a speculator Stevens added the enthusiasms and strivings of the builder. Hoboken was to be a monument to his energy, acumen, and civic-mindedness. If the social-consciousness and civic-mindedness were not always remembered in Stevens' various schemes to make Hoboken a profitable venture, if instead of a commercial center he turned Hoboken into a raucous amusement park and pleasure resort for jaded New Yorkers and gaping tourists, nevertheless such motivations formed an essential part of Stevens' powerful drive. As a builder, he established a family dynasty which not only made the history of Hoboken but wielded an enormous influence in the development of the state of New Jersey in the nineteenth century.

Through his business strategy and boundless energy, he had built the foundations for a great business empire in real estate and transportation in New Jersey. His chief frustrations had been caused by opposition from rival business interests, such as Livingston and Stockton, both of whom were related to him by marriage. The former was defeated by Marshall's decision, the latter by compromise and merger. But the greatest blow to the Colonel's ego was that it was Fulton who was popularly known as the "inventor" of the steamboat and not he. Stevens possessed organizational genius and great skill in pecuniary manipulations. His primary contributions, therefore, were in the realm of business techniques and organization. With the reorganization of the Union Line in 1820, the formation of the Hudson River Steamboat Association, and the coalition of the Joint Companies, the Stevens family controlled a transportation empire which dominated the Hudson, Delaware, and Raritan rivers and the state of New Jersey. The sons, well-schooled by their father in business matters, carried on in his tradition.

VI

Henry Noble Day

A Study in Good Works

1808–1890

By R. Richard Wohl

Henry Noble Day's business career was an interruption of his life. It was, so to speak, smuggled into his life behind the irreproachable façade of a perfectly respectable academic venture. He was not intended for business. He had been reared, trained, and educated to be a professional intellectual. At twenty-six he made what was probably his only spontaneous choice of career, and it was not to go into business. He wanted to go to China to lead a mission to convert the heathen.

That choice was dictated by a crisis of baffled ambition. By all standards, he was long past his first youth. Furthermore, he had already experimented with three of the learned professions to no avail. The choice of a life work had become a grating anxiety. His station, no less than his income and his self-esteem, depended on somehow suitably utilizing his exceptional advantages and connections. Now, as he was completing his theological studies, the last respite from decision was drawing to a close. Almost in desperation, he seized on the mission to China. Here was a project fitting to his learning and background, one that complemented his exceptional piety and promised as well a spice of adventure in a faraway place doing strange, difficult, and noble work. As was to happen again and again, moreover, he became convinced that this career had come to his notice through the direct intervention of Providence. It is a gauge

by which to measure the man to know that he announced his intention to
his family and friends in just these terms.

The project was immediately, and firmly, crushed.

"Before you conclude," he was reminded, that this opportunity "is indicative of a sign of Providence respecting you," it would be well to make
sure that "it did not originate in some quarter that you have been thinking of a missionary life." [1] Common sense kept crowding in. He was reminded of his responsibilities to his younger brothers. Besides, his health
was poor, always had been; and, if he could not endure New Haven
summers how could he hope to survive the rigors of the semi-tropical
heat of Canton and Macao. The final verdict was pronounced by his uncle,
Thomas Day. "There is one consideration which is decisive," he wrote,
". . . you are not *constitutionally fitted* for the enterprize." [2] One month
later, after family consultation, a final disposition had been made of Henry
Day's future.

My belief has been [again wrote his uncle Thomas], that the situation
best suited to your health and constitution, the most congenial to the structure
and habits of your mind is a *College Professorship*. This I have reason to think
you may get, or rather your friends may obtain for you. I have had some conversation with Brother J[eremiah Day, President of Yale College] and intend
to confer with Professor [Benjamin] Silliman next week. With this object in
view, should there be no immediate prospect of obtaining it, I advise you to
continue your present situation [as a tutor in Yale College] another year. This,
in every point of view, is a *safe* course. [3]

The family verdict was unanimous and final. The mission to China
left without Henry Day. For a year or two, thereafter, letters came from
Canton, sealed in red wax and sporting exotic Chinese ideographs entwined
about a sea-anchor. Their contents were pious, and must have seemed a
little unreal in safe, stable New Haven. After a while, the letters stopped
coming, and Henry Day forgot about the mission.

He was helped to forget. In an act of signal psychological tact, the
family sent him abroad on a grand tour of Europe. [4] The motive was
plain: perhaps in foreign countries amid strange scenes — but not too
foreign or too strange — he could work off his highly charged restlessness.
Then he could return home and settle down to some useful and respectable
work.

Thus was the magic circle drawn within which Henry Day was meant
to spend his life. He was involved, by habit and decision, in a fierce family
solidarity whose problems and privileges would determine his station and
opportunities in life. He was, by choice and nurture, an intellectual. Finally, there was the fact of his temperament, an elusive quantity to be

sure, but one which was to flicker across his life history like bursts of flame from a banked fire. It sought release in intellectual dilettantism, religious revivalism, and business speculations; constantly ringing the changes on a mind and personality anxious to discipline itself to conformity, but always incapable of effectively controlling the inhibitions which were implied in such an effort.

II

Henry Noble Day was born on the fourth of August 1808, the son of Noble Day, of Washington, Connecticut.[5] His history, so full in other respects, sheds little light on his father. After a short and precarious business career, Noble Day retired to Washington. He left that town only late in life to remove to his son's home in Ohio where he died. His secrets and aspirations, whatever they may have been, are forgotten.[6]

Henry Day remained in his father's house until he was ten years old. He was raised in a simple rural community, in an area which prided itself on being the "land of steady habits." Its impressions on him may have been fundamental, but if so, he never recalled them except in nostalgia. When he left home, he went to Hartford to live with his uncle Thomas Day and to continue his education. He never again returned home except, perhaps, for short visits. The influences which shaped his life and molded his attitudes were those brought to bear by his two uncles, Thomas and Jeremiah Day, who had charge of him until he achieved adult independence. In the role of surrogate fathers they put the boy through a course of specific and intense socialization. Had they been asked, they might have said that they were intent on making him a proper, Christian gentleman. They did more. They defined, in fact, an outlook and a state of mind for the young boy. He never undid their training.

Thomas Day was a Connecticut patrician. Prior to the disestablishment of 1818, Connecticut was ruled in its business, political, ecclesiastical, and philanthropic activities by a tight conservative oligarchy whose power and authority stemmed from its control of, and association with, the established church. Thomas Day was a member of this group.[7] He had friends, "an extensive reputation, blessed with all that is valuable in possession for earth and all that is cheering in prospect for heaven." [8]

He was, to put it most simply, a lawyer. But he was more than that, he was a legal presence. He did not directly engage in litigation or counseling; he was more a legal intellectual, serving as a judge, a court *rapporteur*, and editor of the State Statutes. At one time or another he served in all the Connecticut courts, high, low, and middle, while at the same time holding down the post of Secretary of State for Connecticut.

The latter post, incidentally, was nominally elective; actually it was a sinecure, free from opposition, and Thomas Day filled it for twenty-five years.

As if that were not enough to absorb his energies, he engaged himself further in what was for the time an extensive career in public philanthropy. He was trustee and functionary of a host of asylums, schools, historical societies, and public institutions. His several careers left their imprint on the man. It was said of him, without satire and in pride, that he "brought a consistent life to a consistent close." [9]

This uncle enrolled Henry Day in the Hartford Grammar School of which, incidentally, he was trustee. The institution was a training ground for the elite; it recognized that its students were a chosen body and, in addition to the classical Latin and rhetoric, they received a careful schooling in the outlook on life suitable to a scholar and gentleman. Correct principles were evenly inculcated by mace and maxim. "The MANNERS AND MORALS of the pupils," the catalogue boasted, "are often made the subject of practical remarks, generally, however, in connection with topics of recitation, or occurrences adapted to give them greater effect." The principal, it was announced, "had no confidence in any system of school government which did not exact of the pupil *prompt* and *unconditional obedience*." [10]

Henry Day remained in this school for six years, and its principal lesson, that a highly visible conformity was one of the sovereign principles of his life, was only to be reinforced when "as by natural law" he moved up to Yale College.[11] No real change in milieu took place; he merely passed from the family of Thomas Day into that of Jeremiah Day, the College President. He was the only student who lived in the President's house.

Jeremiah Day was associated with Yale for more than half a century, and though he had a national reputation in his day, in ours he is little known. By profession a mathematician, he turned philosopher on his accession to the presidency. His conception of a proper education was rigid and austere. The Yale report of 1828 established the classical course as the prevailing norm in American colleges, and dealt a blow to the cause of vocational education from which it began to recover only after fifty years.

The whole of Jeremiah Day's life was suffused by a peculiar awareness of the problem of good and evil, to which he was as sensitive as other men are to light and shade. The great drama of human existence, in his eyes, manifested itself in the struggle between these two opposing forces, in which temptation and opportunity for evil were faced resolutely by inflexible will power. The ultimate fact of life was the final judgment of this struggle, a judgment which came unannounced, and lest adequate preparation were made, might find any man vulnerable to a terrifying verdict. This last dreadful alternative was the gauge by which to judge our earthly course.[12]

It might seem strange to find an active career in a modern urban community so suffused by a tightly knit theology, yet such was the case of Jeremiah Day in New Haven and of many others in Connecticut, where, as has been said, the church long wielded political power. Its idiom and phrasing dominated the mind of native intellectuals, in Jeremiah Day's case the more so because of his own background. His father was a famous and articulate minister who had deeply influenced his son.[13]

At Yale, as at the Hartford Grammar School, Henry Day was an excellent scholar, and a popular student. "My general principle," he confided to a friend, "is that correct moral feelings and a tender sensibility are the passports to the affection and esteem of our fellows." [14] Yet there was something about the boy, which, if he did not fully realize it himself, was apparent to his friends. The more he repressed himself to conformity, the more his fantasy reveled in compensating dreams to ease and vindicate these inhibitions. Some of the dreams he must have confided to intimates, for one of them thought it proper discreetly to warn him that: [15]

> Short is ambition's gay deceitful dream
> Though wreaths of laurels crown her brow
> Calm thought dispels the visionary scheme
> And time's cold breath dissolves the withr'ing bough.

The hint went unheeded, though plain enough.

III

Henry Day was graduated in the Yale class of 1828. He was twenty years old. His next eight years were to be *Wanderjahre*, preoccupied with a restless search for a career and the vindication of his hopes. What were these hopes? They were vague, but intense. He had to find useful and acceptable employment. Such a job must provide both an income and a basis for sustaining his social pretensions.

A career was essential; Henry Day's father was not a rich man. All available evidence points to the fact that he was, in fact, poor.[16] Neither was the family, as a whole, rich. Although both his uncles had risen high in the world, their means were limited. In their eyes, an education was a capital investment which, in later years, must yield an income. They had managed readily enough to meet the overhead on the social positions to which their professions committed them, but not much more.

I have little expectation of being able to do more for my children [wrote Jeremiah Day to his son Sherman], than give them an education. . . [S]alary men in Connecticut can not be expected to lay up money. I think you will be under the necessity of depending principally on your own exertions for your future support. I have frequently considered it a circumstance unfavorable to the welfare of my children that my *official* situation renders it necessary to accustom them to a style of living more elevated than they will probably be able to sustain throughout life.[17]

If the Days belonged to an aristocracy it was to an intellectual or even a moral one, not a propertied one, and the continuing test for member-ship was intellectual or moral, not business, achievement. It was for this reason that the vocational aspirations of so many of its members were so narrowly channeled. Money-making was not prized, and this especially for boys who had been sent to college. Such boys had little option but to attempt careers in the learned professions, or else to break with their tradition and sometimes with their families. To all its other disadvantages, moreover, business was peculiarly vulnerable to moral peril and to this none could be more sensitive than the Days.[18] "The acquisition of prop-erty," sternly warned Jeremiah, "will not compensate for the neglect of the great interests of eternity."[19] Business, furthermore, was urban and rootless. It was in the cities that moral standards wilted and evil flourished, encouraged by tolerance and concealment. "I consider you going to such a city as New York," Jeremiah Day hopefully counseled his son, "for the purpose of going into a mercantile business like a young physician going into the midst of pestilence to become proficient in the art of healing."[20]

Business was undergoing a radical change from its traditional forms by the 1830's and had, in recent years, become a most perilous affair in many places. True, in Connecticut the change was coming slowly, so that even by 1850 the state had largely retained its agricultural cast and conservative aspect. But Jeremiah Day looked beyond Connecticut.

I have no patience [he declared] with the rage for speculation that is spread like a pestilence on the community. I believe that some signal calamity will ere long come upon us in a judgment for this insatiable greediness for rapid accumulation. I wish to see honest industry liberally rewarded, but the mere transfer of property from one man to another adds nothing to the wealth of the community. On the contrary, it diverts the capital and talent and activity of the country from productive agency.[21]

This new flood-tide of business brought with it dangerous, individual-izing forces disruptive of stability and order. It was, he felt, nothing short of a moral catastrophe, for which penance was inevitable.

I have been expecting [he wrote his son], some disastrous reaction from the phrensied [sic] spirit of speculation which has run like wildfire from Maine to Wisconsin. The agony to be immediately rich which has seised [sic] so large a portion of the population must have provoked the displeasure of him who looketh on all the sons of men, and who considereth covetousness. To my apprehension, the most alarming feature of our national history of late has been what we have called our unexampled prosperity, our rapid strides in opulence and lavish expenditure . . .[22]

These views were shared, in principle, by Henry's other uncle, Thomas Day, who warned him also to shun business and prefer the academic life, and with it the opportunity for sustaining greater moral worth.[23] Thus if the family could not pass on wealth, it might still transmit its status by controlling the choice of its heirs' careers.

It was under the influence of such considerations as these, phrased in the idiom of propriety, that Henry began to canvass a possible career among his remaining opportunities. With the model of his uncle Jeremiah Day most immediately before his eyes he inclined first to teaching. Naturally this choice was heartily approved; recommendations of his fitness from Professor Benjamin Silliman, then America's greatest science teacher, and a public figure in his own right, accompanied those written by the Yale President himself. It would be difficult to conceive of more exalted auspices for launching an academic career at this time.

A job was found. Henry Day went to Burlington, New Jersey to teach the classics in Mr. Gummere's academy there.[24] Indecisive and troubled at what he might find in his new post, he consulted former classmates who had since become masters themselves. The advice was intended to discourage him. One friend warned him that the students were roughnecks, and that the birch taught as much Latin as the teacher. Henry Day seemed unconcerned; he had heard that there was a pretty, dark-eyed Quakeress at his school.[25]

Two years was all Henry Day could stand of this. He drew no excitement from the daily round of teaching. Burlington, moreover, was a small town without the cultural resources or the society to which he had become accustomed at New Haven. Another course, therefore, had to be taken, and the model of Jeremiah having been found wanting, what better than to try the model of the other good uncle, Thomas Day. Thus young Henry went to Philadelphia, where he would be close to his brother Mills and his cousin Sherman Day, to study law.[26]

But whatever hopes law had held out to him were somehow dashed in a year. There seemed nothing to do but to return again to Yale and draw fresh inspiration there. He went back and was appointed a tutor in the college. Since his own graduation, Henry Day had sampled two learned professions, law and education, and had made a career of neither. He was, furthermore, not inclined to medicine, and, besides, that was a career little esteemed by men of his class. He was too frail to go into the army. Thus the only choice that remained open was the ministry and dutifully, while a tutor in the college, he enrolled in the Yale Divinity School.[27] It was while there in 1834 that Henry Day made his momentous and, as it turned out, quite futile decision to go to China. When that course was closed to him he went, as we have seen, to Europe, with the promise that some place would be found for him when he returned.

Henry Day spent more than a year abroad. When he came back to New Haven, he seemed to have rounded a corner in his life. He brought gifts of lace for the ladies, books for the gentlemen, and oranges from Italy for the children. His journey seemed to have soothed him, and he proceeded, according to plan, to settle down. To do that he needed a job and a wife. In a very short time, he had both.

He had returned to New Haven early in 1836. In a few months, after a brisk courtship, he married Miss Jane Louise Marble. The marriage was eminently suitable. It was also a happy marriage, sustained as much by the gaiety and patience of the wife as by the geniality and gentleness of the husband.[28]

Jane Day was the daughter of a most respectable New Haven family, doubly crowned with a solid economic competence and a reputation for great piety. Her father, Simeon Marble, was a director of the Mechanics Bank, a position of prestige in the commercial community. The family moved with ease in the higher if not actually the highest circles of New Haven society. Mrs. Simeon Marble was president of the Dorcas Club, which, apparently, was just a shade below the Literary Society which boasted the presidency of Mrs. Jeremiah Day and the executive assistance of Mrs. Benjamin Silliman. Adeline Marble, another daughter, had been absorbed into the local martyrology, and her sainted memory pointed a lesson in holy endeavor and "christian character." Her short life had been distinguished by the remarkable pious work of founding the New Haven "Female Juvenile Mite Society." This was the sort of marriage Henry Day's family might have expected him to make.

In a scant six months after his wedding, Henry Day had also found a post. He was installed as pastor of the First Congregational Church in Waterbury, Connecticut. Before that he had been offered but rejected pulpits both at Washington (where he was born) and in New Haven. This Waterbury appointment rounded out an intense period of pulpit-hunting in which the mark of family influence can easily be discerned.[29]

At last it seemed as if the troubled days of uncertainty were over for Henry Day. The family drew an even breath and buttressed his position still further. Recommendations signed by Professors Olmsted, Silliman, and uncle Jeremiah — a veritable academic galaxy — announced to the world that the school carried on by Henry in Waterbury as an adjunct to his pulpit bore their hearty approval. Occasionally, too, bad boys at Yale were sent to rusticate in Waterbury at that school. Henry Day built a fine new house, fronted by white Ionic columns, and seemed himself a very pillar of society.

This era of felicity lasted only twice as long as the earlier one at Gummere Academy. Henry Day called this period one of "four years of pleasant and successful ministry." [30] Actually, his temperament reasserted itself; the ministry was a shade too successful. It was, in effect, a series of three revivals, which whipped up religious sentiment to a frenzy. Each demonstration of zeal called forth another, intended to exceed the fervor of its predecessors. Henry Day's fame spread. It was commented upon in Nev Haven and in Hartford. How much further need fame reach; where else need praise be sought?

Then a circumstance intervened. An accident. Henry Day received an invitation to take up the Chair of Sacred Rhetoric at Western Reserve College, in Hudson. Ohio. On the theological faculty at Western Reserve were two former classmates from Yale; the president of the institution, Pierce, had been chosen after the advice of President Jeremiah Day had been solicited. Western Reserve aspired to be the "Yale of the West." The invitation, as has been said, was an accident, but it was, it appears, such a one as could only occur in a prepared environment.

This was a major change, yet it was no great departure from the norm to which he was expected to adhere. He sought advice from the family. He knew nothing of Ohio, little about Western Reserve College. In response to his inquiries, President Pierce wrote that Western Reserve had an endowment of $100,000, that his annual salary would be $700, and that his was an endowed chair.[31] His friend, Loomis, wrote further that the climate was pleasant and healthful, living costs reasonable, that he would be very comfortable in Hudson. As yet, the student body was small but that need not be a matter for concern. "Moreover," he added eagerly, "the State has women perhaps inferior to no other State in the Union. Here you will see is a field for obtaining students to fill a college to overflowing." Not one in twenty Ohio children were sent out of the state to study at college; Western Reserve, argued Loomis, was the coming school of the West.[32]

Finally, there came a letter from his uncle Jeremiah, the ultimate authority in matters educational. He declined the opportunity of supplying a clear verdict. "It is not infrequently the case," he shrewdly urged on his nephew, "that after an unusual religious interest, there succeeds a state of comparative apathy, and the evil of the change is all charged upon the minister. . . May you be guided by wisdom from above." [33]

That, apparently, settled the matter. After a little dickering, Henry Day sent in his acceptance. The authorities at Western Reserve were delighted. On June 4, 1840, Henry Noble Day was unanimously appointed Professor of Sacred Rhetoric. Uncle Jeremiah must have been deeply shocked when this innocent appointment proved to be the gateway to Henry's extraordinary business career.

IV

When Henry Day came to Hudson, Ohio, he stepped into a frontier community. It had been founded in 1800, and was only forty years old when he first saw it. It was on the frontier if by that term is meant that it was isolated, self-sufficient, and simple. In another sense, it was old and well established, for it was tied firmly and intimately to the culture from which it had sprung.

The founding of Hudson was a direct result of the second great awakening that had swept through Connecticut in the latter years of the eighteenth century. In Goshen, Connecticut, the religious excitement had been particularly intense. David Hudson, a native of the town, who, according to his own testimony, had hitherto been a godless man, caught fire from the prevailing religious enthusiasm, and underwent a psychological crisis. He determined that thereafter he would devote himself to the Lord's purposes. He would go into the wilderness and found there a community which would live according to His ordinances. He never, in after years, wavered from that purpose. In 1799, he penetrated the Western Reserve and carefully explored it. He selected a suitable site, and in the next year brought his family and a few followers to settle there with him.

From the very first he determined that his resolve should not be dissipated under the stress of a frontier life with its attendant hardships. He need not have feared. The isolation, the hard work done in common, sustained the original homogeneity of the group and served, indeed, to provide it with added vitality. The people were farmers and remained farmers. They lived in log cabins, worked hard, and prayed with sturdy zeal. They literally lived off the land, the town being too isolated from a market to allow of commercial agriculture. Thus there was hardly any money in the community except for that which came later on the current of emigration, and that was scant enough; so that, in Jeremiah Day's terms, there was hardly any temptation either. For many years it was considered a stroke of good fortune that David Hudson was postmaster, for in that office he had access to a frank. It would have been rare indeed for twenty-five cents in hard money to be found in the town to pay the postage for letters to Connecticut.[34]

For a long time business was unknown as a distinct calling; there was little need for it. The community was almost entirely self-sufficient and devotedly abstemious. The brides of the town made their own wedding dresses out of seventy-five-cent calico. In their homes, the height of ornamental elegance was a water color (or silk embroidery) of "Moses in the Bullrushes." The early history of Hudson was marked by two economic breakdowns which would have prevented the growth of business and trade, had there been any impulse for them to develop. The embargo of 1807 which convulsed the eastern seaboard produced a sympathetic recession in the West; later, the panic of 1837 stopped what little growth had taken place subsequently.

The main interest of the town was in its church and in the college. The school was the final and most precious flower of David Hudson's holy work. Both church and college, dedicated to substantially the same purposes, formed the social and cultural center of the town; all other activities were referred back to them for relevance. A devout application to work and prayer was the main theme of existence.

> The men prominent in the early church [writes a local historian], were of strong personality, intensely individual, typical Calvinists — men of strong convictions, and from the tenacity with which they held on to them there would have seemed to enter into their composition some of the stuff of which martyrs are made. It would be difficult to overestimate their reverence for the Sabbath and the sanctuary. In summer's heat and winter's cold over roads whose badness no words can adequately describe, every one of them, appeared on the Sabbath, in Zion, before God. They would have regarded inability to stand through a prayer of twenty to twenty five minutes long as an alarming sign of being "at ease in Zion!" [35]

The homogeneity of the community was further assured by a physiological peculiarity. The people who settled in Hudson were exceptionally hardy. Throughout the entire period of our narrative a large proportion of the original immigrants were alive in Hudson. Even by the third quarter of the nineteenth century approximately one in every forty of Hudson's inhabitants were between 70 and 87 years old, survivors of the original wave of settlers.[36]

David Hudson had further assured the continuance of his prospect beyond his own lifetime by making it a condition of the marriage of his daughter that his son-in-law reside with him in Hudson, and ultimately take over his plans and projects after his death.

The community throve in its first years but produced no great accumulation of liquid wealth. In time, the log cabins gave way to more substantial brick houses, because the local clay made cheap brick possible and accessible. Cultivation was not pressed to the full limit of the productivity of the soil, but then only a moderate surplus was sufficient, trade being so difficult. Until 1851, dirt roads offered the only lines of communication and transport and the community concentrated on producing grains, meat, and dairy products for its own use. A few cattle were fattened, some pork packed, and enough wool and flax grown to meet the local demands for textile fiber. For the most part, the town throve modestly, putting its wealth into tidier, better stocked farms, improved flocks, and better houses and barns. Some probably yielded to the farmer's lasting land hunger by taking over a few more acres.[37]

Here then was a community in which Henry Day could transplant himself from his earlier milieu without suffering any ideological shock. It might, in many ways, be more primitive and ruder than New Haven, yet, in another way, it was the Connecticut original in a purer form, undiluted and undistracted by modern worldliness and the change encroaching on the east. The values and the aspirations which had been carefully inculcated into Henry Day from the time he was a boy were regnant and universally accepted in Hudson, itself a perfect matrix for the kind of career that had always been planned for him.

It was fitting for this community that a theological school should be established as a department of the university. Such a move, however, was far in advance of the tendency prevailing in the country at the time. Of the theological schools founded before 1840, only one-third were organized as departments of a college. Few of these had been organized so early in a college's career as had that of Western Reserve, hardly out of the throes of the formalities of organization itself. It had, furthermore, been founded with standards which were equal to the highest then prevailing in the country. These standards were maintained even at the cost of keeping down the student body to a minimum. On such a faculty as this Henry Day could feel himself an equal, by any intellectual or moral standard, to scholars of the universities in the East. But the school's brave show could not win out in the end; the founders had reckoned without their public.

From the first, Western Reserve's divinity school was ringed about with flourishing competitors. Within three hundred miles of Hudson were four other theological schools, all competing for pupils. Two of these were not only definitely Presbyterian, but were independent seminaries as well, and both clergy and laity favored training in independent schools. Western Reserve was not denominational. Two other competitors, Gambier and Oberlin, were determinedly sectarian, and as such preferred. Finally, as if to complete the crown of thorns, the prevailing trend in the religious education of the time was toward a vigorous evangelism which the austere intellectuality of Western Reserve rejected completely. If, indeed, there was a demand to be met for the kind of ministers which it proposed to train, that demand could easily be met from the eastern universities which were continually turning out graduates in this tradition, many of whom showed no reluctance to coming out to the West. In no one year of its seventeen-year existence were there more than twenty-three students enrolled in the Theological Department, the average enrollment was nearer fifteen, often much less.[38]

As a result, Henry Day, as Professor of Sacred Rhetoric, had almost from the very beginning of his appointment a great deal of leisure. In the best of times the college offered insufficient work to absorb his energies, and in 1851 the Theological Department was suspended, ostensibly for lack of funds. His association with the college continued in other lines, but always with a small range of formal duties. Often he worked closely with President Pierce, then primarily engaged in developing the college endowment. Thus, while Day had an established status and an official connection, he was provided with an abundance of free time in which he might give other interests full play. He turned to business.

V

It took Henry Day four years to recognize, and act upon, the fact that his job at the college could not fully occupy him. Yet it was difficult, especially in such a milieu, to effect a transition from his role as educator and clergyman into that of businessman. There was no apparent intervening set of institutions or activities through which such a move might be made. Over all was the further consideration that to abandon his professorship — endowed by the town's leading citizen, Heman Oviatt — his college connection, and the cloth, would have meant certain deterioration of status and standing in the community, as well as an invitation to all kinds of economic uncertainty and family displeasure.

Yet, Henry Day followed a course that seemed to him to offer an opening. He associated himself with the newspaper published in Hudson, the *Ohio Observer*, and on July 12, 1844 a formal agreement was drawn up making him a junior partner in the enterprise. Alvin Upson, the printer, was to produce the paper and oversee its distribution. Professor E. P. Barrows (a Yale graduate) was to write the first two pages, and Day was to supply the third and fourth sheets. The agreement was to run yearly, and to be rewritten after an annual sharing of profits.

It took Henry Day but one year to convert himself from junior partner to publisher in the enterprise. By July 1845, when a new set of articles was written, he took over complete responsibility, retaining the services of Upson and Barrows as employees.[39] He now had a vehicle by which he could make himself known to the community at large and to the whole surrounding area. He became absorbed in all that was news in the region, although the newspaper remained heavily tinged with religious discussion and church affairs. This, far from being a drawback, was a positive advantage not only to the paper but to him personally in minimizing the conflict between his emergent and his past roles. He had, in this way, discovered the principle which he was subsequently to apply in converting himself from an academician to a businessman. He associated himself with new activities, explained these activities in terms of his academic role, and then extended them, further and further, until they embraced a whole series of functions, which had become wholly alien to that role. The newspaper served, too, to provide him with a medium through which he could pronounce his views and opinions on a host of subjects, and establish a presumptive competence in many areas, which had hitherto been barred to him in the classroom.

It is appropriate to pause at this point to attempt to disentangle the paths which his thinking traveled before reaching this solution to his problem. Even before Henry Day had arrived in Hudson, he had been anxious to achieve some success, some tangible accomplishment, which would bulk large in the eyes of his family and friends. There seems no other way to explain the restless search for a profession, and his extravagant pastoral exertions in Waterbury. Yet of all paths to glory, business seemed the one he would least likely follow and the one least likely to receive the avuncular accolade. Moreover, he had no stock of capital of his own to engage, he had no experience, or training, or even occasion for a business venture.

Yet the solid front of opposition which his family had raised to business had already been breached within the family. Cousin Sherman, the son of President Jeremiah Day himself, as we have seen, had gone into business, as did Henry's three brothers, Charles, Thomas, and the younger Jeremiah. There were, in fact, too many sons and too few professional opportunities. The line might always be drawn between the preferred intellectual, learned professions and the less desirable business careers, but the latter had to be embraced by some.

Henry Day's brother, Jeremiah, had not gone to college, but after serving a brief apprenticeship in Connecticut business houses had removed with his brother Charles to one of the hottest fronts of economic development in the country, Apalachicola, Florida, where they set up a commission business. Apalachicola, because of the continually enlarging sales of cotton which took place there, had in a few brief years been converted from a scraggy malarial swamp into a booming little city. Its prosperity indeed soon was so great that in a short time a rival town was established a few miles away, to cut into its cotton traffic. This was St. Joseph, feverishly built up with a railroad, buildings, warehouses, landings. The race between St. Joseph and Apalachicola was a delirium of competition and, in the correspondence that passed between Henry Day, then still at Waterbury, and his brother Jeremiah, the number of bales sold each season were flaunted like scores in a game. The race had its own drama, for St. Joseph was to fail, and Apalachicola grow to greater glory and Charles and Jeremiah with it.[40] Henry Day followed the letters from Apalachicola avidly and Jeremiah reported the struggle in abundant detail. Central to the whole was money, which, in the letters, seems to carry overtones which are utterly romantic. Money ceased to be a concrete object or power, but became rather a vague, but highly charged grail.

Henry Day caught the fever. Even this early, he looked around in Waterbury for such an El Dorado as his brother had found in the south. Later, in December 1838, he quietly boasted to his brother that he had "some attraction for single handed capitalists." Jeremiah quickly replied that if he came across anything "choice" to give him a share.[41] In the meantime, Jeremiah took small sums from his brother to risk in southern speculations. They were successful, and Henry Day ravened on success. Every profit must be greater than the one before; there was no satisfying him, not even 25 per cent on the risked capital. Finally, Jeremiah, smarting under his brother's exhortations to greater gain, cut short one speculation, protesting that "you are a little too hasty to get rich. We southerners are content to make a few thousands a year, but you want to make hundreds of thousands, and do not make anything and lose what you have." [42] The correspondence of course continued. When St. Joseph was finally crushed the commission business flourished so mightily that the two brothers in the South determined to divide their effort. Charles Day would stay in the South, Jeremiah would go to New York and handle that end of the business.[43]

In Hudson itself, therefore, with this heady experience and solid example, Henry soon found other threads which, though more closely related to his academic duties, supported his susceptibility to business. President Pierce, with whom he was intimately associated devoted himself to fund-raising and administering the endowment of the college. From the very nature of his principal duties, his chief concern was with business rather than education. Not only did he have to seek out money, but he also had to watch the state of trade in order to realize on the many gifts of land which formed the most substantial portion of the college capital. By 1839, moreover, when the backwash of the panic of 1837 was decimating land values, Pierce had to find other sources of funds to keep the college growing. His method was to operate on credit, borrowing again and again to meet current needs. This was policy not improvisation. Pierce later explained himself:

In the distracted state of the public mind it was thought necessary that some bold measures should be entered upon and a public demonstration made that the college was to live and prosper. In conducting the charities at that time it was a common sentiment that the best way to procure means was to let expenditures go in advance and create a necessity which would be met when pressure was felt.[44]

The close association between the President and Henry Day drummed this financial principle into the young man's mind. It seemed confirmed by the success it enjoyed.

For all its unworldliness, moreover, there was beneath the placid surface of the frontier town — even among its orthodox elements — a contained enthusiasm for expansion and increased economic activity. Heman Oviatt, Hudson's principal merchant, who had endowed Henry Day's Chair in Sacred Rhetoric, and Judge Van Rensselaer Humphrey, lawyer and politician, with connections in the more expansive parts of the state, had once before challenged the hostile public opinion by being named as founders, in the charter of 1836, of the proposed Cleveland and Pittsburgh Railroad.[45] Now, in the 1840's, when the depression was lifting, they were again responsive to the prevalent enthusiasms, economic and political, in the state as a whole. Both men were intimate with Henry Day and he with their minority opinions.

Thus, even before he had committed himself to any large ventures he had felt the impact of some very suggestive ideas which turned his mind to business. His brothers' southern experience had given a taste of the excitement and rich rewards of economic booming; his association with President Pierce had given him a technique of fund-raising, of anticipating capital requirements by capital commitments; his intimacy with Oviatt and Humphrey, finally, suggested excellent colleagues, powerful and highly esteemed in the community, if he attempted a business career.

VI

If Henry Day's background and upbringing make his ultimate venturing on a business career seem remarkable, the backwardness of the rest of the population of Hudson, Ohio, needing as it did the stimulus of such a man as Day to rouse it to business activity, seems more remarkable still. The communities surrounding Hudson had been booming, more or less evenly, for some time. By 1840, when Henry Day had arrived there, Ohio had become the third most populous state in the Union, and was still growing at a rate that exceeded by far that for the nation as a whole. Even this spectacular increase in the population of the state, however, was outstripped by the surge of people into the whole Western Reserve. Between 1800 and 1810, the population there had increased more than ten times; in the next decade it increased again by two and a half times. Between 1820 and 1830 it barely fell short of doubling itself and in the ten years which followed it more than doubled again. In 1806, the Western Reserve had only 9000 persons scattered over its entire territory. By 1850, it had a population of 340,000 and was in number greater than any one of ten of the thirty-one states in the Union.[46]

And not only did people pour in but they helped create the means to get their produce out. In 1815, Northern Ohio was more or less completely isolated from the East. All the principal roads led into the southern part of the state. The National Road stretched from Baltimore to Cincinnati, or access could be gained from a southern network of roads running through Virginia, Kentucky, and Tennessee. To get to the Western Reserve at that time, it was necessary to go overland via the lake route, from the east, or else to trek inland from Pittsburgh. After 1830, however, the Erie Canal, the Genesee Turnpike, and the roads which rimmed the southern shore of Lake Erie to Cleveland changed all this.[47] The stream of cereals from the West soon destroyed New England grain-growing, and turned fresh hordes loose for western settlement. Moreover, the composition of the nation's population was undergoing a dramatic change which was to augment the market for Ohio grain. Between 1810, the time, approximately, when the factory system was introduced, and 1860, urban dwellers in the United States increased from 7 per cent to 37 per cent of the population! These landless people had to be fed and Ohio farmers were eager to feed them. A state report near the end of this period compared prices and quantities of grain in 1829 and in 1858.

Corn was higher in 1858 than for several years [wrote the Ohio State Commissioner of Statistics] but so it was in 1829. The comparison is, on the whole, fair. The result is that the wheat harvest *doubled*, corn nearly *trebled*. . . The consequence is that the *ultimate* value, *the amount which can be got* for our agricultural products, is more than double what it was thirty years ago. This is not in consequence of any change in currency; for if the enlarged bulk of currency has increased prices it has increased all prices and not those of particular articles. On the contrary, prices of imported articles are less; but the price of our products is greater. The advantage is all on our side. This process must go on for so long as the fabricating and artistic [artisans?] increases faster than the agricultural; or, in other words, the town or [agriculturally] non-producing people increase faster than producers. This is the case now in Ohio.[48]

Thus the Ohio land was aching with prosperity; and only a series of superlatives monotonously repeated can describe what was happening in mining and manufacturing as well. As if overnight, the great Ohio coal seams were opened up and fabulous increases in production were rapidly made manifest. In 1840, 150,000 bushels were received at Cleveland for consumption or reshipment; in 1850 more than fifteen times as much was laid down in that port; and in the next seven years this amount was quadrupled.[49]

To select another from many possible examples, the growth of manufactures in Cincinnati may be cited, if only because the statistics for that city are fuller than for others. Despite declining price levels over the decade, the aggregate increase, between 1840 and 1850, in seventeen manufacturing lines was 200 per cent. Factories and commercial establishments, indeed, were springing up everywhere, so fast that the State Commissioner of Statistics confessed his inability to keep pace with their progress.[50]

Hardly less spectacular was the equally sudden emergence of myriads of businessmen who supplied and serviced these new activities. Farmers who had hitherto been concerned with subsistence and only incidentally with large-scale commercial farming, turned entrepreneurs. Outputs had to be planned and priced to meet the requirements of a market. The fertility of the soil had to be conserved and replenished. Efficiency in production, improvements in stock and seed, all went hand in hand. Farming passed from a simple craft proceeding by hit or miss methods into a determinedly scientific and commercial enterprise with close associations with accounting, soil chemistry, and engineering. The change was organized in a host of agricultural societies, fairs, and journals.[51]

Manufacturers and merchants, too, underwent an apprenticeship to gain their necessary skills. The mysteries of credit and prices, the arts of prudent management and careful planning were learned slowly, and at great cost, by men whose chief qualification for business, at first, was a speculative fever. These phenomena were not confined to Ohio, but were characteristic of the entire West. Morgan Neville, who wrote on the condition of Western manufactures during the tariff controversy of 1832–33, reported to Congress that:

I found that in every establishment in our large towns a mystery was thrown around their operations and in the country a want of experience in some and absence of scientific knowledge in others rendered what information could be gleaned a matter of much uncertainty and distrust. . . As yet, in Ohio, in all the country west of Pittsburgh, manufactures are but beginning to exist. . . Every establishment in the west may be considered as the creation of industry and credit. Many men of reputed wealth have engaged in them, but their wealth was not available but for the purpose of gaining credit. Loans, generally, to the whole amount of the capital were negociated.[52]

It was in this milieu, so vastly and obviously successful, yet at the same time so pragmatic and experimental, that the unlikely Henry Day was to carry on his projects, centered in unlikely Hudson. Both Day and Hudson thus had the background of a time and place in which great plans were exciting commonplaces. One of the key words of that milieu was credit, a somewhat fabulous talisman which could translate hopes into hard cash and large profits. Yet credit, the expansion of production, wealth, all seemed, perhaps, merely different words which in a religious idiom were expressed as faith and good works. Expressed so, both Day and Hudson naturally were susceptible.

VII

Since we have touched on the influences which early conditioned Henry Day's attitudes, it seems appropriate at this point to stop and examine the formal declaration of ideology by which, intellectually at least, he accomplished the transition from the academic role for which he had early been groomed to that of businessman in his mature years. His statement of business purposes, appropriately enough, took the form of a sermon, which he delivered the year before the Theological Department of Western Reserve suspended and released him for his business career. He chose the fiftieth anniversary of the founding of Hudson as the occasion, and on Thanksgiving Day made his pronouncement. For his text he chose Daniel 7 : 13–14 which begins, "In the night I saw visions . . ."[53]

His sermon dwelt on three main points. He opened with a consideration of the holy duty of all earnest Christians to direct their earthly labor in conformity with holy purposes and to work for the advent of God's Kingdom on earth. He proceeded then to point out how the institutions, the location, and the social organization of the country seemed divinely predestined to fulfill just that purpose. He concluded that both the intention and the means were blended in the national American character in such a way as to constitute a Providential directive to the fulfillment of the holy mission.

The task was to give "the Kingdom of Christ universal and perpetual sway on earth and to make all earthly kingdoms 'all nations and languages' subject and subservient."[54] This historic destiny was already in process of fulfillment. "That Kingdom," he exhorted his hearers, "has been established on earth, its conquests have commenced, its power and dominion were extending; and all events are rolling on its perfect consummation in glory and might among men. Every nation — our own — is to serve it and help in its triumph." [55]

This historic destiny may be inferred from a multitude of objective facts, chief among which is our geographical position. The continental spread of the American nation he foresaw as a divine purpose intent on producing a people characterized by "unity, independence, strength, enterprise and greatness." [56] Providence

has appreciated our existence in an age when such physical obstructions as we have to experience in our interchanges of political and social sentiment and interest are made to vanish before the trained and subdued power of more mighty physical agencies; and no reasonable man can doubt that the pushing links of commercial inter-communication and rapid advances of settlers, villages and townships will soon bind us across the Rocky Mountains as closely as they connect us across the Alleghenies . . .[57]

Our political institutions emphasizing the separation of church and state, the freedom of the individual, the very nature of our language and the universal desire for self-improvement and education, all witness our impending greatness. All means are afforded for the carrying out of this great work.

Scarcely a luxury and no real comfort or necessary of life, whether of natural or artificial product is there which we may not obtain without recourse to foreign countries, and so diversified is our soil and climate that that great scourge of contracted countries famine [he struck out the words "even scarcity"] is hardly to be an object of reasonable apprehension.[58]

Confronted everywhere by such magnificent opportunity the nation was required, from consideration of God's will and man's benefit, to bend every effort to realize this potential spiritual and temporal greatness. We must apply our faith in democracy and the promptings of an urgent sense of progress to the affairs of daily life.

Another expression of our national life [he urged], is in our industry and in our arts. The characteristics which Christianity in its present stage seems to require are chiefly vigor of invention, skill in execution and subscribing to the true end of industrial arts — utility. In the activity and vigor of inventive talent and in the general success of mechanical enterprise, the docility with which foreign arts are studied and apprehended, and the restless ambition to press on from present achievements to higher stages of perfection give our countrymen advantages over those countries in which a narrow conservatism veils existing defects and indisposes to further improvements.[59]

All these advantages have their counterparts, he claimed, in corresponding traits in the American character; and for each goal to be achieved there was a predisposing tendency to direct American attention and thought to them.

We must despise all nature's influences [he concluded], if we be not characterized by lofty thoughts, broad views, expanded sympathies, large plans and high aspirations; if our character be not broad, deep and noble in all its elements . . . that we be a united, self-relying, powerful, enterprising and magnanimous people — such a people as the advance of Christianity now calls to its service, such a people, in these respects, as a millennial sun will not blush to look upon.[60]

In this sermon may be observed the intellectual bridge which Henry Day crossed between his two, and hitherto conflicting, roles. He had, by his phrasing of his intended functions, blurred the hitherto sharp conflicts which had emerged in terms of set oppositions between temporal and spiritual interests, between intellectual, selfless devotion to ideas and a preoccupation with wealth. He identified his business projects, his railroad building, with a symbol — militant Christian awareness — which was at the same time the basis of the solidarity of the town of Hudson and the philosophical content of his family's ideas. He had, indeed, phrased business activity in terms of theological fieldwork, he had united progress, utility, and innovation with a historical Christian task, and incidentally made it entirely appropriate for an intellectual and a man of God to participate in business, since this, he pretended, was his customary work with but a slight change in emphasis which the time and place demanded. In sum, the basis of a direct attack on his new projects was removed from the hands of any opposition, since he argued for it on the same grounds on which he might be opposed.

The tactic was eminently successful, although whether it was subterfuge or an honest and sincere conclusion it is impossible to say; we may hazard that it was the latter. His uncle Thomas Day, when he fully realized the implications of his nephew's position, wrote him and recalled his earlier tender of advice to Henry to be an academician. He considered his nephew's new role with some misgivings. His "reflections," he wrote, were of a mixed character:

If you become a *business man* I cannot object to your being a *thorough* business man. . . You consulted me some years ago about your going to China on a mission, and I took the responsibility of advising you not to go . . . I should *hesitate* about advising you to quit the peace and quiet of an academic life for which I know you are well-fitted for a course of life which must be *new to you* and not unattended by *dangers* of some sort. One of the dangers of a business life, which is particularly impressed on my mind at this time, is an injury, if not a total loss of, your simplicity of character. Heretofore, the characteristic of your mind has been to consider everyone as pure-minded and undesigning as yourself. Will not a business life, associating, as you must, with business men, turn you about so that you will regard every man you deal with as having some design upon you, or trying to get some advantage over you? [61]

The transition from professional intellectual to businessman was therefore accomplished with a minimum of tension between the two roles, and without a break with his family or tradition, which, instead of being deterrents were converted to indispensable aids in his proposed new career.

VIII

Henry Noble Day's business plans were double-pronged. They included first a network of railroad lines, and then a series of business enterprises in anticipation of the economic growth which he felt must accrue with the development of his railroads. These businesses were centered in Hudson which he expected the railroad to transform from a pious village to a flourishing metropolis.

The key to Henry Day's railroad activities is to be found in the Cleveland and Pittsburgh Railroad. All the other railroad lines with which he was associated were connected with it, each being viewed as a means of tapping the pool of traffic which the Cleveland and Pittsburgh would carry, or of drawing fresh streams of traffic to it. The Cleveland and Pittsburgh had originally been chartered in 1836, partly under the sponsorship of Humphrey and Oviatt, of Hudson. The panic of 1837, however, intervened, and it was not until March 1845 that a new charter was obtained from the Legislature and active work begun in the organization of the road, completing surveys and laying out a specific route. The line from Cleveland eastward, it was then decided, was to pass through Hudson, and immediately upon the announcement of this decision local excitement was generated.[62]

Henry Day became embroiled in the project almost at once. By the middle of 1846 he became its regular propagandist. The directors sought to rouse enthusiasm for the projected road, and to translate that enthusiasm into financial support. They felt that local subscribers might be reassured if the federal government could be persuaded to make a cash donation toward its construction. Discreet inquiry, however, revealed that this was not feasible, but that there was a possibility that some public land might be donated. Henry Day was commissioned to open a campaign to solicit such support and to prepare a memorial to Congress urging the gift. He was, further, to circulate his petition and to accumulate as many signatures as he could espousing the scheme, in the localities in his immediate vicinity. He acted promptly. The memorial was soon written and signatures collected.

His energy and success must have been impressive, for on August 10, 1846 he was appointed an agent of the road and entrusted with a special task. He was to proceed at once to Philadelphia, Boston, and New York, and such other places as seemed to him profitable to visit, and to inform local financial circles about the road and its prospects. To finance this propaganda tour he was also empowered to solicit subscriptions to the capital stock of the line. For each share of stock sold he was to require the down payment of one dollar, and from this money he was to reimburse himself for his expenses. Should this prove insufficient, the company would reimburse him.[63]

Apparently the journey east was successful, for at the beginning of the following year, he and the eminent P. M. Waddell of Cleveland were placed in charge of the local campaign to raise $200,000 in order to construct the road from Cleveland to Hudson. Again, his success is indicated, for Henry Day was appointed a Director of the Cleveland and Pittsburgh shortly thereafter.[64]

This association with the Cleveland and Pittsburgh transformed Henry Day very quickly from a gifted amateur spokesman to a professional expert in railroad promoting. It also provided him with extensive experience and connections in Eastern railroad financing circles. Beyond that, it initiated him into the mysteries of the promotion of large-scale economic development, for the Cleveland and Pittsburgh was intended, in fact, to develop an entire region, and to relate its economic progress to the eastern seaboard's markets.[65]

The Cleveland and Pittsburgh was to link the Lake Erie port with Pittsburgh, connecting there with the Pennsylvania Central to the eastern seaboard. At Rochester, Ravenna, and Union in Ohio its route lay athwart the paths of existing canals and it was thus in contact with the traffic which passed through and gathered there. But it was primarily concerned with meeting an integrated set of traffic needs hitherto unserved, while at the same time generating new streams of traffic itself. The latter plans had four main objectives: the coal trade, the carriage of the western agricultural and manufactured goods, the lake and river commerce, and finally, the through traffic between its terminals.

In passing through the Yellow Creek Valley, on the Ohio-Pennsylvania border, the Cleveland and Pittsburgh traversed a very rich coal area just being opened to exploitation. The promoters of the road calculated that they could lay down coal in Cleveland, after it had traveled nearly the whole length of the line, for $2.50 a ton. This traffic alone they estimated would yield rich profits for in 1840 Cleveland alone had taken up 164,000 tons at $3.00, or more than 200 tons for every working day of the year. This reckoning left out of account the considerable market they felt could be opened up along the way from the coal fields to Cleveland, especially since many industrial establishments were springing up along that route.

Agricultural produce was to flow westward as well. It was cheaper to grow wheat in Pennsylvania than in the Western Reserve, if the cost of overland transport were added to the price of the Western grain. Wheat was to be gathered up along the way and shipped to Cleveland for rerouting to the east. Other agricultural supplies such as packed meats, butter, and cheese would be directed to the Ohio River ports for transshipment southward. Wool, however, was to go to market in Cleveland.

The future of manufactures in the Western Reserve, it was admitted, was problematical; but it appeared to the projectors of the road that such establishments would increase and prosper in the area. They would, therefore, provide a profitable trade for the road which could bring in raw materials and ship out the finished product. There was, in addition, the "way business" supplying freight and transport services to the population tapped on either side of the main line of track along the entire route.

Lake and river traffic would supply still further revenue. Eastern cottons, shoes, and clothing, as well as a host of other consumers' goods, would require railway service. The record of past demand was impressive: in 1847 imports into Cleveland amounted to more than $4,500,000, while in the same period more than $9,500,000 of goods were exported from that city. And finally, there was the passenger traffic between Pittsburgh and Cleveland, and what freights might come during the winter months when lake traffic was suspended because of the weather.[66]

Here then was a promising plan for the economic development of northern Ohio. It took account not only of the human population in the area, but linked the railroad to the area's entire business system. Most important, it allowed of almost unlimited extension. The Cleveland and Pittsburgh stretched across a wide territory and on both sides of its track were vast areas not served by any railroads. Why not, then, build feeder roads which would tap this hinterland?

This question, indeed, is what stirred Henry Day to elaborate his scheme for making a great city of Hudson. Soon after the completion of the main road, two feeder lines were built, one from Wellesville, along the Ohio River to Wheeling, the other, likewise extending southward, from the canal town of East Rochester to New Philadelphia. The logic of these feeder lines Henry Day elaborated into a whole subsystem of other roads all centered at Hudson, which was to become not simply a center on the Cleveland and Pittsburgh but in its own right a terminus for a distinct railway net.

The whole plan was developed very rapidly, and carried forward with great energy. On the Cleveland end the construction of the Cleveland and Pittsburgh had made slow progress, and it was only in the winter of 1851 that the road had progressed as far eastward as Hudson. Earlier that same year, however, an agitation had been set in progress to build a branch road southward direct from Hudson. This move finally culminated in an amendment to the charter of the Cleveland and Pittsburgh which allowed the formation of a separate, but associated, company to be known as the Akron Branch Line company. On March 11, 1851 this venture was formally organized with Henry Day as Secretary of the new company. Thirteen days later, a law passed the State Legislature authorizing and requiring County Commissioners, in the area concerned, to subscribe to the capital stock of the new company, pending consent of the voters in the area. This subscription was not to exceed $100,000, which they were authorized to raise by the issuance of 7 per cent bonds in denominations of at least $100. Eighteen townships registered 1605 votes against the proposition, while 2432 approved. Shortly after this successful balloting the treasurer of the Akron Branch received the fifteen-year bonds, on which interest was due semiannually. Simultaneously, local tax rates were increased to provide for the payment of interest and to accumulate a sinking fund for the amortization of the principal.

Private stock subscriptions also poured in, and were as promptly paid. By July 4 of the next year the road had been built as far as Akron, and shortly was extended south to Millersburgh. There, a connection was obtained with the Ohio & Pennsylvania Railroad subsequently known as the Pittsburgh, Fort Wayne & Chicago, and an outlet, more or less direct, was available to Columbus, Cincinnati, and even further west and south.[67]

The success of this venture, accomplished with a speed remarkable even for the expectations of the time, drove Henry Day to a further frenzy of activity. He reasoned that if a line between Pittsburgh and Cleveland had turned out so successfully — although at this time the road had not yet conclusively proved itself — how much more successful would a road be which tapped the eastern and western extremities of the country as a whole. Poring over railroad maps, he traced the faint lines which indicated planned railroads and saw for Hudson a strategic niche in a proposed transcontinental system to be arranged by the linkage of short lines. The first step was the Clinton Line railroad, of which he was elected President and which was to extend eastward from Hudson to the Pennsylvania border. There, at Kinsman, Ohio, it was to connect with the projected Venango Railroad, then under construction. The rumored building of a

spur by the Cleveland & Pittsburgh itself to connect it with the projected
Clinton Line at Kinsman gave the latter, on paper at least, the option of
two very desirable routes to the east coast.

A year later, in 1853, a western link to his system was projected. This
was the Clinton Line Extension Railroad, which was planned to run 94
miles westward from Hudson to Tiffin, Ohio.[68] There it was to connect
with a chain of other projected roads reaching, all together, as far west as
Council Bluffs, Iowa, and thence westward again — over further projected
roads, of course. That same year, the last logical link in the Hudson railroad net was supplied by the Hudson & Painesville road, sponsored by
Henry Day's Hudson associate and colleague on the Clinton Line roads,
Judge Van R. Humphrey. This line was projected to run northeastward
to Painesville, a town on Lake Erie, complementing the Akron Branch
which ran southwestward to Millersburgh.[69]

Thus, by 1853, Henry Day's bold railroad empire was not only down
on paper, but it was brought to higher semblance of reality than most such
projects of the time by the initiation of separate corporate organizations,
the raising of capital, and the actual setting of crews to work to survey
and grade the proposed routes.

IX

The maturing of this imperial scheme of Henry Day's can be traced
to the years 1845–1850, the impulse to it apparently coming from his association with the Cleveland and Pittsburgh. As early as 1845, however,
he had written his brother Thomas, in Cleveland, of his ambition to make a
great metropolis of Hudson. Thomas was surprised by the fervor with
which Henry argued for what seemed a completely unstable plan. "I fear
you are a little extravagant," he replied, "in expecting Hudson 'to become
the center of business operations of the west.' It may well become a second
New Jersey 'tapped at both ends' but scarcely can compete with such places
as Cleveland, Pittsburgh, &c." Others were hardly more sanguine. His
wife, on hearing that a railroad was being planned to come to Hudson,
wrote him in 1846 that she was surprised by the move. "I am glad you are
building a Rail Road through Hudson. Henry [Mills Day, their son] says
he hopes it will be done before you come east to New Haven, so you can
come fast. I did not think there was so much interest in Hudson." [70] In
1851, the large negative vote against public support of the Akron Branch
will be remembered. In later years, even after the combined railroad building had generated a great boom, the verdict of the older inhabitants on
the boom was reflected in a comment by a friend of Day's. He wrote that
there was prevalent skepticism of the whole expansion; that Day seemed
to have plenty of money, that he was spending it freely and was engaged

in various enterprises, but that the feeling of the town was that he was going rather too fast.[71]

But for Henry Day himself the dream he had for Hudson had become a sacred reality. He was able to anticipate its completion while the first few spadefuls of earth were taken out for grading. He proceeded therefore to enact the logic of his expectations. He began to create a network of businesses in Hudson to service the demands arising out of the railroad building boom and to cash in on the enlarged market which would result once the roads were completed.

Most of these enterprises were directly related to the railroad plan. As early as 1847, Day promoted the establishment of a telegraph station in Hudson, intended to work in conjunction with the railroad. His method in gaining this point was typical. He subscribed to the stock of the telegraph company and solicited further contributions from the townspeople. Here again, he encountered resistance. Many who, in their initial enthusiasm, entered their names on the stock subscription lists came to regret it and delayed so long in paying up that for a time it was doubtful if the telegraph would come to Hudson at all. "Were it not for your railroad," wrote H. B. Ely, the telegraph line promoter, "the object of which you have steadily in view, it might well be doubted whether an office could be supported in Hudson, but connected with that object there can be no doubt of it." [72]

In 1849, Henry Day began what was to be the seat of nearly a dozen separate businessess. That year he approached Western Reserve College for a loan of $1500 with which he would undertake to construct a large commercial building. Since the railroad was to come shortly to Hudson, there would be a great demand for business floor space, of which there was hardly any available in the town. Against the loan he would pledge the lot on which he intended to erect the structure. In addition, he would pay the going rate of interest and retire the loan as rapidly as he could.

No sooner had he begun the actual building when his plans for the structure were enlarged into something far grander. Less than a year later, the completed building had exceeded its planned cost by $3000. He returned to the trustees of Western Reserve with a fresh proposition. If they would advance the $3000 for which he had committed himself, he would pledge the building as well as the land, and throw in 1000 shares of Cleveland and Pittsburgh stock as additional collateral. He would, in addition, undertake an option to purchase the building from the Trustees within fifteen years, paying, during that interval, the going rate of interest on the additional money advanced, as well as a rental of $176 per year to the college. This investment, Day contended, was certain to be lucrative, since he had already rented the entire structure with the exception of one room for which a large number of eager applicants were waiting. The Trustees proved cool to the proposal; but his plans were not stopped by the rebuff. Before the structure was completed to his satisfaction it had swallowed up $18,000, although the source of this capital remains to this day a mystery which cannot be solved from the tangled, incestuous financing which prevailed in Henry Day's enterprises.[73]

The structure was a magnificent aberration, entirely out of scale with the relatively small, low buildings which filled the rest of the village. It was a five-sided, three-story edifice — an earlier Pentagon — and was soon packed full of a collection of businesses at the bottom of each of which was Henry Day, impartially providing catpital, plans, and enthusiasm. On the broad main frontage of the building was established Sawyer, Ingersoll & Co., a printing and publishing concern which announced its willingness to undertake any kind of job and book printing that might be demanded of it. Henry Day constituted the "company" and into this enterprise were funneled the publication of the *Ohio Observer*, a variety of college printing, and the whole mass of railroad printing which Henry Day's influence could command. Flanking the printing office was the concern of J. W. Smith & Co. — again "& Co." meant Henry Day — a large-scale dry goods store which in a short time blossomed out into a general store sheltering an abundance of the most varied stocks. Wedged between these two businesses was a smaller one — likewise sponsored by Henry Day but not bearing his name — the "Western Reserve Drug Store." On the floor above, immediately topping Smith's store, was the W. T. Norman furniture and agricultural implement business, while reaching around the corner C. M. Knight's watchmaking and jewelry establishment was located, all Day concerns, none bearing his name.[74]

All these concerns were "created," so to speak, by Henry Day. They were established in the names of his partners whose chief contribution, always, was the superintendence of the enterprise. Day himself would have no overt share in managing the routine business details of any of his concerns. In addition to helping found these businesses, Day did take over the problem of bringing to Hudson the necessary instrumentalities for carrying them on. Letters poured in constant stream to his family in Cleveland, New York, and Connecticut, soliciting their assistance in locating expert printers, typefounders, and binders, and ordering them to buy essential machinery, fonts of type, and all manner of paper stock.[75]

In addition, he was constantly preoccupied with recruiting new businessmen and enterprises for Hudson, for his holdings there. Indeed, to fill up his building space (when that need presented itself) he was capable of adding still another side line to his already extensive holdings. Thus, he negotiated with a manufacturer of sacks in Cleveland offering to take his total output if he would establish a plant in Hudson and buy steam-power and rent quarters from Day.[76]

In the meantime the projected railroads brought a great stream of cash and hundreds of workers into Hudson. Of the $200,000 pledged for the Clinton Railroad, $18,000 was expended within Hudson itself, a proportion far greater than it appears, since many of the subscriptions to stock were made in the form of lands, not cash.[77] The numerical expansion of the population also created a host of new problems which boomed business. The greatest demand was for shelter and Henry Day proposed to meet it with a vertically integrated scheme for new housing.

One of the greatest benefits of the railroad boom, its protagonist argued, was to be the enhancement of local land values. Hence Henry Day, associating himself with the most powerful elements in the community, purchased — on credit, of course — large tracts of land outside the main area of settlement in the town, but immediately adjacent to it. Here — in what he labeled "Day's Addition" — he proposed to rear the housing which was to accommodate the present increase in population as well as the further additions which would surely come after the railroads were fully built.[78] To finance construction and sale of his houses, Day conceived a special kind of banking organization, the "Hudson Society for Savings." The real nature of the bank can be inferred from the business interests of those who constituted its directors and officers. Day was President. Harvey Baldwin, the largest local landowner, was a Director; Moses Messer, a local dealer in lumber, was Secretary-Treasurer, the same office which he filled for the Clinton Line Railroad. John W. Smith, Day's partner in the "Pentagon" company, was also the instigator of the lumbering enterprise which Day entered when the building scheme got under way.

Outwardly, the Savings Society seemed to have traditional and rather innocuous purposes. It was to receive deposits from subscribers, to invest such deposits, and pay interest on them according to the length of time they were left in the bank. But this general function was considerably modified in the bylaws of the organization. The bank was also — indeed primarily — to accept deposits from individuals (for their benefit) to be applied against the purchase price of building lots and houses. Depositors pledged themselves to make regular payments which would in the course of a year amount to at least 10 per cent of the purchase price of a home or lot and continue to make regular payments thereafter until the full purchase price was paid. All monies were to be administered as "trust funds" for the sole benefit of the depositors. Officers and directors would receive no compensation, aside from a nominal sum which was to be paid to the secretary-treasurer, apparently the only official with any regular, detailed duties.

The scheme was, however, capable of further elaboration. The depositor might, if he chose, have a lot or house furnished him before he had fully paid up his purchase price. In that event, "he shall pay the institution as rent, in addition to his deposits, 10 per cent on the balance of its cost over the amount he had paid in addition to the interest that may have accrued on his deposits, which balance shall now be reckoned anew for this purpose from year to year." The Society, of course, would retain first lien on his property until all was paid and title fully transferred.

This bank — for such it was to all intents and purposes — therefore constituted an ingenious scheme for erecting houses and capitalizing on effected rises in land values, running ahead of the community's capital for supporting such construction. It was reared on credits, piled on top of one another, and always susceptible to collapse when the weakest segment gave way.[79]

The final element in this development scheme was a building supply business. At the instigation of J. W. Smith, Henry Day found the capital to establish the Hudson Planing & Lumber Company, to be built along the Cleveland and Pittsburgh railroad depot and track. From the first, it undertook to supply a wide line of lumber products and millwork, as well as shingles, lath, sash, and doors. Since it was so close to the railroad track, it engaged, as well, in the sale of coal. As the bulk of new construction was probably clapboard and frame, the Hudson Planing & Lumber Company carried what amounted to an almost complete line of building materials.[80]

X

Thus, in the space of five short years Henry Day became involved in a complex of business firms ranging from newspaper publishing and printing, railroad promotion and housebuilding to selling groceries and running a bank. Over all of them he exercised leadership not from any technical competence, nor from any special business acumen. His authority stemmed from his control over the basic conception of the plan for development which he had devised for the town and the area; and this authority was continuously implemented by his further control over its most strategic element: he had access to capital. Because he brought capital to Hudson from the outside, moreover, he could use it as a lever to elicit local resources all the more effectively. Money came to money.

Where, however, did his outside capital come from?

It came from the Family. Just as he had turned to the family in electing a career, just as he had manipulated their prestige in moving from post to post, so now he turned to them to provide the funds which would translate his business aspirations into fact.

These funds were available to him in various amounts: he took what he could get, wherever he could get it. His father-in-law sent him a hundred dollars to supplement his salary; his brother supplied countless borrowed thousands. The full history of his financial transactions within the family can never be traced. They are lost in a network of bills and notes which were kited from hand to hand and never entered in any central accounting record. Henry Day's conception of credit was shortsighted; he depended always on having a source of readily available borrowings, not on any careful reckoning of the amount of his commitments.

His business enterprises borrowed and lent to one another, then turned about and used their mutual credit to sustain the weakest unit in a moment of crisis. The full amount of his obligations was, it appears, for long unknown to Henry Day himself and only became apparent on the day of final reckoning. It was possible for him to carry on this delirious financing only because in many of his transactions he felt that particular borrowings would be self-liquidating during the life of the loan; and when events proved the contrary, the only resource seemed to be to borrow more to secure the first debt. To his actual borrowings from his family he added borrowings from local banks, creating a jungle of debts which even final liquidation could not sort out.

But if the full story of these multiform transactions cannot be told, it is possible, at least, to trace the main flows of capital on which Henry Day drew for his projects.

Most important of all were the resources which brother Jeremiah, the commission merchant of Apalachicola and New York, placed at his disposal. In New York, this young brother controlled the funds which resulted from southern sales, and accepted the commercial paper of southern clients drawn against the funds accumulated in New York. There was, therefore, a considerable sum always available in his hands pending remittance, as well as considerable credit on which he could draw as required in the normal conduct of his business.

Jeremiah and his brother Henry were beguiled by this arrangement. Why should they not employ these funds and credit to do profitable business on their own behalf while awaiting instruction of their clients? True, the cash might be momentarily called for, but it was more than likely that only a fraction of the whole would be required at any one time, and regular demands could be met quite easily. Thus, if they could use this money for short periods, realize (as they hoped) considerable profits, and replace it, no harm would be done and both would be the richer for it. The scheme, in all its deceptive innocence, was capable of further elaboration. Jeremiah Day & Co. could accept drafts written upon it in Ohio for periods sufficiently in the future to allow a profitable realization on the proposed transactions. In such a way (in theory at least), the monetary resources of the firm would never actually be touched, but its credit would support the business in hand. All that would be required of Jeremiah (again, in theory) would be his signature of acceptance on a draft. In addition, Henry Day sent large amounts of railroad securities to be marketed in New York, and a further deceptive cash pool was created, against which to charge Ohio obligations.

Thus, in all the Hudson enterprises in which Henry Day was the "& Co.," he was working with Jeremiah, who supplied the funds which made these businesses possible. In New York, Henry Day had access, also, to the resources of his cousin Sherman Day's firm, though to a more limited extent since the latter very shrewdly and very soon limited his acceptance of Ohio paper. In New Haven, Henry had further lines of credit in his father-in-law, Simeon Marble, a director of the Mechanics Bank, and his brother-in-law, Edwin Marble, a local businessman. At one juncture when all other sources had failed, both of these assumed between themselves the main burden of providing credit to sustain his enterprises. In New Haven, too, he had further access to capital in the persons of two men associated with Yale College, which, after all, must have seemed to him almost a family appanage. These were Professor Thomas Thacher and E. C. Herrick, treasurer of the college, both regular buyers of Henry's railroad securities.

In Hartford, moreover, uncle Thomas Day was as heavy a security buyer as his funds allowed, and through his influence attracted other buyers to the paper of his nephew's enterprises. It was in Hartford too — and presumably through this uncle's influence — that he found it possible at one point to farm out a bond issue in support of the Clinton Line Railroad.[81]

In addition to all these sources — possibly as a consequence of having them available — Henry Day could also command a varying amount of local credit written against Ohio banks. Their advances, however, were geared to the supply of eastern money with which, it seems, they were consistently bailed out, except at the very end. How much capital he personally raised, directly or indirectly, in Hudson, it is impossible to know, but it seems unlikely that so energetic a promoter as Henry Day would have left this likely source untapped.[82]

It is, as has been said, impossible to state precisely what his total capital was, or to allocate it accurately to the sources he drew upon. Such figures as remain are more indicative of relative magnitudes than of precise amounts. From his brother Jeremiah he received $100,000 — at least this was the final figure of unpaid obligations when the final crash came, though the total amount may have been considerably greater. His father-in-law supplied at least $3500 (to finance the lumber company), the figure

given in an assignment of personal assets to Simeon Marble. Again, the
actual amount might have been far in excess of this. His brother-in-law,
at the very end, underwrote some $15,387 of his notes in a last desperate at-
tempt to salvage him. Within the town of Hudson itself credits were available, but to what extent Henry Day drew upon these personally — as he
must have — and to what extent they represented advances to businesses
he created it is impossible to determine. More than $200,000, at any rate,
was invested by the town in one form or another in the Clinton Line Railroads, and this sum leaves out the other branch lines, and such investments
as were made in the telegraph company. The Hudson Savings Society
swallowed up another $50,000. Personal commitments by the relatively
wealthy townspeople can be estimated from the fate of Moses Messer, by
no means a magnate, who lost $16,000 in the Savings Society and Clinton
Line Railroad for both of which he was treasurer.[83]

XI

The best measure of the effectiveness of Henry Day's role in mobilizing
capital can be found in the fact that these businesses were all actually
brought into being. But more than capital was required to build up this
business network. The very definition of Henry Day's role as a businessman required that he have two sets of collaborators. He needed colleagues
who would oversee the active administration, in detail, of all his ventures.
He needed too, a set of co-workers with established prestige and authority
to help turn Hudson from a small, self-contained village to a booming
railroad metropolis. At least one socially esteemed individual was sought
for each main class of business.

The single most prominent man in Hudson was Harvey Baldwin, son-
in-law of the founder, David Hudson, and by profession and avocation a
highly visible public figure. David Hudson, when he had given his daughter in marriage, had insisted that Baldwin live in Hudson and carry on his
work, and, according to a local historian, Baldwin "thoroughly identified
himself with the business and educational interests of the township and
village, coöperating with them, and as his successor, fully carrying out
Mr. Hudson's benefactions in educational, church and public enterprises,
being a trustee of Western Reserve College for over forty years." As heir
to his father-in-law's holdings he, of course, held much land and was interested in real estate development. He was also interested, however, in such
bodies as the Portage Mutual Life Insurance Company and Day's Society
for Savings, enterprises which were tinged with a concern for the public
welfare. Most of his business connections were rather austere, of a
trustee character, and calculated more to embellish his public standing
than to make him rich. His explicit sponsorship of some of Day's enter-

prises thus afforded the latter a borrowed source of influence which helped overcome local inertia against his expansive plans.

Another important colleague, a fount of prestige and influence over a wider, one might say a regional, area was Judge Van Rensselaer Humphrey. The Judge was well known and respected not only in Summit County (where Hudson was located) but in adjacent counties as well. He knew his way around, too, in Columbus, the state capital. His long experience as a lawyer, judge, and representative in the State Legislature had built up for him a set of wide connections especially useful for Henry Day's railroad network. In an emergency he could be sent down to Columbus to persuade the legislators there of the interests in Hudson which must be met if the public welfare was to be best served.

Henry Day, of course, gained the allegiance of such men, and through them entrée into the tightly knit and socially conservative Hudson community, largely because he could approach them on their own social level. His own background was impeccable, his professional association with the college was eminently proper, his pastoral calling was in consonance with the main ideology of the local culture. These qualities, however, were less important in mobilizing the cadre of managers to oversee the details of each particular enterprise, control sales, order supplies, supervise production, order and maintain equipment, and (however poorly) to keep accounts. Each business needed at least one such man, avowedly an expert in his line, who would run the establishment on a partnership basis with Day. Of all these, the most prominent and — for Henry Day — the most crucial individual was John W. Smith.

Fate, it seems, must have intervened in a conspiracy to keep the history of John W. Smith obscure. His very name makes it impossible to trace his background effectively. Henry Day appears to have known little about him other than that he had been in business in Toledo. He apparently came to Hudson and met Day there. Their temperaments were so much alike they were immediately drawn to one another, and Smith understood, from the first, the role which Henry Day wished him to fill. They established a fatal partnership.

At first this partnership was restricted to Smith's management of J. W. Smith & Co., the general store located in the "Pentagon." But Smith eventually became the main intermediate channel for the funds that were sent westward by Jeremiah Day & Co., and he was soon engaged, more or less directly, in all of Day's businesses which drew on these funds. He purchased goods, expanded into corollary lines, and in general boomed the non-railroad interests in which Henry Day was engaged to fantastic proportions. It is possible to trace in horrified fascination a typical, gradual expansion by Smith. From a modest grocery department, existing merely as an adjunct to the dry-goods business, he drew Henry Day into a monster cheese speculation which, at the end, involved a commitment of more than $30,000.

Of all Day's managerial collaborators Smith was the only one who appeared to have a theory on which to work. He somehow understood the sense of destiny that Henry Day felt for Hudson. He particularized this vision into a gospel of what he called "mutual support" for the mercantile and manufacturing businesses which were being established by Day. It was his feeling that it was safe and profitable to keep adding new lines all the time, since, as the town was bound to grow, each business would "support the other" and the accumulation would strengthen the whole structure. Under this persuasion, so akin to his own beliefs, Henry Day began to go in deeper and deeper, at every turn involving his brother Jeremiah more deeply too.

Henry Day's separation from actual management made it all the more possible for Smith — as it did for the other managing partners to some extent — to take the bit between his teeth and expand at an independently rapid rate. Ashmun, the druggist, Sawyer, Marshall, and the others involved in the printing establishments all outdid themselves. Sawyer and Marshall, especially, passed from flourishing job printers into a massive and frozen publishing business, again independently, and quite possibly to a degree far removed from Day's original intention, for he knew little of the actual day-to-day details of any of his concerns.[84]

Crowning this whole structure of collaboration was the special position reserved for Henry Day himself. His role involved two main functions: planning and persuasion. It was he who conceived the ruling vision which governed all his particular commitments; he was, so to speak, the intellectual who provided the plans and general directives of the working staff of colleagues who were gathered about him.

This was his appropriate function since it was in these terms that he had rationalized the transition of his role as an academic intellectual to that of an active businessman. It was for this reason, obviously, that he spurned active managerial control of any of his enterprises. With his railroad ventures he adopted the same policy as flourished in his mercantile establishments, always having an adjutant who was engaged in active management. Such working colleagues, for instance, were James Butler on the Akron Branch and Moses Messer on the Clinton Line Railroad. It was Henry Day who wrote the manifestoes, made the proposals, and developed the plans necessary to bring his enterprises into being.

Why had he chosen this role? In his case, it might be said that the form of activity which he allowed himself was in fact the only one which his situation would permit. He lacked the aptitude and the training as well as the capacity for a more normal managerial role, as the whole course of his business career indicates in retrospect. But perhaps as important was the fact that his position and authority in business was, in large part, defined by his family, on whom he depended for capital, They, as a group, had labeled Henry Day an intellectual, an academician, a man of words and ideas. He could hardly alienate himself from this definition by plunging into business in a more normal, orthodox fashion. To accomplish the transition, moreover, from academician to businessman (albeit of a special kind) Henry Day had phrased his activities even to himself so as to present them in the light of a practical Christian endeavor appropriate to a minister. He was, he had argued, hastening the millennium, by ripening the conditions whereby the Kingdom of Christ might be achieved — an activity, in his eyes, which was the common task of his entire generation.

The special definition of his own role depended, of course, on a great many supporting factors. It is a tribute to Henry Day's clear-sighted perception of these requirements that he fulfilled them so completely. He gained allies to overcome the inertia and resistance of the town by awakening, as has been seen, the coöperation of its most prominent citizens. He mustered, too, a group of working auxiliaries who, for all their later failure, created almost in a single stroke a large business community fitting to his premises. Finally, he propounded a theory of his own position and the role of his plans which fitted closely to the cultural predisposition of the entire community. The commitment he obtained from the people around him eventually was so complete that when his enterprises finally fell they impoverished everyone. Were it not for the chance (?) loss of some records of their obligations, the town might have been entirely bankrupted.

XII

Between 1850 and 1853, Henry Day pushed his plans for Hudson for all they were worth. And, by 1853, he had constructed a truly impressive façade. A whole string of railroads were under his control. He had acquired almost a round dozen of other businesses, all of them apparently profitable and expanding, all with capital available for their growing needs, all apparently on the threshold of great and permanent prosperity. Within one year, however, the entire structure began to collapse, suddenly, crazily, and completely. Within two years, only the ruins of his empire were left, but for the next two decades scavengers were to hunt among these ruins to retrieve some part of what they had lost, or determinedly to try to resurrect some shattered fragment.

The first crack in the solid front appeared in the printing and publishing business. Begun originally as Sawyer, Ingersoll & Co., this enterprise promised to be among the most profitable of all. Hudson was an intellectual center, the populace in the entire region were great readers, and all the new business firms in the region needed some printing in their work, as did the college, whose business Henry Day himself brought in. With such a prospect Sawyer and Ingersoll, the active managers, fell in with the mania for expansion, A type foundry was added, and the firm went into the business of selling printing equipment and supplies. Finally, it engaged in what proved to be the fatal venture of book publishing on a large scale. The choice of titles was unfortunate and more and more capital was swallowed up in an inventory of unsalable books. Finally, a crisis at hand, Henry Day intervened.

It is typical of his state of mind in such matters that he proceeded to create a new legal entity rather than to remedy the conditions that had brought about the impasse. Since he was aloof from the active management, and since he had but little knowledge of the actual business of printing and publishing, his solution for problems of this kind was standard. At his suggestion David Marshall, a native of Hudson whom he had interested in the enterprise, was appointed Trustee to take over the stock and obligations of Sawyer, Ingersoll & Co. Thereupon, David Marshall, Trustee, transferred the assets and liabilities thus received to David Marshall & Co., Day forming a new firm with the old force. This change brought not one penny of new capital into the business, but it did, for the moment, ease the pressure of creditors. Since no fundamental change had taken place in the direction of the business, however, it dragged on for a short time as it had before, until finally the pressure of debts forced another reorganization. This time Day obtained a new charter under the name of the Hudson Book Company, a new legal entity but again with the same old people. Newly printed stock certificates were pledged where a little fresh credit could be obtained and a steady, but thin, runnel of additional money was being poured into the dying firm from the funds sent to Ohio by Jeremiah Day.

In 1855, all expedients having proved inadequate, the firm fell, assigning its few assets and numerous liabilities to one E. G. Knight to dispose of as best he could for the satisfaction of the creditors. By now, however, this had become but one collapse among many not only for Henry Day, but for the family, for Jeremiah Day & Co. in New York had strained its resources beyond recovery and was forced to a day of reckoning. The terrible year, 1854, had completely constricted the money market, and by this time the firm was committed too deeply in the illiquid Ohio transactions to extricate itself.[85]

Early in January 1854, Charles Day, writing from Apalachicola, Florida, had sent out a caution. The hovering depression, he felt, required a slowing down of the Ohio projects.

Be not *too* fast [he warned Henry], you might break down. There is considerable danger of this in you Western men and with yourselves you might involve the destruction of others. . . Jerry writes in the most despairing mood and we help him all we can, we have already sent him [$] 100,000 but this is not enough, we cannot do much more. You would have a great deal to answer for if Jerry *did* fall.[86]

In New York, Jeremiah was truly in despair. "I am used up here," he mournfully reported to Henry. "I have used up all the means and ways I know of to raise money. . . I do not know what to do, I wish I had given up a month ago." He had, by this time, advanced one hundred thousand dollars, $80,000 of which Smith had put out without any possibility of ready liquidation.

I have been trying for the last two years [he complained], to get Smith's amount down but instead of that we get in deeper every day. . . He will let money fly as soon as he gets it in all directions and when he remits us $1 he draws for 2 so it has been since he has got under way. There is no plan or system for paying the drafts as they mature. . . I suppose every debt he owes far and near is paid, but we are left to shift the best way we can. . .[87]

In sixty days the last agony was over, Jeremiah Day & Co. was forced to suspend:

I have had to succumb a little sooner than I expected [he wrote his brother Henry]. I saw it would be difficult to keep on much longer and as money continues to grow tighter, I am convinced I could not have gone on much further. I have told Smith to continue on if he manages right, but he has to go to work and redeem his stock and do a great deal less and get things down to a manageable condition. . . I have regretted very much to come to this. It may be for the best. I expect there will be a grand smash and the sooner you stop with your railroad work the better — or at least do little. . .[88]

There was a final pathetic P.S. "You must give Smith no peace. You must make him stand firm . . . not give to the first thing that comes up. He needs firmness and unless he has a little put into him occasionally, he will not keep on."

Henry Day refused, at first, to yield to circumstances. He hurried East, pledged such securities as he could lay his hands on to raise cash. Letters flew to New Haven and Hartford pleading for a little ready money, but it seemed as if all the cash had been sponged up by the depression. His father-in-law and brother-in-law raised a little money on their own names to bolster up his tottering ventures, but this lasted only a short time. He turned again to Charles and Jeremiah Day in a final plea for help. "I cannot see," his brother Charles replied coldly, "how either of your brothers can serve you. . . Doing more is not to be thought of. Let us hope, however, that through the assistance of others or some arrangement with your creditors you can continue to float." [89]

Henry Day couldn't continue to float. The printing business suspended. The lumber company suspended with $35,000 liabilities over assets. J. W. Smith & Co. suspended with $100,000 liabilities and $80,000 nominal assets which shrank as ice under a hot sun in the depressed markets of the time. The "Pentagon" block succumbed also, and the Savings Society failed for $50,000 net liabilities and with it all the grandiose plans for real estate development. Nor were the railroads spared. Henry Day, in a final burst of charismatic eloquence, persuaded the contractors to take over blocks of bonds for their work and wait for redemption until the entire roads were completed. But this couldn't last. In after years, late at night, local townspeople stole out to rob the abandoned culverts of the stone of which they were built. Periodically, new hopes would be raised that the roads would be completed and false hopes were cherished to the very end of the nineteenth century, but nothing ever came of them. In time, the grading was effaced and no trace of the proposed lines was left.[90]

Henry Day tried to salvage what he could from the wreckage, but little remained. His personal property he saved from his creditors by assigning it to his father-in-law, using as a technicality an earlier advance by the latter of $3500 to found his planing mill. For the next three years, he remained in Hudson clearing away the tangle of claims and braving the storm of suits which followed his downfall, fixing the terms of the final, painful settlements with his creditors.

XIII

When he saw the full extent of the debacle in Hudson, Henry Day realized, as well, that his short career as a businessman was over forever. He slid back, at once, and apparently without reflection, into the groove that had been carved for him from early youth. Even as his businesses were falling on every side he persuaded his friends to join about him and provide him with a graceful exit from his predicament. On February 13, 1855, a committee was formed to organize a new school in Hudson to be known as the Hudson Female Seminary. Two weeks later, the articles of association were drawn and on March 17 the group (including Humphrey and Smith) met to consider plans for the formal organization of the academy. The scheme bore the cachet of the Day approach to crisis: form a new organization, make new plans, and somehow thereby escape from the dilemmas of earlier, inadequate ventures.

The business collapse, however, was too great, the repercussions of the failure too deep for the town to tolerate such a move. Pressure must have been exerted to disassociate Day from the venture, if not to abandon the project altogether. In any case, on July 14, 1855 Henry Day resigned from the committee formed to organize the school, and the project dissolved.[91]

The pattern, however was steadfast. Three years later, when the wrangling over the remains of his erstwhile empire had somewhat subsided, Henry Day left Hudson to become President of the Ohio Female Seminary at College Hill, near Cincinnati. His business career was finished.

Although his efforts at being an entrepreneur had resulted in failure, his career is instructive for general insight into the roles of men in business. By training and persuasion his role had been that of a professional intellectual. He had been given thorough instruction and by more indirect cues a mental image of what was appropriate and fitting for a man committed to such work. In Ohio, for reasons already given, he had cast himself for another role — one involving clearly deviant behavior from that for which he had been trained. His career explicitly shows how he tried to link that new role — of businessman — to the cultural patterns of his time as viewed by one in his social position, and, in the end, how he failed because his definition of his role as entrepreneur was inadequate to the demands made upon it by the objective projects he chose to pursue.

In later years, he did not reproach himself for what he had done. In sketching his life in a brief biography for the fortieth reunion of his class, he remembered (in the third person) his business career:

> It cannot be supposed [he wrote], that a quarter of a century of the enterprising part of a man's life in Western Society would leave him undistractedly to the quiet pursuits of educational life. . . He yielded to the irresistible pressure from the fermenting elements of a rising civilization . . . so far as to accept controlling positions in the conduct of divers public improvements of great magnitude, in which, very successful in a part . . . he never reaped any pecuniary harvest for himself . . . nor left any void of aching regret in his reminiscences of some years of laborious exertion in this direction.[92]

This was the only public explanation he ever made of his business career, or for that matter, the only apology.

VII

The American Industrial Elite in the 1870's

Their Social Origins

By Frances W. Gregory and Irene D. Neu

Despite the importance of business in the United States, as elsewhere, the social origins of business leaders, the social sources of business leadership, have received but little attention from scholars. A few biographies and autobiographies have tended to point up the spectacular and the unusual, with the result that the origins of a handful have been attributed to the many, though the grounds of attribution have remained vague. What have been the actual origins of American business leaders? And what have been the consequences, for the business community and for society at large, of the actual process of recruitment? These are questions of great magnitude and are not to be resolved by the findings of a single study. It is felt, however, that the information presented in this paper is a contribution toward the eventual answers.

The characteristics of the industrial leader in the United States, as tradition had sketched him, reflect the idealism of the American heritage. Specifically, his was the Carnegie story. A poor immigrant boy arrived on the shores of a new nation which abounded in endless opportunity. As the boy was the son of a workingman, he had little or no formal education and was forced by circumstances to seek employment at a tender age. His first job was a lowly one, but in short order he rose to prominence, usually as a result of cleverness, diligence, or luck. In this manner, the top-level businessman was but a generation removed from poverty and anonymity.

This story was not unheard of before the golden age of American industrial expansion that followed the Civil War. It was already frequently told in the early decades of the nineteenth century when the merchant was at the apex of the business ladder. It is the theme of the short biography of Amos Lawrence, suggestively entitled *The Poor Boy and Merchant Prince*.[1] Nathan Appleton, the Boston textile magnate and backer of Webster, also voiced this thesis of freedom of ascent to financial success and industrial prominence, and always projected himself, indeed with more or less accuracy, as an example of this fluidity of social and economic structure.[2] It was only with the appearance on the American scene of such businessmen as Carnegie, Vanderbilt, and Rockefeller, however, that this thesis found its major exemplars, and in the history books and biographies of succeeding generations their lives continue to be used to buttress the tradition.[3]

Only within the last twenty years has this tradition been seriously questioned. F. W. Taussig and C. S. Joslyn in *American Business Leaders: A Study in Social Origins and Social Stratification*, published in 1932, cast doubt upon the widely held belief in the easy ascent of the poor boy to business prestige and financial power.[4] They showed that the way was considerably more accessible to the sons of the middle and upper classes, and advanced the hypothesis that the absence of representation of the lower classes among business leaders was chiefly the result of a lack of innate ability not lack of opportunity.[5] Studies of this subject by other scholars have appeared from time to time in learned journals. For the most part, these have been concerned with but small groups of businessmen or with but one or two characteristics of larger groups, and their value has been limited for these reasons.

Recently William Miller published two essays in which he analyzed the backgrounds of 190 American business leaders of the first decade of the twentieth century and compared their social characteristics with those of the population generally.[6] In these essays he set forth the conclusion that the men who held the top positions — essentially presidencies or board chairmanships — in the largest industrial and financial institutions in the United States during this period were recruited, in great part, from a highly select segment of the population. Typical of these magnates in the early twentieth century was the son of a professional or business man of colonial American heritage, born in some American city or town of more than 2500 persons. This executive very likely had attended high school and had had a 40 per cent chance of reaching college. Moreover, he certainly was over 16 and was likely to be over 19 before going to work. In all probability, he was a member of the middle or upper class.[7] Unlike Taussig and Joslyn, who offer no acceptable evidence for their thesis of innate ability among the business elite,[8] Miller presents verifiable data to support his contention that certain social characteristics marked a man as good material for the leading business positions.

These findings prompted the Research Center in Entrepreneurial History at Harvard University to conduct an investigation into the origins of a group of business leaders of an earlier period and to compare the findings with Miller's for the period 1901–1910. This is the first report of that investigation.

II

At the outset it was decided that the period for study should be the decade 1870–1879, one recent enough to assure adequate biographical information for a considerable number of men, yet not too close to that of 1901–1910 for purposes of comparison and contrast. To keep the number of business leaders within manageable limits, men were chosen from three major fields only: textiles, steel, and railroads. Textiles and steel were selected because the first was the oldest large-scale industry in America and the second was then the newest. Railroads were an obvious choice for they represented by far the largest agglomeration of capital in the period.

Once these three industries had been decided upon, the next step was to ascertain the key top jobs in the major companies. In textiles the treasurer and agent of each establishment were used. The treasurer was the chief executive officer and had charge of the financial end of the business, including the purchase of cotton from the South. The agent was the local authority on the job and supervised the construction of the factory, the manufacture of cloth, and the employment of labor.[9] In steel corporations the top men were taken to be the president, the vice-president, and the general manager or superintendent. This industry, however, was still organized largely on a partnership basis, and since there was no general way of determining the relative interests of the several partners in an establishment, all known partners were included.[10] The top men in the railroads were taken to be presidents, vice-presidents, and general managers.

The men in textiles represented all cotton manufacturing concerns having an authorized capital of more than $1,000,000 and a spindlage of at least 70,000; all wool manufacturing companies with an authorized capital of $600,000 or more and at least 49 sets of cards; and the single American silk company which had a capital of $1,000,000.[11] The men in steel covered all eleven Bessemer and all fifteen open-hearth plants in the United States in 1878, as well as the six crucible plants which produced 10,000 tons or more that year, or were attached to ironworks having a combined production of iron and steel in excess of 10,000 tons.[12] The railroaders represented all companies in their field capitalized in excess of $24,000,000 and having construction and equipment accounts in excess of $38,000,000, according to the census of 1880.

In all, seventy-seven companies supplied men for the list. These were the thirty largest textile companies, the thirty largest steel manufacturers, and the seventeen largest railroads in the country. The names of the leaders themselves were found, for the most part, in industrial directories.[13] The final aggregate of 303 men includes 102 from textiles, 100 from steel, and 101 from railroads. No men known to have held the positions named above in any of these companies were omitted from the list,[14] though, of course, for some not all the information sought could be found.

A list of the men and the companies used in this study is presented in the Appendix to this article, pp. 204–211.

III

Though the men with whom this study is concerned were all industrialists and represented but three industries in an economy which was already highly diversified, these three industries were among the four largest in the United States.[15] Since the results of this study will be compared with Miller's for the period 1901–1910, other things should also be noted here. While about 20 per cent of Miller's men were bankers and life insurance executives, and an additional 15 per cent were in public utilities, these activities are represented in the present study only by executives who were also in textiles, steel, or railroads. Further, it must be remembered that Miller writes largely of the bureaucratic business hierarchies which had become common by 1910, while the present essay is concerned with an age when even some of the topmost companies were still organized as family concerns. This certainly was largely the case in steel but much less so in textiles in which most firms were already incorporated and career lines of a professional, managerial type could be found. A bureaucracy, it is true, was emerging in railroads by the 1870's but even here its organization was far from complete.[16]

Whether bureaucrats or family-made men or general entrepreneurs, however, it is clear that the men both in Miller's sample and our own were among the topmost business leaders of their time.

IV

The businessmen in Miller's group, averaging approximately 50 years of age in 1900, were considerably younger than men in similar positions today.[17] The men of the 1870's, in turn, were younger still; their average age, brought down, to be sure, by the sizable representation of men other

than those at the very top, was 45.[18] But even these men were already
in the prime of life, nor had they, as the tradition would have it, spent
much of their time in becoming accustomed to a strange culture in a
strange land. Some, of course, like English-born John Fallon in textiles,
and Scotsman Thomas Carnegie in steel, were born abroad. That these
men, however, were exceptional, not typical, among the industrial elite
of the 1870's, as among the business leaders of the later decade, the
accompanying table attests.

TABLE 1

American Industrial Leaders of the 1870's by Industry and Region of Birthplace *

Birthplace	Textiles	Railroads	Steel	Total	Miller Totals ** (1901–1910)
	%	%	%	%	%
New England	90	39	24	51	18
Middle Atlantic	1	40	50	29	37
East North Central	1	4	7	4	22
South	1	6	1	3	9
West	..	1	..	1	4
U. S., Unspecified	..	..	4	2	..
United States	93	90	86	90	90
Foreign	7	10	14	10	10
Total Cases † (= 100%)	87	80	80	247	187

* These are census regions. Combined in "South" are south Atlantic, south central, west south central; in "West" west north central, mountain, Pacific.
** Statistics in this column, in all the tables, are taken from Miller's "American Historians and the Business Elite," unless otherwise credited.
† As stated in the text, the total number of men in the 1870's group is 303: 102 in textiles, 101 in railroads, and 100 in steel. The number in the Miller group is 190. In this and all succeeding tables where total cases are fewer than just stated, the difference indicates the number of men about whom information was unavailable.

Besides Fallon, five other textile men are known to have been born
abroad. Two were the Cumnock brothers (a third brother was born in
America) whose father, a freeholder of Glasgow, was "a man of fair
estate." [19] Andrew F. Swapp, another immigrant, like Fallon, was from
a working-class family. Of all those born abroad, only Alexander G.
Cumnock ever reached the treasurership and he, of a company too small
to be included in this study. The others were agents only. In steel, ten
men in addition to Carnegie were born outside the United States. At
least six of these — the three Chisholms, Reginald H. Bulley, William
Butcher, and Otto Wuth — appear to have come from substantial middle-
class backgrounds. In the railroad group there is not a single instance of
a "poor immigrant" working his way up the ladder. Of the eight men
known to have been born in foreign countries, Jacob D. Cox, John
Murray Forbes, and Azariah Boody were the children of American parents

and therefore could hardly be called "immigrants." Of the five men who may properly be so labeled, James B. Hodgskin, James McHenry, and Gustavus A. Nicolls were the sons of well-established professional men, Alexander Mitchell was the son of a "well-to-do" [20] farmer, and Peter H. Watson apparently had been trained in the law before the time at which he arrived in the United States, after having been forced to leave Canada for his part in the rebellion of 1837.

Not only were few of these business leaders immigrants; but few were the sons of immigrants. Of the native-born in the group about whom information is available, only 3 per cent were the sons of foreign-born fathers.

TABLE 2

American-born Industrial Leaders of the 1870's by Industry and Region
of Father's Birthplace

Father's Birthplace	Textiles	Railroads	Steel	Total	Miller Totals * (1901–1910)
	%	%	%	%	%
New England	98	49	36	65	29
Middle Atlantic	1	32	42	22	34
East North Central	..	..	..	..	5
South	..	4	2	2	13
West	..	..	..	..	..
U. S., unspecified	..	13	12	8	8
United States	99	98	92	97	89
Foreign	1	2	8	3	11
Total Cases (= 100%)	72	53	50	175	158

* These totals, which do not include the father's birthplace in the case of men who were themselves foreign-born, were compiled by Miller especially for this table, and are not the same as those which appear in Table III of "American Historians and the Business Elite," where fathers of foreign-born leaders were included.

It would seem, therefore, that the top-level leadership in American industry in the 1870's, as in the 1900's, was native-born and of native families. Indeed, the immigrant ancestors of these families, in all likelihood, had come over to America in the seventeenth century.[21] Not John Fallon, therefore, who came to this country as an expert in calico-printing, but George Atkinson, Edmund Dwight, or Augustus Lowell, men born in New England whose fathers and grandfathers were also born there, would seem to be characteristic of the topmost men in textiles. In steel the typical leader was not Thomas Carnegie, but such a man as James I. Bennett or William Sellers, both born in Pennsylvania to fathers who were native Pennsylvanians. A typical railroader might be John H. Devereux, who was born in Boston, and whose father was a native of

Massachusetts; or Charles E. Perkins, who was born in Cincinnati of New England parents and whose relatives were still prominent Bostonians.

Perkins' history, moreover, illustrates the shift in the geographic origins of American business leaders away from storied New England, a shift that took place, perhaps, a good deal earlier than has commonly been supposed. By the 1900's, indeed, as Miller's totals show (see Table 1), fewer than two in ten of the men studied were themselves born in New England; more striking, fewer than three in ten of their fathers had been born there (see Table 2). For the 1870's, of course, the proportions of New Englanders are considerably greater; but even so, including the

TABLE 3

American Industrial Leaders of the 1870's by Industry and
Paternal Family's Origin *

Family Origin	Textiles	Railroads	Steel	Totals	Miller Totals (1901–1910)
	%	%	%	%	%
England and Wales	80	59	69	71	53
Ireland	9	10	13	11	14
Scotland	9	13	2	7	7
Canada	..	1	5	2	3
British Empire, other or unspecified	..	..	..	..	5
British Empire	98	83	89	91	82
Germany **	2	4	9	4	12
Other countries	..	13	2	5	6
Total Cases (= 100%)	65	52	58	175	162

* Or country of leader's own origin if he was the first in the family to settle in America. In either case, *last country* before settlement in America.
** In this category are included those states which in 1871 were united to form the German Empire.

almost 100 per cent representation of the textile sample,[22] about half the whole group was born there; and of those not in the textile group, considerably less than half had New England-born fathers.

The decline of New England as a source of business leadership is paralleled by the falling off between the 1870's and the 1900's in men of British but especially of English origins. Even so, such men continued to be represented at the top of American business far out of proportion to their representation in the population generally.[23]

Most of the leaders of the 1870's had been reared in a period of religious ferment and fragmentation of some of the older established sects. Aside from the Unitarians, however, most of whom must either have embraced this faith themselves or been the sons of men who did, only fourteen of the group are known to have shifted from one denomina-

ROCKMONT COLLEGE LIBRARY

tion to another, and among these it was more often a shift to the older elite Episcopal church than to any one of the more zealous or more intellectual ones.[24] This, as Table 4 shows, served to bring those who shifted into closer conformity with their associates in the business community.

TABLE 4

American Industrial Leaders of the 1870's by Industry and
Religious Background *

Denomination	Textiles	Railroads	Steel	Total	Miller Totals ** (1901–1910)
	%	%	%	%	%
Episcopal	24	21	29	25	25
Presbyterian	..	16	26	14	21
Congregational	42	18	6	22	.. †
Unitarian	20	9	2	10	6
Methodist	4	5	8	6	9
Baptist	..	5	8	4	5
Quaker	4	7	13	8	.. †
Other Protestant	..	12	6	6	8
Protestant, unspecified	6	7	2	5	16
Protestant	100	100	100	100	90
Catholic	..	..	..	..	7
Jewish	..	..	..	..	3
Total Cases (= 100%)	50	43	51	144	174

* In almost all instances this is the religion of the leader himself and probably of his family as well. In instances where a shift of religion is known to have occurred, only the religion in which the subject was reared is counted.
** Statistics in this column are taken from Miller, "The Recruitment of the American Business Elite," p. 249.
† An insignificant number included in "other Protestant."

V

There is in American literature considerable evidence of the view that the business leader, if not a refugee from abroad, was at any rate a refugee from the farm. Nor is this theme confined to fiction. Andrew Carnegie, himself the son of a city worker, was but stating a popular belief when he wrote in 1886, "Most great men, it is true, have been born and brought up in the country. . ."[25] In speaking of the 1870's, one of the outstanding historians of our own day has said, "the cities were full of wealthy newcomers of rural antecedents. . ."[26]; but he cites as his only reference William Dean Howells' Silas Lapham, a fictional Boston capitalist who was born and reared on a Vermont farm. Certainly there were such cases in real life, too, in the 1870's as in all periods of American history, but the statistics in Table 5 show that these cases were hardly representative in our period, and this at a time, be it remembered, when by far the larger part of the nation's population was composed of farm dwellers.

According to the table, half the industrial leaders of 1870–1879 were born in places with more than 2500 persons as compared with 59 per cent of the business leaders of 1901–1910. But even the remaining half in the 1870's was not necessarily of rural origin. A population below 2500 is roughly the measure used by the Bureau of the Census, both in designat-

TABLE 5

American-born Industrial Leaders by Industry and Size of Birthplace *

Size of Birthplace	Textiles	Railroads	Steel	Total	Miller Totals (1901–1910)
	%	%	%	%	%
Under 2500	38	59	57	50	41
2500–8000	26	21	20	23	19
Over 8000	36	20	23	27	40
Total Cases (= 100%)	80	71	66	217	174

* Population is from the census nearest each man's date of birth. The Miller totals include a few instances in which the place where a man was reared, rather than his birthplace, was used.

ing modern rural areas and in going back into the past for purpose of comparison. Yet it is scarcely sound to suggest, on that account, that every community having a population of less than 2500 in 1825 (the year in which the "average" industrial leader of 1870–1879 was born), was essentially rural. Take, for instance, St. Albans, Vermont, which even as late as 1830 falls into our "rural" category population-wise, but which, when J. Gregory Smith, the railroad man, was born there in 1818, was already a flourishing community with many of the refinements of the urban life of the time.[27] Smith's father was a lawyer and businessman, and of Smith himself it has been said, "established position and affluence were his birthright." [28] Another example is Erie, Pennsylvania, in which railroad man John F. Tracy was born in 1827. With a population of 1465 in 1830, Erie was a bustling lake port, and a rapidly expanding business center. Tracy's father was a railroad contractor; the academy which the boy attended had been a feature of Erie life since 1806.[29]

Nor are Erie and St. Albans the only examples. It is perhaps a fairer measure, therefore, to count as having been brought up in rural surroundings only those men actually born on farms. When this is done, the rural classification in the 1870's, as shown in Table 6, drops from 50 to 25 per cent, and the farm boy who becomes a successful businessman appears a much less frequent phenomenon.

The prevalence of businessmen among the fathers of the leaders in our group is noteworthy. While the term "businessman" is interpreted to include such widely separated occupations as bank president and peddler,[30] only two fathers fit into the first category and but one in the second. One-third of the fathers designated as businessmen were merchants; another third were manufacturers. Among the remaining third were three contractors or builders, two sea captains, a supercargo, a river captain, a railroad superintendent, a gristmill operator, the owner of a country store, a newspaper publisher, and a bookseller. The fathers of

TABLE 6

American Industrial Leaders of the 1870's by Industry and
Father's Occupation *

Occupation	Textiles	Railroads	Steel	Total	Miller Totals ** (1901–1910)
	%	%	%	%	%
Businessman	57	49	48	51	55
Professional	7	16	16	13	22
Farmer	19	31	27	25	14
Public Official	2	4	..	3	7
Worker	15	..	11	8	2
Total cases (= 100%)	67	70	57	194	167

* Some fathers engaged in more than one occupation. The one used here was dominant in the period in which each leader was reared.
** These figures adjusted by Miller, in line with the criteria used for the 1870 study. The adjustments result in but very slight changes.

seventeen textile leaders were themselves textile men, while the fathers of a like number in the steel industry had preceded their sons as iron and steel manufacturers. Only seven railroaders were the sons of men who had engaged in railroading.

Such crude occupational categories as we have used are not necessarily precise criteria of social status in any of its various meanings. "Farmer" may include men who were able to afford education for their children, while some petty businessmen could not do so. And if, at one end of the scale among business and professional men we find those who could not give their children higher education, at the other end are fathers who were already at the top in their respective fields and men of more than local power and prestige. Precise calculations of class or status do not seem feasible, but every effort to take all known factors into account reëmphasizes the general impression that most — perhaps 90 per cent — of the industrial leaders in our group were reared in a middle- or upper-class milieu.

That the education of most of these men was not limited to what the little red schoolhouse had to offer is indicated by Table 7, which shows that the large majority at least attained the equivalent of high school training, while a sizable number also had a taste of college. This is particularly apparent in the textile group, almost half the men whose edu-

TABLE 7

TABLE 7

American Industrial Leaders of the 1870's by Industry and Highest
Educational Level Attained *

Education	Textiles	Railroads	Steel	Total	Miller Totals (1901–1910)
	%	%	%	%	%
Grammar School	25	22	43	30	22
High School	31	48	20	33	37
College	44	30	37	37	41
Total cases (= 100%)	59	64	60	183	183

* The many types of older schools have been reduced to modern terminology. Included in "grammar school" are institutions called by that name, as well as district, public, common, and similar schools. In "high school" are included academies and other institutions of similar rank. Counted among grammar-school boys are those who had little or no formal education as well as graduates; among high-school boys, all those who attended whether graduates or not. The same rule was followed for college men. A few leaders who had private tutors well into their teens but did not attend college are with the high-school group.

cation is known having attended college. Among the railroad men, moreover, while not as many had gone to college, almost half had had professional training, usually in law or engineering.

A natural consequence of a longer educational period is delay in starting to earn a living. Table 8 shows that almost half the men for whom data were to be had did not go to work before they had reached their nineteenth birthday. Less than one-quarter were set to work when they were younger than sixteen. These figures and Miller's for the later decade point up the fact that in the earlier period, as in the later, we are dealing with a favored segment of the population.

TABLE 8

American Industrial Leaders of the 1870's by Industry and Age on Going to Work *

Age	Textiles	Railroads	Steel	Totals	Miller Totals (1901–1910)
	%	%	%	%	%
15 or under	30	23	18	23	20
16–18	21	35	38	32	35
19 and over	49	42	44	45	45
Total cases (= 100%)	57	62	57	176	179

* This is age on taking first regular business, professional, or other job (except work on father's or other relative's farm) after leaving school.

VI

Was the typical industrial leader of the 1870's, then, a "new man," an escapee from the slums of Europe or from the paternal farm? Did he rise by his own efforts from a boyhood of poverty? Was he as innocent of education and of formal training as has often been alleged? He seems to have been none of these things. American by birth, of a New England father, English in national origin, Congregational, Presbyterian, or Episcopal in religion, urban in early environment, he was rather born and bred in an atmosphere in which business and a relatively high social standing were intimately associated with his family life. Only at about eighteen did he take his first regular job, prepared to rise from it, moreover, not by a rigorous apprenticeship begun when he was virtually a child, but by an academic education well above average for the times.

APPENDIX

Men and Companies Used in the Study of the Industrial Elite of the 1870's *

THE TEXTILE LEADERS

Cotton Mills	*Men*
Amoskeag Manufacturing Company	Amory, William
	Clark, Daniel
	Livermore, Thomas L.
	Straw, Ezekiel A.
Atlantic Cotton Mills	Battles, Joseph P.
	Gray, William
	Gray, William, Jr.
	Saltonstall, Henry
Boott Cotton Mills	Cumnock, Alexander G.
	Lowell, Augustus
	Rogers, Richard D.
Continental Mills	Abbott, Stephen I.
	Davis, Ezekiel S.
	Wood, William B.
Dwight Manufacturing Company	Balch, Edward F.
	Bedlow, George W.
	Cumnock, James W.
	Freeland, Charles W.
	Nichols, J. Howard
	Nye, George H.

* Each man is listed with the company in which he first attained the highest position he held in this decade, and only there.

Great Falls Manufacturing Company	Burleigh, George W.
	Dalton, Charles H.
	Cumnock, John
	Hussey, Daniel
Harmony Mills	Johnston, Robert
	Thorn, William E.
Laconia Company	Codman, Edward W.
	Dexter, George
	Haines, Augustine
Lawrence Manufacturing Company	Coolidge, T. Jefferson
Lonsdale Company	Goddard, William
	Kilburn, George
	Pratt, George A.
Lyman Mills	Bush, Samuel L.
	Davis, Jones S.
	Lovering, Quimby W.
Manchester Mills	Amory, Charles
	Chapman, George R.
	Palfrey, John C.
	Smith, Waterman
	Stone, Joseph
	Thompson, H. M.
	Thompson, William H.
	Wade, A. M.
Manville Company	Bowen, Holder B.
	Handy, Russell
	Taft, John A.
	Tucker, William A.
Massachusetts Cotton Mills	Atkinson, George
	Bartlett, Homer
	Battles, Frank F.
Merrimack Manufacturing Company	Crowninshield, Francis B.
	Ludlan, Joseph
Nashua Manufacturing Company	Amory, James S.
	Crombie, Daniel D.
	Hussey, Oliver
	Maxfield, Rufus A.
Naumkeag Steam Cotton Company	Dwight, Edmund
	Kilburn, John
	Sullivan, Henry D.
Pacific Mills	Chapin, William C.
	Edmands, J. Wiley
	Fallon, John
	Little, James L.
Pepperell Manufacturing Company	Blanchard, John A.
	Haines, Ferguson
	Haines, William P.

Ponemah Mills	Atwood, James S.
	Taft, Edward P.
A. and W. Sprague	Chafee, Zechariah
	Dyer, Henry
	Sprague, Amasa
Tremont and Suffolk Mills	Ayer, James C.
	Battles, Charles F.
	Birdseye, John C.
	Shaw, Thomas S.
Wamsutta Mills	Bennett, Thomas, Jr.
	Kilburn, Edward
	Kilburn, Hiram
	Pierce, A. Granville

Woolen Mills

Assabet Manufacturing Company	Browne, T. Quincy
	Maynard, Amory
	Maynard, Lorenzo
Harris Woolen Company	Boutelle, Newell A.
	Cole, Joseph E.
	Farnum, Darius D.
Lowell Manufacturing Company	Fay, Samuel
	Jewett, David B.
	Swapp, Andrew F.
Middlesex Woolen Company	Avery, William C.
	Fay, Richard S.
	Fox, Gustavus V.
Salisbury Mills	Francis, Charles
	Gardner, John
	Steere, Marcus D. T.
Washington Mills	Coe, Henry F.
	Kirk, Parker C.
	Salisbury, W. H.
	Scott, Robert
	Scott, Robert S.

Silk Mill

Cheney Brothers	Cheney, Charles
	Cheney, Frank W.

THE RAILROAD LEADERS

Company	*Men*
Central Pacific	Stanford, Leland
Chesapeake and Ohio	Dunn, W. M. S.
	Hatch, A. S.
	Huntington, Collis P.
	Wickham, William C.

Chicago and North-Western	Dunlap, George L.
	Howe, James H.
	Hughitt, Marvin
	Keep, Albert
	Pierson, Henry R.
	Porter, Henry H.
	Sykes, Martin L.
	Tracy, John F.
Chicago, Burlington and Quincy	Forbes, John M.
	Harris, Robert
	Joy, James F.
	Perkins, Charles E.
	Walker, James M.
Chicago, Milwaukee and St. Paul	Merrill, Sherburne S.
(consolidation of Chicago and Milwaukee and	Mitchell, Alexander
Milwaukee and St. Paul)	Sage, Russell
	Wadsworth, Julius
Lake Shore and Michigan Southern	Clark, Horace F.
	Newell, John
	Schell, Augustus
	Vanderbilt, William H.
New York Central and Hudson River	Rutter, James H.
	Vanderbilt, Cornelius
	Vanderbilt, Cornelius, II
	Vanderbilt, William K.
New York, Lake Erie and Western	Blanchard, George R.
(successor to the Erie)	Clarke, James C.
	Diven, Alexander S.
	Dix, John A.
	Fisk, James, Jr.
	Gould, Jay
	Jewett, Hugh J.
	Robinson, Lucius
	Tyson, Henry
	Watson, Peter H.
New York, Ontario and Western	Culver, Delos E.
(successor to the New York and Oswego	Littlejohn, DeWitt C.
Midland)	Opdyke, George
	Stevens, John G.
	Wheeler, Elisha P.
New York, Pennsylvania and Ohio	Clark, James F.
(successor to Atlantic and Great Western)	Devereux, John H.
	Gardner, John
	Hodgskin, James B.
	McClellan, George B.
	McHenry, James
	O'Brien, Robert E.
	Sweetser, Henry F.
	Wright, George B.

Northern Pacific

Billings, Frederick
Cass, George W.
Rice, Richard D.
Sargent, Homer E.
Smith, J. Gregory
Stark, George
Wright, Charles B.

Pennsylvania

Cassatt, Alexander J.
Lombaert, Herman J.
Roberts, George B.
Smith, Edmund
Thomson, Frank
Thomson, J. Edgar

Philadelphia and Reading

Gowen, Franklin B.
Jones, J. Wyman
Nicolls, Gustavus A.

St. Louis and San Francisco
   (successor to Atlantic and Pacific)

Baker, James
Coffin, William H.
Crocker, Uriel
Dulaney, Woodford H.
Fish, James D.
Griswold, William D.
Hayes, Francis B.
Hays, Samuel
Peirce, Andrew, Jr.
Stockwell, Alden B.

Southern Pacific

Colton, David D.
Crocker, Charles
Crocker, Charles F.

Union Pacific

Ames, Oliver
Atkins, Elisha
Dillon, Sidney
Duff, John
Scott, Thomas A.

Wabash, St. Louis and Pacific
   (consolidation of the Wabash and the St. Louis,
   Kansas City and Northern)

Anderson, Adna
Bates, Barton
Blackstone, Timothy B.
Boody, Azariah
Cox, Jacob D.
Drummond, John N.
Field, Cyrus W.
Fox, Elias W.
Hoge, William
Hopkins, Amos L.
Jackson, John
Lewis, B. W., Jr.
Roosevelt, James A.

THE STEEL LEADERS

Bessemer Works	*Men*
Albany and Rensselaer Iron and Steel Company (consolidation of Albany Iron Works and Rensselaer Iron Works)	Corning, Erastus Corning, Erastus, Jr. Griswold, Chester Griswold, John. A. Walker, James E.
Bethlehem Iron Company	Fritz, John Hunt, Alfred Linderman, Garrett B. Thurston, William W.
Cambria Iron Company	Morrell, Daniel J. Townsend, Edward Y. Wood, Charles S. Wurts, Charles S.
Cleveland Rolling Mill Company *	Chisholm, Henry Chisholm, Wilson B. Stone, Amasa B.
Edgar Thomson Steel Company, Limited	Carnegie, Thomas M. Jones, William R. McCandless, David
Joliet Steel Company	Brooks, William S. Leith, Alexander J. Meeker, Arthur B. Scott, John G. Smith, Horace S. Torrence, Joseph T.
Lackawanna Iron and Coal Company	Hatfield, Edwin F. Scranton, William W.
North Chicago Rolling Mill Company	Burt, S. P. Potter, Orrin W.
Pennsylvania Steel Company *	Bent, Luther S. Felton, Samuel M.
Union Iron and Steel Company	Chisholm, William H. Stubbs, Jabez B.
Vulcan Steel Company	Ferguson, David K. Garrison, Daniel E. Garrison, Daniel R. Shinn, William P.
Open Hearth Works	
Bay State Iron Company	Crooker, Ralph Dexter, F. Gordon Hooper, Samuel Richards, J. Avery Whitmore, Charles O.

* This company also manufactured open-hearth steel in the 1870's.

Beaver Falls Steel Works
   (Abel, Pedder and Co.)

Abel, George (?)
Pedder, John

Canton Steel Works
   (Bolton, Bulley and Co.
   Bolton, Myers and Co.)

Aultman, Cornelius
Bolton, Ogden
Bulley, Reginald H.
Myers, Isidore
Wuth, Otto

Midvale Steel Works
   (successor to William Butcher Steel Works)

Brinley, Charles A.
Butcher, William
Durfee, William F.
Huston, Samuel
Sellers, William

Nashua Iron and Steel Company

Sweeney, Alfred
Wellman, Samuel K.

New Jersey Steel and Iron Company

Cooper, Edward
Stokes, Joseph

Norway Iron Works
   (Naylor and Co.)

Huntington, Edward B.
King, George P.
Schlesinger, Barthold
Schlesinger, Sebastian B.

Otis Iron and Steel Company

Otis, Charles A.
Wellman, Samuel T.

Pittsburgh Steel Casting Company

Hainsworth, William
Irwin, James
Patterson, Alfred
Patterson, Henry W.

Roane Iron Company

Chamberlain, Hiram S.
Rathburn, William P.

St. Albans Iron and Steel Company

Gustin, A. J.
Osgood, Isaac
Remington, Philo
Smith, Edward A.

Singer, Nimick and Company

Nimick, William K.
Singer, William H.

Washburn Car-wheel Company

Barnum, William H.
Healy, William A.
Hyde, Salisbury
Washburn, Nathan

Crucible Works

Black Diamond Steel Works
   (Park, Brother and Co.)

Black, Alexander W.
Hancock, John
Park, James, Jr.
Park, William G.

Fort Pitt Iron and Steel Works
   (Graff, Bennett and Co.
   Reese, Graff and Woods)

Bennett, James I.
Dull, Andrew J.
Graff, John
Reese, Jacob

Hussey, Howe and Company
  (successor to Hussey, Wells and Co.)

Pittsburgh Steel Works
  (Anderson and Co.
  Anderson and Passavant
  Anderson and Woods)

Swift's Iron and Steel Works

Wayne Iron and Steel Works
  (John H. Brown and Co.)

Howe, Thomas M.
Hussey, Curtis, G.
Wells, Calvin

Anderson, Robert J.
Cosgrave, Sylvester A.
Lavely, John
Passavant, Walter
Woods, William

Clymer, George E.
Hubbard, L. T.
Swift, Alexander

Brown, John H.

VIII

Frank Julian Sprague

Father of Electric Traction

1857–1934

By Harold C. Passer

Between 1880 and 1900, a revolution occurred in urban transportation. In 1880, motive power for the 18,000 streetcars in the United States was supplied by 100,000 horses and mules. The elevated railroads of New York used steam locomotives. By 1900, electric power had been successfully applied to both streetcars and elevated trains. This clean and reliable form of power reduced costs, increased schedule speeds, and enlarged the carrying capacity of the urban transit systems. The result was an appreciable easing of the transportation difficulties which were beginning to restrict urban expansion. The electrification of city transportation allowed rapid growth of American cities to continue into the twentieth century.

Urban transit systems have their origins in the horse-drawn omnibuses which began to appear on the streets of American cities in the 1830's. These were superseded in the 1850's and the 1860's by street railways. Like the omnibuses, the streetcars were pulled by horses and mules but the rails permitted larger vehicles and faster speeds. The street railway companies prospered in the period after the Civil War, and street railways became an accepted part of urban life. They were such an improvement over alternative methods of city transportation that their service was considered low-cost and rapid. The maximum average speed which could be maintained was only six miles per hour but this speed was satisfactory for all but the largest cities.

By 1870, New York City was beginning to feel acutely the need for faster transportation. New York was the largest city in the United States and, at the same time, one which for geographical reasons had to expand largely in one direction. Before the opening of the Brooklyn Bridge in 1883, the natural and easiest direction for expansion was northward on Manhattan Island. It soon became evident that horsecars were inadequate. Travel time for the thousands of people who crowded into southern Manhattan on each business day was nearly at its limit. Unless speedier transportation could be provided, an independent metropolis would arise to the north.

The only land transportation then in use other than animal-drawn vehicles was the steam railroad and it was to steam that urban transportation men gave their attention. In 1867, construction of an elevated railroad was begun on Greenwich Street in lower Manhattan. Financial, legal, and technical troubles nearly caused the abandonment of this project, but by 1871 steam trains were in regular operation and the line had been extended northward on Ninth Avenue as far as Thirtieth Street. Five years later, the elevated railroad reached Fifty-ninth Street. Fifteen locomotives and twenty-one cars were then in use and forty trains were operated daily over the five-mile structure.

The success of the Ninth Avenue road led to the construction of elevated steam railroads on Second, Third, and Sixth Avenues. The New York Elevated Company, owner of the Ninth Avenue line, built the Second Avenue road and the other two were projects of a second firm, the Metropolitan Elevated Railway Company. Street railway companies and property owners bitterly fought the new roads. The former were alarmed by the prospective loss in revenue and the latter objected to the noise, dirt, and vibration of the trains and to the unsightly structures which darkened the streets. The courts, however, ruled in favor of the elevated companies in 1877. From that time on, construction proceeded rapidly.

The urgency of the need for rapid transportation in New York City is indicated by the actions of the municipal Board of Transportation which was established in 1875 to further elevated development. The Board fixed a limited number of elevated routes in order to make them valuable and of interest to investors, and made route franchises conditional on immediate development. As an additional safeguard against delays, the Board formed the Manhattan Railway Company. Its capital stock was subscribed by private investors and the company was in every sense a private one, but unlike the other two elevated companies, the Manhattan firm had no regular routes to develop. It was to become active only if the other two companies should have construction or operation difficulties. When such difficulties arose in 1879, the Manhattan Railway Company purchased the two elevated companies and their four elevated roads. By 1881, these roads were operating under one management from South Ferry to the Harlem River.

During the 1880's, the New York elevated lines were extended northward. The growth of Chicago led to the construction of elevated railroads there by 1893. As traffic on these lines rapidly increased, it became clear to transportation engineers that steam-operated railroads had nearly reached the limit of their carrying capacity. The number of trains could not be appreciably enlarged because they were being run as close together as safety permitted. Faster or longer trains would be possible only if heavier locomotives were employed. But heavier locomotives would require a stronger elevated structure and that would mean a substantial increase in capital expenditures. An alternative to such expenditures would be the construction of additional elevated lines. But the city inhabitants objected strongly to the erection of more elevated structures and it became almost impossible for the elevated railway companies to secure permission from municipal governments to build additional lines.

The growth of New York City was so rapid that the steam-operated elevated trains which in the 1870's had seemed to be a satisfactory solution to the city's transportation problems were no longer adequate by 1890. Similarly, the smaller cities which had found the horse-drawn streetcars a big improvement in urban transportation were looking for a faster and less costly transport system by the middle of the 1880's. The streetcar managers hoped that a substitution of mechanical power for animal power would give them an economical increase in schedule speed. Because very few cities would permit steam locomotives on the streets, it was necessary to resort to a more indirect use of steam power. The technique finally developed was the cable system. This permitted the application of steam power to streetcars without a locomotive. A stationary steam engine was employed to revolve an endless steel cable which ran in a slot between the two street rails. On each streetcar was mounted an arm which reached down into the cable slot. The arm could be made to grip the moving cable and the car was thereby put into motion. The operation of this gripping mechanism involved considerable physical exertion and could be undertaken only by men of above average strength.

The cable railways had the prime advantage over horse railways of faster speed. A ten-miles-per-hour average speed was readily attainable. Another advantage was a reduction in cost but this was true only in areas of heavy traffic. Where traffic was light, the horsecar was still cheaper because the cable installation and equipment costs were high. The cable system was therefore of restricted applicability. It was never used in more than fifteen cities in the United States and in these cities it was used only in the downtown areas. Cables could not be a general solution to the need for a faster and cheaper surface transit.

Another disadvantage of the cable system was its inflexibility. It could be applied only to straight, double-track sections. Curves were difficult to handle. Turnouts and sidings could not be used. A single-track cable system was uneconomical because it required the movement of a cable which was long relative to the number of cars which were pulled. Since the movement of the cable itself represented energy wasted, the length and weight of the cable had to be minimized by having both the outgoing and incoming parts of the cable pull cars. An even more serious disadvantage of a single-track cable system was the necessity for all cars on the line to travel in the same direction at any one time.

Cable cars were difficult to operate as a transportation system. The cars could not make up lost time. No car could travel faster than any other car because they were all propelled by the same cable. Once the cars were bunched together, the proper and safe distance between cars could be obtained only if the back cars waited for the ones ahead to move forward. Since bunching of cars is unavoidable during the hours in which traffic is extra heavy, the cable system proved to be peculiarly incapable of adapting to daily and hourly variations in urban transportation needs.

The mechanical problems which arose in the operation of a cable system were not easy to solve. The cable wore out rapidly and had to be repaired or replaced frequently. As the cables weakened, it was common for individual strands to break. These broken strands sometimes caught the gripping arms of the cars so securely that the arms could not be loosened. When this happened, the cable car was dragged through the streets and struck whatever was in its path. The only remedy was for the conductor or grip man to jump from the moving car and communicate with the power station to stop movement of the cable. When the cable was halted, all cars on that cable would also come to a standstill. The runaway cable cars were so common that most of the cable railway companies installed special telegraphs and telephones along the cable routes at frequent intervals. The conductor of a runaway car could communicate very quickly with the power house and the time during which a car was out of control could thereby be reduced.

The cable railways were not very satisfactory and, except where special conditions prevailed, the costly and slow-moving horsecars still provided the cheapest, safest, and most reliable urban transportation. In surface traction, as in elevated traction, the techniques of the 1880's were unable to meet in a satisfactory way the transportation needs of the urban population. Into this situation, ripe for major changes in transportation methods, stepped an electrical engineer named Frank Julian Sprague. The need for improved urban transit was so great that had Sprague not lived or had he given his attention to other problems, someone else would undoubtedly have worked out a solution to city transportation difficulties. But the fact remains that it was primarily one man who perceived these difficulties and devised the means of overcoming them.

What Sprague did was to substitute electric power for animal and cable power on the street railways and for steam power on the elevated railroads. He was not the first to envision the use of electric power on street railways nor was he the first to install an electric streetcar system. But he was the first to show that electric power was the general solution to surface transit problems. He did this at Richmond, Virginia in 1888. Similarly, he was not the first to apply electric power to elevated railroads but he was the first to conceive of and install a modern rapid-transit system. He demonstrated that electric power was the general solution to the rapid-transit needs. He did this at Chicago in 1898. Sprague's outstanding work at Richmond and Chicago is the subject of this essay.

II

Frank Julian Sprague was born July 25, 1857 at Milford, Connecticut where his father was the plant superintendent of a hat-manufacturing firm. After the death of his mother in 1866, Sprague and his younger brother were placed in the care of a maiden aunt who taught school at North Adams, Massachusetts. Sprague continued his education there and in high school showed a marked aptitude for science and mathematics. The school principal advised Sprague that he would benefit greatly from an engineering education. Because he realized that Sprague's financial means were limited, the principal suggested that Sprague take advantage, if possible, of the free but excellent engineering training given at West Point. Sprague went to Springfield to take a competitive examination for a West Point appointment but on arrival he learned that the examination was not for West Point but for Annapolis!

Sprague had not planned on a career afloat but he took the examination anyway and secured the appointment. Borrowing four hundred dollars to meet immediate expenses, he went to Annapolis in 1874 to begin his naval career. Even though this choice of Annapolis instead of West Point was the result of pure chance, it was exceedingly wise. To train for a career in electrical engineering, Sprague could not have attended another institution in the entire United States which gave as good a course as the United States Naval Academy. The United States Navy was then extremely interested in electricity because of its possible naval uses. At Newport, Rhode Island and at Annapolis, naval officers and civilian scientists were carrying on extensive electrical research in the 1870's. The Navy was collecting, testing, and comparing more dynamos than any other organization in the United States. This pioneer work enabled the Naval Academy to offer better instruction in electricity than any of the colleges or universities.

Sprague had the ability and the desire to profit from the Naval Academy engineering course. In four years at Annapolis, he received theoretical and practical training in basic engineering and electricity. This training and his native inventive talents were the factors primarily responsible for his brilliant career as an electrical engineer.

Sprague did well at Annapolis and was graduated seventh in his class of fifty in June 1878. He then spent two years at sea on a ship attached to the Asiatic Squadron. Although limited in time and materials, he carried on extensive inventive activities during his tour of sea duty, particularly in electrical devices. An interest in electricity had been developed by his Annapolis courses and by his visit to the Philadelphia Centennial Exhibition of 1876. He followed the activities of Edison and other electrical inventors closely and by the time he had done his own experimenting on shipboard he became convinced that a period of great electrical development was about to begin. He was anxious to return to the United States to take part in this development but it was 1880 before he could get back. In the spring of that year, he took his ensign's examination.[1]

Sprague was given a short leave during which he experimented with an arc lamp mechanism at the Stevens Institute of Technology and carried on electrical work at the Brooklyn Navy Yard. He then received several shore assignments including one at the Newport Naval Station, center of the Navy's electrical activities, where he was permitted to do independent research and development in dynamos and motors. When he learned of the 1881 Paris Electrical Exhibition he requested duty as the assistant to the officer representing the United States Navy at the exhibition. This attempt failed but he secured orders for temporary duty on a naval vessel which was sailing from New York to join the Mediterranean Squadron. Because the ship was delayed, he did not reach Europe until the spring of 1882, after the close of the Paris exhibition. Fortunately for Sprague, the Crystal Palace Electrical Exhibition had just opened in London and he went there instead. Although only twenty-five years of age, he was given the opportunity to serve as secretary of an award jury which included a number of distinguished scientists. As a jury member, Sprague was in an excellent position to study and test the numerous electrical devices on display.

In London, Sprague rode occasionally on the Metropolitan District Railway, an underground steam railroad. The smoke, gas, and dirt emitted by the locomotive in the small confines of the tunnel led him to consider the possibility of a cleaner kind of power, electricity. The basic principles of the electric motor were well known to the scientists and engineers of 1882 but the number of motors in service was negligible. The absence of motors from the London exhibition and the other electrical exhibitions was good evidence that electric power was not seriously considered for commercial purposes. In thinking of applying electric power to an underground railroad, Sprague was at the frontiers of electrical engineering. Electric traction was then a very new idea with implications hard to foresee.

Sprague worked out his plan for electrifying the underground railway in considerable detail. He first contemplated carrying the current to the car motor by means of a conductor at track level but the probable complications of switching led him to abandon that method. He finally decided on an overhead conductor. The current would be picked up by an underrunning contact mounted on the roof of the car.

Sprague became so engrossed in his electrical activities that he overstayed his leave by nearly six months. This was a court-martial offense and when ordered to rejoin his ship, he decided to comply. En route to New York, where he arrived in May 1883, he wrote a complete account of the engineering work he had done in England. He carefully described each test, giving all relevant data. The report made a volume of 150 pages and included Sprague's recommendations concerning the kind of electrical equipment (generators, batteries, arc lights, incandescent lights) that should be installed on naval vessels. The report proved beyond doubt that Sprague was a competent electrical engineer. One section related the results of his test of the three-wire system of electrical distribution. This had been invented almost simultaneously by Edison and Hopkinson, an English engineer and inventor. The purpose of the three-wire system, as opposed to the two-wire system it replaced, was to save copper in incandescent lighting circuits. Edison and Hopkinson disagreed on exactly how much copper was saved and Sprague ran tests to settle the controversy. He also tested the Hopkinson short-cored dynamo which was an improved model of the standard Edison dynamo.

The most noteworthy part of Sprague's report was a description of experiments with a device not primarily electrical, the gas engine. It was then very new and not well understood. As a test, Sprague operated a gas engine without outside ignition. This was probably the first demonstration of the principle Diesel later incorporated in the engine which bears his name. Sprague's discussion of gas engines was so complete and timely that the Navy Department printed this part of the report in a small pamphlet and distributed it among the technical and scientific personnel of the Navy. The Navy Department's opinion of Sprague's report is further indicated by the fact that on the basis of the report Sprague was forgiven for taking too much leave.

One significant feature of the report, in view of Sprague's later work, is that no material on electric motors was included. This omission reflects the fact that no motors were exhibited at the Crystal Palace and further indicates that elsewhere in England none came to Sprague's attention. In preparing the report, Sprague in effect surveyed the most advanced devices of electrical science. What he saw strengthened his belief that a period of electrical development lay ahead and, even more important, clearly revealed that almost nothing had been done in designing and perfecting a motor for commercial use.

III

At the London exhibition, Sprague met E. H. Johnson who, as Edison's representative in England, was in charge of the Edison exhibit of incandescent lighting. Johnson was favorably impressed by Sprague's knowledge and interest in electricity and suggested that he work for Edison on his return to the United States. Sprague accepted this offer and resigned from the Navy in order to devote all his time to electrical work. On arriving in New York, he entered Edison's employ.

Sprague was first assigned to Edison's central station planning department. This department prepared the plans for the street mains of projected central stations and determined the size and location of the various conductors. The procedure used was long and tedious. A large map of the district to be served by the central station served as the basis for a model of the central station circuits. Spools of wire were mounted at the locations of residences or other buildings which were to receive electric current. The resistance of each spool was made proportional to the number of lights to be used at that location. Wires to represent the street mains were run from the central station site to the various spools. A battery was then placed at the central station site and technicians measured the voltage drop along each of the street mains. By trial and error, the proper size for these conductors was determined.

Sprague saw very quickly that the model method was not only time-consuming and expensive but also inaccurate. He developed methods by which the conductor sizes could be determined correctly and easily. The model was no longer necessary and the time was reduced from two weeks to four hours. Sprague used the general principle that the cross section of the conductors should be proportional to the current they were expected to carry and showed how the correct conductor sizes could be determined by calculation alone. His ability to work out this procedure was good evidence that he had an excellent grasp of the basic principles of electrical engineering. The value of his Annapolis training in electricity was amply demonstrated by the fact that although Edison had other employees with scientific and engineering training, Sprague was the first one who had the benefit of advanced training in electricity. He was consequently able to eliminate a cumbersome method which the other Edison employees had accepted as a necessary evil.[2]

From the planning department, Sprague went to the construction department where he helped in the installation of a number of Edison central stations. After completion of a station at Brockton, Massachusetts, he remained there as operating engineer. In his free time he carried on motor experiments and constructed a railway motor. He made such good progress in developing a practical and efficient motor that he resigned from Edison's employ in the spring of 1884 and thereafter did nothing but motor-development work. Edison was stressing electric lighting to the exclusion of all other uses of electricity and Sprague was pessimistic about opportunities in the Edison organization for anyone interested primarily in electric power.

Sprague continued work on his motors during the summer of 1884. By fall he was ready to market a motor explicitly designed for industrial use. The motor was well engineered and contained several new features. It did not spark and the speed was constant regardless of changes in load. Sprague displayed the motor at an electrical exhibition in Philadelphia in the fall of 1884 where its merits were quickly recognized. The reception given the motor encouraged Sprague to go ahead with plans to market it. In November 1884 he and Johnson formed the Sprague Electric Railway and Motor Company, with an authorized capital stock of $100,000. Except for a few shares owned by Johnson, for which he paid cash, Sprague held all of the stock. The company undertook to sell its motors through sales agents located in all sections of the United States. The manufacturing was done by the Edison Machine Works and Sprague continued to spend most of his time on development work. He obtained the necessary funds from Johnson who received stock in return.

For several years, Sprague's enterprise was not much more than a paper one. Since the manufacturing was subcontracted to Edison, no manufacturing personnel or facilities were needed. The selling was handled by independent agents who invested their own funds in the inventory they carried. The operation of the Sprague firm consequently required very little capital investment and almost no employees. Johnson and Sprague could easily take care of the administrative problems that arose. Sprague was truly operating on a shoestring, for the company was established with less than $20,000 paid in. Even this small amount was not required for ordinary business operations and Sprague was able to apply the funds to research and development work. Profits which arose as sales expanded were used in the same way.

Sprague's enterprise prospered. His motor was well designed, gave good performance, and was endorsed by the Edison central stations who believed it to be the best motor available. By 1886, sales had increased appreciably. Sprague decided to establish his own manufacturing plant and leased a New York factory in October 1886. To finance this expansion and to provide additional working capital, the authorized capital stock was increased to $1,000,000 a few months later. The factory was acquired to make motors designed for special purposes; the standard types of motors which were made in quantity were still manufactured by the Edison Machine Works.

The Sprague motors were sold for industrial uses but Sprague was spending almost no time on industrial motor design and development. He was concentrating on the problem of electric traction, and, in particular, on the application of electric power to the New York elevated railroads. He made a thorough study of the elevated lines and their operating problems.[3] In 1885 be began experimenting on a short elevated test track at Twenty-ninth Street. He soon realized that a longer track was desirable for realistic test runs and he switched to the Thirty-fourth Street branch of the Manhattan Elevated Railroad to continue his experiments. By the end of 1886, Sprague was giving successful demonstrations of his electric car which showed reliability, good pulling power, and fast acceleration. These tests were so impressive that the Edison Electric Light Company considered purchasing the Sprague Company. Although this purchase was not carried out, several Edison directors invested a total sum of over $50,000 in the Sprague firm. The elevated railway officials, however, could not be convinced that electric traction was the answer to their problems.

Just why the management of the New York elevated railroads was so uninterested in electric power is not easy to explain. The existing elevated lines had nearly reached the limit of their carrying capacity and the elevated officials were aware of this. They were also conscious of the objections of the people of New York to the noise and dirt of the steam locomotives. In the early 1880's they commissioned Edison to make a study of the effects of the noise and vibration on the residents and structures along the elevated lines. But no changes were made. It is probable that the elevated officials hoped that the public would overlook the discomforts resulting from steam locomotives and that permission would be granted for the erection of additional elevated structures, particularly on Broadway, and with these hopes in mind, they refused to take any other steps

either to increase carrying capacity or the comfort of the New York populace.

Jay Gould was one of the financiers who controlled the Manhattan Elevated Railway Company and his prejudice against electric traction may
have been a factor in the attitude of the elevated management. Gould
was present at one of the elevated demonstrations given by Sprague and
was riding on the motor car when, as a result of a heavy surge of current,
a fuse blew with an explosive flash. Gould was so startled that he attempted
to jump from the car and he refused ever again to take the slightest interest in electric traction.[4]

Unable to interest the elevated railroads in electric traction after nearly
two years of experiments and tests and unwilling to finance more such
development work himself, Sprague turned to urban surface traction in
the hopes of achieving more success. He secured his first street railway
contracts in the spring of 1887. One of these contracts — the one calling
for electrification of a new street railway to be built in Richmond — was
to decide whether the horse, the mule, and the cable were to give way before electric power. The significance of this contract derived mostly from
its size. The Richmond railway marks the first attempt in the United
States to electrify a large-scale streetcar system. Forty cars, twelve miles of
track, a power plant of 375 horsepower — no electric railway then in operation even approached these figures.

IV

Electricity, of course, had first come into common use not as a source
of power but as a source of illumination, when the electric arc light began
to replace the gas street lamp about 1880. Several years later, Edison's
incandescent bulb introduced electric light into homes and offices. The
next commercial application of electricity was in power transmission. By
1885, a number of inventors were already attempting to electrify street
railways, and by the time Sprague signed the Richmond contract in 1887,
a few electric railways were actually operating in the United States.

All of these railways, however, were still in the experimental stage,
and none was giving satisfactory service. They were small and had few
features in common. Some employed a third rail to carry the current to
the motor; others used two overhead conductors; and still others a single
overhead conductor. Techniques of motor control, motor mounting, and
motor design were equally diverse. Operation of the railways was costly
and unreliable and a superiority over animal and cable power was yet to
be demonstrated. Furthermore, even if one or two of the small electric railways were successful, the managers of the large street railways would cor-

rectly have said that such success implied little about possibilities of applying electric power to the large street railway systems.

Sprague realized that previous efforts to electrify street railways had
not been successful, but he believed that he could design a large-scale
electric railway system which would be economical and reliable and which
would demonstrate the real worth of electric traction. His disillusioning
experience with the elevated in New York led him to accept the contract
to electrify a street railway in Richmond in 1887.

Early that year, a group of New York capitalists, including Maurice
B. Flynn, visited Richmond in search of a site for a manufacturing plant.
They noticed that Richmond had only one street railway and thought that
a second one could be profitably operated. But the route they chose in
cluded steep grades, sharp curves, and unpaved clay streets. In these conditions the use of horses, except at prohibitive cost, was almost impossible.
In order to be reasonably sure of a profit, they needed more power than
horses could provide, and turned to electricity as a possible solution
to their problem.

Flynn contacted Sprague, who had received considerable publicity as
a result of his elevated experiments, and suggested that he electrify the
street railway to be built in Richmond. The track was not yet laid nor was
the route completely determined and therefore the exact conditions in
which the cars would operate were not known. In spite of this uncertainty,
Sprague signed a contract early in May 1887. He agreed to bear all the
risk of failure and to guarantee an early completion date. The contract
stipulated that Sprague was to supply forty cars with two motors and ac-
cessory equipment for each car, a complete overhead current supply system
for twelve miles of track, and an electric generating plant of 375 horsepower. Thirty of the forty cars were to be operated simultaneously and
grades of 8 per cent were to be ascended. The completion date was to be
ninety days after the track construction had proceeded far enough to permit the electrical installation work to begin. When the railway had operated satisfactorily for sixty days, Sprague was to receive $110,000 in cash.[5]

The problems Sprague faced in trying to fulfill the Richmond contract
were numerous and difficult. He had only blueprints and some rough experimental apparatus which he had used on the elevated railroad. The
many details essential to the success of a forty-car system had not been
worked out. As a further handicap, Sprague contracted typhoid fever in
July and was unable to work for over two months. Precious time slipped
by and it was early fall before Sprague could give his personal attention
to the Richmond project.

The condition of the track and roadbed was a major obstacle. The
track was light, poorly jointed, and insecurely fastened. Moreover, it was

unevenly laid on red clay and there were twenty-nine curves — including five of less than thirty feet radius — and grades as high as 10 per cent. A wet fall and winter converted the red clay into a sticky mass which often submerged the rails and made travel impossible. A more unfavorable situation in which to place the first large-scale electric street railway can hardly be imagined.

The technical problems encountered by Sprague were even more difficult. He had set out to show that electric power could be economical and reliable for a large street railway system. This goal guided him in the design of what became the prototype of the modern street railway but numerous and costly experiments were required. Sprague's predecessors, the builders of the eight small and experimental electric railways in the United States, had employed techniques which could never be successful on a large scale. They had used chain drives to connect motor and axle. But the chains were inefficient power transmission devices and broke frequently. The motors were mounted on the car platforms for easy repair and adjustment. This technique reduced the car space available for passengers, encouraged time-consuming and awkward methods of speed control, and permitted the use of unreliable motors. Furthermore, it was almost impossible to mount two motors on a car or control the car from both ends. The use of only one motor meant that the power was insufficient for heavy loads or steep grades. Single-ended car control complicated car scheduling and operation because the cars had to be turned around at the end of the line.

The early electric railways also employed the overrunning trolley. This was a small-wheeled carriage which ran along on top of the overhead conductor and was connected by a flexible cable to the streetcar. This type of current pick-up device worked satisfactorily only under ideal conditions — a straight, level section of track and the car proceeding at low speed. Curves, hills, switches, and high speeds had to be avoided.

The overrunning trolley and the other devices and techniques of the first railways had one thing in common. They were temporary and makeshift. They were awkward, expensive, and unreliable. They could not be used on a large street railway system if that system were to provide speedy and efficient service over many miles of track. Equipment was needed that could give reliable and inexpensive service under all operating conditions. Until such equipment was designed, the electric street railway would remain in the experimental stage. Sprague understood the fundamental errors of his predecessors. He knew what a large-scale system needed; he had the technical ability to meet these needs; and he was ready to overcome any obstacle that might stand in his way.

The first serious technical trouble Sprague encountered was in the motors. An attempt to climb the 10 per cent grades burned out the armatures and field coils. To obtain more power, Sprague was forced to alter the gearing. He contacted Brown and Sharpe, machine makers of Providence, Rhode Island, who agreed to manufacture the new gears as rapidly as possible. The first test runs were made in November 1887, but by the following January it was apparent that Sprague could not meet the ninety-day deadline. The owners of the railway were disappointed, and, even more important, considerably alarmed. They threatened to cancel the contract. To obtain an extension of time, Sprague was forced to make financial concessions. The total payment was reduced to $90,000 and only half of that was to be in cash. The remainder was to be in bonds of the street railway company.

Early in February, streetcars were in operation and gave free rides to the children of Richmond. On February 8, 1888, in a drizzling rain, the line opened for regular service. During the succeeding months, service was maintained but only with great difficulty and enormous expense. Overhead switches, insulation, lightning, and the motor brushes gave the most trouble. Of these four, the last was by far the most serious. The metal brushes wore out rapidly and were very hard on the commutators.[6] It was a common sight to see a loaded car climb a grade with a lurid green glare lighting up the track. The result would be at least $100 damage. The continual starting and stopping, together with occasional reversing, subjected the railway motors to a kind of abuse almost never experienced by stationary motors. The brushes had to be replaced frequently and the commutators machined. Each car was inspected after every trip and the necessary repairs were made. The Edison factory in Schenectady and the Sprague factory in New York continuously shipped motors and motor parts by the fastest available means in order to keep the cars running.[7]

Sprague realized that his career, his financial solvency, and the future of electric railways were at stake. He knew that he had to keep the line in operation once regular service had begun and he spared no expense. Night and day work was the rule. The efforts of Sprague and his crew were successful. After the February opening, animal power was never used to propel a streetcar on the Sprague railway in Richmond. The electrical and mechanical problems were matched by difficulties with the track and roadbed. The rails often spread apart or sank into the mud. There were no guard rails on the curves. As a result, derailments were common and each car was equipped with a large timber and a scaling ladder. The timber was used to place the car back on the tracks, and the scaling ladder enabled a man to connect the trolley pole to the overhead wire. The ladder and the timber, which resembled a battering ram, gave an amusing medieval appearance to the parties of men who pushed the derailed cars back on the tracks.

Thunderstorms, snowstorms, and sleet also interfered with operations. Gradually these and other troubles were overcome; mudholes were filled and the tracks were straightened. A special electric connector and sections of rail were designed so that a derailed car could get back on the track under its own power. The substitution of carbon brushes for metallic ones solved the brush-commutator difficulties. Lightning arresters were installed and it was learned that if the car lights were turned on during a thunderstorm, most of the lightning would discharge harmlessly through the lighting circuit. Over fifty different trolley poles were tried before the underrunning, universal swiveling pole which exerts an upward pressure was developed. The armatures and field coils of the motors were completely redesigned and rewound. Lubrication was found to loosen the motor gears which tended to lock. By the fall of 1888, reliable and economical operation had been achieved.

v

The real significance of the Richmond installation was that it contained the technical features which permitted successful operation on a large scale and set the pattern for electric street railway development. A single overhead conductor was used and the current was picked up by an underrunning trolley. The motors — two on each car — were mounted beneath the car and suspended by what was called wheelbarrow suspension. Each motor was mounted by three points, two on the car axle and one on the car. This arrangement made it possible for the car to move relative to the axle and motor without misaligning the gearing. The motor brushes were fixed in position and motor control was achieved by a series-parallel controller. One controller was mounted on each end of the car so the car could be operated from either end. Lightning arresters were installed. The current supply system employed 450 volts, a parallel circuit, and a main conductor which fed the trolley wire at 1000-foot intervals. All these features became standard on American street railways and have remained so until the present. The motor mounting, the positive mechanical gearing, the current pick-up device, the method of motor control, the motor brushes — all these were so well chosen and so well adapted to reliable and economical operation that the improvements that remained to be made in later years were not fundamental.

The Richmond installation cost Sprague over $160,000 or nearly twice what he was paid. The high cost is easily accounted for. Sprague had not worked out the technical details when he took the contract and the necessary experimentation was expensive. Furthermore, he was working against time and the attempt to achieve results in a minimum of time was very costly. Changes in equipment were frequent and had to be decided upon instantly, without careful deliberation. Motors and other apparatus were manufactured quickly and sent by express to Richmond. When Sprague ordered the special gears from Brown and Sharpe, he told them to make them as soon as possible without regard to expense. The race against time led Sprague to open the road for service to the public in February, long before operation was reliable. As a result, much effort and expense were necessary to keep the cars running.

It is plain that Sprague did not exercise ordinary business prudence in accepting the onerous conditions of the Richmond contract. When the contract was signed he knew very little of the conditions of the route, he had not worked out a complete system, and the time allowed was exceedingly short. He later said that had he been able to foresee the troubles he was to encounter, he would never have taken the contract.[8] He overestimated his chances of success. He thus evidenced a strong faith in his own ability as an engineer and a willingness to stand behind his ideas on electric traction. He was an independent thinker and possessed the qualities of determination and perseverance to an uncommon degree. Enormous obstacles did not defeat him nor shake his belief in ultimate victory. His business success was attributable to more than outstanding technical ability and keen perception of profit possibilities; his personality characteristics were essential, for had he been cautious and prudent, he would never have accepted the Richmond contract.

Flynn and the other New York capitalists who formed the Union Passenger Railway Company of Richmond were not willing to accept unusual risks. Although they needed electric power to operate their street railway profitably, they would have refused to construct the railway if Sprague had not been willing to bear the risks of installing electric traction. They were ready to accept the ordinary risks which accompany the establishment and operation of a business but beyond that they were not willing to go.

Sprague was able to withstand the heavy Richmond loss because of the good earning capacity of the Sprague Electric Railway and Motor Company, and he made up the loss many times over when the success of the Richmond installation became known. Not only was continuous service by a large number of cars maintained at Richmond, but, even more important, operating costs were only 40 per cent of what they would have been with horses. When thirty cars were first in operation at one time, on May 4, 1888, the Union Passenger Railway Company notified Sprague that the "satisfactory operation" clause had been fulfilled and the electrical equipment was formally accepted. By July the operation of the electric cars was so satisfactory that Flynn was willing to expand their use. He ordered forty more cars from Sprague for the Union Passenger lines and he purchased control of the other Richmond street railway company and announced plans to electrify it. This was the Richmond City Railway Company, which had been established in 1865 and which by 1888 was using 225 horses and mules to operate fifty cars over thirteen miles of track. Flynn was particularly anxious to gain control of this company because it had a much better route than his new Union Passenger Company and the prospects for high profits as a result of electrification were very good.

The excellent performance of the Sprague Richmond installation exerted a powerful influence on the growth of electric street railways in the United States. One example of this influence is provided by the West End Street Railway Company of Boston. This company, formed in 1887 through the amalgamation of seven street railways, operated the largest street railway system in the United States. It used 8000 horses to pull 1700 cars over 212 miles of track. Henry M. Whitney, president of West End, decided that a motive power better than horses was needed and plans were made to install a cable system. Land for the power stations was purchased and some of the construction contracts were awarded. Then Whitney heard of the Richmond railway. He halted all cable preparations, and made a thorough study of electric traction. He visited Richmond three times. On one of these visits, Sprague staged a special demonstration for him in which twenty-two cars were lined up and started at once. Whitney decided that electricity, not cables, should provide the motive power for his street cars and he awarded Sprague the contract for the Boston-Brookline section of the West End system. Twelve miles of track and twenty cars were involved.

The impetus which the Richmond railway gave to the business of the Sprague Company and to electric railways in general is indicated by the following data. In the spring of 1887, at the time that Sprague signed the Richmond contract, there were in operation in the United States eight electric street railways, which used a total of sixty-five cars on thirty-five miles of track. By 1890, two years after the Richmond road began regular operation, there were over two hundred electric street railways in operation and under construction. Of this number, Sprague supplied the equipment for about one-half.[9]

The expansion of the sales of the Sprague Company, as its industrial and railway business grew, necessitated a second increase in its capitalization by 1889. An additional $200,000 of common stock and $400,000 of preferred stock were issued. The preferred stock was purchased by the Edison Electric Light Company. A few months later the Sprague Company was merged into the newly formed Edison General Electric Company. By absorbing Sprague, Edison General Electric made certain that its largest customer would not take his business elsewhere. Over 65 per cent of the motors manufactured at the Schenectady plant were sold to Sprague in 1889. Sprague went along with his company and assumed the post of consulting engineer to Edison General Electric. He soon came into sharp conflict with the top management over several technical matters, however, and resigned.

VI

Sprague repeated in 1890 his course of action of 1884. He left an Edison organization and went into business for himself. In 1884 he had begun to design and make motors for industrial purposes. In 1890 he turned to electric elevators and in 1891 formed the Sprague Electric Elevator Company. During the following years he developed and installed electric elevators for fast passenger service in the tall buildings in New York. Vertical transportation did not occupy all his time and he continued to show an interest in electric traction and especially in urban rapid transit. As early as 1890 he strongly advocated a four-track underground electric railway in New York. In June 1891 he publicly offered to install on the Second Avenue elevated line, at his own financial risk, two six-car trains, one to be powered by an electric locomotive and the other by electric motors under each car. He repeated these test-train offers to the New York Elevated Railway management in 1895 and 1896 but each time was refused.

In working with electric elevators, Sprague devised various methods for controlling the elevator motors from within the elevators and from outside. Outside control was used to test new installations. He worked out a system whereby he could use a single master switch, placed in the basement of a building, to control the movement of any single elevator or all of them together. He soon realized that he could apply the same control methods to electric motor cars and proceeded to develop what he called the multiple-unit system of control.

If this system were installed on an elevated railway, every car would be equipped with electric motors and each car could be operated alone or with any others in any number, in any end relation, and in any sequence. The entire train could be controlled from either end of any car. The maximum conceivable flexibility in train make-up and car handling would be achieved. Each car would be powered, lighted, heated, and braked independently, reducing train make-up time, permitting trains of any length, and making storage, inspection, and repair very easy. Another and even more important advantage was that each car would possess the correct amount of power for it alone. No heavy locomotives which waste power on short trains and deteriorate the elevated structure would be needed. Tractive power on a railroad is a function of the weight on the driving wheels. When a locomotive is used, it must be heavy enough to give the desired traction. But if each car is self-powered, the entire weight of the train, including the passengers, can be used for traction. Furthermore, individually powered cars allow much faster acceleration. This increases the average running speed with no decrease in safety and gives greater economy in energy consumption.

All of these advantages are permitted by no form of motive power except electricity. With the growth of New York and Chicago, the elevated railroads in those cities were faced with the problem of increasing their carrying capacity. But they were using steam locomotives and the size of the elevated structure limited the weight of the locomotives and therefore the length of the trains. Because the trains were already running at very short intervals, additional trains could not be operated with safety. The Sprague system would provide the extra capacity by permitting trains of any length (up to the limit set by the length of the station platforms) which could run fast and close together. No expensive changes in the elevated structure were needed. Moreover, the electric system, with the power generated in a few, large stationary steam plants instead of in hundreds of locomotives, would reduce fuel costs.

The first application of electricity to the elevated railways employed the locomotive principle. In this respect, electricity was not a radical change from steam and did not utilize the primary advantage of electric power. General Electric included an electric elevated railway with a third rail in its exhibit at the Chicago World's Fair in 1893. Several elevated railways had been partially electrified before the Fair; afterward, General Electric secured the first contract for the complete electrification of an American elevated railway. This line was the Metropolitan Elevated Railway of Chicago. The Metropolitan electrification and others of that period utilized the so-called locomotive car. This was an ordinary passenger car, fitted with two or four motors, which pulled one or two trailer (non-powered) passenger cars. The locomotive car was used in preference to a locomotive because it was lighter, which meant less wear on the elevated structure, and it carried passengers, thereby saving track space. The locomotive car was still in principle a locomotive, however, even though it was also a passenger car. As long as the locomotive principle was used, the advantages of electric power over steam power for elevated trains were restricted to fuel savings and the lack of noise, fumes, and dirt. The realization of the essential limitations of the locomotive method and how they could be avoided by the use of electricity occurred to only one man.

Sprague believed that his system of multiple-unit control could provide the needed increase in carrying capacity. He had a vision of what multiple unit control could do and he had the ability and the determination to make that vision a reality.

Sprague's opportunity to carry out the multiple-unit control scheme came in 1897. The South Side Elevated Railway of Chicago was reorganized in the spring of that year and decided to adopt electricity. This decision was undoubtedly a result of witnessing the operation of the electrified Metropolitan Elevated line. Equipment bids were called for. General Electric, Westinghouse, and a Chicago firm, Siemens and Halske, responded. All the bids proposed locomotive cars. The South Side Company was not satisfied, however, that locomotive cars could provide the increased schedule speed which was desired. A. D. Lundy, an electrical engineer who was acting as a consultant to South Side in connection with the proposed electrification, suggested that Sprague, whom Lundy had worked for in Richmond, be called in.[10] At first Sprague refused. He had made plans to go to London to try to secure a $500,000 elevator contract for a new underground railway under construction from the Bank of England to Shepherd's Bush. Furthermore, he had recently fallen while installing elevators at the Waldorf Hotel in New York and had suffered serious injury. He was still on crutches when Lundy asked him to draw up plans for the South Side electrification.

His friendship with Lundy plus the chance to propose his multiple-unit system of control induced Sprague to accept Lundy's offer. Sprague suggested to the South Side management that his control system was the answer to their need for greater carrying capacity. The novelty of his proposal and the opposition of the equipment companies who ridiculed it as impractical led to some hesitation before it was accepted. Sprague finally secured the electrification contract, early in April 1897, by agreeing to take upon himself all risk that his plan might fail. He signed the contract as an individual, and the elevated company, for its protection, required Sprague to furnish a $100,000 bond for penalties in case he failed to fulfill it. He agreed to have six cars completely equipped and ready for testing on or before July 15 on a standard track, at least one mile long. He was to supply the test track at his own expense. Further tests were to be conducted when the remaining 114 cars had been equipped. The officers and the engineers of the elevated railway were to prescribe the tests in detail. If they were unsatisfactory to any of the South Side officials or if the cars were not ready for testing at the specified times, the company could cancel the contract without recourse by Sprague. A further condition was that all testing and installation was to be accomplished without interrupting the regular elevated service. For supplying and installing on the 120 cars, motors, lights, heaters, cabs, control mechanisms, and braking systems, and for fulfilling all performance and testing conditions, Sprague was to receive $300,000.

VII

When Sprague accepted the South Side contract, his plans were no more fully developed than they had been when he signed the Richmond contract ten years before. The multiple-unit control system existed only on paper. No controlling mechanism had been constructed and tested. But the large amount of developmental work to be done was only part of Sprague's difficulty. He was physically handicapped and he decided to go ahead with his London trip. His chances of making the July 15 dead line thus did not seem very good. The negotiations for the London elevator order went slowly and Sprague could not get back to New York until June. On his return, he found that the small amount of development work that he had been able to direct by cable and letter from abroad was nearly at a standstill because of a strike in the Sprague shops. It is not surprising that Sprague later referred to 1897 as "one of my most difficult years." [11]

W. J. Clark, manager of the General Electric railway department and a good friend of Sprague's, followed him to England in the hope of securing the order for the 240 motors that were needed for the South Side electrification. Clark promised Sprague the use of the General Electric test track at Schenectady and got the order although the generators for the power station were purchased from Westinghouse. By very intensive labor, Sprague was able to put two cars in operation on that track on July 16. Ten days later, he demonstrated a six-car train there before South Side officials and engineers. To indicate the ease with which the six cars could be operated, he permitted his ten-year-old son to handle the controls. In November, a five-car train was put into service for test purposes on the track of the Metropolitan Elevated Railway in Chicago. The operation of this train for several weeks proved that the Sprague control mechanism was reliable. The following April twenty cars were placed in operation on the South Side tracks. Seventeen of these — one in flames — had to be taken off during the first day because of defective rheostats but after that no serious trouble was encountered. By August 1898, 120 cars were in operation and the steam locomotives had been removed from service.

The South Side installation worked remarkably well. From the beginning, it gave efficient and reliable service. The increase in average speed to fifteen miles per hour, the better adjustment of train lengths to variations in traffic, and the greater facility in car handling resulted in increased revenues and lower costs. The earnings of the South Side Elevated

Railway before and after the conversion to electricity are shown in the
accompanying table.[12]

Month	Year	Motive Power	Net Earnings
November	1897	steam	$10,603.80
November	1898	electricity	39,448.56
December	1897	steam	14,691.69
December	1898	electricity	45,355.68

The effect of the multiple-unit control system on South Side Elevated's
earnings was quickly reflected in the value of its stock. Before reorganization, the stock was selling at $32 per share. After electrification, the market
price rose to $105. Capitalists and elevated railway officials could not af-
ford to ignore the Sprague installation in Chicago. It was evident that the
basis for the increase in the South Side's earnings was the multiple-unit
system of control. Even the most conservative business management will
alter its production methods if the change will reduce costs and increase
revenues and if it can be put into effect with no risk of failure. The adoption of the Sprague system by other elevated railroads in the following years
was practically a certainty because of its effect on costs and revenues. It
is important to realize that the electrification of the elevated railways
did not come about because the elevated managers wanted to add to the
comfort of city residents by dispensing with steam locomotives. Both
steam power above the surface and animal power on the surface of city
streets were dirty and unpleasant but neither was abandoned until it was
proved that electric power was cheaper.

Sprague's success in Chicago not only led to the electrification of other
elevated railways but also aroused the interest of the two largest firms
manufacturing electrical equipment, General Electric and Westinghouse.
Both supplied equipment for the Chicago installation and each was quick
to see the advantages of multiple-unit control. The two firms soon were
marketing their own elevated electrical systems. The General Electric
system was an all-electric one, very similar to Sprague's, while the Westinghouse system was electro-pneumatic. Compressed air was used in conjunction with electricity in the controlling mechanism. In spite of this
competition from two well-established companies with large engineering
staffs, Sprague secured a number of elevated electrification contracts, including the Boston Elevated Railway and the Brooklyn Elevated Railway.

General Electric soon came to the conclusion that Sprague was infringing its motor control patent in his multiple-unit control system, and
refused to supply him with any more motors or other equipment. To

counteract this measure, Sprague purchased his motors from Westing-house. General Electric's next step was to bring suit against Sprague for infringement of the General Electric series-parallel controller patent. Oddly enough, this patent was originally Sprague's, granted to him for one of the inventions he had made while working on the Richmond contract in 1887. Sprague had assigned the patent to the Sprague Electric Railway and Motor Company, which had been absorbed by Edison General Electric which, in turn, had been merged into General Electric. Sprague countered this second move by bringing suit against General Electric for infringe-ment of his multiple-unit system of control. This suit proceeded very well for Sprague. It began to appear that Sprague would win. General Elec-tric became alarmed because it had made important installations of its multiple-unit control system — on the Manhattan Elevated Railway, the Brooklyn Heights Railroad, and others — and these installations as well as future business would be jeopardized by a Sprague victory. In 1902 General Electric purchased the Sprague Electric Company, the firm Sprague had formed to make elevated installations, "as in no other way could we get possession of a patent which was absolutely necessary to our business." [13] Sprague received over $1,000,000 for the multiple unit con-trol system patent.

Sprague's multiple-unit system became the prototype for urban rapid transit. Not only the elevated railroads but also the subways which began to be built about 1900 utilized this system. A later use for it was on those mainline railroads which were electrified. When two or three power units were coupled together to act as a locomotive, the Sprague control system was used to synchronize operation of the various motors.

VIII

Sprague was twice a pioneer innovator in electric traction. In each case, he stepped in after electric power had been applied for several years to commercial installations. By reorienting the development of electric power devices, he altered completely the commercial significance of elec-tric motive power. In street railways, he envisioned large systems with many cars, in contrast to the small ones which had been electrified, and he designed the motor and auxiliary equipment for large-scale operations. Before Sprague, the electric streetcar had shown no superiority over the cable and only a slight superiority over the horse. After Sprague, it was clear that horses and cables would be replaced by electricity. In elevated railways, he perceived the limiting element in traction — the weight upon the driving wheels — and saw how the entire weight of a train could be used as driving wheel weight through electricity. He discarded the locomotive principle, which had been carried over from steam practice into elevated electrification work, and designed the multiple-unit system of control. This gave electricity such an advantage over all other forms of motive power that it was soon recognized as the only motive power suitable for rapid transit systems. Before Sprague, the electric elevated had not shown much superiority over steam. After Sprague, it was clear that no elevated railway could continue to use steam power. In both street railways and elevated railways, Sprague showed outstanding vision, stamina, technical ability, and courage. He signed large contracts with hardly more than ideas and blueprints. Yet within relatively short periods, he developed reliable, practical, and economic systems of electrical transport.

Sprague was an engineer-entrepreneur. He gave economic worth to scientific advance by using newly discovered scientific principles to solve economic problems. The pattern of his entrepreneurship, as revealed by his work in street and elevated railways, can be viewed as a three-stage schema. First he visualized a place in the economy that electric power could occupy. With this vision before him, he decided what technical features an electric power system had to have to achieve commercial success. In street railways, the concept of a large-scale system guided him in choosing those features. In elevated railways, his guide was the desire to abandon the locomotive principle. He then invented a street railway system and an elevated railway system which possessed the necessary technical features.

The Richmond and the Chicago contracts show without question that Sprague assumed the risk of failure in his schemes for electrification. Rigid time limits were set in order to remove the risk of long delays. The operation had to be satisfactory before Sprague could receive payment. His willingness to assume the entire risk grew out of his conviction that his ideas were sound. Even though standard engineering practice served as the basis for severe criticism of his plans, he knew that the plans were practical and he was willing to work against great odds to prove it. His ability to take the risk in the two rather large contracts rested in the fact that in 1887 and in 1897 he had a successful and profitable business which provided financial support, experimental facilities, and the required technical personnel. The success of his industrial motor business in the 1880's made it possible for him to sustain a huge loss at Richmond. The success of his electric elevator business in the 1890's made it possible for him to post a $100,000 bond.

Like every pioneer innovator, Sprague met considerable resistance. Some came from fellow engineers who labeled his proposals as impractical, unscientific, and contrary to good engineering practice. Resistance also came from the owners and managers of the street and elevated rail-

236 Harold C. Passer

ways because they were reluctant to alter traditional methods of operation. It is significant that Sprague did not make his pioneer installations
in existing street railways or in the New York elevated lines. He succeeded
in breaking the wall of resistance by securing a foothold in a new firm or
one with new management. Richmond had one street railway in 1887
but this company had shown no intention of discarding animal power.
A new firm was formed that year to operate a second railway and because
the firm was new, starting from the beginning to lay out and construct a
street railway system, Sprague could argue for his plans without the resistance of a management successfully operating an existing system.
Similarly, in Chicago a new management was in charge of the South Side
elevated in the spring of 1897 because the road had gone through bankruptcy and reorganization. The new officials were reviewing the operation
of the railway without prejudice and consequently were receptive to new
ideas. Sprague's experiences seem to indicate that major innovations first
appear where there is a new firm or a new management which because it
is new does not feel committed to traditional patterns of business behavior.

Once the wall of resistance to change has been pierced sufficiently for
the act of pioneer innovation to be accomplished, it is important that other
firms learn of the success of this innovation and readily adopt it. Otherwise
the innovation may spread so slowly as to have little effect on the economy.
Sprague's innovations in Richmond and Chicago were extremely successful in breaking down the economy-wide wall of resistance. One reason
was the large investment involved in each instance. Another was the
wide publicity Sprague received. Whitney of the Boston West End
Street Railway Company heard of Sprague's work in Richmond and, after
an investigation, decided to adopt electric power. When the largest street
railway system in the United States abandoned horses and cables and was
ready to invest millions of dollars in electric traction, the smaller street
railways were not longer hesitant about electrifying. When Sprague secured a $300,000 contract for installation of his multiple-unit system on a
Chicago elevated railroad and when that installation proved to be technically and financially successful, the other elevated railways were ready to
invest millions of dollars in the same system.

As an engineer entrepreneur and pioneer innovator, Sprague was not
interested in routine business administration or in building a huge industrial enterprise. In 1890 he sold his motor and railway equipment business
to Edison General Electric. Ten years later he disposed of his elevator
company and in 1902 he sold the Sprague Electric Company to General
Electric. In the succeeding years he continued to invent and to advance
electrical engineering. He became interested in automatic railroad signal-
ing and in 1906 formed the Sprague Safety Control and Signal Corpora-

tion. He played a prominent part in the electrification of the steam railroad terminals in New York. During World War I he served on the Naval
Consulting Board and assisted in the development of depth charges and
delayed-action fuses. In 1927 he invented an automatic control system
which permitted two elevators, one express and one local, to operate in the
same shaft. He continued to be active in business and electrical engineering until pneumonia caused his death on October 25, 1934.

IX

Capital Accumulation in Life Insurance between the Civil War and the Investigation of 1905

By Douglass North

Life insurance companies came into permanent existence in the United States in the 1840's[1] and were well established financial institutions by the end of the Civil War. However, the period between the end of the war and the early years of the twentieth century mark the "coming of age" of the industry. In the thirty-five years after 1870, life insurance in force for all reporting companies increased by 577 per cent. Between 1865 and the Armstrong Investigation[2] of 1905 the total annual income of all reporting life insurance companies grew from $25 million to $642 million, the excess of total annual income over total expenditures from $14 million to $230 million.[3]

These quantitative measures of expansion, however, impressive though they are, only add interest to the more crucial qualitative changes in the business of insurance which were so instrumental to its growth. Such changes were the means by which the insurance industry itself profited so hugely from the expansion and development of the entire American economy, in which process it also played an important part.

The growth of American industry and transport utilizing new technological means was the core of this general economic expansion. Between 1860 and 1910 capital invested in manufacture increased from one to twelve billion dollars, while the value of manufactured products rose from almost two billion to more than twenty billion dollars.[4] The Bessemer and open-hearth processes made possible an age of steel, and the application of new techniques in other fields of metallurgy created other large-scale industries. The development of oil refining, the expansion and improvement of machine-tool manufacture, and the vast growth of railroad transportation marked the development of an industrial society. With the creation of large-scale industry came the population increases of the four decades following 1870 [5] and the swift urbanization of large sections of this population.

By the end of the nineteenth century the assets of the life insurance companies had become an important part of the capital accumulation financing the expansion and consolidation of transport and industry. The petty savings of millions of wage and salary earners, representing over $1,700,000,000 in 1900, were by this means made available to the expanding capital market in New York.[6] The large companies had become closely linked with the large financial complexes around the major investment banking houses; and the character and size of their investments, particularly in railroad securities, indicated the important place they occupied in the New York financial market. The investment portfolio of the Mutual Life may be taken as typical of the large companies. Of almost $500 million of assets in 1906, 57 per cent were in securities (as contrasted with 11.3 per cent in 1871) and railroad securities alone made up 41.4 per cent of this securities portfolio.[7]

The growing industrial society not only used the accumulation of life insurance, but also created the need for such insurance. The self-sufficiency of the family unit in an agricultural and domestic economy gave way to the economic interdependence of an industrial capitalist order.[8] Loss of the working member increasingly meant destitution for the rest of the family, there being no hereditary livelihood left to the survivors. The creation of a large section of the population without property and dependent on a money income in a society where specialization and division of labor minimized hereditary crafts and skills resulted in family insecurity. Life insurance was a contrivance to mitigate this insecurity.

If the development of an industrial capitalist society, however, created the need for life insurance, in itself this development provides but little explanation for the rapid accumulation of insurance funds that took place. For although the whole industry grew substantially after the Civil War, it was the spectacular expansion of only a small number of companies which accounts for much of this over-all growth. By 1905 the big three, the Mutual, Equitable, and New York Life, had approximately $5 billion worth of insurance in force compared to but $150 million in 1865.[9] They now dominated the life insurance world and in 1905 possessed assets of

$440, $412, and $391 million respectively.[10] By then two industrial companies, the Metropolitan and the Prudential, had assets of over $100 million each.[11] The growth of these companies can only be accounted for as a result of (1) a number of innovations in insurance forms coupled with sharpening and improving of marketing methods and (2) a significant shift in the political strategy and devices to which these companies turned in the interests of rapid accumulation. Both the technical innovations and the new strategic policies represented sharp departures from announced, purposed functions of life insurance.

The radical character of the policies pursued by the big three can be more clearly realized when contrasted with the unusual "prehistoric" firm that remained outside the main stream of competitive accumulation. Colonel Jacob Greene of the Connecticut Mutual epitomized the entrepreneur of the conservative firm who conscientiously performed the manifest functions of life insurance. According to Greene the function of a life insurance company was limited simply to providing family protection at its mathematically ascertained cost. The development of scientific actuarial methods had removed speculation from insurance and guaranteed the safety of the policy. It continued to be generally necessary, to be sure, to overcharge the policyholder in order to provide a margin of safety, but this overcharge, in Greene's view should be, and in the practice of firms such as his actually was paid back each year in the form of annual dividends.[12] Those policyholders, moreover, who could not keep up the premiums on their contracts and had to surrender them to the company were given a paid-up policy in proportion to the premiums actually paid in.[13]

When Greene became president of the Connecticut Mutual in 1878 it was the second largest life insurance company in America, surpassed only by the Mutual. By 1905, the New York Life wrote as much business in six months as the Connecticut Mutual had totally in force.[14] Even more striking is the contrast in growth between the old-fashioned companies that continued to write annual dividend insurance and those that changed to the new tontine type, which is described below. The five leading annual dividend companies[15] in 1868 had $443 million of insurance in force as contrasted to $352 million for the four leading companies that later shifted to tontine insurance.[16] In 1905 the five annual dividend companies had $998 million in force compared to $5,779,000,000 for the four tontine companies.[17] Thus the former had hardly more than doubled insurance in force while the latter had grown almost twenty times. The differences between them were due largely to the innovations in insurance forms, marketing methods, and political activity of the tontine firms.[18] Underlying these innovations was a fundamental departure from the avowed functions of a life insurance company. Accumulation rather than provision of family protection became the new orientation of the dominant life insurance firms.

II

The most important innovation of these accumulative firms was the development of tontine insurance, so called because it came from an old scheme proposed to Mazarin in 1656 by one Lorenzo Tonti for the purpose of raising revenue for the crown. Equal contributions were solicited from a large number of people, and after a stipulated period of time the survivors divided up the accumulated interest and the crown kept the capital fund. As first adopted by Henry B. Hyde, the founder of the Equitable Life Assurance Society, the tontine policy embodied three features: [19] (1) beneficiaries of those who died received the face value of the policy without any accumulated dividends; (2) those whose policy lapsed received nothing (i.e., no surrender value); (3) those who kept their policy in force until the end of the period (ten, fifteen, or twenty years) received the face value of the policy plus their own accumulated dividends for the whole period, plus a share of the dividends of those who died, plus a share of the accumulation of those who lapsed.[20]

This system of pure tontine was one in which the participant wagered on his own longevity, with the survivors of a particular class dividing up the total accumulation at the end of the given period. As adopted by Hyde in 1868, it had a short existence, but the almost equally speculative modified deferred dividend system that it gave rise to became the major source of company accumulation,[21] and the large companies, by lower commissions to agents, discouraged the selling of other types of policies.[22] The main distinction between the pure tontine and the modified deferred dividend policy was that whereas the former carried no surrender value at all, the latter after a stipulated period of time provided a small cash (or paid-up insurance) surrender value based on the reserve built up by the premiums.[23] The accumulation potential of such insurance was enormous, especially under the high-pressure salesmanship of the new type of life insurance agent who came in along with it.[24] The high lapse rate coupled with small surrender values and the guarantee of these large accumulations of funds not subject to division for periods of five to twenty years were the major advantages of this business to the companies that promoted it.

There are no comprehensive figures on the lapse rate of policies during this period although most estimates are that approximately 60 per cent of all policyholders received no dividends (either died or lapsed).[25]

Actuarial testimony during the 1877 investigation brought out that, of all terminated policies, but one in ten matured by death while the other nine were forfeited.[26]

The value to life insurance companies of lapsed contracts, even in the old days, is shown by the fact that the entire expenses of the Mutual for the five years preceding 1863 were more than paid for by proceeds from forfeited policies.[27] The pure tontine policy of ten years later which embodied total forfeiture when lapsed was also very profitable. So too in this respect was the subsequent deferred dividend policy even when it paid some surrender value in cash or better still for the company, in the form of small paid-up insurance.[28] However, it was particularly the failure to provide any return on accumulated dividends which was significant. The contrast between a deferred dividend policy of the Equitable and the annual dividend policy of an "old-fashioned" company such as the Connecticut Mutual illustrates the difference. On similar $10,000 policies that lapsed after fifteen years, the surrender value from the Equitable was $2784 while that from the Connecticut Mutual was $2550 on the accumulated reserve [29] plus $1214 that the policyholder had received in dividends.[30]

Even if total forfeiture on the first tontine policies and small surrender values on deferred dividend policies were harsh on the lapsed policyholder, in themselves they should have meant simply a larger accumulation for the continuing policyholders who would expect to share it ultimately as dividends. In fact, however, the results for these policyholders were very disappointing. Actual paid dividends were approximately one-half the estimated ones that had been so effectively used as a device by agents in soliciting new business.[31] The companies were not held to such estimates by law, and the system of division was their own.[32] They could keep the total accumulation, including forfeited dividends, for periods of ten to twenty years. This meant not only that they could use the people's money for such periods but also that they could only with the utmost difficulty be held accountable for how they used it. Annual dividends provided a frequent test of the efficiency and economy of the company, whereas deferred dividends postponed accountability for surplus, thus concealing low net earnings. Deferring dividends, moreover, meant not only that companies did not have to worry about favorable results each year, but also that they could use the cumulative surplus to borrow against in the tremendous drive for new business. A committee of the Board of Directors of the Equitable, investigating company practices in 1905, pointed out that "growth beyond the normal rate can be had only through unusual exertion, and this increased costs." [33] This committee went on to point out:

The deferred dividend company is never held to accountability by the whole body of its policyholders, and is so held by its individual policyholders only when their opportunity for action has passed. The absence of accountability makes possible the pursuit of rapidity of growth at undue cost, because the effect of that cost is not felt by the policyholder until, as said before, it is too late for his availing protest.[34]

It was the existing policyholder, therefore, who bore the brunt of these increased costs. Company accumulation and surplus continued to expand as a result of the new business. At this time the Equitable, with assets of approximately $412 million, had a surplus over $80 million.[35]

The conservative companies, dividing the overcharge annually, could accumulate no such surplus against which to borrow to finance the quest for new business. Moreover the annual dividend policy lacked the speculative appeal of the deferred dividend one; salesmen of the former could not match the extravagant estimates of future returns promised by the agents for tontine companies. That these promises were not fulfilled fifteen years later was of little consolation to the company that insisted upon issuing simple life insurance and saw the purchase of annual dividend policies drop to almost nothing. The liberal surrender values offered by such companies as the Mutual Benefit of New Jersey as early as 1879, although attracting considerable attention, had little effect on the tontine policy. Each prospective policyholder was persuaded by his agent that he would not be the one to lapse.

While tontine and deferred dividend insurance exploited one market for life insurance, another innovation, industrial insurance, tapped an entirely new and ever-growing stratum of the new industrial capitalist society, namely the working class. The earlier development of a factory system in England provided a potential market which was first exploited in 1854.[36] In 1875 John F. Dryden of the Prudential Insurance Company of America introduced industrial insurance into this country. The significant differences between the new form of insurance and ordinary insurance was that the former was available in small units (the average face value of a policy was about $100), it was available to any member of the family from age one to seventy, usually without a medical examination, and premiums were normally collected weekly by house-to-house calls.[37] Although the individual premiums often were as little as five or ten cents a week, the aggregate from a rapidly growing working force was large; and as the factory system spread, the market expanded accordingly. Between 1876 and 1905 industrial insurance in force in the United States rose from $443,072 to $2,309,885,554.[38] With industrial insurance even more than with deferred dividend insurance, a major source of accumulation was a high lapse rate and little or no surrender value.

Of the Metropolitan Life Insurance Company policyholders, 51.46 per cent lapsed within a year (1904) [39] and 63.74 per cent within five years.[40] The Prudential paid no surrender value on policies that lapsed before the end of three years, which meant that over two-thirds of the policy-holders received no return.[41] After three years a small paid-up insurance policy was given as surrender value, and policies that lapsed after fifteen years received a cash surrender value.[42] Industrial insurance, unlike de-ferred dividend insurance, was usually nonparticipating; that is, the policyholder was not entitled to dividends. Therefore any gains from lapses and surrendered policies contributed to company accumulation. For 1904, the Metropolitan gained more from surrendered and lapsed policies than from all other sources.[43]

The contrast between the liberal policies of the Mutual Benefit of New Jersey and the liberal promises of the Prudential (also of New Jersey) indicate clearly the accumulative potential inherent in the contracts of the latter. Between 1875 and 1904 the Mutual Benefit received in premiums $204 million and paid out $181 million. During the same period the Prudential received $287 million and paid out $92 million.[44] As an official of the Prudential pointed out, the difference is primarily to be accounted for by the rapid growth and the high lapse rate (and small surrender values) of the Prudential.[45] While Senator Dryden, the president of the Prudential, was using part of the gains from the tremendous lapse rate and low surrender values [46] to pay for the increasing cost of new busi-ness,[47] the Mutual Benefit was adopting liberal surrender values on policies to provide as high a return as possible to those who were unable to keep up their policies. Amzi Dodd, the president of the Mutual Benefit, made nonforfeiture a basic feature of that company's policies.

III

Neither tontine nor industrial policies could have caused the rapid expansion in life insurance assets without the work of the life insurance agent. No matter how attractive the contract offered, the market was narrowly limited without high-pressure selling.[48] The life insurance agent was not new. Person to person solicitation became the most important marketing method as early as 1843.[49] However, with Henry B. Hyde tontine insurance and a new type of aggressive marketing were combined to produce a revolution in the industry.

Hyde's father was himself a successful agent for the Mutual Life and at an early age the younger Hyde became a clerk and then cashier of that company. At the age of twenty-seven he was fired for proposing to the president of the Mutual that another company be set up to handle larger risks. Within a week he had created the Equitable Life Assurance Society;

and in the ten years following its inception in 1859, it moved to first place in annual sales.[50] In the early years Hyde devoted all his energy and money to the development of an elaborate field force.[51] He increased the pay of his agents by raising their commission rates, circularized them with suggestions for more aggressive methods of reaching every insurable person, and continuously traveled throughout the country to improve and expand agency organization. When he could not find trained agents, he stole them from other companies by offering them double the usual commission.

The rapid development of a large and active agency force was expensive from the start, and as a result Hyde and his new Equitable could not compete with the annual dividends of other companies such as the Mutual and the New York Life. Cutting down the cost of new business so that his dividends might compare favorably with those of other companies, however, meant a retrenchment of expenses and of agency forces — quite the opposite to what Hyde had in mind. The drastic alternative was to eliminate the annual dividend.[52] Hyde had heard of Tonti's scheme and in 1868, as the way out of his dilemma, introduced tontine insurance. A necessary requirement was the rescinding of the law which required ascertainment of surplus every five years. Hyde got the New York State legislature to repeal this law in 1868. This combination of political action, an agency force aggressively selling the new insurance with its particular speculative appeal, and the accumulation potential of such insurance itself formed one basis for the spectacular growth of the Equitable.[53] Other companies quickly took the cue, some of course with more success than others.

Though faced with this new and rugged competition, the Connecticut Mutual and a few other conservative companies persisted in trying to sell annual dividend insurance. Greene refused to raise agents' commissions to compete with the tontine companies. More important, he insisted that life insurance be sold as such. While the big three emphasized policies that were investments, guaranteed incomes, Consols, and Gold Bonds, the Connecticut Mutual continued to sell insurance simply as family protection. Many of the conservative companies, faced with the clear decision of making concessions toward the new types of insurance and all its concomitant requirements of increased agents' commissions and other high costs or suffer a substantial decline in new business, compromised. They issued variations on the tontine policy (with such conservative qualifications as annual calculation, but not distribution, of dividends) and attempted to provide more attractive agents' contracts. Men such as President Ide of the Home Life, while roundly denouncing many of the policies and tactics of the big three, nevertheless considered themselves forced to modify their views on life insurance in order to obtain any new business at all.[54] While tontine insurance meant the accumulation of surplus, Ide kept this surplus at less than 10 per cent of assets and distributed anything above that figure to policyholders as dividends. Because the company, moreover, made more in the case of lapse of the deferred dividend policy, it could now afford a more liberal contract.[55] Ide conceded that the lapsing policyholder received less in a deferred dividend than in an annual dividend policy, but claimed that he chiefly wanted policies that would not lapse.[56]

Companies such as the Home Life, which compromised with the new orientation of life insurance, survived and expanded. However, their growth was circumscribed by the many conservative policyholder welfare provisions which they adopted or retained. Their costs and net premium payments, on the other hand, were substantially higher [57] than those of companies which completely abstained from tontine insurance or other policies oriented to rapid accumulation.

While Hyde developed an aggressive agency force, it remained for the industrial companies to first utilize the agent in a "retail" capacity. Weekly premiums which had to be collected in person required a vast army of agents, each with an area exclusively his own. When industrial insurance was first introduced into the United States in 1875, the Metropolitan Life Insurance Company was a small company with but twenty-five million dollars of insurance in force.[58] In 1880 Joseph Knapp, the president of the company, sent to England for experienced men to act as superintendents and agents. In the next five years he imported 819 men who were to form the nucleus of the vast field force necessary for marketing the new type of insurance. By the end of 1904 this company had $1,470,421,281 of insurance in force, of which over one billion dollars was industrial insurance.[59]

IV

Hyde's aggressive entrance into the life insurance field touched off the bitter struggle for control of the rapidly expanding industry. In this struggle, the manifest functions of a life insurance company were increasingly neglected by the competing titans whose tactics, strategy, external policy, and internal organization proved to be remarkably similar. Supremacy of tactical position first required supremacy in size, and every effort was directed to writing new business. But to supremacy within the industry had to be added security against legal and political attacks from outside by discontented policyholders and corporations in other industries which persistently strove to shift tax burdens to insurance firms. Thus sustained domination by the large company, besides requir-

ing unremitting exploitation of the market, also required extensive political connections, intimate relations with regulatory bodies such as the
New York State Insurance Department and similar bureaus in other
states, and close affiliation with or control of investment outlets.

In the struggle for size, since more and more agents were needed to
increase sales, higher and higher commissions were offered.[60] Agents'
earnings, however, did not increase.[61] In the competition for each prospective policyholder, agents had to offer such substantial rebates on first
year premiums that real commissions remained on the old level. Gradually
adding to costs of both agents and companies, and leading therefore to
the increased loading of premiums, was another by-product of the drive
for new business, called "twisting." This consisted of an agent convincing
a policyholder in one company to shift his policy to another company.
Successful agents of one company, moreover, were made attractive offers
of double the commission rates and substantial money advances by competitors, and frequently a general agent would go over to a competing
company with his entire field force.[62] Thus the New York Life received
notice one morning that its entire Manhattan office consisting of a general
agent and over two hundred agents had gone over to the Equitable.[63]

Such tactics were common among the large companies; however, they
were a major hardship to the small or conservative company which found
that every good agent would be tempted away by the high commission
rates of the major companies.[64] Greene claimed that every one of his
good agents had received lucrative offers from the big three. The Connecticut Mutual not only continued to lose agents to the tontine companies, but also faced the competition of almost universal rebating and
twisting. Policyholders had come to expect that part or all of their first
year's premiums would be returned to them in rebates. Greene continued
to point out that the aggressive competition of the big three was causing
rebating and that ultimately the policyholder paid for it in the form of
higher premiums and smaller dividends.

The search for new business caused the three largest companies to
extend their business outside the United States, and by 1906 the Mutual
had twenty-five agencies in over twenty countries.[65] The Equitable and
the New York Life had preceded the Mutual and had equally extensive
overseas forces. Each country, however, presented new difficulties in
adapting insurance to local conditions, and frequently expenses consistently exceeded new premiums. The Equitable had a ratio of expenses to
new premiums of 126.5 per cent in Australia in 1904 and it was as high
as 137.5 per cent in 1900.[66] In Great Britain it was 130 per cent in 1904.[67]
Despite the expense, foreign business made up between one-fourth and
one-third of the new insurance of the Equitable in 1888.[68]

Advertising rapidly became one of the biggest expenses of the companies. It had a twofold purpose: (1) to indoctrinate the population with the fundamental necessity of life insurance, and (2) to promote the individual company in the fiercely competitive war. This propaganda was done through the clergy and religious papers, college professors, prominent military figures, and esteemed representatives of other highly sanctioned activities.[69] One of the most extensively used methods was newspaper editorials and news stories featuring life insurance, for which the newspapers were paid, usually $1.00 a line.[70] Such editorials and stories were also frequently used for individual company promotion, as were circulars attacking the reliability of competitors.[71] In 1904 the Mutual expended $1,134,833.76 for advertising, printing, stationery and postage.[72]

In the ceaseless effort to achieve the dominant position in the industry, the major companies hired insurance journals not only for advertising purposes but particularly to attack other companies and to publicize any malpractices. The most celebrated journalist in this field was Stephen English, whose *Insurance Times* was an organ of the Mutual primarily aimed at attacking Hyde and the Equitable. In 1872 English changed sides and armed with extensive material[73] proceeded to attack F. S. Winston, the Mutual's president. A libel suit was instituted and the editor jailed. English appealed to the New York State Assembly, and the subsequent investigation cleared him and substantiated most of his charges.[74] Subsequently Winston paid English a sum sufficient to regain his friendship and his rather hazardous editorial support.[75]

Although the war between the large companies continued in such personal ways as journalistic attacks and through more orthodox economic methods such as premium reductions[76] and public offerings of premium rebates,[77] the larger companies more and more found that they jointly faced the rapid increase in small companies and the growing hostility of policyholders.[78] Therefore, even while they fought among themselves, they began to coöperate in the face of such external threats to their joint position. The first organization of life insurance companies, the Chamber of Life Insurance, was at one time an instrument of the companies opposed to the Mutual's rate-cutting proposal during the Winston-English-Hyde struggle.[79] Subsequent to the settlement of that dispute, however, the Mutual joined the organization and it turned its attention to legislative action. However, such organized group tactics were less effective at that date than the large companies' informal domination over the State Insurance Department in New York and the state legislature.

The New York State Insurance Department was organized in 1859. The first Superintendent of Insurance was William Barnes,[80] who remained in office for ten years and was displaced by George Miller, a

Tweed appointee. In 1870, Miller, at the behest of a Mutual policyholder, conducted an investigation of that company. Midway through the examination the investigation was suspended and no report was ever given. However, the policyholder, James W. McCullough, received a letter from Sewell and Pierce, the law firm representing the Mutual, which read:

> I beg to present you herewith a copy of the examination of witnesses before George W. Miller. You will please take notice that the same has been duly entered in the clerk's office of the district court of the United States for the Southern District of New York by the Mutual Life Insurance Company and that a copyright thereon has been secured by the company. I am instructed to inform you that any violation of the copyright by the publication of the whole or any part of the said examination will be prosecuted by the company to the full extent of the law. Very respectfully, Robert Sewell.[81]

The apparently intimate relationship between Sewell and Pierce, attorneys for the Mutual, and Miller was one of the factors that provided the Republicans with ammunition to institute impeachment proceedings against Miller. The resultant investigation substantiated the close association among the latter, the law firm, and the Mutual.[82] It also brought out that Miller, with the substantial financial support of the large companies, had introduced the "Miller Life Bill" with the objective of crushing the small companies.[83] In 1870, at the request of the president of the Mutual, Miller called a convention of state insurance superintendents. One of its primary objectives was to prevent the enactment of legislation increasing surrender values.[84]

Miller was not an atypical insurance superintendent, and if more insurance superintendents were not impeached it was not for lack of evidence of their direct functional relationship to the dominant companies, but rather because of the increasingly powerful influence of these companies over the state legislature.[85] A friendly insurance superintendent guaranteed favorable examinations which had both large advertising and publicity value and also frequently forestalled more critical examinations.[86] Moreover he could advance discriminatory legislation against assessment insurance companies,[87] and out-of-state or foreign companies. Finally he provided a bulwark against policyholder discontent and threats to accumulation. The position of superintendent of insurance early became one of the top political appointments of the Tammany machine and the succeeding Republican machine, under Senator T. C. Platt, carried on the tradition. The three big insurance companies occupied key positions in financing the Republican machine and to some extent the Democratic one also and thus guaranteed to themselves not only friendly legislators but coöperative insurance departments as well.[88]

Policyholder discontent, attacks on forfeiture, attempts to require division of surplus, and numerous requests for investigation were more directly the concern of the legislature than the insurance department. The numerous failures of life insurance companies in the seventies had particularly aroused policyholders.[89] These failures were due partly to the depression of the period and partly to the aggressive tactics of the dominant companies. However, a large number had simply been plundered by their own management.[90] In 1877 an extensive investigation was conducted by the New York Assembly Committee on Insurance, but, as in previous investigations, several members of the assembly committee were representatives of the principal companies,[91] and the investigation was discontinued.[92] The leading representative of the large companies in the legislature was James W. Husted,[93] who occupied a key position on the insurance committee for many years and then became speaker of the Assembly.

Domination of state legislatures and insurance departments by the big three was primarily oriented to sanctioning and protecting their acquisitive policies. To a lesser degree political control was also oriented toward the advancement of discriminatory legislation and rulings against other companies. The most consistently effective weapon employed by the big three in attacking the conservative company and particularly Greene and the Connecticut Mutual, however, was the insurance press. At first the Connecticut Mutual was attacked because it was one of the largest firms. Long after the big three had left that company far behind, however, it remained a primary target of the controlled insurance journals. Greene's outspoken and relentless attack on the policies of the leading tontine companies was more of a threat to the position of the big three than he could ever have been as a business competitor alone. His letters in the New York *Tribune* and other newspapers attracted wide attention. He attacked the speculative elements in the tontine policy, the growth of large surpluses from withheld policyholder dividends, and the tremendous increase in expense that came from the ceaseless drive for new business. The Equitable, Mutual, and New York Life countered both through their insurance journals and extensive circulars discrediting the Connecticut Mutual and attacking Greene personally.[94] In 1885 the pages of the New York *Tribune* contained numerous letters from the presidents of the big three on the one hand and Greene on the other. This controversy over the policies of the leading tontine companies, coming as it did at a time of increasing policyholder dissatisfaction, led Hyde to seek a truce with Greene. The president of the Connecticut Mutual refused, maintaining that he had an obligation to acquaint the public not only with the benefits of legitimate life insurance but also with the perversions of life insurance.[95]

In the early eighties the first tontine policies matured with a marked discrepancy between the estimated dividends and the actual results. In part this decline was a result of a falling interest rate; however, it was the tremendous increase in expenses which was the primary cause of small dividends. A large part of this expense was incurred in obtaining new business where commission rates had risen from 20 to 25 per cent in the sixties to 50 to 80 per cent by the turn of the century, where advances to agents were in the millions,[96] where advertising outlays had increased many fold, and where overseas business and the cost of erecting and maintaining large overseas office buildings was substantial. In 1904 the total expenses of the Mutual were almost $17 million. Approximately $10 million of this was attributable to the cost of new business that year.[97]

However, if the expenses of new business were high, the cost of maintaining a dominant position in the industry in the face of the internal warfare and the external threats to accumulation were almost equally expensive. The New York Life paid at least $1,312,197.16 to one man to subvert inimical legislation between 1895 and 1905.[98] The Equitable contributed $10,000 a year to the Republican State Committee; $50,000 to the Republican National Committee in presidential years; $20,000 a year to Republican Senator C. M. Depew; $5000 a year to Democratic Senator David B. Hill; and $6000 a year to a Tammany official. In addition there was $1,874,916.60 in one account (of several) which was used in good part for political control.[99] The expenses of the legal department also increased many times, and by 1904 the Mutual was expending over $360,000 a year in this department alone.[100] All these increased expenses could not help but greatly reduce dividend payments. Subsequent efforts to investigate tontine insurance were either defeated[101] or conducted by the actuary of the leading tontine insurance company himself.[102] Discontented policyholders instituted suits to demand an accounting from the companies; however, in 1890 Section 56 of the insurance law was enacted prohibiting a policyholder to demand an accounting from a company without the permission of the attorney general.[103]

The comparison of the net cost (premium less dividend) of policies issued by the big three with those issued by the Connecticut Mutual shows the effects of the increased expenses of the leading tontine companies. On a twenty-year endowment policy, for example (age 25, issued in 1893), the net cost in 1906 was $36.67 for the Connecticut Mutual, $38.64 for the New York Life, $41.79 for the Equitable, and $42.40 for the Mutual.[104] On other types of policies, as well as dividends on paid-up insurance, the leading tontine companies were consistently at the bottom

of the list.[105] The cheapest insurance was issued by the Connecticut
Mutual, the Mutual Benefit, the John Hancock, the Union Central (of
Ohio), and other similarly conservative companies. In these terms they
should have been the most popular companies for prospective policyholders. Obviously the key to rapid expansion was not simply the lowest
net cost to the policyholder. Speculative policies which promised large
rewards, extensive advertising, an aggressive agency force, and large
rebates were far more persuasive. Such practices required an almost unlimited expenditure in the acquisition of new business. The entrepreneur
who insisted on liberal surrender values and annual division of surplus
in the interests of existing policyholders lacked the funds necessary for
the rapid acquisition of new business.

This history of life insurance in the last half of the nineteenth century
is really a history of the large firm in the main stream of competitive
accumulation. While the entrepreneurial orientation of Greene, Dodd,
and other conservative life insurance executives was toward the welfare
and protection of existing policyholders, Hyde, McCurdy, and McCall
of the big three were oriented to acquisitive accumulation in the interests
of size and dominance of the industry. While the proponents of reform [106]
were setting up the conservative company as the ideal type, it was the
big three (and in the twentieth century the industrial companies) who
were responsible for the expansion of life insurance and the capital accumulation which was of material importance to the American economy.
Adherence to the strict manifest functions of life insurance would permit
no such expansion as took place. The innovations in insurance, particularly the tontine policy in the nineteenth century, provided the speculative
appeal. The aggressive methods of agency forces coupled with other selling techniques brought the tontine policy to the attention of every prospective policyholder. While the innovations and the selling methods
expanded the market, the characteristics of the policy guaranteed that
the assets of the companies would directly benefit. The retention of surplus for long periods, low surrender values, and the division of surplus
depending on company discretion were the directly contributing factors.
To implement such policies a wider and wider area of control was necessary to forestall the competitive threats of other companies, and the discontent of policyholders. Control of newspapers, legislatures, and regulatory bodies not only served the negative purpose of preventing hostile
publicity and legislation, but also served the positive purpose of favorable
publicity, the repeal of restrictive legislation and regulatory measures, and
enactment of such measures as would implement company accumulation.
Therefore, in addition to the speculative character of tontine insurance

and the low surrender values of both tontine and industrial insurance, the political domination of regulatory bodies and the legislatures were necessary requirements for such swift expansion. By 1905 life insurance companies, with assets of $2,924,253,848,[107] had become an essential part of the financial structure of the American economy.

X

Henry Varnum Poor

Philosopher of Management

1812 — 1905

By Alfred D. Chandler, Jr.

Henry Varnum Poor is best remembered for his pioneer work in providing investment information and services. The great mass of accurate information gathered by him about the railroads of the United States, first as editor of the *American Railroad Journal* from 1849 to 1862 and later as publisher of Poor's *Manual of the Railroads of the United States*, was long used by men in business to determine the value of railroads and other corporations as investments. Yet Henry Poor strongly believed that the information he compiled and edited had a far greater value than just as an aid to the investor. Describing his work to his wife in 1860 shortly before his *History of the Railroads and Canals of the United States*, the forerunner of the better known *Manuals*, went to press, he remarked:

> To tell you what I am doing would be to show you columns of figures to be added, divided, or subtracted, or the memoirs of some rr. or canal, which is little else than a record of names, and dates, and distances — this is the most prosaic business possible. It may lay the foundation by the by, for something better. First comes the form — then the soul, the natural sequence must be respected. . . I am getting along well though slowly. The work I am doing will never be done over again. So I am making it as valuable and complete as possible. It will be the record of a great achievement — of the greatest achievement the world has yet seen.[1]

Recording the "greatest achievement" the world had ever seen was indeed rewarding; but even in the years before 1860 while he was collecting data — laying the foundation — Henry Poor was also analyzing and interpreting his compiled information, trying to understand the soul. Deeply interested in how this great railroad achievement was being accomplished, what it meant for the country as a whole, and how the problems currently impeding its further progress might be met and solved, Poor made special studies of construction, finance, operation, and administration. Of the major problems discussed in the pages of the *Journal* those raised by the beginning of large-scale private finance, at first fully occupied his attention. It was not long, however, before the more lasting and the much more complex questions of large-scale business organization began to take precedence in his mind and in his writings. He was the first American to analyze with care and intensiveness many of the basic problems of modern big business. This would of itself be reason enough for focusing this essay on Poor's studies of railroad operation and administration were not his descriptions, analyses, and insights, written for and widely read by the businessmen of nearly a century ago, still of interest and of use today.

II

Henry Poor was particularly well qualified to analyze the complex and often completely new problems faced by the youthful railroad industry in the 1850's. His intellectual background gave him a broad vision of the over-all function of the railroad in the American economy, while his business experience provided him with insight into ways by which this function might be most efficiently carried out.

Poor's intellectual and business experience were both the results of a New England training. During the years 1845 to 1849 he had actively helped his brother, John Alfred Poor, build one of New England's most important railroads, the Atlantic and St. Lawrence, which connected Portland with Montreal. In this work he acquired a valuable firsthand understanding of what the construction of a railroad in a semi-frontier area of the United States involved and what specific problems of promotion, organization, construction, and financing had to be met.[2] But even more significant than this business experience was the contribution of New England to Poor's intellectual training. As a young man he had been in close contact with the stirring new ideas of Unitarianism and Transcendentalism.[3] Through his brother-in-law, Frederick Henry Hedge, one of the initiators of the Transcendental movement, Poor came to know personally Ralph Waldo Emerson, the Channings, Theodore Parker, George Ripley, and other intellectual leaders of the day. It was quite natural, therefore, that he became imbued with their buoyant, optimistic belief in man's progress and perfection.

Like these men Poor believed that God had given man a mind as the means for his perfection. Man's mind was stronger than man-made institutions and could alter these institutions which had brought sin and evil into the world. Yet the mind, in order to progress toward perfection, must be carefully trained and disciplined both intellectually and morally. As he was closer to Emerson than to Spencer, Poor's belief in progress was a positive rather than a negative faith involving creative action rather than automatic or mechanistic laws. This faith, moreover, was fully developed before Poor became closely acquainted with the amazing technological developments of the nineteenth century.

To Henry Poor the coming of the industrial and transportation revolutions was, in fact, a magnificent verification of his basic concepts. Here men by creatively applying their minds to the labor-saving machine were making strides towards the physical perfection that was the first and necessary step to intellectual and spiritual perfection. Of all the new technical instruments that were furthering the progress of mankind, the railroad was having the most profound effect.[4] By lowering the cost of transportation and by making possible widespread commercial agriculture and large-scale industry, the railroad was making food, clothing, and the other necessities of life plentiful to all classes of people. By breaking down the barriers of place and time, by permitting the interchange of ideas and beliefs as well as goods, the railroad was allaying petty regional antagonisms and narrow provincialism. In time it would even bring an end to the more traditional national boundaries and usher in the millennium of universal peace and prosperity. For Henry Poor, then, the efficient construction and operation of the American railroad system was even more a moral than an economic necessity, and throughout his life his moral indignation was thoroughly aroused when incompetence or dishonesty hampered effective railroad operation.

When Poor became editor of the *American Railroad Journal* in 1849, the American railway system was on the verge of its first great period of expansion, and it was largely the problems raised by this expansion that were to occupy the major part of his attention during the 1850's. In that decade some 25,000 miles of railroad were constructed, nearly three-fourths of all the mileage built before the Civil War. This expansion, concentrated in the Old Northwest, laid down the basic transportation system east of the Mississippi. Unlike earlier transportation developments, it was carried out largely by private enterprise and private capital. Its building and operation required, for the first time on a nation-wide scale, the use of the big corporation in its modern institutional sense as an instrument for the administration of large amounts of men, money, and materials. Its private financing not only created for the first time in this country a sizable investor class, but the requirements of the roads for relatively simple and standardized methods of raising large amounts of money also brought about the rapid institutionalizing of the American investment market. Largely because Wall Street successfully financed the new roads in the South and West in the 1850's, New York, where Poor had come to live and work, became and remained the dominant financial center of the United States.

When the decade of the fifties opened, however, the investment market had not yet been standardized. Thus finance was the first major problem of the railroad industry. The new western roads were coming en masse to the eastern cities to raise money and if the funds were not forthcoming many lines so essential to the growth of the United States could not be built. For this reason Henry Poor, writing from his office just off Wall Street, turned his attention in 1850 to helping the railroads, especially the western roads, raise the required funds. This he did first by popularizing the railroad mortgage bond, the comparatively new financial instrument that was to finance the construction of the roads in the West and the South. Secondly, in the pages of the *Journal*, he analyzed conditions of the New York investment market, advising the roads when to float their securities and explaining to them the intricacies of getting an equitable price for western railroad bonds. Poor repeatedly advocated that the methods of buying and selling be systematized. He urged reliable banking firms to enter the railroad security field and advocated the adoption of the sealed bid system then in use by the national government as the fairest and least exploitable way of selling securities.

By 1852, however, conditions had changed so rapidly that construction finance was no longer the major problem in the railroad industry. The New York investment market was becoming systematized along the lines Poor had been advocating. Even more important, the western railroad mortgage bonds which in 1850 could only be sold at a heavy discount were now the most popular securities in the New York market — too popular, Poor thought, fearing that a speculative boom in railroad securities would surely lead to overconstruction in railroads.

In keeping with his fundamental concepts, Poor now shifted his policy from aiding the railroads on Wall Street to advocating a program which might assure a more healthy even if slower expansion of the American railroad system. "Our real danger has just commenced," he warned in December 1852, and emphasized that:

There is great danger that taking advantage of the confidence known to exist in railroad investments, and the abundance of money, some projects not entitled to aid from their inherent strength, and others of purely speculative character may succeed in affecting large loans, not only involving great risk of loss but bringing discredit and suspicion upon the whole railway interest and productive of the most injurious consequences.[5]

He urged the investors not to put their money into roads about which they had little information, and asked the roads not to come to the market unless the soundness of their financial position was made explicit in their printed prospectuses. To implement this policy Poor began to make careful analyses of the prospectuses and exhibits of roads coming to the New York investment market, pointing out to investors any discrepancies, omissions, or other facts that might give a speculative or otherwise un-reliable tinge to these proffered securities. In this way, by carrying out a policy that he felt to be for the best interest of the railroad and the country at large, Henry Poor began his life work of serving the investor.[6]

The panic of 1854 soon emphasized the validity of Poor's warnings, and the depression of 1857 fulfilled them. No longer was it necessary to warn the investor and the general public against overconstruction; they now only too clearly appreciated its dangers. During the mid-1850's Poor therefore turned his attention from finance and financial reform to the second major problem raised by the expansion of the railroad system at the time — that of operation and management.

III

By the middle of the 1850's the roads which had been successfully financed earlier in the decade were all going into operation at about the same time. These included many of the nation's key railroad lines such as the great trunk lines which joined the East to the Old Northwest and the roads that extended the trunk lines to the major cities in the Mississippi Valley. The Erie was completed in 1851, the Baltimore and Ohio and the Atlantic and St. Lawrence in 1853, and the Pennsylvania in 1855. The year 1852 saw the entrance of the Michigan Central and the Michigan Southern into Chicago, and by 1855 the Mississippi had been reached at several places. By that date the Old Northwest which in 1849 had only some 600 miles of road could boast that nearly every sizable town in the area had rail connections with the Atlantic seaboard.[7]

As the roads became connected, the development and handling of through traffic became an important factor in their survival or success. One result was the consolidation of smaller lines. The most important of these amalgamations were those which formed the New York Central in 1853, and the Pittsburgh, Fort Wayne and Chicago in 1856.[8] Fre-quently where formal consolidation did not take place, companies put themselves under a single operating management as did the roads connecting Cleveland and Cincinnati in 1852, the roads joining Toledo and Cincinnati in 1854, and those uniting Columbus and Indianapolis in 1856.[9] This period also saw, beginning in 1854, the holding of regional and occasional national railroad conferences to discuss ways and means of facilitating the flow of through traffic, of establishing rates for this traffic, and of considering the numerous other problems raised by the coming of rapid large-scale, long-distance transportation.[10] Having built a railroad network from the Atlantic to the Mississippi with amazing swiftness, the railroad entrepreneurs of the 1850's were now faced with the complex problem of how to operate it most effectively.

By far the most serious and most novel of the problems of operation were raised by the greatly increased size of the new operating units. It was size — size in terms of mileage operated, capital raised, men employed, and traffic transported — that strikingly differentiated the new railroads from those that began operations before 1850. In 1849 no company in the United States was managing as many as 250 miles of road and few more than a hundred miles. By 1855 close to twenty operating units were working more than 250 miles of road, and five of these were administering lines at least twice the size of the largest road in the country in 1849.[11] In 1849 only two roads were capitalized at over ten million dollars; by the middle of the fifties at least ten companies were larger than this and five of these were capitalized at over twenty million. The same pattern held for the number of operatives employed and the amount of freight and passenger traffic carried.[12]

This development of large individual operating units which accompanied the sudden growth of the railroad industry in the 1850's presented the American businessmen for the first time with the many modern problems of large-scale business management. In meeting these problems the railroad managers of the day had comparatively few precedents upon which to rely. The older transportation companies which governed canals and turnpikes were not operating organizations. They constructed and maintained canals and turnpikes for the use of common carriers on payment of a toll. On the other hand, a contemporary manufacturing company like a Lowell or Pittsburgh mill involved only a comparatively simple type of operation, usually with but a single plant that could be physically inspected in the space of half an hour. Even the experience of the earlier and smaller railroad companies could not offer much aid in solving the problems of large-scale management. Daniel C. McCallum, superintendent of the Erie, pointed out that actually in management methods the smaller roads were closer to the small manufacturing firms of the day than to the new roads of the fifties:

A Superintendent of a road fifty miles in length can give its business his personal attention and may be constantly on the line engaged in the direction of its details; each person is personally known to him, and all questions in relation to its business are at once presented and acted upon; and any system however imperfect may under such circumstances prove comparatively successful.

In the government of a road five hundred miles in length a very different state exists. Any system which might be applicable to the business and extent of a short road would be found entirely inadequate to the wants of a long one; and I am fully convinced that in the want of a system perfect in its details, properly adapted and vigilantly enforced, lies the true secret of their [the large roads'] failure; and that this disparity of cost per mile in operating long and short roads, is not produced by a difference in length, but is in proportion to the perfection of the system adopted.[13]

Henry Poor quite agreed with McCallum that system rather than size determined the efficiency of a road, and therefore, its productiveness. Like McCallum and the Erie's Board of Directors, his attention had been turned to the problems of large-scale management by the realization that many small roads, old and new, were making better net returns than the large new ones.[14] But even on some small ones, especially in New England, where profits were relatively low, Poor felt that the failure to systematize administration and operations, rather than the roads' traditional excuse of low rates, was most responsible for their unfavorable financial record.[15] In 1854, therefore, as the new problems of administration and operation were becoming increasingly acute, Poor decided to turn the attention of his paper to the study of management:

We believe that the science of *management* is the most important in its bearings upon the success of the American Railroads — that it includes facts and principles which are deserving a full statement and an elaborate discussion. . . In this field the *Journal* will ever strive to be a faithful laborer.[16]

IV

To the editor of the *Journal* the science of management fundamentally resolved itself into three principles — organization, communication, and information. Of these organization was basic. Organization to Poor meant the careful division of labor, from the president to the common laborer, with each man having his own specified duties and responsibilities, and each being directly accountable to his immediate superior. The words responsibility and accountability appear constantly in Henry Poor's discussions of management. By communication Poor meant primarily a method of reporting throughout the organization which would give the top management an accurate and continuous account of the progress of operations, and which in so doing would assure the necessary accountability all along the line. Information in an administrative sense was to Poor recorded communications — that is, a record of the operational reports systematically compiled and analyzed. This information was to be used for deriving a clearer understanding of such basic matters as fixed costs, running expenses, operational performance, rate-making, and so forth, and also to provide data necessary for more scientific experimentation to improve service.

In formulating these ideas Poor relied on the experience of the foremost railroad managers of the day including John Brough, manager of the jointly operated roads between Columbus and Indianapolis, Benjamin H. Latrobe of the Baltimore and Ohio, J. Edgar Thomson of the Pennsylvania, George B. McClellan of the Illinois Central, and Daniel C. McCallum of the Erie, each of whom Poor knew personally. Of all these men he was closest to McCallum of the Erie, and it is in his discussion of McCallum's work that Poor's views on management are best revealed.

"Mr. McCallum's strong point," wrote Poor, "lies in his power to arrange and systematize, and in his ambitions to perfect his systems. To this end he has untiringly devoted his energies since he was appointed in charge of this great work." [17] In September 1854, not long after McCallum had become General Superintendent, Poor who had been highly critical of the Erie since its completion in 1851, reported that thanks to the new superintendent the road was finally getting on its feet.[18] Already McCallum had reorganized the service so as to eliminate much duplication of work and thereby had actually made the road more efficient by cutting down the number of paid hands. Further measures had been "taken to put every employee at '*hard work*,'" if only by putting men temporarily unoccupied to cleaning machinery and making minor repairs on the rolling stock and equipment. He had systematized the methods of repairing locomotives so that more than forty engines which were normally lying idle could be on the road. More important was McCallum's proficiency in adapting the telegraph to railroad operations — an improvement that was soon to attract world-wide attention.[19] Not only did the telegraph make for safer and far more efficient operations but it was also used to facilitate over-all administration. Poor concluded his remarks on McCallum's initial reforms by pointing out that:

By arrangements now perfected, the superintendent can tell at any hour of the day, the precise location of every car and engine on the line of the road and the duty it is performing. Formerly, the utmost confusion prevailed in this department, so much so, that in the great press of business, cars in perfect order have stood for months upon the switches without being put to the least service, and without its being known where they were. All these reforms are being carried out as fast as the ground gained can be held.[20]

These first reforms were part of a larger and more fundamental reorganization of management along the lines of organization and communication so favored by Henry Poor. McCallum's careful "division of management" was best expressed in an organization chart of the Erie which he had drawn up for purposes of reference.[21] The design of the chart was a tree with the roots representing the President and the Board of Directors; the branches were the five operating divisions and the service departments: engine repairs, car, bridge, telegraph, printing, and so on; while the leaves represented the various local agents, subordinate superintendents, train crews, foremen, and so forth. McCallum's subdivision went even further than indicated on the chart. The smaller units such as the repair and machine shops were "managed with the same careful system that characterized the general superintendence of the Company's affairs."[22] Within these subdivisions the duties of each grade in the hierarchy not only were carefully specified, but the grade of each individual in the organization was indicated on the prescribed uniform worn by all employees.[23]

The line of command within the organization followed closely the lines indicated on the organization chart. Orders must go from roots to the leaves via the proper branches. "All subordinates," McCallum insisted, "shall be accountable to and *be directed by their own immediate superior only*; an obedience can not be enforced where the foreman in immediate charge is interfered with by a superior officer giving orders directly to his subordinates."[24] In the same way McCallum pointed out when discussing the powers of the more senior officials, "their subordinates cannot communicate with higher office, but through them [the senior officials] and can only be communicated with through them."[25]

McCallum realized that the most essential communication in his organization was from subordinate to superior rather than vice versa; and on the Erie this communication was achieved by a thoroughgoing system of reports. This system which provided accountability as well as communication received Poor's strongest commendation. "This plan involves on the one hand a very considerable trouble and expense," the *Journal* admitted, including "the maintenance of a large office of eight active clerks, but on the other hand it depicts faithfully in the general office every fact of practical importance."[26] This plan included hourly, daily, and monthly reports. The hourly reports were mainly operational, giving by telegraph a train's location and the reasons for any delays or mishaps. This "information being entered as fast as received on a convenient tabular form, shows at a glance, the position and progress of the trains, in both directions on every Division."[27] Just as important, the tabular forms were filed away to provide an excellent source of operational information which among other things proved especially useful in determining and eliminating "causes of delays."

Daily reports — the real basis of the system — were required from both conductors and station agents. They covered all important matters of train operations as well as the more general movement of freight and passenger traffic. Moreover reports from two different sources on train movements, car loadings, damages, misdirected freight, and so forth acted as a reliable check on the efficiency and the honesty of both conductors and agents. Daily reports were required from the engineers also. These were compiled in a monthly statement giving for each engine the miles run, running expenses, cost of repairs, and work done, and were submitted as part of the monthly report required of each division superintendent. The superintendent's reports included an account of all operations of the division including cost, expenses, work done for all types of equipment. Similar monthly reports were required from the heads of all the service departments. Like the hourly reports, wrote McCallum, "the information thus obtained is embodied in the statistical accounts kept in this office and from it we deduce" a mass of information useful in improving the effectiveness of operations.[28]

To Henry Poor the recording and filing of the operational and administrative information in statistical form was almost as important an aspect of McCallum's reporting plan as was its provision for communicating the progress of operations to the head office. Poor had long considered operating statistics the basic tool for scientific management, and McCallum's plan appeared to be the most effective one yet devised to acquire such data.[29] Intelligent action could be taken to reduce expenses and improve performance only when it was known what the expenses of a road were and just how equipment and personnel performed. Comparative studies of the monthly engine reports, for example, clearly showed what engines were best suited to the different tasks, which engineers operated their machines most efficiently, and where changes should be made.[30] The Erie and then other roads printed such engine reports, distributed them throughout their companies, and had them published in the *Journal* and occasionally in other railroad periodicals.[31] Thus not only the company but the whole railroad world was able to make full use of these first reliable operating statistics.

Statistics so necessary in determining running expenses were also essential in ascertaining the specific cost of carrying the different classifications of freight traffic and in fixing a fair rate for each classification.[32] Statistics, Poor insisted, were the only basis on which sound principles of rate-making could be evolved. Unless rates were thus scientifically determined, unless running and fixed expenses were carefully understood, no road could be sure just what its net receipts were or how its profits and loss really stood. These determinations, in turn, could not be made until a careful system of organization and communication was devised.

For these reasons Poor considered that the current discussions on railroad management and reform which centered about the question of high as opposed to low fares were unrealistic and superfluous.[33] Such contemporary writers as Captain William H. Swift, William Appleton, Elias H. Derby, James M. Whiton, and E. B. Grant seemed to be missing the point. It was not a question of whether high or low fares would bring the best return. It was rather to determine whether rates were remunerative in relation to the costs and expenses of transportation. Moreover the solution of Swift, Appleton, and others which would raise the rates on the transportation so essential to American economic development went against Henry Poor's basic principles. Instead of increasing the rates Poor urged the American railroad men to apply their minds to reducing expenses so that the apparently low fares could bring a profitable return. "The true remedy," he wrote, "is one we have always insisted upon — an *economical* administration of the roads. With such an administration we believe the usual rates of charges can be rendered sufficiently remunerative." [34]

In calling on the roads to meet their financial problems by adopting more efficient and economical operating and administrative techniques rather than by raising rates, Poor was the first to voice a demand that railroad engineers and reformers would take up and carry on for decades to come. In Poor's own day such engineers as Charles Ellet, Jr., John B. Jervis, Daniel C. McCallum, and Zerah Colburn, Poor's one-time assistant editor, all made extensive efforts in different fields of railroad operation to carry out Poor's principles of a more scientific management.[35] After the Civil War their efforts were expanded and refined by the brilliant work of Charles Francis Adams, Albert Fink, and Marshall Kirkman. Nevertheless, as considerations other than improved management influenced the policies of the financially minded railroad executives of that day, too often innovations and improvements in management methods were ignored or laid aside. Thus even as late as 1910 Louis D. Brandeis, expressing the views of many of the country's leading engineers, insisted in language strikingly similar to that used by Poor a half century earlier that the railroads should meet their financial difficulties by improving their administrative and operational efficiency rather than by raising rates.[36]

v

If Henry Poor's enunciation of the principles of a more scientific management — the principles of systematic organization, communication, and information — anticipated and indeed indicated the most constructive nineteenth-century developments in big business organization, his understanding of the problems involved in putting these principles into practice foreshadowed the twentieth-century pragmatic analysis of big business management. Poor's keen appreciation of the problems involved in the effective operation of a large-scale organization was unique for his own day, and for many decades thereafter no analysis approached his in depth or realism. Indeed it was not until big business came to dominate the American economy that analyses similar to those made by Poor when big business was still in its formative stage would again be written. Much of what Poor had said then was paralleled in the writings of Thorstein Veblen, Adolf A. Berle, Chester I. Barnard, Robert A. Gordon, and others. Perhaps this is because objective analysis of an economic institution and organization is easier when it is still new and experimental or after it has reached full maturity rather than during the period of its most dynamic development.

Poor first turned his full attention to analyzing pragmatically the problems raised by the operation of a carefully structured business enterprise in the later years of the 1850's. The depression following the panic of 1857 had shown that a careful "division of management" did not necessarily mean a rise in net receipts or even an increase in operating efficiency. Moreover in 1858 Poor, during an extended visit to England, made a thorough study of the more mature British railroad system which verified his suspicions raised by the depression in America concerning the ineffectiveness of large-scale administration.[37] These lessons did not change his belief that systematic organization, communication, and information were indispensable for large-scale railroad administration; but they did impress upon him the grave difficulties of adapting human capabilities and current business practices and institutions to the severe requirements demanded by the efficient operation of large-scale administrative units.

Of these difficulties the most obvious to the public eye was the problem of getting railroad employees to accept the strict discipline and rigid regulations that were an essential part of large-scale administration. The employees took no pains to hide their dislike of the new model management. In fact several early strikes of skilled operatives on American railroads came in protest against administrative and operational regulations rather than over matters of wages and hours; and these strikes were most serious on the Erie where the organization had been most thoroughly established.[38] The tightening of control was also a primary cause for the founding in 1855 of the National Protective Association of the Locomotive Engineers of the United States. The call for the Association's first regular meeting registered a strong protest against "the blind system requiring implicit obedience" to all rules and regulations and asked:

shall we longer submit to the tyrannical will of a few men who strive to aggrandize themselves and build themselves up the title of "Napoleons" and "Able Managers" by grinding down the pay and trying to suppress our rights as a free and independent class of men for the purpose of adding to their already enormous salaries for their *"Able Management"*? [39]

Henry Poor believed that the engineers were rather extreme in their statements and felt strongly that the new rules and regulations must be faithfully followed, for "we can see no other way in which such a vast machine can be safely and successfully conducted." [40] Nevertheless he stressed that the engineers had a valid point and urged that the regulations be given flexibility and that discretion within certain limits be allowed. He warned railroad managers of the danger of "regarding man as a mere machine, out of which all the qualities necessary to be a good servant can be enforced by the payment of wages. Duties cannot be always prescribed and the most valuable ones are often voluntary ones. . ." [41]

Less obvious but, to Poor, far more dangerous than the reaction of the employee against the tightening of control was the deadening effect of fixed wages and prescribed duties on the initiative and interest of the men in the organization. Poor had always found it difficult to believe that any man on a salary would do more work than was absolutely necessary to collect his regular wages. Incentive was even less when a man was in the pay of a large organization, for here "all of a similar grade receive nearly the same rate of compensation although some of the parties, instead of being valuable officers, may possess no qualification whatsoever for their duty." [42] Thus with salaries determined by grade rather than by ability shown or work accomplished and with the functions of each grade specifically prescribed, Poor saw little reason for the railroad employee or official to exert himself to improve the company's service. The inevitable tendency was for administration to bog down into mere routine. Railroad management, Poor feared, was following the pattern of military and governmental administration and with the same damaging effect on employees. Writing from London in 1858, he compared railroads to the English bureaucratic institutions and asked:

Do the regular establishments in this country, the army, navy and church ever produce superior men? Seldom or never. Yet these establishments contain the best and most cultivated minds in the country. But their duties being prescribed according to a given routine, they soon become little better than servile copyists or imitators, lose all desire and faculty to act up to their former ideals, and turn out to be little better than dead rubbish. [43]

The English army, Poor continued, was only aroused from this condition by the Crimean War. At first individual heroes were sacrificed by an incompetency engendered by bureaucracy, but finally:

The capacity for success grew out of the experience gained during the war which forced the leaders to quit a routine which they had followed all their lives, to shape their actions to the exigencies of the moment, and the conditions in which they found themselves placed. Is there not sóme method by which railroads can be taken out of the category of red-tapeism, by which a living principle can be introduced to take the place of prescription or habit? There is one way in which it can, and that is to supply an adequate motive to good conduct, by rewarding merit at its worth. Till this is done, railroads, wherever they may be, will drag along in their beaten tracks of dullness and routine, and become worse managed and less productive year by year.[44]

Poor admitted, however, that the tendency toward routine and dullness was not inevitable as long as top management provided genuine leadership. Leadership infused an *esprit de corps* into the organization, which stirred the interest and initiative of subordinate officials and made strict regulation more acceptable to the employees.[45] At the same time leadership was essential to keep the organization operating as a single unit. The minds of the top management, wrote Poor,

must become the soul of the enterprise, reaching and infusing life, intelligence and obedience into every portion of it. This soul must not be a fragmentary or disjointed one — giving one direction to the head, another to the hands, and another to the feet. Wherever there is a lack of unity there will be a lack of energy — of intelligence — of life — of accountability and subordination.[46]

Such leadership, however, demands the highest talents. Not only must the top managers know how to handle men, but they must, in Poor's view, have an expert knowledge and training in all aspects of railroad administration and operation. Yet this was rarely the case in American companies, for, as Poor wrote, railroad executives and superintendents, while understanding their own specific duties, too often were

unacquainted with those of every important department under them; there is consequently no connecting link between the different departments of service, and no intelligence to guide them to a common end. In such a case it will not be long before the *morale* necessary to a high state of discipline will be completely broken. Instead of a unit, the different departments of service will often be arranged in hostile attitude towards each other. Parties in influential positions, being left to themselves, soon come to regard their own interests as the chief objects of concern.[47]

The lack of knowledge and training in the top management which hastened this type of organizational breakdown did so, Poor emphasized, because it disrupted the lines of accountability, communication, and information. A superior could hardly be expected to exact accountability down the line if he did not comprehend the type of work being accounted for. Nor could he make use of a carefully systematized supply of hourly, daily and monthly reports if he were not competent to interpret and understand the data he received. His subordinates finding it unnecessary, indeed often useless, to make reports and rarely receiving explicit orders were soon carrying out their own work without supervision from above. The ultimate result was that the railroad was administered from the bottom rather than the top and that a "sort of *imperium in imperio* grows up which really controls the conduct of all connected with the road." [48]

If the American railroads were, therefore, to operate efficiently it was obvious that they must be managed by men of the highest ability and training in railroad management. Yet it was just as obvious that this was rarely the case. In trying to account for this deficiency, Poor suggested that, in the first place, railroad companies did not provide incentives enough to attract and hold the most able men; and, secondly, they too often used other criteria than ability and training in the selection of men for the top managerial posts. Finally, railroad companies too often failed to detect inadequate leadership within their organization. This blindness Poor blamed primarily on the inability of the roads to exact proper accountability and responsibility from their managers. The breakdown of managerial leadership in Poor's view, was, thus, not so much the inability of human capabilities to meet the multitudinous responsibilities of top management; it was rather the failure of current business methods and organization to meet the requirements of large-scale administration. And this organizational failure was, in Poor's mind, sharply intensified by the sudden rise of a new business phenomenon — the separation of ownership and management within the railroad corporation.

By the end of the 1850's the editor of the *Railroad Journal* was tracing nearly all the problems of railroads to the one underlying fact that their managers did not own and their owners did not manage. The complex requirements of large-scale railroad operation necessitating as they did, for the first time in American business, the development of a technically proficient administrative hierarchy had created a managerial class. The huge financial demands of railroad construction and operation, on the other hand, requiring a vast amount of capital from private individuals, had created an investor class and had spread ownership among a large number of persons many of whom lived at great distances from each other and from their property. Henry Poor was uncertain whether the resulting division of the business unit between management and ownership could be resolved within the accepted framework of the corporation. Writing from England in 1858 he noted that:

> A great obstacle to the success of railroads in both countries is the fact they are controlled by *joint-stock companies.* . . It is an axiom that corporations have no soul. They certainly have more soul than sense. Now in business there is no success that is not earned, — that is not the product of good sense united to a steadiness of purpose, kept alive and active by a direct interest in the result of a person's labor and efforts. The servants of a joint-stock company seldom bring with them such qualities as these. . . As I have remarked before — if we would reform our management, and bring it to a state of efficiency and economy, we must supply to every person employed, the motives and sanctions that are necessary to success in the ordinary walks of life.[49]

While the managers did not have the incentives of ownership, the owners, Poor continued, had neither the good sense, interest, nor steadiness of purpose necessary for effective business management. Lacking the technical knowledge or "sense" necessary to understand railroad management and often not having the time or interest to acquire it, the stockholders were unable to locate or remedy inefficiency, incompetence, or dishonesty on the part of management.[50] Nor were they able to suggest practical reforms or improvements. At first Poor, like other writers of the day, tended to take the stockholders seriously to task for not trying to understand more clearly the problems of management in general and the financial and administrative status of their own railroad property in particular.[51] As the decade passed, however, he realized that this lack of knowledge and interest could hardly be avoided.

Behind the indifference on the part of management

> is . . . that of the owners of our roads. Among these there is little interest felt as to the manner in which they are conducted. It is natural that it should be so. Almost every person in the United States is deeply immersed in his own business or calling, the duties of which take all his capacities. We all know nothing more annoying or wearisome to a person so engaged to have his attention called to matters entirely foreign to his ordinary pursuits.[52]

A paucity of information as well as lack of time and inclination made it difficult for the stockholder to learn the facts of railroad management even on the roads in which he had placed his funds. There were no good general works on the subject, and the reports of individual railroad companies were rarely of any help.

Moreover a new type of stockholder tended to appear, with even greater ignorance and indifference than the earlier ones. When many of the roads were first constructed their stock was held by farmers and merchants living along the line of the road. These men considered the road a community project built to improve the value of their lands and businesses by providing essential transportation services. However, Poor noted that "with the lapse of time the tone of management is apt to relax. The zeal and disinterestedness displayed in the earlier stages of its progress gives place to indifference and selfishness." [53] The stock was increasingly purchased for investment purposes rather than to promote local transportation facilities and the business enterprises which stood to profit from them. It was scattered in all parts of the country, and the owners no longer had personal contact with one another. Concerted, vigorous, and intelligent action by the stockholders was, therefore, almost impossible; and when it did come it was only because the dividends on their investment had greatly diminished or ceased altogether. Then, of course, it was too late for remedial action. At such a time, commented Poor, the "stockholders are loud and often in their denunciations, but they are entirely unintelligent and would be no more successful were they placed in charge of their line." [54]

If the managers did not have the incentives of ownership and the owners did not have the knowledge of management, Henry Poor feared that the Board of Directors, the connecting link between ownership and management, had neither.[55] Directors, often owning but a few shares of stock and serving on a part-time, no-pay basis, tended either to give too little attention to the affairs of the company or to exploit their position for their own benefit. When, as was often the case, a man was elected because he was a successful merchant, manufacturer, or banker, he was by the very reason of his success sure to have his own extensive affairs to handle. Resulting inattention on the part of a number of the directors permitted a small clique to control the company and often to make large personal gains by contracting with themselves for construction or materials, by taking commissions for favors rendered, by using their inside knowledge to manipulate the price of the company's securities on the stock exchange. Such exploitation meant a serious loss to the company both in the effectiveness of the management and in the return on the investment.

Far more common and thus more dangerous than dishonest or negligent directors were incompetent ones. Too many directors lacked the knowledge or ability to perceive and rectify inefficient or inadequate performance on the part of management. Nor were they able to select capable superintendents and department heads. A glib tongue rather than real ability too often proved the criterion for managerial selection and promotion. Worse still such directors, not understanding the problems of administration, tended to make sweeping changes in personnel for relatively minor reasons. The result was that:

The great body of superintendents are *peripatetics*, wandering around from one road to another, without being allowed to remain in one place a sufficient time to get fairly warm in it. Should one not prove acceptable to the president or directors who may be entirely unfit to form any opinion of his qualifications, he must go. This is one of the worst features about our roads. No efficient encouragement is offered to young men to enter the service of companies, in the expectation that qualifications will regularly lead to preferment — thus offering the highest position as the rewards of merit. As it is, merit and position have no necessary connection.[56]

Poor felt that in this way the Board of Directors was primarily responsible for the breakdown of large-scale railroad management. Such management demanded the highest competence at the top level. Because the Board failed to recruit men properly, to supervise them efficiently, or to set stable policies for them to follow, this competence often was lacking. Moreover, even when competent men were found, the Board usually failed to provide the owners with the information so essential if they were to have an intelligent understanding of the condition and operation of their property. Poor once wrote in exasperation:

Directors tell us nothing for the best of reasons — that they generally know nothing about their roads. They are a medium of communication between the force employed on it and the stockholders. But the medium through which a correct idea of the condition of their road, the necessary link — that of intelligence — is wanting. The public have gone on ignorant of the condition of their property, and the manner in which it is managed. All have suffered in a greater or less degree, while many have been totally ruined.[57]

Failing to keep open the channels of communication between ownership and management not only meant that the directors had failed to supply adequate information but also had failed to make management accountable to the stockholders. Without such accountability Poor insisted that management, working without the incentives of ownership, could not possibly operate efficiently. If a large railroad was to be administered within the traditional framework of the corporation "the employees must be responsible to an intelligent board of directors; and those in turn to an intelligent board of stockholders. If either link in the chain is wanting the road will fall. Nobody can be trusted without exacting such accountabilities." [58]

Yet, as Poor pointed out, the difficulty of exacting such accountabilities was still further increased by the impersonal nature of the railroad corporation. Corporate organization made for a diffuseness and vagueness of responsibility which was not true of other business organizations and which not only made easy but actually encouraged the avoidance of responsibility and accountability. The difficulty, wrote Poor, is that:

The moment a person assumes an official position [in a corporation] it is very rare that he does not feel and act as if absolved from those moral responsibilities which he acknowledges and respects in his private or personal relations. A corporate body has no eye to detect the first departure from duty, and no indignant presence to rebuke and awe the offender. Those that sustain relations to it, are consequently without the motives and sanctions which enforce a certain degree of good conduct from parties who are rather influenced by a sense of shame, or desire to stand well with the public, than any love of principle, or sense of duty. In his own affairs, every person suffers the penalty of his misconduct. The conviction that he cannot escape it renders him vigilant and watchful over all his acts. But as servant of a *corporation*, the latter alone is the sufferer for any wrong or mistakes he may commit. No matter how great these, and the consequent loss may be, he never can be made to feel or appreciate its extent. It is so widely distributed, and the loss to each individual may be so small (though great in the aggregate), that the necessary relation between cause and effect is, in his mind, entirely obliterated. He may be dishonest or incompetent without a sense of guilt or dread of loss, and without fear either of exposure or punishment. Incompetency or dishonesty is usually only discovered from its effects, and then perhaps not till after a lapse of years.[59]

It was in describing the connection between the nature of the corporation and the nature of management — in understanding the broad implications of the separation of ownership from management — that Poor made his most original contribution to the business thought of his day. Most of his contemporaries whose views were recorded in print appreciated clearly that the nature of the corporation made the control of a company by its owners difficult. They wrote much on the need for reforms that would give the stockholder stronger control of the corporation and prevent exploitation of the type Schuyler, Kyle and Kilbourn had made so notorious.[60] Yet in their discussions of ownership and control these men rarely mentioned its connection with management. On the other hand the few men who did discuss management rarely considered its relation to ownership and control. Henry Poor was one of the very few persons who saw the problem as a single unit.[61]

With McCallum, Poor agreed that a carefully structured administrative hierarchy with carefully defined channels of accountability, communication, and information was absolutely necessary for large-scale business administration. Like the editors of other railroad periodicals and more general magazines and newspapers, he realized that owners usually did not control their property. But unlike the rest of his contemporaries, Poor saw that a failure of control very often meant an administrative breakdown and that this breakdown occurred because the lines of accountability, communication, and information did not reach from the management to the owners of the roads. Far more serious in Poor's mind

than the sensational frauds of a Schuyler or a Kilbourn was the breakdown in the later eighteen fifties of some of the greatest American lines
such as the Michigan Southern, the Rock Island and the Erie — failures
which occurred less from fraud than from mismanagement.[62] It was this
problem and these roads that Henry Poor had in mind when he made
his radical proposals for railroad reform.

VI

To Henry Poor the primary purpose of analysis was to suggest reform;
and reform, he strongly believed, must be quickly instituted if the railroad
was to play its destined role in the growth of America and the progress
of the human race. Since, according to his analysis, railroad mismanagement resulted fundamentally from the breakdown of the lines of accountability, communication, and information between the managers and the
owners, Poor saw two antithetical though, in his opinion, quite logical
courses of reform. On the one hand he proposed, by means of publicity,
a systematic strengthening of lines of accountability and information. On
the other hand he suggested, in the contract system of management, a reorganization of the corporation which by distinctly separating management from ownership would remove the need for such strong lines of accountability and information.[63]

Through the contract system Poor hoped to separate ownership from
management largely by replacing salaries with contracts or leases. Top
management would lease a road or contract for its operation from its
owners at a fixed rent or at a stipulated sum per miles operated. Top
management in turn would contract out the work on the lower level, or
if salaries were preferred, pay a premium or bonus according to the work
accomplished. In December 1854 when Poor first proposed this plan, he
told his readers to consider for the moment how such a scheme would
improve the operations of even the best-managed roads:

Suppose the Erie Company were to lease their road for a period of five
years, say, at 50 percent of its receipts, to a private company composed of ten
men, all of them as competent in their respective departments to be assigned
them, as is the present superintendent. To one, would be allotted the superintendence of repairs of track; to another, of machinery; to a third, the passenger
traffic; to a fourth, the freight; to a fifth, the reception and disposition of freight,
etc., etc.; each of the departments to be also subdivided, with a proper interest
to various subordinates. Suppose for instance, that in addition to their ordinary
salaries, a premium of $500 be offered to every engineer who should, during
the year, run a given number of miles at a *minimum cost*; (taking fuel, wear
and tear, and accidents, etc., into consideration); $400 to another limit;
$300 to those that come within the *third*; etc., etc. Does anyone doubt that vast
savings would be effected? [64]

By such a plan Poor hoped to restore incentive and initiative to management and at the same time to guarantee the security holders a certain return on their investment. Since the management would receive all it made beyond the stipulated rent or contract price, there would be every incentive to increase the efficiency of operations. Besides bringing the road out of "their beaten track of dullness and routine," this system, if widely adopted, would, Poor believed, help bring about the professionalization of management that was so badly needed in the railroad industry. For in the first place only qualified and competent men would take or be given such a lease or contract. They in turn would be careful to select the best men as their subordinates. Qualifications could be easily determined by a study of records of returns made by an employee or manager. Selection all along the line could be made on merit. Moreover there would be a strong incentive to work up the ladder, for every skilled employee and managing official "would have his eye on the best roads in the country, and make the control of such a road the height of his ambition. Any person employed on a railroad would have a constant stimulus to improve himself, according to his capacity." [65] Thus the railroads would now for the first time be assured of having trained and energetic younger men on hand to fill the higher posts.

Furthermore, Poor pointed out, this plan by freeing the directors from problems of management would permit them to devote their full time to the financial affairs of the road — the only subject that they were normally competent to handle. Thus the security holders, with an assured rent and with directors to manage the sinking funds and other financial matters, would be as sure as anyone can be in business of a certain and steady return on their stocks and bonds. And this was, after all, their primary interest in the company. By the contract plan, then, the owners would no longer need a knowledge of management nor would the managers any longer lack the incentives of ownership.

There were several precedents for Poor's plan. From 1849 on the editor of the *Journal* had been observing with interest English experiments in operating locomotives by contract. [66] These experiments proved so successful that by the early fifties such great lines as the London and Northwestern and the Eastern Counties had wholeheartedly adopted the system. [67] In America the contract method was being instituted at this time by leading states like New York and Ohio for the repair and maintenance of their canal systems. [68] Contracts, too, had built most of the railroads in this country, for their construction was let out to small contractors "who were paid by the *piece* at a reasonable profit." [69] Like contracting, the leasing of roads to other railroads for operation was also becoming common, especially the leasing of feeders and branch roads by the larger lines. The Atlantic and St. Lawrence, the very road that Poor himself had helped build in the late forties, was itself leased in 1853 by the Grand Trunk Railroad of Canada. Poor's original contribution was in suggesting that the contract and the lease might now be specifically adopted as a management technique to restore incentive and with it efficiency to the American railroads.

While Poor first proposed the contract plan late in 1854, he did not strongly advocate it until after the depression of 1857 and his trip to England in 1858 had impressed him with the need for management reform.[70] By that time too he could cite the example of an important American railroad that was actually being operated successfully in this way. That road, the Philadelphia, Wilmington and Baltimore, reported in 1858 that "nearly all the service excepting the repairs of bridges, the Treasury department and that of the conductors and supervising officers, is performed by contract instead of fixed salaries."[71] The operation of the trains, the handling of freight and repairs, the furnishing of fuel, and so forth were all let out at a fixed rate usually on a per mile basis. Samuel M. Felton, president of the road and one of America's leading railroad engineers, reported uniform improvement of service since the adoption of the system, with the ratio of net receipts to current expenses rising from 47 in 1856 to 58 in 1858, and with the dividends remaining steady despite the panic of 1857.

Throughout 1858 and 1859 Poor urged other roads to follow Felton's example; and no road could benefit more by the adoption of the contract system, Poor believed, than the Erie. Since the departure of McCallum in early 1857, that road under the administration of financier Charles Moran had been going from bad to worse; and by the summer of 1859 Poor believed that only sweeping changes could revive it. He urged the security holders to lease the road to a competent operating company. That June he was authorized by a company of engineers headed by Charles Minot, a former superintendent on the Erie, to make an offer for the lease of the road for a period of ten years at the price of $18,500,000 to be paid in ten annual installments.[72] The security holders and the management seemed to favor the plan, but the Board of Directors headed by Daniel Drew was able to block any action until the road went into bankruptcy that August.[73] Failing in this specific attempt to get a road managed by the contract method, Poor returned to advocating the most significant of his reforms — publicity.

Through the contract system Henry Poor hoped to solve the problems raised by the separation of ownership and management by placing each into a separate business unit. By publicity he hoped that these problems might be solved within the structure of a single corporation. Since it is easier to make use of accepted practices, the latter reform was a more realistic solution and it continued to be advocated as an important business reform long after the all too radical contract plan had been forgotten.

As editor of the *Journal*, Poor had been advocating publicity long before he had taken up the study of management. In 1849 he urged that state railroad commissions annually inspect the railroads so that the investors, the public, and the company all would know just where the road stood in its finances, safety of its operations, and so forth.[74] In 1850 and 1851 he had advocated publicity in the sale of railroad securities on Wall Street; and after 1852, when he had become spokesman for the investor, he repeatedly urged states and stockholders to insist on full, uniform, and accurate reports from railroad companies. Besides protecting the investor such reports would help prevent speculation and the over-construction of railroads.[75] Quite naturally, then, when Poor began to look for an answer to the problems of large-scale management, he turned to this favorite idea.

By publicity, especially in its relations to management, Poor meant a system of published reports by which "every important act of the managers would be laid before the public."[76] "Full and complete statements of every act must be required. Daylight should be let into every department of service."[77] Poor's aim basically was to enlarge and extend McCallum's system of internal reports. Such a reporting system would be instituted on all railroads and would be extended beyond the superintendent to the directors and then to the stockholders. The information recorded in the internal reports would be carefully compiled and synthesized by the department and division heads. From this information each official would make at specified intervals, preferably semiannually, a complete report to the president who in turn would include them in the annual report of the company to the stockholders.

To be of real value, for comparative study and analysis, Poor believed, the methods and forms of reporting should be uniform for all the roads and should be submitted by them on approximately the same date. Only by such a system of uniform and regular reports, he insisted, could the flow of accountability and information from management to ownership that was so necessary to large-scale management be assured. The managers and the directors, knowing that all their important acts were to be made public, would do their best to fulfill their prescribed duties and responsibilities. "No man would enter the service of the company, without determining to qualify himself for the discharge of his duties in a creditable manner, well knowing that exposure and censure would await him, were he to be negligent or incapable."[78] Besides, such publicity might well provide a real incentive to management; for each man, knowing that the result of his work would appear in print and would be compared to that of similar officials all over the United States, would strive to make the best showing possible.

Almost more important than providing incentive and accountability, such publicity would give directors and stockholders an accurate knowledge of railroad management. Full, accurate, and regular reports would permit directors untrained in railroad management to get a complete and sound over-all picture of their roads; would provide them with instruction on the technicalities of railroad operation; and make possible the rapid detection of incompetency or dishonesty. Such reports would in fact "furnish a sort of platform in which they [the directors] can meet and mingle with the force employed in conducting the operation of our roads." [79] This would in turn restore the "rapport" between the directors and employees that was so necessary for good morale in a large organization.

The stockholders, too, would gain. They would now have available the information necessary for taking a discerning interest in the affairs of their company; for evaluating the work of the directors and managers; and for making intelligent suggestions and decisions at its annual meetings. Moreover, with such information readily available security holders might even develop an inclination and find the time to study railroad affairs; for complete reports "would lay the foundation of a proper conception of what a road is and what it should be, and inspire an interest which would render the study of the economy of railroad management as attractive and agreeable as it is now repulsive and disgusting." [80]

Finally publicity, in Poor's opinion, would make the railroad corporation official once again responsible to public opinion and public criticism. No longer would the impersonal structure of the corporation allow a double standard of business ethics that permitted the railroad director to be during office hours "absolved from those moral responsibilities which he acknowledges and respects in his private and personal relations." Besides restoring personal responsibility, the criticism of an informed public might well provide constructive suggestions for the improvement of railroad management. Thus Poor observed that:

Were directors obliged every six months to publish what they had done, and what they proposed to do, they would have the benefit of a constant public criticism; and as men so situated are predisposed to make their statement as favorable as possible, they would be forced to act with a good degree of honesty and discretion, to save their *reputation*, about which most men are much more concerned than about integrity of character. The only way to render wholesome a noxious hole, is to let in the sun-light. So the only way to introduce honesty into the management of railroads, is to expose every thing in or about it, to the public gaze. Concealment in either case is certain to breed disease. Instances are very rare in which integrity is preserved unless strict accountability is exacted.[81]

There was no question in Poor's mind of the real need for publicity; the great problem was how to attain it. One way was by government regulation. From 1849 on, Poor had urged that the state and national governments require railroad companies to make full and accurate reports at least annually to the state or national legislature. By the mid-fifties, however, Poor had begun to lose hope of getting effective action by legislation. In the first place few states seemed interested in requiring any reports from railroads, and the requirements of most of those which did were condemned by the editor of the *Journal* as "a mere mockery." [82] Moreover, even if adequate reports had been universally required and faithfully submitted, Poor felt that the information gained would not have been enough. "Legislative reports," he wrote, "merely give *results*. What we want are the process by which they were reached. These must be given voluntarily, and with a desire to communicate information, not to suppress it." [83]

For a time Poor had hopes of getting such voluntary action from the railroads themselves. He constantly pointed out that the railroads had everything to gain from making full and complete reports. Such reports, by giving the investing and general public confidence in the roads and in their management, would make it much easier to raise money and to avoid hostile and discriminatory legislation. Moreover, such important roads as the Baltimore and Ohio, the Pennsylvania, the Pittsburgh, Fort Wayne and Chicago, the Philadelphia, Wilmington and Baltimore, Illinois Central, and a few of the Southern roads made excellent reports to their stockholders.[84] If they could set such an example, why, asked Poor, could not the others follow? Admitting that competitive considerations — "secret diplomacy" as he called it — might be a factor, he believed that far more often the failure to issue public reports was the result of indifference, incompetence, and occasionally dishonesty on the part of the railroad directors.[85]

By the end of the fifties Poor thus found himself facing a dilemma. By now he admitted that the best systems of accountability and information through publicity were to be found in the government-owned roads in Europe, especially in Prussia.[86] Yet the rigid government control which was exercised on those roads was patently impossible in America. On the other hand, publicity of the sort Poor desired was not to be had from the great majority of the American roads without outside pressure. As he remarked:

In this country the railroad managers have not assumed a duty which the government has entirely ignored. What should be gained by a greater degree of freedom has been lost by neglect. The government archives furnish little information of value in reference to railroads, because these companies, not being compelled to, will not furnish it. The records and publications of companies are equally barren of everything like useful intelligence, because the subordinates are not required to present to their chiefs accurate accounts of the operations of their departments. The freedom enjoyed by the railroad companies of this country has, consequently to a very great extent, excited a disastrous influence. That the intelligence of the individual is higher than that of government and better fitted to manage all commercial enterprises, there can be no doubt. But it is better that government should look after railroads, than that they should be entirely committed to a set of managers responsible to no one but themselves and between whom and the stockholders no intelligent link of communication exists.[87]

In the United States, then, the government would not or could not enforce publicity by law and yet the individual roads would not voluntarily make their acts public.

As a possible solution to this dilemma, Poor, backed by several of the leading investment houses in New York, offered a publicity plan of his own in February 1858. By this scheme Poor planned to send out annually to all the roads in the United States a uniform questionnaire of some six hundred questions covering all aspects of railroading. "These interrogatories," he wrote, "call for no information that should not be reported annually to the stockholders, and that is not of the highest value to both them and the directors of the roads." [88] At the same time a commission of engineers would make an inspection of the condition of each road. Poor planned to compile and edit the information thus gathered from these two independent sources in the following manner:

The reports of the examining parties, and the answers of the railroad companies, will be printed in convenient form (quarto), for reference and binding, and will be accompanied by maps of the routes of the roads and plans of such kinds of work as cannot be sufficiently understood without illustrations. To the reports will be added a sketch of the history of each road reported upon, showing the annual increase of its construction account since it went into operation, its earnings and expenses, with such other information as may be necessary to a correct idea of its value.[89]

The cost of this scheme was to be covered by the investment houses backing the plan. These firms included such leading bankers and banking firms as Winslow, Lanier and Company; Duncan, Sherman and Company; DeCoppet and Company; Marie and Kanz; Herman Gelpke; Joseph W. Alsop; John Ferguson; and Robert Benson & Company of

London. These bankers, who were among the most important agents marketing American railroad securities in Europe, had been deeply troubled by the startling defects in railroad managerial competence and financial honesty revealed by the panic of 1857. Quite naturally, therefore, they backed Poor's plan which aimed at reforming railroad management and finance and which in doing so would give them valuable investment information.

Poor believed that financial pressure from the investing houses would force any recalcitrant roads into line. He hoped, however, that the roads on realizing the advantages of such a plan to themselves would coöperate without pressure. He expected that the compiled and edited reports would become "a manual covering the whole of railroad economy" and through such a compilation "the experience of the best managed roads may become the property of all." [90] This manual, he hoped, would serve as the primary source of data for the scientific study of finance, administration, operation, and engineering which would bring the efficiency of American railroads to their maximum peak.

Despite these apparently obvious advantages, few roads favored such a pooling of information. Although the questionnaire did not ask for anything that should not be reported to the stockholder, it certainly asked for data which most railroad companies would prefer to keep from their competitors, shippers, and the general public. The roads would have probably been willing, if they had the data readily available, to answer the engineering, technical, and even some of the financial questions. On the other hand, Poor was certainly naïve if he expected the railroad officials to answer honestly questions on drawbacks granted, discriminatory rate charges, directorates held in other companies, and the speculative activities of the directors, or if he expected them to furnish complete and accurate data on every aspect of their companies' financial affairs. Useful information would have been almost as difficult to obtain from the answers to his questions on the "tone" of the roads' management and the "morale" of their employees.

Nevertheless the questionnaire was an excellent check-off list for the investigator determining the value of a railroad as an investment and its efficiency as an operating unit. Undoubtedly Poor used a similar form when, during the 1860's, he investigated the productivity and the financial standing of the Pittsburgh, Fort Wayne and Chicago and other roads for Winslow, Lanier and Company. Two decades later Charles H. Coster probably used much the same type of list for his examinations of railroads prior to their purchase or reorganization by J. P. Morgan and Company.

Morgan, in fact, brought a type of reform to the railroad industry through personal action much in the way Poor hoped to do it through institutional methods. In reorganizing large sections of the American railroad industry, Morgan insisted upon having accurate information and strict accountability and responsibility from the managers and directors of a road to him or his associates as agents for the road's security holders. The bondholders whom Morgan represented were, significantly enough, largely European investors. However, where Poor, whose primary interest was efficient operation, would have revealed all information to competitors, shippers, and general public, Morgan, chiefly concerned with protecting his and his clients' investments, never dreamed of allowing his information to leave the files of his Wall Street office.

Poor realized in the 1850's what Morgan was to demonstrate in the 1880's and 1890's — that the most available power for reform in American business during the second half of the nineteenth century was financial rather than political. During the fifties, however, the New York banking houses were not strong enough or unified enough to enforce their views on American railroad corporations, and therefore Poor's plan was never put into action. The effective use of financial power had to wait until one house, indeed one man, dominated the railroad-investment field.

Despite his failure to secure concerted Wall Street support for his plan, Poor continued to advocate and work for increased publicity of railroad affairs. He revived his old campaign of obtaining strong state legislative requirements for the publication of full and accurate reports; and, in fact, expanded his demands to make mandatory reports from all incorporated companies.[91] At the same time he did his best to compile and analyze all available information on railroads himself. In 1859 he published a series of comparative statistical studies in the *Journal* covering several of the major roads. Statistics were given for a period of years showing cost, expenses, and earnings, all broken down as far as possible into the component figures and then reduced to ratio and per mileage data so as to make comparison easy. Along with these statistics Poor gave a carefully written analysis pointing out what they showed in the way of comparative costs of fuel, repairs, and machinery, and about the matter of depreciation, renewals, and so forth and what they indicated about the financial soundness and operating efficiency of the individual companies.[92]

Poor now planned to publish in book form this and other data he had collected. Early in 1860 he outlined an ambitious task of publishing a three-volume work that would embody

within convenient compass a statement of the organization and the condition of our companies, [and] at the same time present a history of their operation from year to year, which would necessarily reflect the character of their management, the extent and value of their traffic and supply abundant illustrations, with which to compare similar enterprises that might be made the subject of inquiry and information.[93]

The first volume of this work, the *History of the Railroads and Canals of the United States*, came off the press in October 1860. Before the second reached the printer, the Civil War had broken out and turned Poor's attention completely to wartime matters.

Owing to the war Poor gave up his position as editor of the *American Railroad Journal*. Although he continued working in the railroad field, he never again had the opportunity of making so important and unique a contribution to the railroad development as he did as compiler and analyzer of railroad information while editor of the *Journal*. His earlier work, however, was carried on in part by the publication, beginning in 1868, of the *Manuals of the Railroads of the United States*. In the introductions to the *Manuals* and elsewhere he continued his campaign for publicity. He praised the efforts of Charles Francis Adams of Massachusetts and George B. Wright of Ohio towards obtaining better state action; and he recommended to the Cullom committee the setting up of a National Railroad Bureau "to which all railroads should make full returns of their financial condition and of the results of their operation." [94] Poor's recommendation was carried out in the Interstate Commerce Act of 1887 which incorporated such a bureau into the Interstate Commerce Commission as its Bureau of Statistics. The work of the Interstate Commerce Commission, especially after the Hepburn Act of 1906, and that of some of the state commissions carried forward Poor's efforts towards effective publicity. It was not, however, until the passage of the Securities Exchange Act of 1934 that Poor's reforms reached their real fruition.

VII

The fact that Poor's demands for publicity remained a basic business reform for close to a century demonstrates the validity and usefulness of his analyses and of the suggestions stemming from them. On the other hand, the outright rejection of his basic reforms and the slow, reluctant adoption of his suggested improvements in systematic organization, communication, and information indicate that the dominant railroad manager of Poor's day failed to recognize or acknowledge the validity and usefulness of these analyses or suggestions. This repudiation is all the more significant in view of the widespread support these reforms received within the railroad industry. Prominent railroad superintendents like McCallum and Jervis did their best to put them into practice. The strongest non-managerial group in the industry — the investor class — heartily endorsed them. It was, for example, to the investment houses rather than to the state or the shippers that Poor turned for active backing of the publicity plan he presented in 1858. Nevertheless while the financially minded investor was a major source of support for Poor's reforms, the financially trained railroad manager was primarily responsible for their rejection.

The sudden domination of the railroad industry in the 1850's by managers whose business training and experience was financial rather than technical was one of the most significant developments in the early history of America's first big business. The growth of large-scale organization in the railroad industry necessitated a division of management between two types of managers. The demands of administration and operation required the full-time attention of a technically trained manager who normally held the post of general superintendent. The need for large funds was met by the president and the board of directors, men trained in the ways of finance. The president, interested chiefly in improving management, was highly sympathetic to Poor's ideas and suggestions; the board of directors, whose paramount concern was profit, tended to ignore or reject them. Since in any conflict of policy between the two, the financier almost always won out over the engineer, Poor's suggestions were rarely put into practice.

The reason for the dominance of the financially trained executive is obvious. A railroad in the 1850's might exist without good management; but it could not possibly do without a steady and ample flow of funds. Large sums of money were essential if the road was to be built at all, if it was to expand its physical equipment as the traffic grew, if it was to build feeders and branches necessitated by competition, or if it was to survive sudden contractions of the money market such as occurred in 1854 and 1857. An executive who could command large sums of money was, therefore, an invaluable asset to a railroad company. There seems little question that the financier was more essential than the engineer for the survival of the railroad firm as a business organization.

The trouble, as Poor so often pointed out, was that a man who could command large amounts of capital rarely knew anything about railroad management.[95] Such a man was usually a successful manufacturer, banker, or most frequently a successful merchant whose previous business achievements had not only given him surplus funds for investment but, more important, had won for him the confidence of the average investor. Such a background, however, had not prepared him to understand either the more technical matters of railroad operation and administration or the more fundamental problems of large-scale organization; and, therefore, he rarely appreciated the full import of Poor's analyses and suggestions concerning these problems. Rather than study improvements in management, this type of railroad executive generally adopted the standard mercantile practices of solving financial problems by raising the price of the product and extending the area of its market. Higher rates and extension of mileage seemed a far more "practical" solution than lowering cost and bettering service. Moreover he differed from Poor and many of the technically trained managers, in considering that the company's primary aim was to assure the security holders a steady return on their investment rather than to provide the most efficient transportation services. To sacrifice present dividends to pay for long-term improvements in management and equipment appeared, therefore, unwise. Thus, while not directly antagonistic to Poor's views, indeed often professing sympathy with much of what he was trying to do, the financially trained railroad executive tended to set aside Poor's analyses and reforms as being of secondary importance and as having uncertain practical value.

A second type of financially oriented entrepreneur was the financial operator or speculator who could acquire funds and short-term credit by skillfully manipulating the machinery of the money market. Unlike the successful businessman turned railroad executive, the speculator cared little for the future of his company and still less for assuring the security holder a return on his investment. Certainly he gave no thought at all to improving the transportation services it provided. His aim was to make the most out of the company for the personal benefit of himself and a few close associates. Reforms like careful and uniform accounting, accurate reporting, and general publicity would be a major stumbling block in achieving such an aim. The Wall Street operator had little use for Poor — a feeling that was strongly reciprocated.

The differentiation between the motives and aspirations of the railroad executives in the 1850's was apparent on many of the American railroads but nowhere was it more clear than in the early history of the Erie. McCallum's brilliant administrative work proved too radical for the president and many of the directors. In the resulting conflict over policy the stockholders, despite Poor's repeated urgings to the contrary, stood by President Charles Moran with the result that McCallum was forced to resign his post early in 1857. Moran as senior partner of the highly successful importing and banking firm of Moran and Iselin fitted perfectly the currently accepted picture of the business leader. Moreover, he professed to be a strong believer in publicity and other reforms that Poor advocated. Nevertheless neither his past business success, his present capacity for hard work, nor his sincere ambition to make the road a success could overcome a lack of knowledge of the more technical side of railroading and his failure to understand the primary problems of large-scale organization.[96] By the summer of 1859 the Erie was bankrupt. Moran's failure was hastened by the machinations of Daniel Drew who, profiting from Moran's mistakes, was now able to rig the receivership proceedings so that he gained control of the road. In doing so he blocked

Poor's proposition that a company of engineers take over the operation of the company. Once in control Drew began his shameless exploitation which reached its notorious climax just a decade later.

The story of the Erie in this decade could be repeated with only minor changes for the Michigan Southern and the Rock Island by merely substituting the names Jervis, Flagg, and Litchfield for McCallum, Moran, and Drew. This same pattern of changing executive leadership held true although in less clear-cut outline for many other American roads. There were, of course, exceptions, but it is significant that on the most notable exception, the Pennsylvania Railroad, the president, J. Edgar Thomson, was an outstanding engineer as well as a highly competent financier.

The pattern of the fifties was to be continued in the railroad world until well into the twentieth century. As long as the procurement of funds remained the paramount need in the industry, the financially oriented executive dominated the American railroads. It was only with the completion of large-scale railroad construction and with lessening of the need for an increasingly large expansion of the physical plant that the technically trained manager finally began to control policy and that interest in management reform began to receive a significant share of entrepreneurial attention. It is this comparatively recent revival of interest in the principles and problems of large-scale organization that makes Henry Poor's writings of value today. As the philosopher of large-scale business management when such management was new, he set forth many principles which nearly a century later have relevance for an economic system now dominated by big business.

XI

The Business Elite in Business Bureaucracies

*Careers of Top Executives in the Early Twentieth Century**

By William Miller

By 1902, when the Morgan spokesman, George F. Baer, made his prideful remark about how "God, in his infinite wisdom," had "given control of the property interests of the country" to "the Christian men" who then managed them,[1] many of these Christians had already learned that what God might give, men might take away. Among them, indeed, was Baer himself whose career as Morgan's "confidential legal advisor,"[2] though it had brought him to the head of numerous great enterprises, resembled a new type in American business life. Louis D. Brandeis said in the 1890's, "I would rather have clients than be somebody's lawyer," and to a con-

---

* This essay is the fourth by the writer, on American business leaders of the period 1901–1910, and forms part of a larger project of the Research Center in Entrepreneurial History for a study of American business leadership since the 1870's. Chapter VII of the present book, on the industrial leaders of the 1870's, by Miss Gregory and Miss Neu, is also part of this work.

A full discussion of the method used in selecting the business leaders of 1901–1910 and a list of the men and their companies appear in William Miller, "American Historians and the Business Elite," *Journal of Economic History*, vol. IX, no. 2 (November 1949), the first essay in the series. The others are, "The Recruitment of the Business Elite," *Quarterly Journal of Economics*, vol. LXIV, no. 2 (May 1950), and "American Lawyers in Business and Politics," *Yale Law Journal*, vol. LX, no. 1 (January 1951).

siderable degree he satisfied his preference.[3] Baer's career, as was especially plain during the coal strike which was the occasion of his Calvinistic utterance, was more like that of a trained professional no longer free to have clients or to reject them, but tied to the service of a single business interest that could move him about like an ordinary employee.

Even more representative of this type of "captive" professional — for these men engaged in fewer independent ventures than Baer — were such company lawyers as Vanderbilt's Chauncey M. Depew, Huntington's Charles H. Tweed, Harriman's Robert S. Lovett, each at some time president or board chairman of one or more of his sponsor's firms and always on call to the great man himself. Properly classified here too are the counterparts of company lawyers in the "law factory" of a Paul D. Cravath, George W. Wickersham, or William N. Cromwell, which by the end of the nineteenth century had become "virtually an annex to some group of financial promoters, manipulators, or industrialists." [4] Of Cravath, his associate Robert T. Swaine tells this story:

> Early one morning when he had not yet arrived at the office, [Otto] Kahn [of Kuhn, Loeb] wanted to see him in a great hurry. One of the younger associates sought to locate Cravath by telephone, but in vain; going downstairs at 52 William Street to tell Kahn of the futility of his efforts, he met Cravath coming in the door and rushed up with: "I've been looking all over for you; Mr. Kahn wants to see you at once." Cravath broke into a broad smile: "You make me feel just like my father did when he used to say to me: 'Paul, come to the woodshed.' " [5]

This new ubiquitousness of lawyers at big businessmen's elbows, not to say under their thumbs, reflects an epochal change in the structure of American big business enterprises and in their relation to their employees and to society at large. First among the railroads, but by the turn of the century in many other lines as well, the characteristic big business firm had become a big bureaucracy. Functions at each level of operation, supervision, and policy making had become more or less strict and specific, channels of authority and communication had been set up, and hierarchies of ascent had become articulated. Lifetime, salaried careers thus had be-

---

This essay is the fourth by the writer on American business leaders of the period 1901–1910, and formed part of a larger study of American business leadership since the 1870's, of which Chapter VII of the present book, on industrial leaders of the 1870's by Miss Frances W. Gregory and Miss Irene D. Neu, is also a part.

The first two essays by this writer were "American Historians and the Business Elite," and "The Recruitment of the American Business Elite," both reprinted here in the Appendix to the Torchbook Edition with appropriate citations (see below, pp. 309–337). A fourth essay, "American Lawyers in Business and Politics," appeared in the *Yale Law Journal,* Vol. LX, No. 1 (January, 1951). For a full discussion of the methods used in selecting the men studied here, and a list of the men and their companies, see below, pp. 312–319.

come attainable, leading all the way to the top, albeit, as Max Weber has pointed out, "the bureaucratic official" is always "appointed by a superior authority" [6] — a higher functionary, a college of cardinals, a board of directors, the "organization" itself.

In such bureaucracies, ideally, as Weber said, "control" is exercised "on the basis of knowledge"; the "development of bureaucracy . . . tends to eliminate . . . the occupation of offices on an honorary basis or as an avocation by virtue of wealth." [7] The upshot, however, is not "democratization" but rather the rise of a new elite: "The most decisive thing here . . . is the *leveling of the governed* in opposition to the ruling and bureaucratically articulated group, which in turn may occupy a quite autocratic position." [8] This new elite, in Weber's terms, may "increase its power by the knowledge growing out of experience in the service." [9] To become even more firmly seated it may enlist expert technicians not the least useful of whom were those qualified to serve as intermediaries with the leveled populace. Knowledgeable lawyers, expert in their own field, also fitted this second role. Trained in advocacy and persuasion as well as in the law, they were among the first professional lobbyists and public relations men as well as the first formally certified business experts. Their new importance by the turn of the century reflects the growth of bureaucratic managements typically in need of help in navigating legal and political labyrinths and in conciliating public groups often made hostile by the results.[10]

II

That men risen to power as bureaucrats or as their professional adjuncts had not wholly superseded independent entrepreneurs in the key positions in the American economy by 1900 is indicated by the histories of some of the leaders who were still at the head of great business enterprises. Of 185 men so placed in the decade 1901–1910,[11] 14 per cent either started the firms through the development of which, by expansion or more commonly by merger, they had attained their peak positions,[12] or bought these firms or high places in them with resources accumulated in independent ventures. Hugh J. Chisholm of the International Paper Company, Anthony N. Brady of the Brooklyn Rapid Transit Company, and Frederick Ayer of American Woolen, were such men. So, too, though each ultimately paid for his independence by being squeezed out of his own firm, were John C. Osgood, one of the organizers of the Colorado Fuel and Iron Company; Frederick A. Heinze, founder of the United Copper Company; and George Westinghouse, founder of the Electric and Manufacturing Company which still bears his name.

Twenty-seven per cent of these 185 business leaders, moreover, and certainly not the least able ones, may be said to have inherited their high positions. This suggests that while kinship ties may have become more honored in the breach in the transfer of business power, and inherited wealth and tradition less convincing than "self help" and bureaucratic "rationality" as legitimations of such power, dynasties still could be established and maintained.[13] Most of the men in this group had taken over their father's, father-in-law's, or uncle's firms. Others had used their continuing connection with such firms or funds available through them to gain key positions in major outside companies. In the latter class, typically, are sons, sons-in-law, and nephews of great merchants or private bankers — James Stillman and August Belmont in New York, Gordon Abbott in Boston, Henry A Blair and Henry G. Foreman in Chicago. Among the more direct heirs, besides bankers like J. P. Morgan, Henry Lee Higginson, or Frank E. Peabody, are Daniel Guggenheim in copper, Henry O. Havemeyer in sugar, Morgan G. Bulkeley in life insurance, Cornelius K. G. Billings in Chicago utilities. Even railroad presidents George Jay Gould and Louis W. Hill may be included here, each having reached the top of his father's highly bureaucratized company by a route so direct as to leave him virtually unaware of the articulated channels through which henceforth he was expected to work.

All the rest of these 185 leaders, however, except for the 12 per cent who were lawyers,[14] climbed the bureaucratic ladder, not infrequently, of course, after their family status, education, and other social endowments helped them get the proper start. These bureaucrats make up 47 per cent of the whole group. Typical is Charles S. Mellen, who at the age of eighteen began as a clerk in the cashier's office of the Northern New Hampshire Railroad. From here he "rose in his profession," as his biographer puts it, "through successive positions on the Central Vermont" and other roads.[15] After a novitiate of almost a quarter of a century, during which he never forsook railroading, he became second vice-president of the New York, New Haven and Hartford. In 1897, Mellen was made president of the Northern Pacific, only to be moved seven years later back to the New Haven also as president. After a stormy decade, he was ousted in 1913.

Scarcely any of these bureaucrats ever satisfied the urge, if indeed they ever had it,[16] to launch a company of their own, "to plunge into and toss upon the waves of human affairs," as Carnegie said, "without a life-preserver in the shape of a salary." [17] More than 80 per cent of them never headed an enterprise — never were sole owner, partner, president, or chairman — before attaining the eminent office that makes them of interest here. That is not to say that their ascent, once auspiciously under way, was unfaltering or automatic. Nor does it compromise the designation of their careers as bureaucratic to point out that many of them, like many lawyers, became the favorites — with all the hazards of that predicament — of men of more elevated rank.[18]

Jesse T. Welborn, for example, had "advanced through regular stages"[19] in the Colorado Fuel and Iron Company from bookkeeper to vice-president in charge of sales and traffic, when in 1907 the Rockefellers, who a few years earlier had acquired the company, made him president. James T. Harahan had risen "through successive stages"[20] in railroading from clerk on the Boston and Providence to second vice-president of the Illinois Central, when Harriman in 1906 ousted president Stuyvesant Fish of the latter road and put Harahan in his place. Mellen himself, who soon after becoming president of the New Haven was regarded as "The Railroad Lord of New England,"[21] once said of his experiences there, "I suppose that there is more or less prejudice against me because I wear the Morgan collar, but I am proud of it." After Morgan's death in 1913, Mellen said: "I took orders from J. P. Morgan, Sr. I did as I was told. . . So far as I was concerned, the handwriting was on the wall the moment the old man breathed his last."[22]

The distribution by career types of the 185 business leaders of the decade 1901–1910 is summarized in the accompanying table.

TABLE 1

American Business Leaders by Type of Career

Type of Career	Number	Per Cent
Professional (Lawyers only)	23	12
Independent Entrepreneur	25	14
Family	51	27
Bureaucratic	86	47
Total cases	185	100

III

That this early in the twentieth century almost half of the leaders in American business were men who had been salaried officeholders virtually their entire business lives is remarkable enough. Such men, predominant in railroads, were also most numerous in nearly every major business field, while independent entrepreneurs were fewest in every field but one.

The whole group, nevertheless, remains representative of what appears to have been a transition period not simply in the form of the typical big business career but in the environment that made new careers possible and in the sanctions that eventually made them preferred. Earlier, so great a proportion of American business leaders could not have been subordinates, of however high rank, for so long a term; the rarity before the last quarter of the nineteenth century of companies in which hierarchical careers could be followed makes this certain. Today, on the other hand, the number of great hierarchical organizations and the scope of their activities make it almost as certain that the proportion of bureau-

TABLE 2

American Business Leaders by Type of Career and Business Field

Type of Career *	Manufac- turing and Mining	Railroads	Public Utilities	Commercial Banking	Life Insurance	Investment Banking
	%	%	%	%	%	%
Independent	24	8	12	29	0	0
Family	42	8	40	18	43	89
Bureaucratic	34	84	48	53	57	11
Total cases (= 100%)	55	49	25	17	7	9

* Lawyers are omitted from this and subsequent tables. See note 14, p. 347, below.

crats among business leaders has become far larger than ever before, and that the proportion of great independent entrepreneurs has fallen.

That the latter trend was well under way before the turn of the century is suggested not only by the small representation of independent entrepreneurs among the men studied but also by the distribution of these

TABLE 3

American Business Leaders by Type of Career and Date of Birth

Type of Career	Before 1841	1841–1850	1851–1860	After 1860
	%	%	%	%
Independent	26	19	11	8
Family	22	24	42	36
Bureaucratic	52	57	47	56
Total cases (= 100%)	23	59	55	25

men by period of birth. Considerably more than half of those born before 1840 were to become bureaucrats and this proportion remained more or less unchanged for those born later. The percentage of independent entrepreneurs, however, dropped from 26 to 8, even though such entrepreneurs tended to attain their peak offices at a relatively early age.

How much further this percentage has dropped, how indeed it has tended to disappear, is suggested by a study of presidents of big corporations today. Of 159 such presidents, only four — a scant 2.5 per cent —

"started out as self-employed. Just one of these four was able to boost his company to national significance and remain president — the other three men shortly sought employment with established concerns." [23]

"Starting your own company," says the report of this recent study, "is one way to be president," but "the evidence shows that engineers and lawyers have a much better chance to become president of a successful firm." So great, indeed, is the current demand for such professionals that young men now study law or engineering often with no idea of independent practice and many forego practice altogether and start immediately in administrative posts. In the middle of the nineteenth century, however, such opportunities were rare and in any case grasping them would have been frowned upon.

In that era, when the older leaders in the present study started work, young men, whether professionally trained or not, who had no prospect of inheriting a business and yet who at the age of twenty-five or thirty still clung to wage or salary jobs, merited as little regard in the business community as spinsters of the same age did at home. Roles of a sort, of course, were prescribed for both spinsters and employees, but for the latter at least these were likely still to be such as cramp the spirit and cloud over the blue sky of aspiration. Many businessmen, on the other hand, still took pride in being able to point to rising enterprises started by youths they had trained, and to such youths being in business for oneself still appeared to be worth much immediate risk and effort. As Carnegie put it, "there is no great fortune to come from salary, however high, and the business man pursues fortune." [24]

As the end of the nineteenth century approached, however, many able young men had begun to leave their jobs not only to start their own firms — a venture that would appear quixotic today — but more and more to transfer to competing bureaucracies — a step that already aroused resentment. Thus, as early as 1877, J. N. A. Griswold, chairman of the board of the Burlington railroad, wrote to his vice-president, C. E. Perkins, about the loss of William B. Strong to the Santa Fe, of which Strong later became president:

> This want of candor, to call it by no worse name, leads me to think it just as well that he should go. To me it seems inexpedient to hold men in our employ who are as restless as Mr. Strong seems to be, who without looking far into the future, lets himself out to the highest bidder — irrespective of his well assured position with us in which he stood directly in the line of promotion.[25]

Acts like Strong's eventually forced the heads of older firms to face up to the fact that the defection of promising young men was weakening their own growing organizations and to the need to devise new incentives if they were to keep such men. This was as true in family enterprises which had been able for a time to hold on to competent young relatives—before such practices fell from grace and were branded as nepotic — as in other companies. Andrew Carnegie's perspicacity in recognizing this problem and his originality in dealing with it unquestionably were among his greatest business assets.[26] The princely nature of the incentives he offered to the "young geniuses" of his early executive teams — men contemporary on the whole with the younger ones studied here — is probably the measure of what was first needed to retain the loyalty of ambitious men to organizations not of their own making. The example of most such men, in turn, is probably what was next needed to provide stature for salaried executive positions generally.

That the old individualist sanctions died hard, even so, is suggested by the careers of such erstwhile Carnegie "geniuses" as Charles M. Schwab and William E. Corey. Each had been promoted step by step in the Carnegie company to an eminence just below that of the founder himself. Each next advanced to the presidency of the august United States Steel Corporation. There each held his position until ultimately frustrated by hierarchical protocol and probably by the demands of respectability made even by this most imposing business bureaucracy lest it offend the stock-buying public. It was the private antics of Schwab and Corey that prompted the remark attributed to Morgan: "The trouble with the United States Steel Corporation is to find a president of ability who does not need all his time to spend his salary properly." [27] Thus each was forced out and considerably later in life than would seem to have been usual two or three decades earlier proceeded to acquire (with others, of course) a great new steel company of his own.

Schwab and Corey were offering themselves, so it seems now, as hostages to their image of a freer past. Others among these younger transitional men also struck out independently, one at least to give lessons to ambitious bureaucrats of the future. He was George W. Perkins, who had climbed the ladder in the New York Life Insurance Company and in 1901 was rewarded with a partnership in the House of Morgan itself. Nine years later he resigned the more freely to write and speak of the conflict within men he had known who had been nurtured on the precepts of self dependence and self help only to become ensnared, as they saw it, in the new bureaucratic processes of conference, consultation, and compromise.

Many of their contemporaries, nevertheless, appear to have become better adjusted to the emergent conditions than did Schwab, Corey, or Perkins. One reason for this may be that bureaucratic business careers were already becoming honorific. As early as 1908, William C. Brown, who that year became president of the New York Central Railroad, was widely acclaimed as "the man who stayed on his job" [28] — a slogan which, had it been followed a few decades earlier even in the railroad industry, probably would not have won Brown or anyone else much eminence or much fame. A little later, Edwin Hawley, credited by contemporaries with being "the country's leading railroad man since the death of Harriman," said that " a young man who jumps from one pursuit to another can never become proficient — that is, highly so — in any field of endeavor." [29] His advice, and that of others of his time as different and as differently situated as Henry Lee Higginson and Louis D. Brandeis, was to select a field and remain in it so as to become "expert" or "professional." In the Commencement Day address at Brown University in 1912, since reprinted as *Business — A Profession*, Brandeis said:

> The once meager list of the learned professions is being constantly enlarged. Engineering in its many branches already takes rank beside law, medicine and theology. Forestry and scientific agriculture are securing places of honor. The new professions of manufacturing, of merchandising, of transportation and of finance must soon gain recognition. The establishment of business schools in our universities is a manifestation of the modern conception of business.[30]

IV

Though increasingly honorific, bureaucratic business careers have continued since the time of Schwab and Corey to involve able young men in conflicts between their personal aspirations and the health of their firms. This is partly due to the persistence of the self-help ideology which shames men with slogans such as "always a yes man, never a boss"; and partly to the separation of ownership and management which Weber presented as an ideal of bureaucratic organization but which, given American traditions, has only heightened the war between the self-help ideology and the realities of bureaucratic life.[31]

Largely for these reasons the old difficulty of maintaining the allegiance of able executives has had to be constantly fought. Even as late as 1947, *Nation's Business*, the organ of the United States Chamber of Commerce, featured an article on this theme. To the uncertain though highly placed and highly paid hero of the piece who one day asked himself, "Am I a failure? Where did I make the wrong turn? Did I sacrifice my independence for security? Wouldn't I have done better if I had gone into business for myself?", this article replied: "You're happy with your work and richer than you know." [32] Such pronouncements have served less as balm to disenchanted bureaucrats than as symptoms of their ambivalent position. A striking instance of how this ambivalence might disrupt an organization was the split, early in 1950, between Charles Luckman and Lever Brothers, the American company of Unilever, Ltd., of which Luckman was president. "On the record," said *Business Week* at the time, "shifts in Lever personnel since Luckman took over have been broad and frequent. This is apparently what caused Unilever to lay down its ultimatum for a wider management base. . . To nail down strategic executive posts and prevent turnover, Unilever had a plan for a wider participation in authority and earnings. Luckman wouldn't buy it, and that was the end." [33]

The persistence, nevertheless, with which most American firms have attacked this problem and the means they have employed — liberal executive bonus plans, broader participation of administrators in ownership, and especially noncontributory pensions for management — have added to the seriousness of another and I think even more fateful source of trouble. That is not so much the problem of bridging the conflict of loyalties in able bureaucrats as of disencumbering the bureaucracy itself of incompetents, often risen to key positions, who have proved altogether too loyal. I say more fateful, for this newer problem, especially, mirrors a characteristically closed economy in which huge enterprises are astride the major avenues of opportunity. Top management in such enterprises often appears unable to avoid promoting faithful or friendly men who themselves have no way to go but up. Such men, in turn, even when endowed with exceptional talent for bureaucratic ascent, often prove to be cliquish and otherwise irresponsible as top executives. In emergencies they and their cabals may pull their big firms down, and with them in most recent times the whole rigid system.[34]

The problem of what to do with such men, who nowadays are sometimes raised to board chairman, may already be noted in the transition period around the turn of the century when such chairmanships first were becoming fashionable. Then as now it had become apparent that for many men — for independent entrepreneurs drawn into the bureaucratic vortex as well as for true blue bureaucrats themselves — the greater their business success, the greater their personal insecurity; the higher their ascent, the nearer their approach to failure. How often this paradoxical history marked the careers principally of former independent entrepreneurs is evident from the series of cases in Arthur S. Dewing's *Corporate Promotions and Reorganizations*, written at the end of this epoch.[35] How general it was up and down the line of the emergent bureaucratic organizations is equally evident from Frederick W. Taylor's classic *Principles of Scientific Management*, issued at about the same time.[36]

This situation heightens interest in the general question not only of the structure of big business careers in this transition period but also of the means by which such careers were attained — by the most able big businessmen as well as by others who also rose to the top.

v

For some of the men studied here, an answer to this question is comparatively easily arrived at, though it may itself raise other more difficult questions. Henry H. Rogers, for example, one of the older and most independent of these men, was perhaps more richly endowed than many of his contemporaries with what Peter Cooper once called the "knack for contriving." [37] (Why this was so is one of those more difficult points.) His innovations in oil refining and pipe-line transportation probably gave the early impetus to his ascent. Yet Rogers, by his own description, was also "a gambler" often out to "have a little fun" and "always for fighting." "Once when Rogers had A. C. Burrage [a copper magnate] at the foot of the table with four other guests, one of the guests said to Mr. Rogers: 'How can you tolerate that Mr. Burrage opposite to you at the table?' Rogers said: 'I am enjoying it immensely. I was thinking all the time how he would look after I plucked him.'" "Almost the whole story of his gas interests," says one of Rogers' biographers, "was one of warfare, as was his connection with copper." John D. Rockefeller once said that "in working with so many partners," among them Rogers, "the conservative ones are apt to be in the majority, and this is no doubt a desirable thing when the mere momentum of a large concern is certain to carry it forward." [38] But that was hardly Rogers' view; he abhorred partners and involved the Standard Oil Company in the copper business and other speculations against the wishes of Rockefeller himself.[39] One of Rogers' last enterprises — which probably speeded his death — was the construction, virtually with no outside financial assistance, of the 443-mile, $40,000,000 Virginia Railway tying the rich coal fields of West Virginia to the port of Norfolk.[40]

Equally simple in its way, though different enough to be instructive, is the story of another of these men, Conrad H. Matthiessen, in his own view like Rogers a self-made man. In 1897, at the age of thirty-two — precocious, surely, by this time — Matthiessen became the first president of the "glucose trust," just organized as the Glucose Sugar Refining Company. The following year he was reported to have received the then extraordinary annual salary of $75,000, three times that of the president of the United States.

My success, as you call it [Matthiessen told reporters], is due to hard work and that alone. . . I started at the bottom. [Then he said] My father was president of the old Chicago Sugar Refining Company [the keystone of the new "trust"] and when I came West [from Yale] he put me in as a workman at $1.50 a day. . . I was gradually promoted and in 1890 [just four years out of college] the management of the company was given to me.[41]

Even where other types of careers may be as clearly outlined as those of Rogers (independent) and Matthiessen (family-made), reasons for the successive steps in them may often be more difficult to expose. This is especially true of careers which were largely hierarchical.

In owner-manager and family firms, the individual and the enterprise almost always must rise and fall together. The ups and downs of both, in turn, are largely ascribable to their adaptability — itself often a matter of the personality of the controlling enterpreneur — in meeting objective economic changes such as those affecting the market for commodities or capital, the techniques of production, the size and quality of the labor force, and so forth. Moreover, the competition among such firms and hence among the individuals whose fates are so closely tied to them is largely for advantage in regard to these objective factors. The course of bureaucratic firms and the competition, where it exists, among them, are also affected by changes in their relation to these factors. But the fate of *individual* bureaucrats and hence the competition for preferment *within* the bureaucracy — the firm in Kenneth Burke's terms, becoming less the "agency" and more the "scene" of the drama [42] — appear to involve in addition a host of other variables.

Among bureaucrats, for example, an individual's success, as defined by his progress up the ladder, may conceivably have been won despite a concomitant decline in his firm's position, or, indeed, because of it, such a decline sometimes causing a shuffle in management that results in extraordinarily rapid advancement for whole teams of executives. The careers of many railroad men, risen to the presidency of their firms in this transitional period while the firms were clearly on the way to receivership, are striking examples of this.

Similarly, an individual bureaucrat's failure — failure meaning that ascent ceased below the ladder's top — may have occurred while his hierarchical firm, even largely through his efforts, was itself riding a wave of prosperity and unprecedented growth. Take the career of Theodore N. Vail, who, after making a notable record in government service, joined the Bell Telephone system in 1878. From the start Vail "was doing the creative thinking for the group" that controlled the American Bell Telephone Company (then the parent firm) "and really carried on the functions of president." But even in 1887, when the latter office became vacant, he "was given neither the title nor the prestige of the position. Members of the Boston aristocracy monopolized the honors. Furthermore, the Bostonians brought in a good many of their friends to the various departments. . . friends who were not always in sympathy with the far-seeing ideas of Vail, nor were they attracted by his gruff and blunt forthrightness." Snubbed by these men, Vail quit the firm in 1887, not to return until

1907 when a group of New York bankers supplanted the Bostonians in control and invited him to be the titular head of the American Telephone and Telegraph Company, which had become the parent corporation.[43]

Vail's unsuccessful competition with "members of the Boston aristocracy" is an early illustration of Chester I. Barnard's dictum that "where in a general society a low status is assigned, e.g. on race, nationality, sex, age, education, ownership of property, or family, it is difficult in general to acquire high status in formal organizations in that society." The careers of many other bureaucrats studied here illustrate Barnard's corollary that "where there is high social status it tends to facilitate attainment of high organization status, though less so in democratic than in aristocratic societies." [44]

In either case, it follows that bureaucratic careers must often be explained not only in terms of the firm's success in exploiting traditional market and similar external factors, but also of the bureaucrat's own success in exploiting personal factors derived largely from his personal or family status. As Barnard puts it:

> Perhaps often and certainly occasionally men cannot be promoted or selected, or even must be relieved, because they cannot function, because they "do not fit," where there is no question of formal competence. This question of "fitness" involves such matters as education, experience, age, sex, personal distinctions, prestige, race, nationality, faith, politics, sectional antecedents; and such very specific personal traits as manners, speech, personal appearance, etc.[45]

"Old Corneel" Vanderbilt, late in life, once admonished a photographer: "Here, don't rub out the wrinkles and paint me up that way. I ain't particularly pretty as I know of, but I'm damned if I'll travel in disguise." [46] As early as 1902, however, young aspirants for business success were already advised: "Be manly, and look it. Appear the gentleman, and be the gentleman. What's the good of unknown good? Negotiable intrinsic value must have the appearance of intrinsic worth." [47]

That this change in attitude has spread as business bureaucracies have become more common is apparent from *Fortune's* description in 1940 of criteria for promotion:

> Once a man passes $6,000 through his skill or energy, than a different set of criteria begins to bear. Up to $6,000, perhaps in some cases up to $10,000, mere technical ability and energy can carry him. But. . . after that. . . his superiors begin to consider his character even more than his performance. They even consider how well he looks the part of the executive.[48]

That this change is consistent with the changing structure of the whole economy is suggested by David Riesman's summary:

With the growth of monopolistic competition, the way to get ahead is not so much to make a better mousetrap, but rather to "package" an old mousetrap in a new way, and to sell it by "selling" oneself first. People feel that they must be able to adapt themselves to other people, both to manipulate them and to be manipulated by them. This requires ability to manipulate oneself, to become "a good package." [49]

Early in this century, Edward T. Jeffery admonished young businessmen: "submit cheerfully to authority and learn self-control." [50] Note the facts of Jeffery's bureaucratic career of which this sentiment was the bitter fruit: In 1856, at the age of fourteen, Jeffery went to work for the Illinois Central railroad, and twenty years later "reached his first important position, that of general superintendent and chief engineer. . . He was made general manager in 1885, and although his work was generally recognized as excellent, he resigned in 1889, probably as a result of a conflict with Harriman over certain proposed changes in rates." A few years later he had become president of the Denver and Rio Grande. "He made the most significant decision of his life in the winter of 1900–01 when George Jay Gould bought control" of this road. "Would he accept the orders of the dictatorial Gould or would he insist upon his own idea of sound railroading? His decision to support Gould can undoubtedly be traced to his experiences on the Illinois Central." [51]

What Jeffery lacked in his encounter with Harriman was, in Elton Mayo's words, "the new method of human control," the "capacity to receive communications from others, and to respond to the attitudes and ideas of others in such fashion as to promote congenial participation in a common task." [52] By the time of his encounter with Gould he had acquired this bureaucratic skill. Ten years later the Denver and Rio Grande, which Jeffery had earlier "managed so well that it was able to weather the financial difficulties of the panic of 1893," [53] was in financial straits, and Jeffery moved up from president to chairman of the board.

VI

How did owner-managers or representatives of family firms exploit new products, new markets, technological innovations? Answers for them, as for bureaucratic firms, often are matters of record. How did successful bureaucrats exploit the more elusive factors controlling hierarchical competition and hierarchical ascent? How did they establish "communion" with their superiors, to use one of Barnard's terms? How did they become "clubby" with the latter, as N. R. Danielian expresses it? [54] With what measure of boldness or restraint did they display their status appurtenances, those who had favorable ones; with what techniques and what guile did the others compensate for or cover up their lack?

In describing recruitment in his Bethlehem Steel Company and other firms, Schwab once said: "I never allow any of my relations to work or to be connected with any of my organizations in any capacity. . . Neither do I ever go outside of any of my organizations for men to fill a vacancy, but take them right from the inside. People often ask me, 'How do you know which men to promote?' I tell them, 'I don't have to know; their associates pick them.'"[55] Give such picked bureaucrats as much competence as anyone in the development of the firm's business opportunities. The question remains, how did they become the elect in what C. Wright Mills has called "the personality market" within great bureaucratic structures?[56]

The state of the historical literature on business and businessmen makes it futile at present to try to answer such questions systematically; yet simply to ask them is to call attention to major factors, heretofore neglected by historians, in the recruitment of American business leaders, the course of their careers and perhaps most important the course of the whole economy. Certain popular preconceptions about the history of American business leadership, moreover, can now be systematically cleared away and some outward characteristics, at least, of bureaucratic as of other types of careers presented so as to prepare the ground for more penetrating work.

One of these preconceptions, expressed most felicitously, perhaps, by Charles and Mary Beard and given currency by the legitimation implicit in it, is that until late in the nineteenth century, "the government of American railroads and staple industries, with exceptions of course," had been in the hands of "men who had grown up in the roundhouses and the mills through all the technical processes."[57] But who were these men? The merchants and traders who governed the early textile establishments? Surely not. The industrialists and financiers, then, who governed the early railroad companies? Obviously not these either. Indeed, for a considerable part of the nineteenth century and for most of the industries then pursued, it is relevant to ask what were "all the technical processes"? "Tinkering" aside as a lifelong avocation, what technical processes were there, the mystery of which required an apprenticeship of more than a few years?

Among the men in the present study, moreover, whose careers on the whole did coincide with a vast and complex technological development, the Beards' "exceptions" outnumber those who started in mill or roundhouse by almost three to one, and of the latter more than half were out of the shop by the age of twenty-five. Mine, to be sure, are largely men of a later period than the Beards refer to; of the few among them, nevertheless, who did start in a shop of some sort, the smallest proportion (though only scarcely smaller than their representation in the whole group) is that of independent entrepreneurs. And these, on the average, are the oldest men in my selection and the ones whose careers were in the oldest tradition. Were professionally trained engineers not counted in the technical group but in the managerial one to which most of them quickly moved, the proportion of shop-trained independent entrepreneurs would be significantly smaller still, while that of independent entrepreneurs in the "managerial and clerical" category would be significantly increased.[58]

TABLE 4

American Business Leaders by Type of Career and Type of First Regular Job *

Type of Career	Managerial and Clerical	Technical and Manual
	%	%
Independent	18	13
Family	33	15
Bureaucratic	49	72
Total cases (= 100 per cent)	109	39

* First business, professional, or other job (except work on family's farm) after leaving school or, in very few cases, the Union or Confederate army. In "Managerial and Clerical" are included officers, general managers, superintendents, and the like; and clerks, bookkeepers, telegraphers, and similar office workers. In "Technical and Manual" are hourly workers of various degrees of skill, and draftsmen, engineers, surveyors, and other trained technicians.

The largest cluster by far of those who did start in mill or roundhouse, and one much greater than would be expected by their representation in the whole group, is that of bureaucrats — as the table shows. This is especially striking in view of the fact that the Beards introduce their proposition about nineteenth-century men with technical "know how" mainly to decry the latter's loss of place to adventures with less legitimate claims to power — a second untenable preconception. "By the end of the century," they write, "captains of industry were as a rule no longer evolved by natural selection; they were chosen by the dominant bankers." [59] But what sort of men did the bankers choose? The Beards only answer by innuendo; yet if by "natural selection" they mean long exposure and successful adaptation to conditions of work, the "bankers' men" and the other bureaucrats fit the case much better than the lamented nineteenth-century captains. This is true even if shop work, as the Beards imply, were the only honest kind of preparation for business leadership. It is all the more true if other categories of experience are admitted, as they must be.

Were this not the case, of course, my designation of these newer types of executives as "bureaucrats" would be less justified. To see how well justified it is, take first the question of the number of industries in which these men worked before attaining their peak positions. As the next table shows, relatively few in the whole group jumped from industry to industry. But in this category the independent entrepreneurs are to be found much *more* frequently, the so-called bureaucrats considerably *less* frequently than in any other. Scarcely any of the independent entrepreneurs, on the other hand, remained in the industry in which they started. Among the men who never forsook this industry those I call bureaucrats are relatively more numerous than anywhere else.

TABLE 5

American Business Leaders by Type of Career and Number of Industries Worked In

Type of Career	One Industry	Two Industries	Three or More Industries
	%	%	%
Independent	4	17	32
Family	38	31	22
Bureaucratic	58	52	46
Total cases (= 100 per cent)	66	59	37

Take next the ages at which these men entered the industry in which they attained their peak position, to remain in it. Table 6 only confirms what Table 5 suggests: as the entering age groups get older, the greater is their representation of independent entrepreneurs; as they get younger, the greater is their representation of bureaucrats.

TABLE 6

American Business Leaders by Type of Career and Age on Entering Listed Industry

Type of Career	Under 20	20–25	26–39	40 and over
	%	%	%	%
Independent	4	10	28	28
Family	29	32	30	36
Bureaucratic	67	58	42	36
Total cases (= 100 per cent)	52	38	33	34

The relatively greater experience of the newer men — the bureaucrats — in their particular industries is made most abundantly clear by Table 7, which is concerned with the years spent by these men in their industries before attaining the peak job in them.

The idea of an almost frictionless mobility of labor and capital — of great freedom in jumping from one industry to another — was one of the pillars of nineteenth-century economic theory, just as the warm sanction for risk taking was one of the factors that operated to make the theory seem representative of life. Walter Bagehot's statement of this idea in 1879 may be cited: "The first assumption I shall take is that labour and capital circulate readily within the limits of a nation from employment to employment, leaving that in which remuneration is smaller and going to that in which it is greater." [60]

Bagehot felt that "no assumption can be better founded" than this. He was aware of the problem of inexperience but brushed it aside.

In modern England [he wrote, and he could even more appropriately have spoken of the United States] there is a great speculative fund which is always ready to go into anything which promises high profits. The largest part of this is composed of the savings of men of business. . . who have made money rapidly, and who fancy that the skill and knowledge of a special trade which have enabled them to do so will also enable them to judge of risks, and measure contingencies out of that trade.[61]

TABLE 7

American Business Leaders by Type of Career and Years in Listed Industry
before attaining Listed Job *

Type of Career	Under 20 years	20–29 years	30 or more years
	%	%	%
Independent	24	12	4
Family	38	32	14
Bureaucratic	38	56	82
Total cases (= 100 per cent)	58	43	44

* Board chairmen are not included in this table.

Evidence already presented attests to the strength of Bagehot's dictum, as it applies to the men in the older, independent group. Typically, these men ranged from their specialty; their listed industry was but one of many they engaged in, they entered it comparatively late in life, and they entered it at or near the top.

The striking thing about the experience of the great proportion of the rest of these men is the degree to which it was white collar in character. This is especially noteworthy in view of the universal neglect by historians of the development of the business office and of the preconception implicit in this neglect, that modern technology is possible without modern administration.[62]

As the evidence given in Table 4 shows, almost three out of four in the whole selection, almost two out of three of the bureaucrats, never did any but white-collar work. The remaining few, almost without exception, got white-collar jobs as soon as they could. One was Frank A. Vanderlip, who in 1909 became president of the National City Bank in New York. "I took this job" as a machinist, he said later, "not because it was the kind of work I wanted but because it was the only job I could get." [63] Another was told by the president of his railroad: "It seems to me that you have as Fireman with the prospect before you of being an Engineer, a much better position than would be a clerkship among many others in a railroad office." [64] Yet he insisted upon and got the clerkship. Representative of the predominant type is John A. Topping, who, beginning as "an office boy in the Youngstown district," eventually supplanted the former miner and furnace worker, Don H. Bacon, as head of the Tennessee Coal and Iron Company, and in 1907 was made chairman of the board of Republic Iron and Steel. Topping, wrote Herbert N. Casson that year, "is less rugged than Bacon. . . He is a handsome, courteous man of forty-three — a man of the business office rather than of the steelmill." [65]

In white-collar work, especially in the whole range of the executive hierarchy, there are few if any adequate standards of efficiency, few if any accurate measurements of performance. One consequence of this at high levels, as Peter F. Drucker says in his study of General Motors, is that "a false sentimentality" is permitted to operate, "which evaluates executives according to the lip-service they pay to humanitarian principles rather than according to their achievements," especially when the principles are those of a forceful superior like Alfred P. Sloan, Jr. [66] Concerning the lower levels, the Standard Oil Company of New Jersey said late in 1949: "We are still in the dark on how to pre-select potential leaders. . . There is no complete agreement on the exact criteria for discriminating the good from the bad." [67]

In ascent through white-collar channels, therefore, much more than through others, the display and manipulation of personal factors is likely to be most important. "Ability" is likely to be judged, as in the cited instance of Edward T. Jeffery, by the capacity to be congenial with colleagues, compatible with superiors. Barnard writes of this situation: " 'Learning the ropes' in most organizations is chiefly learning who's who, what's what, why's why of its informal society." Yet this process, he adds, often results in "excessive compatibility . . . 'single track minds' and excessively crystallized attitudes and in the destruction of personal responsibility." [68]

Perhaps it was a view of this crippling effect of bureaucratic life and a determination to escape it that impelled Henry H. Rogers and Henry M. Flagler, individualists caught for a time in the Standard Oil Company in this transition period, to undertake their own great private enterprises — Rogers with his $40 million railroad already described; Flagler with his $30 to $40 million development of Florida. [69]

But even such Paul Bunyanesque ventures were unavailable to salaried bureaucrats and their professional retainers to whom, as Mellen said, "the fortune generally comes when it is too late for us to enjoy it." [70] Nor was the spirit likely to move them, even had they the required capital. For early in this century, as the press and politics of the time make abundantly clear, the condition was already growing which *Fortune* in 1950 described in its full development:

The businessman used to get satisfaction out of being the man on the hill, the patron of the arts, the payer of the church mortgage — and did not everyone agree that it was right and proper that he be entrusted with the destiny of the country? Now, satirized in countless novels, politically a prophet without honor, he is stripped of the former dignities and of much of the old feeling of moral contribution. [71]

The question of what alternative modes of self expression, then, conscious or darkly shrouded even from themselves, such "stripped" men of business have employed in the bureaucracies that utterly absorbed them must be answered more fully before the policies of these bureaucracies in the past fifty years toward the different segments of the community at large can be fully understood.

Appendix

To the Torchbook Edition

XII

American Historians and the Business Elite

By William Miller

One might have supposed that historians, largely occupied as they have been with the activities of ruling classes, would have been among the first to study systematically the problem of the recruitment and tenure of elites. This problem is an especially interesting one in a country such as the United States which has had no official caste systems and no legally established hereditary hierarchies. Yet most American historians have shied away from it.[1] Few of them have even raised questions about the locus and transmission of power or status in modern times. Moreover, those who have discussed in particular the ascent of nineteenth- and early twentieth-century business leaders have tended to attribute their success simply to the possession of more shrewdness or trickiness or more pluck or luck or other private qualities than competitors who failed to rise; the very few historians who have considered social determinants such as family background or work experience have, by stressing the alleged values of poverty or of starting business in boyhood, placed their emphasis, as we shall see, quite at the opposite pole from where it belongs.[2]

The present study of 190 business leaders of the first decade of the twentieth century and of 188 contemporary political leaders on whom data are presented for comparison aims to call historians' attention to the critical but neglected field of elite recruitment, to suggest a method by which data may be collected and analyzed,[3] and to present some of the results of applying this method to a particular area in which a few historians have speculated to strikingly misleading effect.

II

This essay is not wholly a pioneer effort to analyze the social characteristics of the American business elite, and a word should be said about the work already done in this field. I am not concerned with full-length biographies of business leaders, of which there are very few of value, nor with popular studies of groups of businessmen, such as Matthew Josephson's *The Robber Barons* or Frederick Lewis Allen's *The Lords of Creation*. Of somewhat greater interest, at least methodologically, are two books by Fritz Redlich — *History of American Business Leaders* and *The Molding of American Banking: Men and Ideas*.[4] These discuss certain "entrepreneurial" characteristics[5] of *sizable numbers* of business leaders; the first, leaders in the iron and steel industry in England, Germany, and the United States, largely in the nineteenth century; the second, American bankers and related politicos, 1781–1840. Unlike the more popular books, Redlich's are long on theory; but, like them, his are short on synthesis. Systematic summaries of his data can be made, but he has not made them.[6]

Most germane to the field of the present essay are the following *statistical* studies of American business leaders:[7] Pitirim Sorokin, "American Millionaires and Multi-Millionaires";[8] Chester M. Destler, "Entrepreneurial Leadership Among the 'Robber Barons': A Trial Balance";[9] C. Wright Mills, "The American Business Elite: A Collective Portrait";[10] and, the only full-length book, F. W. Taussig and C. S. Joslyn, *American Business Leaders: A Study in Social Origins and Social Stratification*.[11]

The first two, by Sorokin and Destler, are suggestive, but certain internal weaknesses reduce their scientific value. Sorokin lumps many kinds of millionaires and near millionaires; his 668 persons selected haphazardly (but not, statistically speaking, at random), over a period of some two hundred years, include actors, preachers, statesmen, and physicians as well as businessmen, and in his tables he seldom distinguishes the last group from the rest. The difficulty with Destler's work lies mainly in the vagueness of some of his categories, though the small number of businessmen studied by him (43) also diminishes confidence in his results.[12]

The essay by Mills and the book by Taussig and Joslyn, while satisfactory as starting points for additional studies, present their own problems, the first mainly because of the nature of its sample, the second partly because of the nature of its questionnaire. Mills selected his men only from the *Dictionary of American Biography,* the subjects for which were named on grounds that made some businessmen eligible for reasons that had little to do with their business achievements and others ineligible however eminent they may have been in the business community of their time.[13] Taussig and Joslyn, in turn, setting out to prove that heredity is more important than environment in business success, asked their respondents for so little information that, as William F. Ogburn said in a review of their book, they have "such a small fraction of the environment measured that they, in the nature of the case, cannot do much toward a solution of the problem."[14] Yet Taussig and Joslyn's initial data were carefully gathered and as presented in some of the tables in their book are available for more scholarly and scientific use.[15]

III

The present study is focused upon "career men" — bureaucrats, that is — who often must have been as occupied with getting and staying ahead in their companies as with keeping their companies ahead of the field. In studying the so-called "robber barons," Destler was impelled to consider also a few early "career men," an odd-sounding designation for "semi-piratical entrepreneurs who roamed the United States virtually unchecked before 1903."[16] I, in turn, have had to include some atavistic captains of industry. Nevertheless, except for a few partners in unincorporated investment-banking houses, the men discussed in these pages were all office-holders; many of them *never* organized a business of any kind.

Yet the dull titles by which these men are called and the bureaucratic maneuvering in which they must often have engaged should not suggest that these were petty men exercising small powers in petty domains. The mere fact that they were bureaucrats should suggest the contrary, for, while there are many examples of petty bureaucracies, generally speaking only large enterprises operating in large theaters need hierarchical structures. The fact is, the men discussed in this essay were at the apex of some of the mightiest organizations the world up to then had seen. In the vernacular of their times, their bureaucratic structures were among the first great industrial, commercial, and financial "trusts."

As late as 1896, except for some railroads, there were probably fewer than a dozen American corporations capitalized at more than $10 million. By 1903, again excepting railroads, there were more than three hundred corporations capitalized at $10 million or more, approximately fifty at $50 million or more, and seventeen at $100 million or more.[17] A similar change may be traced in the modern history of other capitalist nations in which, as in the United States, the startling upward curve in the productivity of workers, attributable in part to the new technology of electricity and alloys, helped bring about an unprecedented speeding up in the accumulation of money and power and in the combination of business firms.

In this period one after another of the key segments of the world's economy was engrossed by the world's business leaders, Americans not least among them. And in the United States as elsewhere it became possible in regard to scores of commodities and key services such as transportation, communication, and the granting of credit to name the corporations or clusters of corporations that dictated the quantities which could be produced or employed and the prices and places at which they could be sold. Such fateful decisions were in the domain of the early business bureaucrats studied here and were communicated to and carried out by the bureaucracies they controlled — organizations that would scarcely have been understood by early nineteenth-century entrepreneurs or by those Jacksonian politicians who had sought, in the name of equal entrepreneurial opportunity, to make the establishment of corporations so easy.

IV

At the start of this work I had decided that two hundred men were all that an individual could study in a reasonable time and that from that number (various contingencies reduced the final group to 190) statistically reliable results could be obtained.[18] If these men were selected from the largest companies regardless of field, the bulk of them would have come from the railroads; if, on the other hand, an equal number were taken from each major business field, representatives of small insurance companies and banks would have mingled with the elite while many from great railroads would have been excluded. This dilemma could be solved only arbitrarily.

The companies from which men were chosen were taken from the following major fields: (1) manufacturing and mining, (2) steam railroads, (3) public utilities, (4) finance (commercial banking, life insurance, investment banking).[19] Companies in the first three fields were ranked by capitalization, the commercial banks by deposits, and the life-insurance companies (no other types of insurance companies approach the life companies in size) by assets.[20] From the *Statistical Abstract of the United States* and other sources summarizing census information, I then took the capitalization of the entire manufacturing and mining, steam railroad, and public-utilities industries in the United States in or near 1910, the total deposits of the national banks, and the assets of the life-insurance companies. These I simply added together and distributed the leaders among the four fields more or less according to the proportion of the total represented by the figure used for each. This total of capital, deposits, and assets came to $57 billion. Table 1 shows how the leaders would have been distributed had the proportions been followed exactly, and how they actually are distributed in this study.

The next step was to choose the topmost positions from which these men should be selected. Should directors be included, or chairmen and members of key panels such as finance or executive committees? What of

TABLE 1

Distribution of Business Leaders by Type of Industry

Industry	Number of Men from Each Industry if Representation Were Proportionate to "Size" of Industry	Actual Number of Men from Each Industry
Manufacturing and Mining	65	64
Steam Railroads	58	58
Public Utilities	29	31
National Banking } Finance	16 } 29	19 } 28
Life Insurance	13	9
Total	181 *	181 *

* The nine investment bankers, selected on a different basis, are excluded from this table. See n. 20.

executive vice-presidents, general managers, or cashiers of banks? Investigation of the locus of different types of power in large corporations has only just begun;[21] for the period of this work it may fairly be said that there are no studies. The decision to limit this work to presidents and board chairmen of corporations and some partners of unincorporated investment-banking houses permitted me to choose men from a larger group of companies than would have been possible had men from more positions been selected; it may have caused some persons of great importance to be excluded, but all of those included, at any rate, were bound to be men of first rank.[22] These men and their companies are listed at the end of this section. No one who was president or board chairman in a listed company in the decade 1901–1910 has been excluded.[23]

One hundred and seventy-four of these men (information on this score is lacking for sixteen) held approximately 2,720 business directorships. A few held more than 100 each; the average was about 16.[24] Clearly, these men were leaders not only in their own companies but in the entire business community.

A List of the Men and Their Companies Used in This Study †

Size, in Millions, 1903	Company	Presidents and Chairmen (* denotes board chairman)

A. Manufacturing and Mining Companies

$1,370	United States Steel Corp.	Schwab, Charles M.
		Corey, William E.
		* Gary, Elbert H.

Size, in Millions, 1903	Company	Presidents and Chairmen (* denotes board chairman)
$503	Consolidated Tobacco Co.⎱ American Tobacco Co. ⎰	Duke, James B.
201	American Smelting & Refining Co.	Nash, Edward W. Guggenheim, Daniel
175	Amalgamated Copper Co.	Rogers, Henry H. Ryan, John D.
170	International Mercantile Marketing Co.	Griscom, Clement A.
145	American Sugar Refining Co.	Havemeyer, Henry O. Thomas, Washington B.
130	United States Leather Co.⎱ Central Leather Co. ⎰	Horton, James Hoyt, Edward C. * Valentine, Patrick A.
120	International Harvester Co.	McCormick, Cyrus H. Deering, Charles
97	Standard Oil Co.	Rockefeller, John D.
84	Pittsburgh Coal Co.	Robbins, Francis L. Taylor, Matthew H. Field, William K.
82	American Can Co.	Norton, Edwin Assmann, Franz A. Graham, William T. * Reid, Daniel G.
74	Pullman Co.	Lincoln, Robert T.
71	Corn Products Co.⎱ Corn Products Refining Co.⎰	Matthiessen, Conrad H. Bedford, Edward T.
60	American Car & Foundry Co.	Bixby, William K. Eaton, Frederick H.
60	Crucible Steel Co. of America	Halcomb, Charles H. Smith, Frank B. Ramsey, Charles C. * Park, William G. * DuPuy, Herbert
58	United States Rubber Co.	Colt, Samuel P.
56	National Biscuit Co.	Crawford, Benjamin F. Green, Adolphus W.
56	Lackawanna Steel Co.	Scranton, Walter Clarke, Edmund A. S.

Size, in Millions, 1903	Company	Presidents and Chairmen (* denotes board chairman)
$52	International Paper Co.	Chisholm, Hugh J. Burbank, Alonzo N.
50	United Copper Co.	Heinze, F. Augustus
50	American Locomotive Co.	Pitkin, Albert J. Marshall, Waldo H.
50	Distillers' Securities Corp.	Curley, Edmund J.
50	Cambria Steel Co.	Stackhouse, Powell Price, Charles S.
49	American Woolen Co.	Ayer, Frederick Wood, William M.
48	Colorado Fuel & Iron Co.	Osgood, John C. Kebler, Julian A. Hearne, Frank J. Welborn, Jesse F.
47	Republic Iron & Steel Co.	Thompson, Alexis W. Topping, John A. Guthrie, Tracy W. * French, G. Watson
46	General Electric Co.	Coffin, Charles A.
45	Associated Oil Co. of Calif.	Canfield, C. A. Chanslor, J. A. Herrin, William F.
44	Westinghouse Electric Corp.	Westinghouse, George Atkins, Edward F. * Ives, Brayton

B. Steam Railroads

Size, in Millions, 1903	Company	Presidents and Chairmen
873	Pennsylvania Railroad Co.	Cassatt, Alexander McCrea, James
490	The Rock Island Co.	Leeds, William B. Mather, Robert Walker, Roberts * Yoakum, Benjamin F.
460	The Southern Pacific Co.	Hays, Charles M. * Tweed, Charles H.
458	Atchison, Topeka & Santa Fe Railway Co.	Ripley, Edward P.
451	Union Pacific Railroad Co.	Burt, Horace G. Harriman, Edward H. Lovett, Robert S.

Size, in Millions, 1903	Company	Presidents and Chairmen (* denotes board chairman)
$394	The Reading Co.	Harris, Joseph S. Baer, George F.
392	Baltimore & Ohio Railroad Co.	Loree, Leonor F. Murray, Oscar G. Willard, Daniel
382	New York Central & Hudson River Railroad Co.	Callaway, Samuel R. Newman, William H. Brown, William C. * Depew, Chauncey M.
372	Erie Railroad Co.	Thomas, Eben B. Underwood, Frederick D.
365	Southern Railway Co.	Spencer, Samuel Finley, William W.
303	Chicago & Northwestern Railroad Co.	Hughitt, Marvin
297	Atlantic Coast Line Co.	Walters, Henry Elliott, Warren G. Jenkins, Michael
286	Northern Pacific Railway Co.	Mellen, Charles S. Elliott, Howard
233	Missouri Pacific Railroad Co.	Gould, George J.
230	Chicago, Milwaukee & St. Paul Railroad Co.	Earling, Albert J. * Miller, Roswell
226	Illinois Central Railroad Co.	Fish, Stuyvesant Harahan, James T.
205	Great Northern Railway	Hill, James J. Hill, Louis W.
152	Chicago, Burlington & Quincy Railroad Co.	Perkins, Charles E. Harris, George B. Miller, Darius
149	Missouri, Kansas & Texas Railway	Rouse, Henry C. Finney, Frederick N. Allen, Andrew A. * Joline, Adrian H. Hawley, Edwin
142	Norfolk & Western Railway Co.	Kimball, Frederick J. Fink, Henry Johnson, Lucius E.
138	Chesapeake & Ohio Railway	Stevens, George E. * Trumbull, Frank

Size, in Millions, 1903	*Company*	Presidents and Chairmen (* denotes board chairman)
$127	Denver & Rio Grande Railroad Co.	Jeffery, Edward T.
119	Delaware, Lackawanna & Western Railroad	Truesdale, William H. * Sloan, Samuel
118	Western Maryland Railroad Co.	Hood, John M. Pierce, Winslow S. Ramsey, Joseph, Jr. Bush, Benjamin F.

C. Public Utilities

392	American Telephone & Telegraph Co.	Cochrane, Alexander Fish, Frederick P. Vail, Theodore N.
224	Metropolitan Securities Co.	Fowler, Thomas P. Vreeland, Herbert H.
176	Public Service Co. of New Jersey	McCarter, Thomas N.
170	Brooklyn Rapid Transit Co.	Greatsinger, Jacob L. Winter, Edwin W. * Brady, Anthony N.
150	Consolidated Gas Co. of New York	Gawtry, Harrison E. Cortelyou, George B.
127	Interborough Rapid Transit Co. Interborough-Metropolitan Co.	Belmont, August Bryan, Edward P. Shonts, Theodore P.
121	Western Union Telegraph Co.	Eckert, Thomas T. Clowry, Robert C.
117	Philadelphia Rapid Transit Co.	Parsons, John B. Kruger, Charles O.
111	Chicago Union Traction Co. Chicago Railways Co.	Roach, John M. * Foreman, Henry G. * Blair, Henry A.
100	United Gas Improvement Co.	Dolan, Thomas
80	North American Co.	Wetmore, Charles W. Campbell, James
76	St. Louis Transit Co.	Carleton, Murray
70	United Railway & Electric Co. of Baltimore	Perin, Nelson House, William A.
69	Massachusetts Electric Co.	Abbott, Gordon

Size, in Millions, 1903	Company	Presidents and Chairmen (* denotes board chairman)
$68	Boston Elevated Railway Co.	Bancroft, William A.
67	People's Gas, Light & Coke Co.	Billings, Cornelius K. G. Knapp, George O.

D. Finance

1. National Banks

148	National City Bank (New York)	Stillman, James Vanderlip, Frank A.
90	National Bank of Commerce (New York)	Hendrix, Joseph C. Snyder, Valentine P.
84	First National Bank (New York)	Baker, George F.
75	National Park Bank (New York)	Delafield, Richard
74	Hanover National Bank (New York)	Woodward, James T.
59	United States Trust Co. (New York)	Stewart, John A. Gage, Lyman J. Sheldon, Edward W.
54	Mercantile Trust Co. (New York)	Deming, Henry C. Fitzgerald, Louis
92	First National Bank (Chicago)	Forgan, James B.
73	Illinois Trust and Savings Bank (Chicago)	Mitchell, John J.
46	Corn Exchange National Bank (Chicago)	Hamill, Ernest A.
46	National Bank of Commerce (St. Louis)	Thompson, William H. VanBlarcom, Jacob C.
47	National Shawmut Bank (Boston)	Stearns, James P. Gaston, William A.

2. Life Insurance

382	Mutual Life Insurance Co.	McCurdy, Richard A. Peabody, Charles A.
359	Equitable Life Assurance Co.	Alexander, James W. Morton, Paul
322	New York Life Insurance Co.	McCall, John A. Orr, Alexander E. Kingsley, Darwin P.
89	Metropolitan Life Insurance Co.	Hegeman, John R.
63	Aetna Life Insurance Co. (Hartford)	Bulkeley, Morgan G.

Size, in Millions, 1903	Company	Presidents and Chairmen (* denotes board chairman)
	3. Investment Bankers	Partners
	J. P. Morgan & Co.	Morgan, J. Pierpont Perkins, George W.
	Kuhn, Loeb & Co.	Schiff, Jacob H. Warburg, Paul M.
	Kidder, Peabody & Co.	Winsor, Robert Peabody, Frank E.
	Lee, Higginson & Co.	Higginson, Henry L. Lane, Gardner M.
	Speyer & Co.	Speyer, James

† Some of these men served in more than one listed company or in more than one eligible position in the same company. Each man is listed according to the first eligible position he held, and only there. Some of these companies changed names and otherwise were recognized during the decade studied; others expired during this decade. All companies are listed by their names in 1903; for some the new names are included in brackets.

V

As stated earlier in this essay, some general American historians have made enough casual remarks about the recruitment of modern business leaders to form a rough explanatory model. I want now to point out some of the facets of this model and then to introduce some of my own findings to show how obsolete it had become by the first decade of this century, if, indeed, it ever fitted the facts.

Virtually all the generalizations that go to make up this model are based upon a few remarkable life histories from the "robber baron" period; thus in most of the books that are at all concerned with the recruitment of business leaders one finds accounts of Andrew Carnegie, John D. Rockefeller, J. Pierpont Morgan, James J. Hill, and Edward H. Harriman. In *The Growth of the American People 1865-1940,* Arthur M. Schlesinger, Sr., cites in addition such older heroes as Cornelius Vanderbilt and Gustavus F. Swift but not later ones.[25] Charles A. and Mary R. Beard, in *The Rise of American Civilization,* add to the ubiquitous five Jay Gould, William H. Vanderbilt, Collis P. Huntington, Jay Cooke, William A. Clark, and Philip D. Armour.[26] Few general historians discuss a greater number of men than do the Beards; but much more significant, practically none discusses any *later* men.

The last extended discussion of the "typical" business leader by Samuel Eliot Morison and Henry Steele Commager in *The Growth of the American Republic* — a widely used textbook — follows (italics mine):

The *most typical figure* of the industrial age was undoubtedly Andrew Carnegie. A *poor immigrant boy* from Scotland, he followed and helped to *perpetuate* the American tradition of rising *from poverty to riches,* and his success he ascribed entirely to the political and economic democracy which obtained in this country. By dint of unflagging industry and unrivalled business acumen and resourcefulness and especially through his extraordinary ability to choose as associates such men as Charles Schwab, Henry Frick, and Henry Phipps, and to command the devotion of his workmen, Carnegie built up the greatest steel business in the world, and retired in 1901 to chant the glories of "Triumphant Democracy" and to give away his enormous fortune of three and a half hundred millions.[27]

Arthur Schlesinger says vaguely of the latest group of business leaders he discusses that they arose "in most cases from obscure origins and unhindered by moral scruples, they were fired by a passionate will to succeed." [28] In the last discussion of business leaders in *The American Nation,* John D. Hicks says: "Typical of the railroad builders was James J. Hill," who, he points out, was an immigrant from Canada.[29] The Beards' analysis of the life histories of American business leaders ends with the eleven men named above, of whom they write:

Of the group here brought under examination only two, Morgan and Vanderbilt, built their fortunes on the solid basis of family inheritances while only one had what may be called by courtesy a higher education: Morgan spent two years in the University of Göttingen. Carnegie began life as a stationary engineer; Jay Cooke as a clerk in a general store in Sandusky; Jay Gould as a surveyor and tanner; Huntington, Armour, and Clark as husky lads on their fathers' farms; Hill as a clerk for a St. Paul steamboat company; Harriman as an office boy in a New York broker's establishment; Rockefeller as a bookkeeper in Cleveland.[30]

The Beards' inference is that these men, starting from the lowliest jobs as exemplars of the tradition, rose from the most humble origins to the very top. This may actually have been so, not only of these few men but of the large majority of business leaders whom they are taken to represent. But, it may be asked, how many in modern times start much higher than these men did, even among the well-born, college-trained young men who, as *Fortune* put it, spend a few years in "the mummery of 'working in the plant'" before ascending to the highest executive levels?[31] Surely, of itself, an initial low-status job does not necessarily imply lowly origins.[32]

It is instructive to note that even the more perspicacious historians, when they err on the origins of business leaders, do so on the side of the tradition. Thus the Beards describe Rockefeller, the son of a "Barnumesque" itinerant entrepreneur, as "the son of a farmer";[33] and Henry B.

Parkes writes of F. Augustus Heinze, the copper magnate who was born in Brooklyn, New York, into a comfortable business family, as a "young German immigrant."[34]

Though most historians say little about it, there has been in the United States for well over a century a sizable and growing working class, propertyless, segregated, often remarkably apathetic to the alleged opportunities of American business and political life. Into this class most immigrants, starting with the Irish in the 1840's, have been channeled. Historians generally imply by the individuals they select as examples that this class and (for so little is said in this connection of rich men's business-bred, college-educated sons) this class alone has supplied our business leaders, that their school, to quote Carnegie himself, was "the sternest of all schools — poverty," that they were graduated from it early in life into apprenticeships as "mechanics" or "poor clerks," and that "against the boy who swept the office, or who begins as a shipping clerk at fourteen," the college graduate "has little chance, starting at twenty." [35]

Yet to read the lives of business leaders, even of those who presumably are the pillars of this tradition, is to look almost in vain for working class or foreign origins, and even poor and unschooled farm boys are not conspicuous among such leaders. Of Rockefeller and Heinze I have already spoken. The historians themselves have accounted for J. Pierpont Morgan and William H. Vanderbilt. Jay Cooke's father, Eleutheros, was "a lawyer who was sent to Congress." Harriman's father, Orlando, was an Episcopal clergyman, "the one exception of his generation in a family of several brothers" who followed the family tradition of successful "trading and commercial pursuits." Harriman himself married the daughter of a banker and railroad president who started him on his railroad career. Even a farm boy such as Elbert H. Gary, who "experienced early in life the arduous regimen of work on a pioneer farm, an experience which endowed him with excellent health and a robust physique," was raised in a settlement named after his forebears and in a house that "was a large one for the time — the largest in the settlement . . . 'the big white house on the hill' it came to be called." [36]

Doubtless examples can be found in the period emphasized by the historians of men whose life histories more fully substantiate the tradition. What of the men in the later period to which the historians tacitly allow their explanations of origins and ascent to apply and which is the subject of this essay?

VI

Had the "typical" American business leader of the first decade of the twentieth century been an immigrant? Was he best represented in manufacturing, for example, by Franz A. Assmann, the German-born president of the American Can Company; or in railroading by Edward T. Jeffery, the English-born president of the Denver and Rio Grande; or in insurance by Alexander E. Orr, the Irish-born president of the New York Life; or in banking by Jacob H. Schiff, the German-born Jew who became senior partner of Kuhn, Loeb and Co.?

Simply to ask the question is to answer it. Of the 187 businessmen studied here whose birthplaces are known, only 18, or less than 10 per cent, were born abroad.[37] Surely these men were less "typical" of the topmost business leaders of their time than the 55 per cent who were born in the eastern part of the United States, in New England and the middle Atlantic states.[38]

TABLE 2

American Business and Political Leaders by Region of Birthplace *

Birthplace	Business Leaders (Per Cent of)	Political Leaders (Per Cent of)
New England	18 ⎫ 55	22
Middle Atlantic	37 ⎭	27
East North Central	22	27
South	9	11
West	4	7
United States	90	94
Foreign	10	6
Total cases (= 100 per cent)	187	188

* These are census regions. Combined in "South" are South Atlantic, South Central, West South Central; in "West" West North Central, Mountain, Pacific.

Of the eighteen business leaders who were foreign-born, moreover, scarcely two or three fit the historians' concept of the *poor* immigrant who made good, and even these men had been brought to the United States at such an early age that they may be said to have been bred if not born here. Two of the eighteen men were of rich, colonial American business families who happened to be residing temporarily in Canada when they were born. Four more, rich and highly placed abroad, either settled here as representatives of big foreign business firms or were brought over by fathers who represented such firms. At least two others had letters of introduction from their fathers or other relatives abroad to American bankers and merchants who helped to establish them here. Thus it appears to be unsafe in writing of elites to associate immigrant status, even where that fits, with the idea of poverty.

If not typically poor immigrants, were these business and political leaders the sons of foreigners? More of them were, surely, but the next table shows that the typical leader in each field was born into an American family.

TABLE 3

American Business and Political Leaders by Region of Father's Birthplace

Father's Birthplace	Business Leaders (Per Cent of)	Political Leaders (Per Cent of)
New England	27	33
Middle Atlantic	31	28
East North Central	4	5
South	12	17
United States, unspecified *	7	4
United States	81	87
Foreign	19	13
Total cases (= 100 per cent)	176	176

* Fathers of none of these men were known to have been born in the "West" as defined in Table 2. All those known to have been born in the United States, the exact region being unknown, are counted here.

Moreover, these families themselves had, in most instances, been in America for many generations. Almost three fourths of the business and political leaders were at least of the fourth generation of their paternal lines to reside in America; many were of the seventh and even the eighth generations. Colonial families were represented by 73 per cent of the business leaders and 79 per cent of those in politics.[39] Fifty-six per cent of the former and 47 per cent of the latter were of families that had settled in America in the seventeenth century.

TABLE 4

American Business and Political Leaders by Paternal Family's Origin *

Family Origin	Business Leaders (Per Cent of)	Political Leaders (Per Cent of)
England and Wales	53	56
Ireland	14	13
Scotland	7	8
Canada	3	1
British Empire, other, or unspecified	5	5
British Empire	82	83
Germany	12	8
Other countries	6	9
Total cases (= 100 per cent)	162	162

* Or country of leader's own origin if he was the first in the family to settle in America. In either case, last country before settlement in America.

Even were they not of colonial ancestry, most of these leaders could point to British, and many to English, forebears.

They could claim Protestant, and often Episcopal or Presbyterian, backgrounds.

TABLE 5

American Business and Political Leaders by Religious Background *

Denomination	Business Leaders (Per Cent of)	Political Leaders (Per Cent of)
Episcopal	25	12
Presbyterian	21	17
Methodist	9	13
Baptist	5	7
Other Protestant	14	20
Protestant, unspecified	16	25
Protestant	90	94
Catholic	7	4
Jewish	3	2
Total cases (= 100 per cent)	174	165

* In almost all instances this is the religion of the leader himself and most likely of his family as well. In a few instances where a shift in religion is known to have occurred, only the old religion is counted.

If not of recent foreign origin, was the typical American business leader of the early twentieth century a migrant from a farm?

Table 6 shows that the political leaders far more frequently than those in business came from rural areas, that almost 60 per cent of the latter were recruited from the larger towns and cities. Indeed, more than 20 per cent of them were born in cities that around the middle of the nineteenth century had populations of 100,000 or more. Upon these men rural influences even in a predominantly rural society must have been at a minimum.

TABLE 6

American Business and Political Leaders by Size of Birthplace *

Size of Birthplace	Business Leaders (Per Cent of)	Political Leaders (Per Cent of)
Rural (under 2,500)	41	75
Town (2,500–8,000)	19 } 59	9
City (over 8,000)	40 }	16
Total cases (= 100 per cent)	164	180

* Population is from the census nearest each man's date of birth. In a few instances of men raised in places (that is, moved there before reaching the age of 7) sufficiently larger or smaller than their birthplaces to alter their classification in the scale used in the table, that place, not the birthplace, was used.

Yet more significant in answering the question are the occupations of the fathers of these business leaders. Here we find that even of those born in rural areas fewer than one third (and only 12 per cent of the whole group) had fathers who were mainly farmers. Fifty-six per cent of all the business leaders, on the other hand, had fathers who had been in business — often big business — before them; eight of ten, indeed, came from business or professional families.

TABLE 7

American Business and Political Leaders by Father's Occupation *

Occupation	Business Leaders (Per Cent of)	Political Leaders (Per Cent of)
Businessman	56 ⎫ 79	33
Professional	23 ⎭	18
Farmer	12	38
Public Official	7	9
Worker	2	2
Total cases (= 100 per cent)	167	167

* Some fathers engaged in more than one occupation. The one used here was dominant in the period in which each man was raised. In a few instances this was not clear so a choice was made more or less arbitrarily (considering our lack of knowledge of income and status factors in the early nineteenth century) by which business (including higher company positions as well as company ownership) took precedence over farming and professional or public-official positions over both. This conforms roughly to the ascending order of status used in classifying occupations today. In no instance was there a problem of a father who was a worker (including wage as well as salaried occupations). About one third of the professionals were lawyers or engineers who might have been called businessmen, given the nature of their professional work; the others were clergymen, doctors, writers, etc. "Public official" includes professional politicians (even if not officeholders) and lawyers who were chiefly public men.

Darwin P. Kingsley, who was president of the New York Life Insurance Company from 1907 to 1931 and chairman of the board from 1931 to his death two years later, once said of his impoverished early years:

On the 40-acre farm, in Vermont, where I was born, everything we wore and everything we ate was grown on the farm, except a little sugar once in a while in place of maple sugar, which was indigenous, and a little tea. From a dozen sheep came wool which was first spun and then woven by hand into winter clothing. Our garden supplied flax which was made into summer garments . . . I well remember the first time my father took his wool and swapped it for fulled cloth. We all regarded that as an epochal advance into a higher state of civilization.

At Alburg, where I was born, there were not then (1857) enough houses to form even a hamlet. In the summer I attended the old "deestrict" school, a primitive affair innocent of any suggestion of higher education. In our home were very few books. Life there was clean through and through, self-respecting, and full of moral and religious discipline. But it was extremely narrow, uninspiring, and unimaginative. There was little or nothing to fire a boy with

ROCKMONT COLLEGE LIBRARY

ambition or enthusiasm or to acquaint him with the world that lay beyond his "cabined, cribbed, and confined" sphere.[40]

Yet it was not this kind of poverty that Carnegie had in mind when he recommended his "sternest of all schools"; this kind of spiritual and intellectual poverty was probably most prevalent among the poor, but this much at least they shared with large segments of the population at all levels, including those born and raised among the very rich. Call Kingsley's family poor in material things as well; but compared with the sons of many urban and rural wage workers even in the 1850's he and other farmers' sons like him were not worst off.

Nevertheless, in the next table, showing the social status of the families of these business and political leaders, Kingsley and a few others with apparently similar or poorer backgrounds were classified as lower class. Men were classified as of the upper class when it was clear that their fathers, like those of August Belmont, Cornelius K. G. Billings, or Charles Deering, were themselves big businessmen, or where their families, like those of Robert Todd Lincoln or Winslow Shelby Pierce, were politically eminent. Generally speaking, those in between — including some businessmen with no special claims to wealth or power or professionals like the average clergyman, doctor, or lawyer — were ranked as of middle-class origins. This does not mean that their fathers were not of help to them. James B. Duke, for example, rose to wealth and power with a company founded by his father; George W. Perkins moved to a partnership in the House of Morgan — probably the acting head of the house at one stage — from a vice-presidency in the New York Life Insurance Company in which his father, a minor executive there, had given him his business start.

Not all the men ranked in the upper class, of course, had fathers as rich and powerful as those of Belmont or Billings, or families as well connected as those of Lincoln or Pierce. Many in the middle bracket, likewise, probably were not as fortunate in their upbringing as Elbert H. Gary, whose family is classified there; probably few so classified were as poor in material things as the Harrimans.

TABLE 8

American Business and Political Leaders by Family Status

Status	Business Leaders (Per Cent of)	Political Leaders (Per Cent of)
Upper	50	36
Middle	45	50
Lower	5	14
Total cases (= 100 per cent)	179	180

Poor boys, as Carnegie rightly said, usually go to work early in life. Clearly few of these business and political leaders were poor boys. And, as the following table shows, few of them went to work at an early age.

TABLE 9

American Business and Political Leaders by Age on Going to Work *

Age	Business Leaders (Per Cent of)	Political Leaders (Per Cent of)
15 or under	20	13
16–18	35	10
19 and over	45	77
Total cases (= 100 per cent)	179	182

* This is age on taking first regular business, professional, or other job (except work on father's or other relative's farm) after leaving school or, in a very few instances, after leaving the Union or Confederate armies.

Only one in five of these business leaders had a job before he was 16; slightly more than half of them had jobs before they were 19. Delaying the business debuts of most of the others — their late start, according to the tradition, being itself a handicap — was the pursuit of higher education, an undertaking that should so have altered their characters as to make them even poorer prospects for business success. The educational levels attained by all the leaders studied here are shown in the following table.[41]

TABLE 10

American Business and Political Leaders by Highest Education Level Attained *

Education	Business Leaders (Per Cent of)	Political Leaders (Per Cent of)
Grammar school	22	18
High school	37	27
Some college	12 ⎱ 41	11 ⎱ 55
College graduate	29 ⎰	44 ⎰
Total cases (= 100 per cent)	183	188

* I have reduced the many types of older schools to this modern terminology, including in "grammar school" institutions called by that name, as well as district, public, common and similar schools; in "high school," academies and others of similar rank. Counted among grammar-school boys are those who had little or no formal education as well as graduates; among high-school boys, all those who attended whether gradutaes or not. A few who had private tutors well into their teens but did not attend college are counted with the high-school group.

Of the business leaders who did not go to work until they were 19 or older, 76 per cent had gone to college. Four out of five of these, in turn, were of the upper class. No group, if the traditional account of the origins and ascent pattern of the American business elite truly represented the facts, could have been worse off than this one in the competition for business eminence. Yet about 28 per cent of the business leaders are found in it.[42] These men shared *all* the alleged handicaps: upper-class upbringing, college education, a late business start; yet, if speed of ascent be taken as the measure of the *greatest* attainment, these men were actually the most successful of all. Not only did they spend less time after starting to work in getting to the top,[43] but, as the following table shows, they got there on the whole earlier in life than those allegedly most favored. This table shows the ages at which the two polar groups attained the high positions that made them eligible for this study.

TABLE 11

American Business Leaders by Age on Becoming President or Partner
of Major Company *

Age	Late-Starting, Upper-Class, College Men (Per Cent of)	Early-Starting, Middle- and Lower-Class Noncollege Men (Per Cent of)
Under 45	43 }66	26 }48
45–49	23	22
50 and over	34	52
Total cases (= 100 per cent)	40	53

* Board chairmen are a special case in regard to age on attaining the position and were omitted from this table.

Still, one has to stretch a point to attribute to more than two or three general American historians *any* discussion of the speed of ascent of the business elite. More of them stress this elite's typically lower-class, foreign, or farm *origins* and speculate on the forces that impelled men upward from such insalubrious environs. Yet poor immigrant boys and poor farm boys together actually make up no more than 3 per cent of the business leaders who are the subject of this essay. If men with such backgrounds had been in fact representative of the great entrepreneurs of the later nineteenth century, they must have been supplanted with extraordinary rapidity by the higher status, more highly educated bureaucrats of the following generation. More likely, poor immigrant and poor farm boys who become business leaders have always been more conspicuous in American history books than in American history.

XIII

The Recruitment of the American Business Elite

By William Miller

Almost twenty years ago, Professors F. W. Taussig and C. S. Joslyn published their book, *American Business Leaders: A Study in Social Origins and Social Stratification*.[1] Although its appearance was without doubt a landmark in the study of the subject, it is the opinion of the present writer that it has won its reputation, at least in part, by default: there simply have been no other studies of comparable scope in the social origins of American business leaders. Of the few articles that have appeared, none has been addressed directly to Taussig and Joslyn's problem of determining the relative importance of heredity and environment in business success, and none has undertaken to test their conclusions.[2]

My opinion that this book, while original and still useful, is limited in its achievement is supported by leading, if forgotten, reviews that appeared soon after its publication. That by Professor Morris Ginsberg in the *Economic Journal* speaks for many of the others.[3] Professor Ginsberg said at the close of his review that "a study such as that made in the work before us, compelled as it is to confine itself to gross differences in the environment, and completely ignoring psychological and genetic analysis, cannot, it seems to me, hope to establish any reliable conclusions in a matter so intricate and complex as the share of genetic differences in social stratification."

The present paper, concerned with a generation of business leaders earlier than that studied by Taussig and Joslyn, but in objective rather more modest than their work, is one of a series aimed at extending our knowledge at least of the social characteristics of such men.[4] In the first of these,[5] I took issue with the description of the origins and upbringing of the "typical" American business leaders of the period since the Civil War that appears in those few American history books that have said anything at all about them. That description is virtually always of the "poor immigrant" or "poor farm" boy who, barely entering his teens, first found work in the meanest of jobs and, "fired by a passionate will to succeed," rose from "obscure origins" and "from poverty to riches" mainly "by dint of unflagging industry and resourcefulness."[6] In my analysis of 190 of the topmost American business leaders in the first decade of the twentieth century, however, poor immigrant and poor farm boys together are shown to have made up no more than three per cent of this group. The great majority was recruited from higher status families and among themselves shared still other social characteristics.[7]

In this paper the question to be discussed is: to what extent were these shared social characteristics found in large segments of the general population; to what extent were they found among the common run of people with whom business leaders by their own pronouncements on their origins have so often sought to identify themselves, yet over whom they have come to exercise great power?[8]

II

In all classes of society and in all geographical, national, and religious groups in the United States in 1900 there must have been many adults who had not aspired to business eminence. If these could be separated from the rest of the people — and account be taken of them as a group apart — a population of aspirants would remain. This would be a better group than the whole population to compare with the business elite. For here it would be possible to point to the known failures as well as to the successes, and to identify more confidently and examine more closely than is now practicable the social conditions attending disappointment and achievement.

Needless to say, this division of the population cannot be made. In lieu of it, however, one may point to certain social groups in the population which, whether aspiring to business eminence or not, failed altogether to be represented among the topmost business bureaucrats discussed here.

"It was too bad women didn't count in Guggenheim business affairs," writes Harvey O'Connor, the biographer of the Guggenheim family, "for many said that Gladys was the most capable of [Daniel Guggenheim's] children."[9] Their failure to use female talent, of course, scarcely made the Guggenheims unique. Females made up almost 49 per cent of the total population of the United States in 1900 and 47.5 per cent of those 50 years of age — the average age that year of the 190 business leaders. But these figures only make them one of the largest of the absent groups.

About 12 per cent of the population of the United States in 1900 was non-white — Negro, Indian, Mexican, Oriental; of the 50-year-old males that year, such non-whites were 16.2 per cent. None, however, are found among these elite businessmen. Also unrepresented are southern and eastern Europeans and their descendants, but they were only a relatively small proportion of the whole population. Sizable numbers of men from European countries south and east of Germany had begun to settle in the United States by 1880, but by 1900 they and their adult offspring as yet accounted for only about two per cent of the adult white population.[10] Another small fraction of the population, made up of white immigrants and their descendants, from South America, Asia, Africa, and the islands of the seas, also are missing from the business elite.

These unrepresented national and racial minorities, however small in some instances, are worth mentioning if only for the sake of completeness of presentation. But there is also a better reason. Though their absence from the group studied here may be due simply to the smallness of this group,[11] it may also point up other conditions governing elite recruitment, conditions suggested by the ascent of men from minorities actually represented in the group under view — notably the ascent of Jews.

Although in 1850 Jews accounted for only a small fraction of one per cent of the white population of the United States and although by 1900 their share had not yet risen much above one per cent, six of the business leaders studied here, or about three per cent of those whose religious heritage is known, were of Jewish descent — a better than average showing if it may be supposed that it would remain the same in a much larger sample.[12] None of these six Jews, however, was in a non-Jewish firm. All attained the high positions that make them eligible for this study not only in Jewish enterprises but in those started by their fathers or other relatives.

It is the operation of this factor in particular, this apparent tendency toward religious and national[13] and even family segregation within the business elite[14] — shown as much by the failure of most firms to recruit for their executive hierarchies members of religious or national minorities, as by the practice of men in such minorities, when in power, of favoring their own people — which seems to be indicated most sharply by the history of the absent minorities. Among the latter there appears to have been no one as yet to affirm that their normal lower class goals could be transcended, no one to serve as a model for their sons' or their compatriots' aspirations, and, perhaps most important, no one to serve as the direct instrument of their ascent.

It is worth noting, too, that the envelopment by 1900 of many of the key areas of the economy by the extant business bureaucracies must have made the outlook all the more restricted for those seemingly excluded at once from these bureaucracies and from those key areas in which almost alone great business success could be won.

III

Published census information being what it is for the period of the lives of the men studied here, many distinctions less subtle than that between aspirants and nonaspirants to great business success also are impractical. In only a few categories, for example, can information on the 50-year-old white males in the population, as of 1900, be separated out from that on the population as a whole. In the following pages, where information on this age and sex group is unavailable, less exclusive comparisons are made between the business leaders and the population generally; and where census data are altogether lacking, other sources are used.

The twelfth census, 1900, does report the birthplaces of the population insofar as they may be identified as native or foreign, by sex, color, and age groups. These figures reveal a considerable disproportion between the foreign-born among all 50-year-old white males and the foreign-born in the business elite under view, those in the first group comprising 34.8 per cent, those in the second only 10 per cent.[15] This census also reports on parents' birthplaces and shows that of all 50-year-old white males, 45.6 per cent had at least one foreign-born parent. Those of foreign-born or mixed parentage in the business elite make up only 19 per cent.[16] It appears, therefore, that as many as four out of five among the business bureaucrats studied here, as against only slightly more than half of the 50-year-old white males generally, were native-born of native parents.

Predominantly of old American families,[17] these business bureaucrats naturally were largely of British descent, 79 per cent of them tracing their origins to England, Scotland, the north of Ireland and other places in the British Empire, exclusive of the south of Ireland. Exactly how this proportion compares with that among the 50-year-old white males in 1900, or even with that in the population as a whole, is difficult to determine. Satisfactory estimates of the national origins of the American people are available only for 1790 and 1920.[18] These are presented in Table 1, together with the national origins of the business elite.

The proportion of persons of British (exclusive of south Irish) descent in the United States probably was never higher subsequent to 1790 than it was that year, while the proportions of those of south Irish and of German descent probably were never lower. Thus, the excess of the first group in the business elite in 1900, as compared to the proportion of this group in the population even in 1790, would appear to indicate a sizable over-representation in the elite of persons of British (exclusive of south Irish) ancestry. A comparison, on the other hand, of the estimates of persons of south Irish and of German origin in 1790 and 1920 with the relative size of such groups in the business elite, seems to disclose a marked under-representation in the elite of persons of such ancestry.

TABLE 1

National Origins of the American Population and of the Paternal Lines of the Business Elite

Country [1]	American Population 1790 [2] (Per Cent)	American Population 1920 [3] (Per Cent)	Business Elite Born about 1850 (Per Cent)
England and Wales	60.1 ⎫	⎫	53 ⎫
Scotland	8.1 ⎪	⎪	7 ⎪
North of Ireland	5.9 ⎬ 74.1	41.4 [4] ⎬ 47.2	11 ⎬ 79
Canada	5 ⎪	5.6 ⎪	3 ⎪
British Empire, other or unspecified	5 ⎭	.2 ⎭	5 ⎭
South of Ireland	3.6	11.2	3
Germany	8.6	16.3	12
Other Countries	13.7	25.3	6
Percentage Total	100.0	100.0	100.0
Numerical Total	3,226,944	94,821,000	162

[1] Last country before settlement of paternal family or businessman himself in colonies or the United States.
[2] American Council of Learned Societies, "Report of the Committee on Linguistic and National Stocks in the Population of the United States," in *Annual Report of the American Historical Association, 1931* (3 volumes, Washington, D.C.: Government Printing Office, 1932), I, p. 124.
[3] Thompson and Whelpton, *op. cit.,* p. 91. For explanation of why total cases in this column does not equal total population in 1920, see *ibid.,* p. 84.
[4] This includes England and Wales, Scotland, and north of Ireland.
[5] Numbers too small to count.

This seeming disproportion in the elite in favor of persons descended from the *national* majority appears to be somewhat reversed in the statistics on *religious* heritage. Here again only approximations are available. The twelfth census, 1900, does not report the religious composition of the 50-year-old white male group. The census of 1850, in turn, the one nearest the median year of birth of the business elite, reports only "church accommodations," that is, the seating capacity of the buildings used for worship — probably only a rough index of the actual size of the religious bodies in the United States that year. A comparison of these figures with those on the religious affiliations of the business elite discloses in the latter a somewhat above normal representation of Catholics and Jews (though the numbers involved are small) at the expense of the Protestant majority in general. The greatest differences between the elite and the population, however, as Table 2 shows, appear to be in the under-representation of

William Miller

the largely middle and lower class Protestant denominations, Methodist and Baptist, and the over-representation of Episcopalians and Presbyterians, denominations more often associated with higher status.

TABLE 2

The Religious Heritage of the American Population and the Business Elite

Denomination [1]	American Population, 1850 [2] (Per Cent)	Business Elite [3] (Per Cent)	
Episcopal	4.5 ⎫ 19.1	25 ⎫ 46	30 [4] ⎫ 55
Presbyterian	14.6 ⎭	21 ⎭	25 ⎭
Methodist	30.5 ⎫ 53.2	9 ⎫ 14	11 ⎫ 17
Baptist	22.7 ⎭	5 ⎭	6 ⎭
Unitarian	1.0	6	7
Other Protestant	22.0	8	11
Protestant, Unspecified	00.0	16	—
Total Protestant	95.3	90	90
Roman Catholic	4.6	7	7
Jewish	.1	3	3
Percentage Total	100.0	100	100
Numerical Total	14,270,139	174	174

[1] In almost all instances this is the religion of the businessman himself, though most likely of his father too. In the few instances in which a shift is known to have occurred, the old religion only is counted.
[2] Based on seating capacity of buildings used for worship. Actual total reported is about 61.5 per cent of the entire population, 1850. See J. D. B. DeBow, *Statistical View of the United States* (Washington: A. O. P. Nicholson, 1854), pp. 136-137.
[3] All the businessmen about whom this information is known are included here, native-born as well as foreign-born. The distribution of religions among the latter is not sufficiently different from that for the whole group to affect the figures as shown in any significant way.
[4] This column shows the distribution of the business leaders by religious denomination, on the assumption, safe enough it seems, that the "Protestant unspecified" group was distributed in the same proportions as the known specified Protestants.

IV

The immediate surroundings in which these great business bureaucrats were raised probably were as important in shaping their careers as were their national and religious inheritances in opening such careers to them.

Since these men not only were of old American families, but were businessmen as well, they might be expected to have come not from the farms but largely from the older commercial and industrial sections of the country. And so they did, indeed even in greater proportions than would normally be expected. Sixty-one per cent of the native-born among them originated in New England and the Middle Atlantic states, which area should, statistically speaking, have supplied only about 39 per cent.[19]

These figures and the others for the population generally, in Table 3, are based on reports of births in the seventh census, 1850.

TABLE 3

Native-Born Business Leaders and Native-Born Free Population
by Region of Birthplace

Region [1]	Whites and Free Negroes Born in the United States, 1850 [2] (Per Cent)	Native-born Business Elite (Per Cent)
New England	11 ⎫ 39	20 ⎫ 61
Middle Atlantic	28 ⎭	41 ⎭
East North Central	25	25
South	31	10
West	5	4
Percentage Total	100	100
Numerical Total	548,837	169

[1] These are census regions. Combined in "South" are South Atlantic, East South Central, West South Central; in "West," West North Central, Mountain, and Pacific states and territories.
[2] DeBow, *op. cit.*, p. 111. Though free Negroes are combined with whites in the census tabulation, there were not enough of them, even were their regional distribution much different from that of the whites, to alter materially the distribution as shown.

Even more striking, in comparison to the distribution of the whole population in 1850, is the proportion of the business elite born or raised in the business atmosphere of American cities and larger towns.[20]

Statistics on the occupations of the American population or any large segment of it in the nineteenth century are scanty, and those that are available, especially for the period before 1870, are notoriously unreliable. Still, none of the earlier ones suggest the need for any revision of the impression of an extraordinary concentration in the business elite of men with business family backgrounds, an impression given by the geographical origins of these men as compared with the geographic distribution of the population generally.[21] Occupational statistics for 1870, in turn, are close enough to the period when the men in the business elite were being raised and launched on their business careers to afford relevant comparisons with the occupations of the fathers of these men. And the 1870 occupational data only strengthen the conclusions drawn from those on regional and city-size origins. Two summaries of 1870 occupational statistics are given in Table 5, together with the occupations of the fathers of the business elite. As shown there, well over half of these fathers were businessmen. Business and professional men together make up a remarkable 86 per cent.[22]

These occupational statistics must make it clear that, as compared to the American population generally, few of the business leaders under dis-

TABLE 4

Business Leaders by Size of Birthplace or Place where Raised and the American
Population by Size of Community

Size of Community	American Population, 1850 [1] (Per Cent)		Business Elite [2] (Per Cent)	
City (over 8,000)	12.5	⎱ 16.8	41	⎱ 60
Town (2,500 to 8,000)	4.3	⎰	19	⎰
Rural (under 2,500)	83.2		40	
Percentage Total	100.0		100	
Numerical Total	23,191,876		170	

[1] Thompson and Whelpton, op. cit., p. 20.
[2] The size used here for each man's place of birth or upbringing is its size according to the census nearest the man's year of birth, not the census of 1850. Place of upbringing is used for all men who moved, before the age of seven, to places sufficiently larger or smaller than their birthplaces to alter their classification in the scale used in this table.
    Of the 18 foreign-born business leaders, six who were brought to the United States before the age of seven and raised here are included in this tabulation. Of those excluded, only one was born in a rural place; most of the others were born in great cities.

TABLE 5

Occupations of American Males and the Fathers of the Business Elite

Occupation [1]	American Males, 1870		Fathers of the Business Elite (Per Cent)	
	Taussig and Joslyn [2] (Per Cent)	C. Wright Mills [3] (Per Cent)		
Businessman	6.2	8.1	56	⎱ 86
Professional	2.5	2.3	30 [6]	⎰
Farmer	32.0	28.2 ⎱ 58.7	12	
Rural Worker	⎱ 56.7 [4]	61.4 ⎰ 30.5 ⎰	0	
Urban Worker	⎰	⎰ 30.9	2	
Other	2.6	5	5	
Percentage Totals	100.0	100.0	100	
Numerical Totals	9,420,000	11,007,505	167	

[1] "Professional" includes independent as well as salaried men; most of those among the fathers of the businessmen were lawyers, engineers, or men engaged in politics, even if not always office holders. "Urban worker" includes wage as well as lower salaried occupations, manual as well as clerical and sales jobs.
[2] From F. W. Taussig and C. S. Joslyn, op. cit., p. 273.
[3] This distribution is adapted from White Collar: The American Middle Class (Oxford University Press, 1951) by Professor C. Wright Mills, who was generous enough to permit me to use his occupational data before the book's publication.
[4] Taussig and Joslyn do not distinguish between rural and urban workers.
[5] Only Taussig and Joslyn use this miscellaneous category.
[6] In my earlier paper, where a comparison of the backgrounds of business and political leaders was made, this figure appeared as only 23 per cent, for the 7 per cent of these business leaders whose fathers were public officials were listed separately. Here it seemed sensible to include them with professionals.

cussion were born or raised in lower class families.[23] The fact that, in a period when most American boys went to work very early in life, only 20 per cent of these business leaders had business jobs before they were sixteen, only strengthens this conclusion.[24] It gains more strength still from statistics on education. In an age when the educational level of the American population generally certainly was no higher than elementary school graduate,[25] only 22 per cent of these business leaders had terminated their formal schooling at that point. Thirty-seven per cent could point to a high school education or its equivalent. The remaining 41 per cent had gone to college, approximately three out of four of them graduating. How far this 41 per cent exceeded the proportion of college men in the population generally is indicated by the following statistics. In 1870, the census year nearest that in which most of these college-educated business leaders would have been in attendance, there were in the United States 2,067,144 white males between the ages of 15 and 20. That year there were 67,350 males in the colleges and universities of the country — a scant 3.3 per cent of the white males of college age.[26]

V

If it be true, as leading American businessmen and leading American historians continue to assert, that, so to speak, anyone can become president of large business firms, it appears to be true also that at least in the early twentieth century most of the successful aspirants had certain social characteristics that distinguished them sharply from the common run of Americans of their time. Such distinguishing characteristics may have been less marked among American business leaders in the first half or three-quarters of the nineteenth century, though too little is known about that period to generalize with safety. In the bureaucratic twentieth century, however, many of these characteristics were so prevalent among the business leaders, and so rare among the rest of the population, that the presumption, at least, is strong that they constituted genuine advantages in the competition for business eminence.

I. The Entrepreneur and the Social Order

By John E. Sawyer

1. A phrase from the citation used in awarding degrees to students of the Harvard Graduate School of Business Administration.

2. It is striking to see the extent to which American officials engaged in the European Recovery Program and Point IV programs have come to recognize "operationally" the role of social structure in economic behavior.

3. From Arthur Smithies' probing "Memorial," *American Economic Review*, XL, no. 4 (September 1950), p. 639. That a renewed interest in this whole subject appears to be developing just after Schumpeter's death is an irony which he would have savored.

4. Cf. *The Theory of Economic Development* (Cambridge, Mass., 1934), pp. 20–22, chap. ii, and remarks scattered throughout Schumpeter's writings, including the more qualified statement in *Business Cycles* (2 vols.; New York, 1939), I, 102ff. His recurrent discussions of this theme suggest that projections of power and creation, as well as aristocratic preferences, were involved in his distinction between Economic Superman and the rest of lesser breed. (The "Lords of Creation," as Frederick Lewis Allen has called them, were, after all, lords of a sort, at a time when the species was rapidly becoming extinct.) Here there is no need to enter the battle of definitions. Our interest is in analyzing the behavior of a social group — loosely, those who made business decisions and otherwise performed "entrepreneurial" functions. To draw the line precisely would be difficult, but the marginal member of such a group is sufficiently similar to the central tendency to make it a problem of little importance for our purposes.

5. Some entrepreneurial functions, of course, exist in all actual economies, but how far the *same* set of concepts of this role can be meaningfully extended over time and space is a question requiring careful examination.

6. Cf. *Theory of Economic Development*, pp. 65f.

7. Schumpeter, *Capitalism, Socialism and Democracy* (2nd ed.; New York, 1947), p. 156. Cf. Part II generally.

8. *Theory of Economic Development*, p. 93.

9. The idiosyncratic factor, including the constitutional and psychic composition of each unique individual, is of course important, but is less relevant to understanding different *patterns* of economic behavior — happily, in that it is infinitely less knowable.

10. The word institution is here used comprehensively to embrace patterns of accepted and expected conduct and orientation that are supported by normative sanctions. In any going society these patterns necessarily interlock to a considerable degree. A number of significant papers developing and applying this so-called "functional-structural" approach in contemporary sociology have been collected in:

Talcott Parsons, *Essays in Social Theory, Pure and Applied* (Glencoe, Ill., 1949), and Robert K. Merton, *Social Theory and Social Structure* (Glencoe, Ill., 1949).

11. Cf. concepts developed in Abram Kardiner, *The Individual and His Society* (New York, 1939) and *The Psychological Frontiers of Society* (New York, 1945).

12. I am indebted to a friendly critic, Professor Alexander Gerschenkron, for emphasis on these differential rigidities, and for other perspectives and cautions. May I here also express thanks to Professors Carl Kaysen and James S. Duesenberry for a number of helpful discussions, and to members of the Research Center in Entrepreneurial History for their useful comments.

13. A delightful example of these variations is the sketch of a distinct and important economic elite in France given in Jean Dufourt, *Calixte, ou l'introduction à la vie Lyonnaise* (Paris, 1926).

14. Over the centuries since the fall of Rome, "France perhaps approaches nearer than any other national state to being co-central and co-extensive with the whole of our Western Society." (Arnold J. Toynbee, *A Study of History* (London, 1935), I, 12.) This seems to be one of the few points on which Frenchmen agree and a point on which a wide range of "good Europeans" would assent, taking the whole span of time from the Völkerwanderungen to the twentieth century. This choice of the French example also reflects my good fortune in having had a certain amount of official and unofficial residence and travel in France and North Africa, before, during, and after World War II.

15. The direct importance of these responses to French output and productivity has increasingly impressed itself on those most directly concerned with reactivating the French economy; by 1950 the problem had become something of an official preoccupation.

16. Our concern here is with those characteristics most relevant to later entrepreneurial behavior. A concurrent paper briefly discusses some of the effects of this medieval heritage on the whole range of economic actors; cf. Part IV, John E. Sawyer, "Social Structure and Economic Progress: The European Inheritance," *American Economic Review, Papers and Proceedings*, XLI, No. 2 (May 1951). Both papers owe a large debt to the economic sociology of Max Weber. I have attempted to analyze related problems somewhat more elaborately in "Strains in the Social Structure of Modern France," Edward Meade Earle, ed., *Modern France: Problems of the Third and Fourth Republics* (Princeton, 1951). This volume includes several interesting and relevant papers.

17. This antipathy to trade, typical of societies based on land, was conspicuous in the Western tradition as received by the Middle Ages. It had been sharply formulated in the writings of Plato and of "The Philosopher," as Aristotle was known to Medieval Europe, and can be traced through Christian and Roman as well as feudal value systems. Cf. Charles A. Foster, "Honoring Commerce and Industry in Eighteenth Century France," Ph.D. thesis, Harvard University, 1950.

18. R. H. Tawney, *Religion and the Rise of Capitalism* (London, 1926), p. 23. That the Church was itself extensively involved in financial affairs does not alter the impress of its teachings.

19. For a most subtle and penetrating analysis of this difference, and of the evolutions in Catholic thought see B. Groethuysen, *Origines de l'esprit bourgeois en France: I — L'Église et la Bourgeoisie* (Paris, 1927). Cf. also the massive work of Ernst Troeltsch, *The Social Teachings of the Christian Churches* (2 vols.; London, 1931), I, chap. ii, esp. sec. 8. The classic statement of the Puritan thesis is, of course, Max Weber's, *The Protestant Ethic and the Spirit of Capitalism* (London, 1930).

20. The comparative experience derived from working with the European (and other) economies since World War II has greatly fortified a familiar insight.

21. Perhaps "permanently" so, in the sense of "social" time, to use for a moment the intermediate of the three kinds of time — geographical, social, and individual — into which Fernand Braudel has recently tried to analyze the historical process: *La Méditerranée et le monde méditerranéen a l'époque de Philippe II* (Paris, 1949), a book now stirring up the waters of contemporary historiography.

22. A nobility that was beginning to engage in economic activity in the era of the "bourgeois king," Louis XI (1461–1483), in later centuries developed a doctrine of *dérogeance* that was sufficiently powerful to frustrate the subsequent efforts of even a Colbert to elevate the prestige of trade. Cf. Foster, "Honoring Commerce and Industry in Eighteenth Century France."

23. Cf. Georges Lefebvre, *The Coming of the French Revolution*, trans. by R. R. Palmer (Princeton, 1947), chap. ii.

24. Entering in relatively large numbers through the *noblesse de robe*, as well as some assimilation through marriage, though rarely breaking into the highest ranks of the *noblesse d'epée*. The polite literature of the period also undoubtedly exercised an influence in the process.

25. It is unquestionably significant that well before the end of the Middle Ages the English merchants had come to constitute a social class identified with the wealth and prestige of the national capital, in which their institutions and values reigned supreme. Cf. Sylvia Thrupp, *The Merchant Class of Medieval London, 1300–1500* (Chicago, 1948).

26. That these policies and characteristics of the Monarchy did not cease with the Revolution can be seen in Shepard B. Clough, *France: A History of National Economics, 1789–1939* (New York, 1939).

27. This set of institutions is examined at some length in Part IV of my earlier paper, "Strains in the Social Structure of Modern France," *Modern France: Problems of the Third and Fourth Republics.*

28. This discussion will have to be kept at a very general level. It would require considerable space to present the evidence that is available, and much more needs to be done. A great deal that is familiar has not had the kind of systematic analysis or quantification needed for clarifying the questions involved.

29. Into very recent times the higher levels of French education have reflected and reinforced the European status system in their selection and training. The diversion of an elite need not of itself create a shortage of entrepreneurial talent; more significant, probably, has been the effect of this example at the top on the behavior of those below.

30. The quoted phrases are from Schumpeter's discussion of the peculiar relevance of these motivations to entrepreneurial action, *Theory of Economic Development*, pp. 93–94.

31. This whole question of withdrawal needs to be studied much more systematically than it ever has been, preferably on a comparative basis. Among the conspicuous exceptions would be the dynastic business families discussed below, an aspect of things that David S. Landes has developed in his two excellent papers, "French Entrepreneurship and Industrial Growth in the Nineteenth Century," *Journal of Economic History*, IX (1949), 45–61, and "Business and the Businessman in France," in Earle, ed., *Modern France.*

32. Quoted in André Maurois, *Edouard VII et son temps* (Paris, 1933), p. 72.

33. Cf. Lefebvre, *The Coming of the French Revolution*, pp. 42–43. Historical

accidents, such as the participation of the nobility in certain fields, have entered into this social ranking.

34. Although again statistical data is lacking, it is probably a safe judgment to say that relatively few enjoying the better educational, social, and economic opportunities have chosen this field. Both the casual visitor to France and the economic statistician find some of the most striking contrasts in the "tertiary" field. Cf., for example, Colin Clark, *The Conditions of Economic Progress* (London, 1940), pp. 318ff, with appropriate cautions as to the problems of comparative measurement.

35. Georges Boris, "Reforming the Bank of France," *Foreign Affairs*, XV, 156–157. Cf. Pierre Frédérix, *Etat des Forces en France* (Paris, 1935), pp. 111ff. Again we need more systematic study of these patterns in large- and small-scale firms, with less focus on a plot theory and more basic data than the writers of the Third Republic provided.

36. The extreme stability and centrality of family patterns in French society is strikingly evident in the *Code Civil*. For a century and a half of shifting political regimes and changing economic foundations the spirit and to a remarkable degree the letter of family and property law has resisted all change; and in their day the framers of the *Code* under Napoleon were themselves concerned only with preserving traditional patterns. Cf. L. C. Jouanneau, ed., *Discussions du Code Civil dans le Conseil d'Etat* (2 vols.; Paris, 1805).

37. There is an old joke in France that if a Frenchman agrees to expand his plant in order to handle a larger order, he must be either a Jew or an Alsatian.

38. The American visitor to France readily sees by example what ECA reports establish statistically. Figures quoted by Bettelheim indicate that in 1928 the value of French machinery per head was less than half of the average for Europe's industrialized countries: Charles Bettelheim, *Bilan de l'economie francaise 1919–1946* (Paris, 1947), p. 46; cf. also Part II. And incomplete surveys indicate great inefficiencies in the use of such equipment.

39. For a particularly violent protest against American practices, cf. Georges Duhamel, *Scènes de la vie future* (Paris, 1930).

40. On the latter cf. Malcolm MacLaren, *The Rise of the Electrical Industry during the Nineteenth Century* (Princeton, 1943), pp. 68–69, 91–92, 114–119.

41. We are here again isolating the factor of social structure, neglecting the basic differences, physical and economic, that have combined to make American economic development unique. Our focus is on the dominant patterns of the nineteenth and early twentieth centuries, and inevitably involves sliding over great diversities in time and region.

42. Cf. for example the recurrence of these themes in the National Association of Manufacturers' full length statement, *The American Individual Enterprise System* (2 vols.; New York, 1946), p. 271 and *passim*.

43. While these institutionalized goals and ways of behaving have probably always operated most directly on middle class groups, in the classic period they appear to have been very broadly diffused.

44. Cf. Chester I. Barnard's remarks on the problem of maintaining morale and effort in an American business that is not felt to be the innovator, the pusher in its field — briefly summarized in the Research Center for Entrepreneurial History's *Change and the Entrepreneur* (Cambridge, 1949), pp. 7–10. This institutionized emphasis on seeking the new, on finding *new* ways and combinations and products, is particularly significant. The competitive struggle for success within highly bureaucratic patterns need not by itself have had any such effect on economic development

as the example in John P. Marquand's novel, *Point of No Return*, so tellingly shows. For a discussion of related points, see the papers by Alfred D. Chandler, Jr. and by William Miller, in the present book.

45. George Bernard Shaw hit out at this wider sense of mission, this talk of "service," in his celebrated comment on a movie negotiation with Samuel Goldwyn: "But there was really never a chance of agreement. While I was solely interested in money, Mr. Goldwyn kept talking of art." Quoted by William S. Schlamn, "European Business is Different," *Fortune*, February 1950, p. 97.

II. Bankers and Pashas

By David S. Landes

1. The best single work on the cotton famine is W. O. Henderson, *The Lancashire Cotton Famine, 1861–1865* (Manchester, 1934). For the effect of the shortage on continental industry, see Henderson, "The Cotton Famine on the Continent, 1861–1865," *Economic History Review*, 4: 195–207 (1933). Still useful are R. Arnold, *History of the Cotton Famine* (London, 1864–65); J. Watts, *Facts of the Cotton Famine* (London, 1866); and E. Reclus, "Le coton et la crise américaine," *Revue des Deux-Mondes*, 2d series, 37: 176–208 (1862).

2. On the last point, see K. Marx, *Capital* (3 vols.; Chicago: Chas. Kerr, 1909), I [Modern Library ed.]: 500–501; 3: 153f.

3. The most convenient source for Egyptian cotton production and the famine is E. M. Earle, "Egyptian Cotton and the American Civil War," *Political Science Quarterly*, 41: 520–545 (1926). There is an excellent general history of Egyptian cotton cultivation, which gives considerable attention to wider economic and political considerations: F. Charles-Roux, *La production du coton en Egypte* (Paris: A. Colin, 1908).

4. Free traffic in grain and other commodities, both imported and domestic, was permitted in Egypt in principle as far back as 1838, under the terms of the treaty of that year between the European powers and the Ottoman Empire. But this commerce, which was conducted mainly by itinerant Greek and Levantine peddlers, was quite limited under Mohammed Ali and Abbas, neither of whom was ready to abandon the system of monopolies. Even where the pressure of foreign governments made overt suppression difficult, indirect techniques of curtailment proved almost as effective. P. Merruau, "L'Egypte sous le gouvernement de Saïd Pacha," *Revue des Deux-Mondes*, 2d period, 11: 347 (1857).

5. A. E. Crouchley, *The Economic Development of Modern Egypt* (London, 1938), p. 77. This is the only convenient general treatment of Egyptian economic history. Though somewhat laconic, the book covers the ground and features some excellent statistical appendices. For those interested in detailed research, there is a superb *Bibliographie économique, juridique, et sociale de l'Egypte moderne, 1798–1916*, by R. Maunier (Paris, 1916).

6. L. Bréhier, *L'Egypte de 1798 à 1900* (Paris, 1901), Ch. i. Other general treatments of the renaissance and rise of modern Egypt are A. Hasenclever, *Geschichte Aegyptens im 19. Jahrhundert* (Halle, 1917), and J. C. McCoan, *Egypt as It Is* (London, 1877). M. Rifaat, *The Awakening of Modern Egypt* (London, 1947), is not always accurate and is marred by chauvinism.

7. Egyptian population statistics for the nineteenth century are at best approximate. Thus the *Essai de statistique générale de l'Egypte* of the Bureau de la statistique of the Egyptian Ministère de l'Intérieur (Cairo, 1879) gives the population of Alexandria in 1846 as 164,000. Crouchley, *Economic Development*, p. 52, gives the figure as 143,000 in 1848. And H. Thuile, *Commentaires sur l'Atlas historique d'Alexandrie* (Cairo, 1922), pp. 47 and 51, gives the number as 100,000 in 1848, 100,000 in 1854, and 250,000 in 1866.

8. Today, Mohammed Ali Square.

9. Theoretically, as a part of the Turkish Empire, Egypt had always been governed by the various Ottoman capitulations of the fifteenth century on. In reality, she had been wholly independent of these agreements until 1841, when the applicability of Turkish law to Egypt was made a condition of hereditary rule. The best legal treatment of the capitulations and the legal status of foreigners is to be found in J. H. Scott, *The Law Affecting Foreigners in Egypt* (Edinburgh, 1907). For the abuses of consular privileges, see M. Sabry, *L'Empire égyptien sous Ismaïl et l'ingérence anglo-française, 1863–1879* (Paris, 1933), which is based in large part on the archives of the French and British foreign offices.

10. This apocryphal adventure has been variously attributed to both Saïd and his successor, Ismaïl. Cf. Sabry, *L'Empire égyptien*, p. 43, and Viscount Milner, *England in Egypt* (London, 1904), p. 44.

11. Most of the above is derived from Commandant Dervieu, *Monographie d'une famille lyonaisse; la famille Dervieu* (Mâcon, 1908).

12. International trade was feeling the after-effects of the sharp commercial crisis of late 1857. Crouchley's figures on Egyptian foreign trade for 1856–1858 are as follows (in thousands of pounds Egyptian, equals approximately £1 0s. 6d. sterling):

	Imports	Exports	Total Commerce
1856	2,569	4,030	6,599
1857	3,149	3,105	6,254
1858	2,715	2,534	5,249

Economic Development, p. 266.

13. This was the first Egyptian state loan to be offered to the European public. The standard history of the Egyptian public debt is A. M. Hamza, *The Public Debt of Egypt, 1854–76* (Cairo, 1944). Still invaluable is J. C. [Jean Claudy], *Histoire financière de l'Egypte depuis Saïd Pacha, 1854–1876* (Paris, 1878), an intimate, impressionistic work which, for lack of documentation, has been accepted, and justly, by later writers as a sort of original source. See also Sidi Lokman El-Hakim [John Ninet], *Les mille pertuis des finances du Khédive* (Vienna, 1873), and L. H. Jenks, *The Migration of British Capital to 1875* (New York, 1927), chs. ix and x.

14. Nephew of Saïd and younger brother of the heir presumptive, Ismaïl.

15. The talent of the family was not limited to banking. For American and British readers, the best-known representative of the line will be the gifted but unfortunate Major John André of the Royal Army, who was captured by the American forces in 1780 while negotiating the betrayal of West Point with Benedict Arnold and convicted and executed as a spy. Major André was the second cousin, twice removed, of Alfred.

16. This brief summary of the history of the André family and the career of Alfred André is derived in large part from the archives of the bank itself, which contain some of Alfred André's personal correspondence. Printed materials include

an excellent piece in the *Dictionnaire de biographie française*, 2: 898–99, concerned mainly with André's political career, and an anniversary history of the firm, *De Neuflize et Cie. Notice historique publiée à l'occasion du cent vingt-cinquième anniversaire de l'établissment à Paris de leur maison de banque* (Paris: privately printed, 1926).

17. This was the balance of a loan of 28 million francs in 1860 from the private bank of Charles Laffitte et Cie and the Comptoir d'Escompte in Paris. The loan, which was made with the blessing and guarantee of the French government, was represented by Egyptian treasury bonds, secured in turn by the revenues of the Alexandria customs. Sabry, *L'Empire égyptien*, p. 90.

18. Possibly the old merchant banking house of that name in Le Havre, the center of the French cotton trade.

19. The best history, though somewhat colorless, of Ismaïl's reign is G. Douin, *Histoire du règne du Khédive Ismaïl* (2 vols.; Rome, 1933). Unfortunately, Douin's work is exasperatingly lacking in footnote references, even when citations are involved. Less detailed, though much stronger on the less savory aspects of the period, is Sabry's *Empire égyptien*. On Ismaïl himself and his responsibility for the bankruptcy of 1876, there is a whole literature pro and con. Following the spectrum from most favorable to most censorious, some of the more important works are P. Crabitès, *Ismaïl, the Maligned Khedive* (London, 1933); G. Zananiri, *Le Khédive Ismaïl et l'Egypte, 1830–1894* (Alexandria, 1923); S. Keay, *Spoiling the Egyptians; a Tale of Shame* (London, 1882); E. Farman, *Egypt and Its Betrayal* (New York, 1908); E. de Leon, *The Khedive's Egypt* (New York, 1878); [M. Bell], *Khedives and Pashas* (London, 1884); E. Dicey, *The Story of the Khedivate* (London, 1902); *idem, England and Egypt* (London, 1881); Lord Cromer [Evelyn Baring], *Modern Egypt* (New York, 1908), vol. III; Milner, *England in Egypt*; Anon., *Egypt for the Egyptians* (London, 1880); W. B. Jerrold, *Egypt under Ismaïl Pacha* (London, 1879).

20. Several writers assert that Ismaïl was on poor terms with Saïd, spending his uncle's reign in prudent seclusion on his estates, far from the intrigues of court. Cf. De Leon, *The Khedive's Egypt*, pp. 157–158, and Dicey, *The Story of the Khedivate*, p. 56. This would seem hard to reconcile with the facts of his regency and his military command.

21. Among others, Douin, *Histoire*, I, pp. 1f.

22. [Bell], *Khedives and Pashas*, pp. 9f.

23. The visit of Prince Napoleon, accompanied by the Princess Clotilde, in May 1863 combined education and diplomatic fence-building. The tourists inspected the Suez Canal project and the usual monuments, and conferred on Ismaïl the grand cordon of the Legion of Honor. The other visit alluded to was that of the Sultan, Abd El-Aziz, who had been received with prodigious pomp and circumstance only a week before, the first Turkish ruler to see Egypt since Selim I had conquered it in 1517.

24. London *Times*, April 3, 1863, p. 5.

25. The best source for the formation and early years of the new Ottoman Bank is G. Young, ed., *Corps de droit ottoman* (Oxford, 1906), V, ch. lxxxiii, which gives the statutes, including the names of the promoters, *in extenso*. On the story of European financial activity in Turkey, which offers some fascinating comparisons with developments in Egypt, see A. du Velay, *Essai sur l'histoire financière de la Turquie* (Paris, 1903), and D. Blaisdell, *European Financial Control in the Ottoman Empire* (New York, 1929).

346 David S. Landes

26. This firm, organized by a Greek merchant with powerful friends in the English financial world, was the first British joint-stock bank to do business in a foreign country. Among its founders were directors of the East India Company, the London and Westminster Bank, and the Oriental Banking Company. A. Baster, "The Origins of British Banking Expansion in the Near East," *Economic History Review*, 5: 78 (1934).

27. A French firm capitalized at 30 million francs. On January 19, 1863, the London *Times*, p. 12, had reported: "Solicitations have been made by the promoters of the Société financière d'Egypte for Government support, but the Viceroy has steadily refused to depart from the declaration he made when it was first attempted to start the undertaking at Paris last year, or to grant even such nominal privileges as might be construed into Government patronage. The Société financière, it is replied, has the same authorization to enter into commercial operations in Egypt as is open to any other establishment whatsoever. The company is under French jurisdiction; but the French consul has declined giving either his official or personal support to its demands." Ismaïl was not long in abandoning this position of unprofitable, if noble, impartiality.

28. The oldest British merchant house in Egypt.

29. Ruyssenaers was the Consul-General of the Netherlands as well as a leading merchant.

30. A large French deposit and investment bank.

31. One of France's most important shipping firms, the creation of a syndicate of stagecoach companies which had seen the handwriting on the wall in a new age of railways.

32. A shipbuilding corporation closely bound by interest and leadership to the Messageries maritimes.

33. Ismaïl had apparently increased his share by 500,000 francs.

34. The epidemic struck the delta in the summer of 1863 and destroyed almost every bovine in the region. The disease spread up the Nile in the fall and was halted only by an exceptionally cold winter. Estimates of the losses range from 250,000 to 700,000 head, depending on the total number of cattle assigned to Egypt at the time. Douin, *Histoire*, I, 233f.

35. Nubar Pasha, an Armenian of Christian faith, had come to Egypt in 1848 in the entourage of Ibrahim, the son of Mohammed Ali, and had risen under Ismaïl to a position of power second only to that of the Viceroy himself. In October 1863, he was in Paris negotiating for a revision of the terms of construction of the Suez Canal. There is a brief, superficial biography by A. Holynski, *Nubar-Pacha devant l'histoire* (Paris, 1886).

36. The Société agricole et industrielle de l'Egypte was formed in 1864 by a syndicate of businessmen of London, Paris, and Alexandria to introduce farm and irrigation machinery into Egyptian agriculture. Frühling and Goschen were the company's agents for Europe. *Economist* (July 9, 1864), p. 887.

37. Partner with Hermann Oppenheim in Oppenheim, Alberti & Co. of Constantinople.

38. That is, the bonus to be given Dervieu amounted to £200,000, or five million francs at twenty-five francs to the pound sterling.

III. A New Way to Pay Old Debts

By Hugh G. J. Aitken

1. "Memoirs of Thomas Merritt, Esq." in J. J. Talman (ed.), *Loyalist Narratives from Upper Canada* (Toronto, The Champlain Society, 1946).

2. Lorenzo Sabine, *Biographical Sketches of Loyalists of the American Revolution* (2 vols.; Boston, 1864), II, 79.

3. Thomas Merritt to Thomas Merritt, Sr., April 1804, in Talman, *Loyalist Narratives from Upper Canada*.

4. J. P. Merritt, *Biography of the Hon. W. H. Merritt, M.P.* (St. Catharines, Ont., 1875), pp. 9–14.

5. W. H. Merritt, *Journal* (1823), Public Archives of Canada, Merritt Papers, vol. 17.

6. Catharine Rodman, daughter of Dr. Jedediah Prendergast of Mayville, N. Y., whom he married on March 13, 1815.

7. *Journal* (1823).

8. W. H. Merritt to Catharine Merritt, St. Catharines, June 3, 1817, Public Archives of Canada, Merritt Papers, vol. I; W. H. Merritt to Mary Hamilton Merritt, St. Catharines, Sept. 18, 1817, *ibid*.

9. *Journal* (1823).

10. *Journal*; Thomas Adams to W. H. Merritt, Bond, March 27, 1816.

11. *Abstract of Invoices of Merchandize (1815)*, Public Archives of Canada, Merritt Papers, vol. 17.

12. J. P. Merritt, *Biography*, pp. 38–40.

13. Cf. F. M. Jones, *Middlemen in the Domestic Trade of the United States, 1800–1860* (Urbana, Illinois, 1937); N. S. Buck, *The Development of the Organisation of Anglo-American Trade, 1800–1850* (New Haven, 1925); Lewis E. Atherton, *The Pioneer Merchant in Mid-America* (Columbia, Miss., 1939); E. A. Cruikshank, "A Country Merchant in Upper Canada," Ontario Historical Society, *Papers and Records*, XXV (1929), 145–190.

14. Cartwright to Davison & Co., Kingston, Nov. 4, 1797, in C. E. Cartwright (ed.), *Life and Letters of the late Hon. Richard Cartwright* (Toronto, 1876), p. 76.

15. W. A. Langton (ed.), *Early Days in Upper Canada: Letters of John Langton* (Toronto, 1926), p. 201.

16. John Howison, *Sketches of Upper Canada* (Edinburgh, 1821), p. 81.

17. *Memorandum Book* (1816), Public Archives of Canada, Merritt Papers, vol. 31.

18. *Merritt & Ingersoll, account current with estate of R. Armour & Davies on Judgement Bond granted by them (1820)*, Public Archives of Canada, Merritt Papers, vol. 2.

19. Niagara *Gleaner*, Jan. 1, 1818.

20. References to Davies' letters to Merritt are from vol. 2 of the Merritt Papers in the Public Archives of Canada. Since this collection has not been indexed, no further references will be given in the following pages.

21. *Report of Select Committee on the Civil Government of Canada* (Great Britain, House of Commons, July 22, 1827), Evidence of Simon McGillivray, p. 99.

22. J. P. Merritt, *Biography*, pp. 44–45.

23. Adam Shortt, "Economic Effect of the War of 1812 on Upper Canada," Ontario Historical Society, *Papers and Records*, vol. X (1913).

24. James Stevenson, *The War of 1812 in Connection with the Army Bill Act* (Montreal, 1892), p. 56.

25. Army Bills in circulation declined from £1,300,000 to £396,778 between February 19 and December 4, 1815. (Stevenson, *The War of 1812 in Connection with the Army Bill Act*, pp. 58–63.)

26. D. G. Barnes, *A History of the English Corn Laws from 1660–1846* (London, 1930), chs. vii and viii.

27. R. L. Jones, *History of Agriculture in Ontario, 1613–1880*, University of Toronto Studies, History and Economics Series, XI (Toronto, 1946), 39–40.

28. The famous English Corn Law of 1815 gave a nominal preference to the British North American colonies, for their wheat and flour was admitted when the English price reached 67*s.* a quarter, while foreign produce was excluded till it reached 80*s.* But this preference was of little use to the Canadian farmer when a good British harvest brought the price below 67*s.*, thus closing the ports to all imported breadstuffs, whether colonial or foreign. The trouble with the British market in this period was its unpredictability, not the size of the preference. See Jones, *History of Agriculture in Ontario*, p. 38.

29. T. C. Keefer, *The Canals of Canada* (Montreal, 1894), pp. 1–6.

30. A *minot* was a French measure, containing 39 liters; a *tierce* (*v.i.*) was originally a liquid measure containing 42 wine gallons, and hence a cask holding that amount, larger than a barrel, but smaller than a hogshead.

IV. The Entrepreneur and the Community

By Robert K. Lamb

By permission of its editors, I have used here in considerably altered form certain material published under the title "Entrepreneurship in the Community," appearing in *Explorations in Entrepreneurial History*, vol. II, No. 3, pp. 114–127, a publication of the Research Center in Entrepreneurial History, Harvard University, Cambridge, Massachusetts. See also my essay on "Entrepreneurship and Community Development," in *Explorations in Economics* (Notes and Essays Contributed in Honor of F. W. Taussig, New York: McGraw-Hill, 1936); and my unpublished doctoral dissertation at Harvard's Widener Library on "The Development of Entrepreneurship in Fall River, Massachusetts: 1813–1859," submitted to Harvard University in 1935.

1. The reader will find in the following biological analogies a first approximation of what I mean by social structure, function, and change:

Structure: those social institutions whose operations at a moment of time may be compared with the skeleton, the nerves, and the tissues of the human body: for example, the family as an economic group, the corporate organization of economic life (or its individual enterprises, including the firm, the association, etc.); the banking system; the public agencies of the national economy, including the Treasury, the First and Second Banks of the United States, etc.

Function: something analogous to the circulation of the blood in the human body, as described by Harvey and his successors, or the operation of the nervous system, as described by Rosenbluth and others (out of which cybernetics has developed). The social analogies include: in a primitive economy, the use of barter; in advanced societies, the circulation of money, the day-to-day operations of markets, the transfer of paper claims, the flow of goods through the factory system and the sale of its products, or indeed the whole system of economic circulation and intercommunication.

Change: both quantitative and qualitative change over time. To indicate the characteristics of qualitative changes consider the biological analogy of the hormones or endocrine glands; they are strategically located in the body so as to stimulate it at periods of transition from infancy to childhood, to adolescence, to maturity, to senescence. The bodily changes they helped to regulate are analogous to the changes from a society rooted in the soil (organizing its economic, social, and political life around the family as its principal social institution, its basic building block) into a city-state community; and the federation of a number of city-states into a nation. When a major economic and political decision-maker appears at a strategic point in the history of a community, his decisions change its structure and function fundamentally: Alexander Hamilton enabled Philadelphia — and later New York — to unify the city and state economies of our original colonies into a national economy. The process of change is most readily observed as it unfolds within a community; for example, from city-state to nation-state to world-metropolitan economy.

2. On the Browns of Providence, I am indebted to the work of Professor James B. Hedges of Brown University; and on the relations of Moses Brown and Samuel Slater, I have referred to G. S. White, *Memoir of Samuel Slater* (Philadelphia, 1836).

3. On the Lowells of Boston, I rely especially on Ferris Greenslet, *The Lowells and their Seven Worlds* (Boston: Houghton, Mifflin, 1946).

4. As a boy Francis Cabot Lowell visited his uncle George Cabot's horse-driven cotton factory at Beverly, and may have gained there his continuing interest in the possibilities of American manufacture of cotton textiles. That Beverly mill was in operation a year before Moses Brown hired Samuel Slater to work with Ozias Wilkinson at Pawtucket, and Brown knew about the Beverly experiment. George Cabot was one of the three appraisers of John Lowell's estate (the old Judge, drawer of wills, died intestate).

5. On the career of Patrick Tracy Jackson, cf. K. W. Porter, *The Jacksons and the Lees*, vols. I and II (Cambridge: Harvard University Press, 1937), *passim*.

6. Of the stock of the new Merrimack Company, 25 per cent was subscribed by the Boston Manufacturing Company, and in later years Francis' nephew John Amory Lowell and Francis' sons John, "Junior" and Francis, Jr. were to become large stockholders; John Amory Lowell served from 1827 to 1844 as its Treasurer and thereafter until 1877 as its President. Patrick Tracy Jackson felt he could not leave the Waltham mill, and recommended instead Kirk Boott, who was made treasurer and clerk, and engaged to lay out the new manufacturing community. The Boott family, English merchants in Boston, had given John Amory Lowell his first job.

7. Appleton had been chiefly responsible in 1808 for bringing down the financial house-of-cards created by Andrew Dexter among country banks through the Boston Exchange Office, which manipulated their notes circulating in Boston. During similar crises in 1814 and 1819 Appleton, as a director of the Boston Bank, held his fellow bankers to the payment of specie, and in 1819 when suspension was general he wrote a number of newspaper articles, contrasting the sound banks of Boston with the unreliable banks farther south.

8. When Appleton's daughter married Professor Henry Wadsworth Longfellow of Harvard, her fortune assisted him in buying Craigie House, where he settled

down to the writing of poetry; Lawrence's daughter Katherine married Augustus Lowell, promising son of John Amory Lowell, who fulfilled his promise during the panic of '57 and succeeded his father in his many directorships and trusteeships after the panic of '73. The greatest contributions of Augustus and Katherine Lawrence Lowell to the Lowell family were their famous children: Percival, the astronomer; Amy, the poet; and Abbott Lawrence Lowell, President of Harvard.

9. Nathan and Abbott each attended the private academy in his town, each missed out on more advanced education; both were to become benefactors of Harvard; their monuments were Appleton Chapel and the Lawrence Scientific School. The first Appleton and the first Lawrence, both Puritans, came from the county of Suffolk, England in 1635. Deacon Appleton had twelve children who grew up in New Ipswich, New Hampshire; Deacon Lawrence had nine who farmed his acres in Groton, Massachusetts. The families of the Appletons and Lawrences were joined on March 31, 1842, by the marriage of Abbott's nephew, Amos Adams Lawrence, son of his brother Amos, to Nathan's niece, Sarah Elizabeth, daughter of William Appleton.

10. In the party of fourteen there were, besides Jackson and Appleton, three Lawrences — Abbott, William, and Samuel — two Lowells — John Amory and his cousin Francis Cabot Lowell, Jr. — and Charles Storer Storrow, a civil engineer trained at the Ecole des Ponts et Chaussees in Paris, who was to build their new industrial city. Storrow's qualifications as an engineer entitled him to an appointment as builder of Lawrence, but his wife was Lydia Cabot Jackson, granddaughter of Jonathan Jackson, and daughter of Dr. James Jackson and Elizabeth Cabot; hence she was the niece of Patrick Tracy Jackson.

11. K. W. Porter, *The Jacksons and the Lees*, I, 125.

12. The year 1835 saw the formal celebration of the completion of three railroads, the Boston & Providence on June 11, the Boston & Lowell on June 27, and the Boston & Worcester on July 4. It also marked the opening of a drive to connect Boston, through Worcester, with Albany and the Hudson River over a line to be called the Western Railroad. At a mass meeting held in Faneuil Hall on October 7, 1835, Abbott Lawrence presided, and Nathan Appleton offered a report and resolutions, starting the new campaign for subscriptions. The road was completed in 1841.

13. Perkins was first interested in a railway to the Hudson in 1825, during the effort to complete the Bunker Hill Monument, when he helped underwrite the tramway for hauling granite from Quincy, and became convinced that a railway would be more feasible than the canal then being projected to join Boston and Albany. In 1826 he petitioned the Legislature to make a survey for what later became the Western Railroad; he succeeded during the next few years in blocking a parallel movement for a canal — the fever of the Erie Canal was in Boston's blood.

14. The late seventies saw recovery and new expansion in the multifarious enterprises and social and charitable institutions over which John Amory Lowell had so long presided, including Harvard College, then headed by Charles William Eliot. By 1877 Lowell had served on the Harvard Corporation for 40 years, with six different Presidents of the College; the year of his retirement from the Harvard Corporation he saw his grandson, Abbott Lawrence Lowell, graduate 32 years before that grandson succeeded Eliot as President of the University.

15. This phrase, "the Boston associates," is used on p. 54 and thereafter in Vera Shlakman, *Economic History of a Factory Town: A Study of Chicopee, Massachusetts*, Smith College Studies in History (Northampton, Mass., 1936). This excellent study goes far beyond the story of Chicopee in its description of the pre-Civil War

generation of Bostonians who founded its regional textile industry. Our essay cannot hope to describe the leaders of the post-Civil War generations in Boston. We can note only that many of the most important of their members were drawn from the families with whom John Lowell formed his connections by marriage in the years before and during the Revolution.

16. Throughout this discussion of entrepreneurship I have neglected the problems inherent in the bureaucratic operations within the institutions over which entrepreneurs preside, or from which they depart when their jobs are done. We need parallel studies of entrepreneurship and of bureaucracy, of routine decision-makers within private and public social institutions. One of the problems of entrepreneurs is to create bureaucracies, to deal with them, and where necessary to by-pass them.

V. John Stevens

By Dorothy Gregg

Most of the original data for the present article were collected from the Stevens Collection Manuscripts housed in the Stevens Institute of Technology, Hoboken, New Jersey, and parts of the Fulton and Livingston manuscript papers. The writer is particularly grateful to Professors Carter Goodrich and Joseph Dorfman of Columbia University for their help and encouragement, although neither is responsible for the contents of this article.

1. Letter from James Chestnut to Stevens, May 10, 1812, Stevens Collection MSS, S810.

2. See the earliest correspondence in the Stevens Collection.

3. Letter from Lord Stirling, August 2, 1778, to John Stevens, Sr., Stevens Collection MSS, S510f.

4. For John Stevens, Sr.'s views about the Revolution and the Constitution, see the early correspondence in the Stevens Collection, particularly the correspondence between Stevens and his son and Stevens and Robert R. Livingston.

5. See the early deeds and mortgages in the Stevens Collection.

6. In 1824 the Pennsylvania Society for Internal Improvements sent William Strickland to England to secure all available information about railroads. After his return, Strickland published a pamphlet entitled *Reports on Canals, Railways and Other Subjects* (Philadelphia, 1826), which lauded the superiority of railroads over canals. This pamphlet was distributed by the Society as propaganda for the railroad.

7. Taken from a pamphlet which Stevens wrote under the pseudonym of "A Farmer of New Jersey," entitled *Observations on Government, including some Animadversions on Mr. Adams' Defense of the Constitution of Government of the United States, and Mr. De Lolme's Constitution of England*, Stevens Collection MSS, n.d.

8. Letter by Stevens, November 25, 1788, to unknown person, Stevens Collection MSS, S4165f.

9. Stevens, *Observations on Government* . . .

10. Letter from Colonel Stevens, December 4, 1788, to John Stevens, Sr., Stevens Collection MSS, S437f.

11. Stevens, *Observations on Government* . . .

12. Letter from Stevens, June 18, 1818, to Tsar Alexander, Stevens Collection, MSS, S1725f.

13. Memorial from Stevens to New Jersey legislature, 1814, Stevens Collection MSS, S5022. In opposing a grant to one of his rivals, the Brunswick Company, Stevens argued that such a grant would "put down all competition, depress the spirit of improvement, and be detrimental to the public convenience." He maintained that he was content to stand on equal grounds of competition with others, as long as neither party to the contest enjoyed the unfair advantage of an exclusive grant.

14. Stevens' petition to United States Military Departments, Stevens Collection MSS, S8282.

15. Letter from Robert Stevens, June 18, 1818, to U. S. Ordnance Department, Stevens Collection MSS, S1725f.

16. Letter from Stevens, February 3, 1818, to Robert Stevens, Stevens Collection MSS, S393.

17. Letter from Stevens, February 17, 1818, to Robert Stevens, Stevens Collection MSS.

18. Stevens Collection MSS, S2213. Stevens accused the Navy Board of squandering millions of dollars.

19. Stevens Collection MSS, S5172, n.d.; letter from Stevens, March 22, 1830, to Andrew Jackson, Stevens Collection MSS, S7509T2.

20. See early correspondence in the Stevens Collection, particularly the letters between John Stevens, Jr., and his father during the revolutionary era.

21. It would be revealing to know the family and economic backgrounds of all of those involved in the auctioneering of confiscated Tory estates. For example, Governor Livingston of New Jersey favored Stevens' purchase of Hoboken and actively discouraged rival buyers. (See the Stevens Collection.) The Livingston family was related to the Stevens family by marriage.

22. For examples, see Stevens Collection MSS, S403, S631–41f, 5036, S8421, S5071, S5085.

23. It is true that Stevens secured permission from the New Jersey Legislature to hold a lottery to help his joint-stock company raise funds for dredging the Delaware, but this was not a regular practice of his. (Stevens Collection MSS, S8178, 8485.)

24. For examples, see Stevens Collection MSS, S5071, 5085, 5015, 5013, 5012, S4251, 5028.

25. In defense of Stevens' own contributions, it has been argued that if he was not a mechanic-inventor he at least possessed some technological knowledge and insight. That is, he had enough knowledge to know which inventions, such as the steamboat and the railroad, could be successfully exploited. However, if we examine the total list of his attempts we note that his failures far outweighed his successes. In the face of such adversities his perseverance in seeking opportunities and his business acumen in managing those "inventions" that ultimately proved practical appear to have been the most decisive factors in his career.

26. Letter from Stevens, November 21, 1809, to Fulton and Livingston, Stevens Collection MSS, S7488.

27. Despite assertions to the contrary (see A. D. Trumbull, *John Stevens: An American Record*, New York: The Century Company, 1928, p. 108), the writer has found no evidence that Stevens was the chief figure behind the passage of the federal patent law in 1790.

28. Letter from John Fitch, July 9, 1795 to Stevens, Stevens Collection MSS, S855f.

29. Letter from Fulton, April 2, 1813, to Cadwallader Colden, Stevens Collection MSS, S7069. This letter Colden was to convey to Stevens.

30. It is true that the early entrepreneur probably knew more about technology than the present-day corporation executive, but his knowledge, usually acquired from books and dilettante experiments, did not make him an "inventor." In a day when there was no established body of mechanical science the innovations came out of the daily work of practicing mechanics.

31. S. C. Gilfillan, *Inventing the Ship* (Chicago: Follett Publishing Company, c1935), pp. 92, 95–97.

32. Thomas C. Cochran and William Miller, *The Age of Enterprise* (New York: The Macmillan Company, 1943), p. 14.

33. Louis C. Hunter, *Steamboats on the Western Rivers: an Economic and Technological History* (Cambridge: Harvard University Press, 1949), p. 384. The generalizations about steamboat navigation of the Mississippi which are presented here are drawn from Dr. Hunter's comprehensive study, particularly chap. 8.

34. But Fulton's *Clermont* had to be completely rebuilt after a few trips and the machinery of the Colonel's *Phoenix* had to be replaced within a year. The later boats were better built, but the Colonel complained constantly about heavy operating costs.

35. Hunter, *Steamboats on the Western Rivers*, p. 362; Robert Fulton, *New York Public Library Bulletin 13*, January 22, 1810, p. 573. Fulton estimated the operating expenses of a $25,000 steamboat on the Hudson at $7000 per year. (See Stevens Collection MSS, S1134f, November 19, 1810.) In these estimates it should be noted that there is a difference of from ten to twenty years because of the later introduction of the steamboat on the Mississippi. The steamboat was first introduced on the Mississippi in 1812 and became important in numbers only after Fulton's and Livingston's attempts to secure a monopoly of steamboat traffic on the Mississippi were defeated in 1818.

36. Hunter, *Steamboats*, p. 362. Fulton, *New York Public Library Bulletin 13*, January 22, 1810, p. 573. Fuel was a heavier charge in the northeast, for many of the Mississippi steamboat captains used driftwood and cut their own timber along the banks of the river.

37. Hunter, *Steamboats*, p. 384.

38. Stevens Collection MSS, S5080.

39. Stevens Collection MSS, S1132f, S833f, S5045, S843f, S4410, S5035.

40. Stevens Collection MSS, S5080.

41. Stevens Collection MSS, S4234f.

42. Letter from Fulton, January 2, 1811, to Stevens, Stevens Collection MSS, S891f.

43. Letter from Fulton, May 8, 1809, to Stevens, Stevens Collection MSS, S874f–875f.

44. Contract between R. R. Livingston, R. Fulton, and Stevens, December 1, 1809, Stevens Collection MSS, S4190f.

45. Letter from Horace Binney, April 13, 1818, to Robert Stevens, Stevens Collection MSS, S1996.

46. In the 1820's Stevens had three steam ferries operating on the Hoboken-New York run. Up to 1824 there were about sixteen steamboats operating on the Hudson, all under licensing agreements with Fulton and Livingston. Until 1824 Stevens was second in importance in the steamboating industry in the northeast only to the North River Steamboat Company (the Fulton-Livingston company); and after 1824 the Stevens family emerged as the dominant force in steamboating in the northeast. By 1825 Stevens' sons had bought out most of their father's stock on the Delaware and

allied with the New Brunswick operators had an integrated line of steamboats and stages between New York and Philadelphia.

47. Stevens, "Documents Tending to Prove the Superior Advantage of Railways and Steam-Carriages over Canal Navigation" (New York: Printed by T. and J. Swords, No. 160 Pearl Street, 1812).

48. For Struik to simplify the debate on canals *vs.* railroads to a class conflict of merchant-industrialist (railroad promoter) *vs.* landed country-proprietors (canal backers) is to overlook the fundamentally complex nature of the business-enterprise activities of such figures as Stevens, who was surely a landed proprietor. (See Dirk J. Struik, *Yankee Science in the Making*, Boston: Little, Brown and Company, 1948, p. 241).

VI. Henry Noble Day

By R. Richard Wohl

I would like to acknowledge the kind help of the staff of the Yale University Library in the preparation of this paper. A special debt of thanks is due to Mrs. Zara Jones Powers, Librarian of the Historical Manuscripts Division, in which the Henry Noble Day papers are deposited, who spared neither time nor trouble in locating and making available all pertinent materials; and to her assistant, Miss Rosemary Smith.

1. Oliver Jones to Henry Noble Day (hereafter abbreviated HND), March 31, 1834. Cf. also Henry B. Wright, "Professor Goodrich and the Growth and Outcome of the Revival Movement," in J. B. Reynolds, S. H. Fisher and H. B. Wright (eds.), *Two Centuries of Christian Activity at Yale* (New Haven, 1901), pp. 73–98, esp. pp. 83, 84–85, 299–302.

2. Thomas Day to HND, March 31, 1834.

3. Thomas Day to HND, April 26, 1834.

4. A file of bills for charges incurred on his European trip are in HND Papers for 1834, also a summary account of all his expenses for the journey drawn up by Sherman Day and Daniel Day. The total cost of the trip abroad was $1,329.42.

5. Biographical materials on HND are few and sketchy. There is a four-page autobiography in his papers which he drew up in 1868 for the fortieth reunion of the Yale Class of 1828, and which he revised on June 29, 1878 for the fiftieth class reunion. The *Dictionary of American Biography* has a short account. A long obituary, more an appreciation of his life than a biographical account, appeared in the New Haven *Journal and Courier*, January 13, 1890.

6. Ellen Day Putnam, *Some Chronicles of the Day Family* (Cambridge, 1893), p. 34. Apparently a business failure forced his retirement for on November 2, 1830, Thomas Day of Hartford wrote to HND, "I send you herewith as I promised you a statement of my account with your Father since his failure in 1819. At that time he owed me for cash advanced and paid for him a balance of $9,705 on which I have since received no dividend other than what is credited on the enclosed account. . . The support of his family will continue to be, as it has always been, an object of deep concern." In return for these and perhaps other advances, Thomas Day received mortgages on real estate owned by Noble Day in Washington, Connecticut. On May 20, 1848, Thomas Day issued a power of attorney to HND em-

powering him to manage "the rents, proceeds and profits of real estate in Washington, Connecticut formerly mortgaged to him for sale, proceeds to go into a trust fund, proceeds and income of which to maintain Noble Day and Elizabeth Day, his wife, for life and after the principal to pass to the Trustees of Western Reserve College." Noble Day's retirement, however, was dignified. In 1842 he was justice of the peace in New Preston (Washington), Connecticut. Cf. *Connecticut Annual Register* (East Windsor, 1841) p. 58.

7. Henry Purcell, *Connecticut in Transition, 1775–1818* (New Haven, 1918), particular references to Thomas Day will be found on pp. 184, 230, 304, 322, 326 and 349. Purcell's brilliant monograph is matched by Jarvis M. Morse's *A Neglected Period of Connecticut History, 1818–1850* (New Haven, 1933), which carries the story down to the middle of the nineteenth century. For Thomas Day cf. pp. 62, 87, 282–283.

8. Thomas Mills Day, "Thomas Day," in *Memorial Biographies of the New England Historic Genealogical Society* (Boston, 1881), p. 338.

9. Thomas Mills Day, "Thomas Day."

10. *Catalogue of the Trustees, Instructors, and Pupils of the Hartford Grammar School, October 1837* (Hartford, 1837), pp. 8–9. The exclusive character of the school and its methods of training are best reviewed in a series of recollections of graduates contemporary with HND. One of them notes that the school was known as the "Rugby of Connecticut," another stresses the social exclusiveness of the pupils. "Edward Hopkins and the Hopkins Foundations," *American Journal of Education*, 28: 171–224 (1878). For material mentioned above see pp. 218 and 208 respectively.

11. "I do not remember," writes President Barnard in 1878, "a single instance of really malicious misconduct, nor a single manifestation on the part of any lad of a persistently sullen, morose or defiant disposition. But in saying that they were good boys, I do not in the least mean that they were *goody*, they were good-natured, frank and honorable." [Italics in original.] "Edward Hopkins and the Hopkins Foundations," *American Journal of Education*, p. 210. The phrase "as by a natural law," is used by the author of the sketch in the *Dictionary of American Biography*.

12. Strangely enough there is no full-length biography of Jeremiah Day. For his early life and career cf. Charles E. Cunningham, *Timothy Dwight, 1752–1817* (New York, 1942), pp. 145, 199, 233, 240. The best account of his administration as President of Yale is in William L. Kingsley, *Yale College, A Sketch of its History* (New York, 1879), I, 124–146. A short contemporary biographical sketch appears in the *Yale Literary Magazine*, 4: 1–2 (1838). The report on curricula was issued under the title, *Reports of the Course of Instruction in Yale College by a Committee of the Corporation and the Academical Faculty* (New Haven, 1828). The synoptic view of President Jeremiah Day's outlook is drawn from a reading of his correspondence with his son Sherman during the years 1819 to 1826. (These letters are in the Jeremiah Day Papers at Yale University.) The following excerpt taken from a Christmas letter to his son at school is typical. It is the closing paragraph of the letter dated December 25, 1819. "Instances daily occurring warn us that young and old are continually liable to sickness and death. The great point is to be ready to depart whenever it pleases God to call us. May we all be prepared to leave the world in peace."

13. W. B. Sprague (ed.), *Annals of the American Pulpit* (New York, 1857), I, 688ff.

14. Inscription in the album of Oliver Hubbard, a classmate. *Yale Memorabilia Collection, Class Books of Class of 1828.*

15. Inscription in HND's album by E. P. Barrows, Jr., dated July 11, 1826.

16. Cf. note 6.

17. Jeremiah Day to Sherman Day, October 4, 1825. (This and all subsequent letters between these two are in the Jeremiah Day Papers at Yale, and will hereafter be cited as JD to SD").

18. "Business vs. Professions," *Yale Literary Magazine*, 29: 169–173 (1864), cf. especially p. 172.

19. JD to SD, October 4, 1831.

20. JD to SD, October 12, 1826.

21. JD to SD, November 18, 1836.

22. JD to SD, May 20, 1837.

23. Cf. letter cited hereafter in note 61.

24. Gummere's letter to HND, June 25, 1828 refers to the recommendations of President Jeremiah Day and Professor Benjamin Silliman and acknowledges HND's appointment to the school.

25. Horace Bushnell to HND, October 20, 1827 and H. B. King to HND, April 21, 1828.

26. Cf. certificate by Charles Chauncey dated Philadelphia, March 7, 1831: "Mr. Henry Day entered my office as a student of law on the 18th November 1830 and has pursued his studies under my direction until the present time."

27. On August 17, 1833 the Association of the Western District of New Haven County issued to HND a certificate declaring that he was a "regularly licensed candidate for the work of the ministry," which was signed by Zephaniah Swift.

28. For Simeon Marble cf. Edward E. Atwater (ed.), *History of the City of New Haven* (New York, 1887), pp. 326–327. For Mrs. Simeon Marble cf. [James M. Patten, ed.] *Patten's New Haven Directory for the Year 1840* (New Haven, 1840), p. 108. A full account of the life and works of Adeline Marble is in the anonymous pamphlet, *Christian Character Exemplified in the Life of Adeline Marble, Corresponding Secretary of the Female Jevenile Mite Society of New Haven, who died May 3rd, 1822* (New Haven, 1822).

29. Joseph Anderson, *The Town and City of Waterbury* (New Haven, 1896), pp. 587–588. The Washington invitation was dated March 29, 1836 and is endorsed with a copy of HND's refusal letter. The New Haven invitation is dated September 1, 1836.

30. The recommendation is dated May 6, 1839 although the school must have been in existence before this date. There is, for example, a letter from J. L. Kingsley to HND dated February 21, 1839 in which Kingsley writes that he is sending one F. W. Miller to rusticate at Day's school until he can go back to Yale.

31. George Pierce to HND, March 9, 1840.

32. Elias Loomis to HND, March 10, 1840.

33. Jeremiah Day to HND, March 21, 1840.

34. Charles Roy Keller, *The Second Great Awakening in Connecticut* (New Haven, 1942), cf. esp. p. 68. "Hudson Centennial Celebration, June 5, 1900," *Ohio Archeological and Historical Quarterly*, 9: 318–371 (1901).

35. Grace Lathrop, *A History of the First Congregational Church in Hudson, Ohio* (n.p., n.d.), pp. 12–13.

36. [Harvey Baldwin, ed.], *Proceedings of the Fifty-Sixth Anniversary of the Settlement of Hudson* (Akron, 1875). Cf. esp. the statistical report by Rev. C. Pitkin, pp. 4–6.

37. William H. Perrin (ed.), *History of Summit County* (Chicago, 1881), pp. 427–428.

38. Frederick Clayton Waite, *Western Reserve University, The Hudson Era* (Cleveland, 1943), pp. 223–227.

39. The original contract was dated July 12, 1844. The second instrument was executed July 12, 1845 and in it HND "assumed all the pecuniary liabilities of said firm [*The Ohio Observor*] of whatever kind" and undertook to "allow said Barrows and Upson whatever may be found to be due them respectively on the books of said firm."

40. James Owen Knauss, "St. Joseph, An Episode of the Economic and Political History of Florida," *Florida Historical Quarterly*, Part I, 5: 177–195 (1927); Part II, 6: 3–20 (1927).

41. Jeremiah Day [HND's brother, none of the subsequent references in this paper refer to President Jeremiah Day, President of Yale, but all refer to Jeremiah Day, HND's brother] to HND, December 21, 1839. Jeremiah quotes from a letter he had received from HND earlier.

42. Jeremiah Day to HND, April 11, 1840.

43. Typical of the letters from Apalachicola which followed this episode are those of March 11, 1842 and June 9, 1843 from Jeremiah Day to HND.

44. Waite, *Western Reserve University*, p. 172.

45. *Report of the Chief Engineer on the Location and Estimates of Costs of the Cleveland and Pittsburgh Railroad* (Hudson, 1849). An appendix gives the original charter of 1836.

46. Waite, *Western Reserve University*, p. 16.

47. Roy Allen Billington, *Westward Expansion* (New York, 1949), p. 295, map entitled, "Settlement of the Lake Plains, 1815–1830"; p. 303, map entitled "Settlement of the Lake Plains, 1830–1850."

48. [Edward M. Mansfield,] *Third Annual Report of the [Ohio] Commissioner of Statistics* (Columbus, 1860), pp. 39–40.

49. [Edward M. Mansfield,] *[First] Annual Report of the [Ohio] Commissioner of Statistics* (Columbus, 1858), p. 34.

50. [Mansfield,] *[First] Annual Report*, p. 20.

51. The reports of the Ohio State Board of Agriculture provide a multitude of examples of the drive to convert agriculture into a businesslike and scientific undertaking. Cf. esp. John H. Klippart, "History and Review of the Condition of Agriculture in Ohio," in *Fourteenth Annual Report of the Ohio State Board of Agriculture* (Columbus, 1860), pp. 450–492.

52. Isaac Lippincott, *A History of Manufactures in the Ohio Valley to the Year 1860* ([Chicago], 1860), pp. 70–71.

53. This sermon is to be found in the Sermon file in the HND Papers, and was delivered before Western Reserve College, on Thanksgiving Day, November 28, 1850. All of HND's sermons are in the form of manuscript pamphlets the first pages of which are usually docketed with the place and date at which the sermon was first delivered and subsequently repeated. The sermon here quoted bears only one such notation and apparently was never repeated. Although the pamphlet sermon is not paginated, I have supplied page numbers commencing with the first leaf of writing. This sermon is hereinafter noted as "Sermon."

54. *Sermon*, p. 8.

55. *Sermon*, p. 9.

56. *Sermon*, p. 13.

57. *Sermon*, pp. 14–15.

58. *Sermon*, p. 19.

59. *Sermon*, pp. 47–48.

60. *Sermon*, pp. 26, 28.

61. Thomas Day to HND, January 27, 1853.

62. Samuel A. Lane, *Fifty Years and Over of Akron and Summit County* (Akron, 1892), pp. 621–626.

63. A. C. Catlett (Secretary of the Cleveland & Pittsburgh Railroad) to HND, August 11, 1846; same to same, August 26, 1846. The latter letter includes a certificate appointing HND agent of the company.

64. J. W. Robertson to HND, January 6, 1847, enclosing a certificate of appointment signed by James Stewart, president, pro tem, of the Cleveland & Pittsburgh Railroad.

65. HND's instructions from the Cleveland & Pittsburgh's officers are illuminating in this connection. "You will therefore urge," they write, "the matter [building the C. & P.] forward, get the Eastern papers to notice the work and take all such measures as yr time will admit to mark out a suitable course and we will have someone take up where you leave it, visit New York and Boston and let your presence as agent of the Company be known and see what interest is manifested in the work. . ."

66. This plan is outlined in the report of the Chief Engineer cited in note 45.

67. Lane, *Fifty Years . . . of Akron and Summit County*, pp. 623–624.

68. Cf. the annual reports of both branch lines which are identically worded, especially, *First Annual Report of the Directors of the Clinton Line Railroad Company with the Report of the Chief Engineer on Location and Construction* (Hudson, 1854).

69. Lane, *Fifty Years*, p. 835.

70. Thomas Day [brother of HND] to HND, January 14, 1845. Thomas was quoting a passage from a letter HND had written him earlier. Jane Marble Day to HND, July 23, 1846.

71. This is an evaluation of HND's activities made by an unknown person whom he had submitted as a credit reference to the Boston printing machinery firm of S. & S. Adams. They sent HND a copy of the evaluation made by his reference and a demand for cash before delivery. Cf. the entire correspondence on the matter, especially S. & S. Adams to HND, April 24, 1851.

72. H. B. Ely to HND, February 2, 1848.

73. All these proposals are reviewed in a memorandum which HND wrote to the Trustees of Western Reserve College, "The Pentagon Loans," dated May 1858.

74. Reconstructed from a billhead wood engraving in the HND Papers.

75. Horace Day to HND, October 22, 1846, describing arrangements for the import of a binder to Hudson. Cf. also the agreement between J. J. A. Tiernan and HND, October 29, 1849 whereby the former binds himself or "any person equally competent to do the business of stereotyping" to accept "15 dollars to come Hudson, and ten dollars a week for 6 mos. then 15 dollars if he wishes to go back [to New York]." Tiernan sent W. H. Shain who became active in HND's printing and publishing enterprises.

76. Contract between George Hobart, S. W. Judd, and HND, September 23, 1857. The manufacturer of sacks, Hobart, is to pay $250 rent for a room and steam power to make sacks which will be sold by him to HND and colleagues at prices fixed in the contract.

77. Perrin, *History of Summit County*, p. 435.

78. The HND Papers include a town plan showing the extent of "Day's Addition" and the names and holdings of owners of contiguous parcels.

79. For the Hudson Savings Society cf. the Constitution and By-Laws which were printed in each passbook, an example of which is in the HND papers.

80. For Hudson Planing Mill cf. Perrin, *History of Summit County*, p. 436.

81. Sherman Day to HND, December 9, 1845; Simeon Marble to HND, December 5, 1845; Edwin Marble to HND, July 5 and 6, 1854; Thomas A. Thacher to HND, July 3, 1854; E. C. Herrick to HND, March 12, 1853; Thomas Day to HND, September 29, 1851.

82. The relation of Eastern funds to Ohio bank advances is shown in the statement of the Summit County Bank to HND, April 7, 1855.

83. For the commitments of Jeremiah Day & Co. to HND's enterprises, Charles Day to HND in [January] 1854 cites the figure of $100,000. For Simeon Marble see his letter from HND, August 12, 1855. Edwin Marble to HND, October 25, 1854, sums up all the loans he has guaranteed. Lathrop, *History of the First Congregational Church*, p. 17 gives the figure for investment in the bank, and Perrin, *History of Summit County*, p. 435, cites the town's investment in the railroads, on p. 834, he cites Messer's personal investment.

84. For Baldwin cf. Lane, *Fifty Years*, p. 818; for Humphrey, *Fifty Years*, p. 831; for Smith, Perrin, *History of Summit County*, p. 436, and Smith's letters to HND dated June 23, 1851, August 11, 13, 20, 29, 1851.

85. A brief history of Sawyer, Ingersoll and its subsequent reorganizations is given in Perrin, *Summit County*, p. 436. The HND papers document each step in this history but for the sake of brevity no individual documents are cited; refer to papers on the Hudson Book Company in the HND papers.

86. Charles Day to HND, [January] 1854.

87. Jeremiah Day to HND, January 26, 1854.

88. Jeremiah Day to HND, March 29, 1854.

89. Charles Day to HND, September 27, 1854.

90. For plans to revive the Clinton Line Railroad cf. Lane, *Fifty Years*, p. 634.

91. Memorandum of formation of committee to organize Hudson Female Seminary, February 13, 1855. On February 26, 1855 the articles of association were written and recorded. On March 12, 1855 HND was elected President of the group, and on July 14, 1855 he resigned.

92. Biographical sketch referred to in note 5.

VII. The American Industrial Elite in the 1870's

By Frances W. Gregory and Irene D. Neu

This paper is a report on a project which was carried out at the Research Center in Entrepreneurial History at Harvard University.

1. William M. Thayer, *The Poor Boy and Merchant Prince* (Boston, 1858).

2. Robert C. Winthrop, *Memoir of Nathan Appleton* (Boston, 1861), p. 60; Nathan Appleton, Letters to Thomas Gold Appleton, 1825–1830, in the Nathan Appleton Collection, Massachusetts Historical Society, Boston, Massachusetts.

3. See William Miller, "American Historians and the Business Elite," pp. 309–

328, above. For a detailed and humorous critique of one historian's analysis of the background and early life of John D. Rockefeller, see the essay by Kenneth Lynn, "Allan Nevins: An Algerine Captive," in *Explorations in Entrepreneurial History*, 2: 245–261 (1949–50). It will be recalled, of course, that Alger's heroes did not necessarily achieve what in the present article is termed top industrial leadership. It should also be borne in mind that this article is concerned only with leaders and does not purport to arrive at conclusions in regard to smaller businessmen or men on lower levels of management in large companies.

4. Frank W. Taussig and Carl S. Joslyn, *American Business Leaders: A Study in Social Origins and Social Stratification* (New York, 1932). See also C. Wright Mills, "The American Business Elite: A Collective Portrait," *The Tasks of Economic History* (supplemental issue of *The Journal of Economic History*, 5, 1945), pp. 20–44.

5. Taussig and Joslyn, *American Business Leaders*, p. 264.

6. These two essays by William Miller, "American Historians and the Business Elite," and "The Recruitment of the American Business Elite," are both reprinted in the Appendix to the Torchbook edition, pp. 309–337, above.

7. Miller, "American Historians and the Business Elite," pp. 309–328.

8. On this point see the reviews of their *American Business Leaders* by William F. Ogburn in *The Journal of Political Economy*, 42: 404–406 (1934), and by Morris Ginsberg in *Economic Journal*, 43: 502–505 (1933).

9. Evelyn H. Knowlton, *Pepperell's Progress* (Cambridge: Harvard University Press, 1949), p. 28.

10. If there was no general manager of a given incorporated company, the superintendent was included. This was to prevent the group's being weighted in favor of partnerships, for usually the names of three or four partners were known.

11. *Dockham's American Report and Directory of the Cotton, Wool, Silk and Linen Manufactures and Dry Goods Trade* (Boston, 1876).

12. Two steelworks used both the Bessemer and the open-hearth processes, so the total number of companies in these two categories is 24. For the crucible plants, production rather than capitalization figures had to be used because the latter are not available for all companies. See *Directory of the Iron and Steel Works of the United States* (Philadelphia, 1878).

13. In textiles, *Dockham's American Report and Directory* supplied the greatest number of names. This directory appeared under various titles, the volumes available being for the years 1870–71, 1874–75, and 1876–77. To supplement this work a decidedly inferior book, the *United States Industrial Directory, 1879* (published by the National Association of Wool Manufacturers and the New England Cotton Manufacturers Association along with the Silk Association of America) had to be used. A few additional names were found in the *Annual Statistics of Lowell and Neighboring Towns*, published in Lowell in 1883, and in the *Acts of Incorporation and By Laws* of the Merrimack Manufacturing Company, published in Boston in 1901.

The names of the steel men were gleaned for the most part from the directories published by the American Iron and Steel Association of Philadelphia in 1875, 1876, 1878, and 1880. The first of these appeared as part of the *United States Textile Manufacturers' Directory* (Boston, 1875); the other three were separate publications of the Iron and Steel Association. The names from this source were supplemented by a small number which were found in city directories and local histories.

The railroad men were derived entirely from Henry V. Poor's *Manual of Railroads*, of which there is a volume for each year of the decade.

14. By position the record is as follows: in textiles, 52 treasurers and 50 agents; in steel, 30 partners, 30 presidents, 12 vice-presidents, 10 general managers, and 18 superintendents; in railroads, 47 presidents, 44 vice-presidents, and 10 general managers. In the search for information concerning these men, the standard biographical dictionaries proved of little help, only 25 per cent of the names appearing in the *National Cyclopedia of American Biography* and but 20 per cent in the *Dictionary of American Biography*. To a large extent, the same names were found in both. Most data, therefore, had to be sought in other places. A systematic examination was made of city, county, and state histories, as well as industrial histories and company records. Other fruitful sources were obituary notices and memoirs in publications of historical and professional societies and in contemporary newspapers. College archives and catalogues also proved helpful, as did probate records and death certificates. Genealogies, when available, went far to supply family background. Although the data unearthed in this manner were by no means complete, the search was successful in that *some* biographical information was obtained for all but 33 of the 303 men in the group.

15. According to the census of 1880, railroads were capitalized in excess of $2,600,000,000, textile mills at $373,000,000, and iron and steel manufacturing at $231,000,000. Between the last two came mining with a capitalization of $365,000,000.

16. While the editors of the first edition of *The Biographical Directory of the Railway Officials of America*, which appeared in 1885, could maintain on one page that "nearly all of the great railway managers of to-day have risen . . . from the humblest ranks in the profession . . . ," two pages further along they had to record that "most of our presidents have occupied no other position in the railway service. . . " (E. H. Talbott and H. R. Hobart, *The Biographical Director of the Railway Officials of America*, Chicago, 1885, iv, vi.) Of the 43 railroad presidents of the 1870's for whom career data were obtained, 23 were general entrepreneurs or financiers or had been for many years engaged in a branch of business other than railroading; 13 were professional men (11 lawyers, one soldier, one public official); only seven rose to their positions "through the ranks." No less than 18 of the 43 presidents had large financial interests in the roads they headed; at least 20 had held public office; six had distinguished political careers behind them.

17. According to a statistical study which appeared in *The Corporate Director* (published by The American Institute of Management), in June 1950, the average age of the chief executives of 204 leading companies at that time was 58 years.

18. The youngest men of all, in the 1870's group, were to be found in the steel industry, their ages averaging 43 years. Textile men and railroad men averaged respectively 46 and 47 years. At first sight this would seem to indicate that steel, being a young industry, attracted younger men, and perhaps this was so. When it is remembered, however, that in many cases, if not most, the new steelworks were attached to old, long-established ironworks, the first facile explanation becomes less tenable. Of the 15 steel men known to be 30 or under in 1870, five were partners in or officers of iron and steel companies headed by their fathers, a circumstance which would seem to indicate that they chose to enter the steel industry not because they were attracted to a new field but because they were joining their fathers in business. Three of the 15 men under 30 were interested in iron manufacture before they turned to steel; only seven, including two who were trained as chemists, apparently made an independent choice of steel manufacturing as a career.

19. D. Hamilton Hurd, *History of Middlesex County, Massachusetts* (Philadelphia, 1890), II, 80.

20. *Dictionary of American Biography*, XIII, 39.

21. Of the 170 men in the 1870's group for whom this information is available, 123 were descendants of seventeenth-century immigrants; 18 of eighteenth-century immigrants; only 29 were either themselves nineteenth-century immigrants, or the sons of men who migrated in that century. In each case, the immigrant referred to was the founder of the subject's paternal line in America. See also Miller, "American Historians and the Business Elite," p. 202.

22. It will be recalled that the large-scale manufacture of textiles in southern mills had not yet become a feature of the American economy in the period of which we are speaking (that is, the 1870's). As late as the middle eighties, Columbus, Georgia claimed the largest cotton mill in the south, with about 50,000 spindles and 1500 looms (Victor S. Clark, *History of Manufactures in the United States*, New York, 1929, II, 400–402).

23. Miller, "The Recruitment of the American Business Elite," pp. 329–337.

24. Seven of the fourteen became Episcopalians, two changed to the Methodist Church, and one each to the Presbyterian, Congregational, Dutch Reformed, Swedenborgian, and Roman Catholic.

25. *Triumphant Democracy* (New York, 1886), p. 46.

26. Allan Nevins, *The Emergence of Modern America, 1865–1878* (*A History of American Life*, VIII, New York, 1927), p. 75.

27. Lewis C. Aldrich, *History of Franklin and Grand Isle Counties, Vermont* (Syracuse, New York, 1891), pp. 359ff.

28. *Dictionary of American Biography*, XVII, 302.

29. *Erie: A Guide to the City and County* (Philadelphia, 1938), pp. 18, 57; American Society of Civil Engineers, *Proceedings*, IV (1878), 72.

30. On the peddler as a businessman, see N. S. B. Gras, *Business and Capitalism, An Introduction to Business History* (New York, 1939), pp. 46–48.

VIII. Frank Julian Sprague

By Harold C. Passer

1. At that time, Annapolis students were graduated as passed midshipmen. They did not receive their commissions until they had served two years at sea.

2. Dugald C. Jackson, "Frank Julian Sprague, 1857–1934," in *Scientific Monthly*, LVII, No. 5 (November 1943), p. 434.

3. Three articles by Sprague under the title "Application of Electricity to the Propulsion of Elevated Railroads," appeared in the *Electrical World* early in 1886. See VII, 27, 36, and 118.

4. John Winthrop Hammond, *Men and Volts* (New York: J. B. Lippincott Co., 1941), p. 84.

5. Frank J. Sprague, "Lessons of the Richmond Electric Railway," in *Engineering Magazine*, VII, No. 6 (September 1894), p. 789.

6. The commutator is a device which is mounted on the armature shaft and whose purpose is to carry the current from the stationary brushes to the moving armature.

7. Frank J. Sprague, "Some Personal Notes on Electric Railways," in *Electrical Review*, XL, No. 7 (February 15, 1902), p. 227.

8. See *Electrical World*, XXXI, No. 7 (February 12, 1898), p. 221.

9. Annual Report of the Edison General Electric Company, January 2, 1890.

10. Frank J. Sprague, "The Electric Railway," in *Century Magazine*, LXX, No. 4 (August 1905), p. 522.

11. Frank J. Sprague, "Digging in the Mines of the Motors," in *Journal of the American Institute of Electrical Engineers*, LIII, No. 5 (May 1934), p. 703.

12. Frank J. Sprague, "The Multiple Unit System for Electric Railways," in *Cassier's Magazine*, XVI, No. 4 (August 1899), p. 460.

13. Letter from A. G. Davis of the General Electric Patent Department to F. P. Fish, General Counsel of General Electric, February 1, 1910; in the historical files of the General Electric Company, Schenectady, New York.

IX. Capital Accumulation in Life Insurance between the Civil War and the Investigation of 1905

By Douglass North

1. However, the Presbyterian Ministers' Fund has had a continuous existence since 1759 (Shepard B. Clough, *A Century of American Life Insurance*, New York: Columbia University Press, 1946, p. 23).

2. *Testimony Taken before the Joint Committee of the Senate and Assembly of the State of New York to Investigate and Examine into the Business and Affairs of Life Insurance Companies* (hereinafter referred to as the *Armstrong Investigation*, after the chairman of the committee). All references are to the seven-volume edition.

3. T.N.E.C. Hearing, part 4, Life Insurance, Exh. 218, p. 1512.

4. Flugel and Faulkner, *Readings in the Economic and Social History of the United States* (New York: Harper & Bros., 1929), p. 485.

5. Between 1870 and 1910 the population grew from 39,818,449 to 91,972,266. *Historical Statistics of the United States 1789–1945*, (Washington, D. C.: U. S. Government Printing Office, 1949), p. 25.

6. J. Schutz and M. R. Caine, *Financial Development of the United States* (New York: Prentice Hall, 1937).

7. Clough, *A Century of American Life Insurance*, p. 183. Mortgage and collateral loans generally declined as securities increased in importance. This essay is concerned primarily with the sources of capital accumulation rather than the significance of life insurance for the expansion and consolidation of the economy during this period. However, for amplification of the important part played by the big three in the railroad and industrial consolidation organized by the large investment banking houses see *Armstrong Investigation Report*, pp. 9–119, also *The Money Trust Investigation* (Washington, D. C.: U. S. Government Printing Office, 1911–1913), also George Edwards, *The Evolution of Finance Capitalism* (New York: Longmans, Green and Co., 1938). Not only did life insurance companies act as a primary reservoir of funds for the investment banker (see, for example, *Armstrong Investigation Exhibits*, pp. 1313–1318, 1332–1335), but almost equally important was the large-scale financing of subsidiary banks and trust companies through which extensive investments were made (see, for example, *Armstrong Investigation Exhibits*, pp. 1323–1331, 1393–1400).

8. The percentage of policyholders in farm areas is far below that in urban areas (Clough, *A Century of American Life Insurance*, p. 8.)

9. J. O. Stalson, *Marketing Life Insurance* (Cambridge, Mass.: Harvard University Press, 1942), pp. 795–799.

10. *Armstrong Investigation*, pp. 11–14, figures are rounded off.

11. See below, pp. 243–244 for an account of industrial insurance.

12. A simplified explanation of life insurance is necessary at this point. The premiums on a life insurance policy were calculated with three factors in mind: (1) an assumed mortality rate; (2) an assumed interest rate (on the accumulated funds of the insured); and (3) an assumed loading factor (the expenses of the company in conducting the business as apportioned to each premium). Should the assumed rates be perfectly correct in all three cases, the premium would be correct and there would be no overcharge. However, there generally was a conservative discrepancy between calculated and actual mortality and between the calculated and actual rate of interest and very often the expenses of the company were less than the loading factor. The result was that the company had accumulated a surplus above the necessary reserve of funds. With some allowance for contingencies this was usually paid back to the participating policyholder in the form of annual dividends (until the advent of tontine and deferred dividend policies).

13. Here the Connecticut Mutual was not as liberal as some other conservative companies such as the Mutual Benefit of New Jersey which provided liberal cash surrender values as early as 1879. Greene's reasons for opposing cash surrender values, however, were very different from those of the big three. He viewed the life insurance company as a trustee of family security. Once the insured set aside these funds for such protection, he should not be permitted to withdraw.

14. *Armstrong Investigation*, p. 1162.

15. Connecticut Mutual, Mutual Benefit, Aetna, New England, and Manhattan.

16. Mutual, Equitable, New York Life, and Northwestern.

17. *Armstrong Investigation*, p. 2661.

18. The big three were not the only companies that pursued the innovations and policies characterized in the following pages, but their leadership was unquestioned. Indeed many small companies went into tontine insurance of necessity in order to survive. See below pp. 245–246.

19. During this period there were many different types of insurance (such as term, endowment, life, etc.). Tontine insurance was not so much an innovation in being another type of insurance as it was an innovation specifically in the distribution of surplus (and in surrender values). In fact the deferred dividend system (which succeeded tontine) was combined with almost all the types of insurance contracts. In the following discussion the significant difference is between the system of annual dividends on insurance policies on the one hand and the tontine (and later deferred dividend) system of dividend distribution on the other hand.

20. There were four classes of the original tontine insurance — one class did provide some surrender value (*Armstrong Investigation*, p. 4697).

21. After the initial success of the Equitable, other companies followed suit rapidly. The Mutual held out until 1885 and as a result had dropped far behind in the competitive race. However, between 1885 and 1905 the deferred dividend system regained for the company all the lost territory and assets increased by over 332 million dollars (*Armstrong Investigation*, p. 1402).

22. Three years after the Mutual adopted deferred dividend policies, less than one-half of 1 per cent of new business was written on the annual dividend plan (Clough, *A Century of American Life Insurance*, p. 146).

23. This perhaps requires some explanation. If a policyholder failed to pay his

premiums the policy lapsed. Total forfeiture, which prevailed under pure tontine, meant that the policyholder received no return. Under the deferred dividend system he received some return on the accumulated reserve which his premium had built up, but none of his accumulated dividends (or overcharge).

24. See below, p. 245.

25. For the year 1872, the Equitable issued 12,491 policies to the amount of $51,911,079. During the same year 8183 were terminated totaling $34,798,871; of this latter amount only 423 (for a total of $9,688,882) were terminated by death; 2108 (for $10,103,598) were surrendered, and 3478 (for $13,333,141) were lapsed. (*Annual Report of the Superintendent of the the New York State Insurance Department*, 1873). The difference between total terminations and the three categories consists of miscellaneous causes such as "not taken.")

26. Testimony of Sheppard Homans (*Testimony Taken before the New York Assembly Committee on Insurance*, 1877 (Albany: W. S. Manning, Publisher, 1877), p. 543.

27. *Armstrong Investigation*, pp. 1702–1704.

28. For a more thorough discussion of the development of surrender values see George L. Amrhein, *The Liberalization of the Life Insurance Contract*, Ph.D. dissertation; Univ. of Pennsylvania, 1933, pp. 248–254.

29. The smaller reserve surrender value from the Connecticut Mutual came from smaller premium payments.

30. Burton J. Hendrick, *The Story of Life Insurance* (New York, 1907), pp. 38–39.

31. For example, tontine estimate (Equitable) of 1873, age 40 for fifteen-year period was $465.50. The actual dividend in 1888 was $232.86 (*Armstrong Investigation*, exhibit 920, p. 1030).

32. W. H. Price, "Life Insurance Reform in New York," *American Economic Association Quarterly* (Cambridge, Mass., 1909), p. 82.

33. Summary of the Frick Report, *The Spectator*, June 8, 1905.

34. Summary of the Frick Report.

35. *Armstrong Investigation Report*, p. 89.

36. The Provident Mutual Assurance, Investment and Loan Association (subsequently renamed the Prudential Assurance Company), J. O. Stalson, *Marketing Life Insurance*, p. 462.

37. Stalson, *Marketing Life Insurance*, p. 462.

38. Stalson, appendix 21.

39. *Armstrong Investigation*, p. 1934.

40. *Armstrong Investigation*, p. 2167. The Prudential had a lapse rate of 72 per cent in five years (*Armstrong Investigation*, p. 3709). The percentage woud be reduced somewhat by the fact that some lapsed policies are revived.

41. *Armstrong Investigation*, p. 3714.

42. Providing paid-up insurance rather than a cash surrender permitted the company to keep the accumulated premiums until the death of the insured.

43. The figures are as follows:

Gains from loading	$1,932,105
Gains from surrender and lapsed policies	$3,931,925
Gains from surplus entrees	$ 116,935
Loss from mortality	$1,540,414

(*Armstrong Investigation*, p. 1938. This is exclusive of changes in the market value of securities.)

44. *Armstrong Investigation*, pp. 3738, 4417 (figures are rounded off).

45. *Armstrong Investigation*, pp. 3738–3741.

46. On surrendered and lapsed policies the Prudential paid out 33.64 per cent of the reserves and dividends, in contrast to 83.83 per cent allowed by the John Hancock, another Industrial company. *Armstrong Investigation*, p. 3744.

47. See below, pp. 247ff.

48. The old Equitable of London, which had no agency force, sold only a few hundred policies a year.

49. Stalson, *Marketing Life Insurance*, p. 353.

50. Stalson, p. 360.

51. For good accounts of Hyde's development of the Equitable, see B. J. Hendrick, *The Story of Life Insurance*, chaps. 3 and 4, and Stalson, *Marketing Life Insurance*, chap. 15.

52. McCall, president of the New York Life, testified that Hyde had told him this was the reason for the development of tontine insurance (*Armstrong Investigation*, p. 1084).

53. *Armstrong Investigation*, p. 1163.

54. See testimony of George E. Ide, *Armstrong Investigation*, p. 3561.

55. Specifically in loan provisions.

56. *Armstrong Investigation*, p. 3568.

57. Primarily as a result of expenses of new business.

58. Stalson, *Marketing Life Insurance*, p. 468.

59. *Armstrong Investigation*, p. 14. Actually the growth of industrial insurance had just begun in 1904. In the fifteen years following the Armstrong Investigation the Metropolitan and the Prudential became the two largest insurance companies in the world. The assets of the Metropolitan today are over ten billion dollars.

60. In the early 70's commissions ranged from 20 to 30 per cent of first year's premium. By 1905 commissions were 50 to 70 per cent of first year's premium (*Armstrong Investigation*, pp. 2597–2600). In some instances they were in excess of 80 per cent (*Armstrong Investigation*, p. 1243).

61. This was not true of general agents. For example, C. H. Raymond and Company (consisting of two partners), general agents of the Mutual for a part of New York City, made $247,826.67 net profit in 1904 (*Armstrong Investigation*, p. 1230).

62. Until about 1900 when the branch manager system under direct company control became prevalent, a general agent would have a contract with a company to sell their policies and receive a certain commission rate. This general agent was semi-autonomous and hired his own agents and paid all his own expenses. See *Armstrong Investigation*, pp. 1204 and 2669 for amplification of this relationship.

63. This was in early 1900 after the New York Life had canceled an agreement not to raid each other's agents (*Armstrong Investigation*, p. 2632).

64. *Armstrong Investigation*, p. 2627.

65. Clough, *A Century of American Life Insurance*, p. 162.

66. *Armstrong Investigation*, pp. 3008–3010. The ratio in the United States was about 65 to 70 per cent.

67. *Armstrong Investigation*, pp. 3008–3010.

68. Clough, *A Century of American Life Insurance*, p. 162.

69. Hendrick, *The Story of Life Insurance*, pp. 263–264.

70. Manning, *Testimony in New York in 1877*, p. 253; also *Armstrong Investigation*, pp. 1757–1760.

71. During the seventies Vice-President McCurdy of the Mutual testified that he got out as many circulars as he could attacking Hyde and the Equitable. For details see Manning, *Testimony*, pp. 312–316.

72. *Armstrong Investigation*, p. 1758. Total expenses were less than seventeen million dollars.

73. From an investigation of the Mutual conducted by the Superintendent of Insurance and a member of the legislature in 1870. The testimony, however, was copyrighted by the Mutual to prevent its circulation.

74. For accounts of this whole affair see *Report of the Committee on Grievances Relative to the Petition of Stephen English, N. Y. Assembly Document # 155*, 1873; also *N. Y. Assembly Document # 169*, 1873.

75. Manning, *Testimony*, p. 436.

76. In 1873 the Mutual reduced premiums by 25 per cent; however, their own policyholders, instigated by inspired newspaper articles from the other companies, objected, and the scheme was withdrawn (Hendrick, *The Story of Life Insurance*, p. 183).

77. In 1878, also withdrawn soon afterwards (Hendrick, *The Story of Life Insurance*, pp. 187–188.

78. This increased hostility of policyholders, while directly oriented to specific life insurance practices, at times became an organized part of the Populist revolt and Bryanism.

79. *The Insurance Spectator*, p. 391 (June 1873).

80. Son-in-law of Thurlow Weed, New York State Republican Party leader.

81. *Assembly Document #169*, 1873. The Mutual paid Miller $2500 in this connection, p. 128.

82. *Report and Testimony on Insurance on Resolution of the Assembly to Investigate into Conduct of George W. Miller, Superintendent of the Insurance Department Relative to His Receiving Fees and Perquisites for His Use and Emolument, etc., N. Y. Assembly Document #65*, 1872.

83. *N. Y. Assembly Document #65*, p. xix; also *N. Y. Assembly Document #169*, 1873.

84. Elizar Wright, *Politics and Mysteries of Life Insurance* (New York, 1873), p. 68. Wright was the first Massachusetts Superintendent of Insurance, an eminent actuary and vigorous reformer.

85. See, for example, *Communication from the Governor Transmitting Charges against the Superintendent of the Insurance Department, New York State Senate Document #26*, 1878. See also *Senate Document #36;* 1879; on company influence over the legislature see Manning, *Testimony*, or those sections of the *Armstrong Investigation* dealing with Hamilton of the N.Y.L. and Fields of the Mutual.

86. *Armstrong Investigation*, pp. 4416, 4497.

87. Assessment insurance, another innovation of the period which enjoyed great popularity, was insurance without premiums. The members of the group were simply assessed at stated intervals to pay for the stipulated insurance of those who died. It was vigorously attacked by the large companies.

88. See *Boss Platt and the New York Machine*, Harold F. Gosnell (University of Chicago Press, 1924), chap. 10 in particular; also *The History of Tammany Hall* by Gustavus Myers (New York, 1917). For a specific relationship between the Republican machine and the Big Three insurance companies, see the testimony of Senator T. C. Platt, *Armstrong Investigation*, pp. 2573–2583.

89. L. Zartman, *The Investments of Life Insurance Companies* (New York, 1906).

90. The failure of the Charter Oak was a noteworthy example; see Manning, *Testimony*, p. 348.

91. Manning, preface and pp. 595–596.

92. However, this investigation had a long sequel. The testimony was revised and corrected by the official stenographer at the request of one W. S. Manning, who then published it along with excerpts from previous investigations. This copyrighted work was purchased by the Mutual, Equitable, and New York Life; and Manning received a "retainer" from 1878 to 1905. (*Armstrong Investigation*, p. 2556.)

93. Manning, pp. 392, 408, 595–596.

94. For an account of the war between the big three and the Connecticut Mutual see Hendrick, *The Story of Life Insurance*, chap. 5, "The Thirty Years War."

95. Hendrick, chap. 5. Greene continued his attack on the Big Three until his death in 1905 on the eve of the Armstrong Investigation.

96. For example, one agent of the Equitable alone had advances of $341,910 (*Armstrong Investigation*, p. 112).

97. *Armstrong Investigation Report*, p. 37.

98. *Armstrong Investigation Report*, p. 42.

99. *Armstrong Investigation Report*, pp. 85–88.

100. *Armstrong Investigation Report*, p. 15. Probably some of this was for politics.

101. *N. Y. Assembly Document #166*, 1883.

102. Hendrick, *The Story of Life Insurance*, p. 209.

103. *Armstrong Investigation*, p. 1479.

104. W. H. Price, "Life Insurance Reform in New York," p. 3. (It is interesting that companies that issued compromise deferred dividend policies such as the Home Life also had high net costs.)

105. See tables of net costs on ordinary, endowment, twenty-payment life, and dividends on paid-up twenty payment life in W. H. Price, "Life Insurance Reform in New York," pp. 3–4.

106. Specifically the muckrakers. The agitation for reform culminated in the Armstrong Investigation of 1905.

107. Clough, *A Century of American Life Insurance*, p. 179.

X. Henry Varnum Poor

By Alfred D. Chandler, Jr.

1. Letter, Henry V. Poor to Mary Poor, July 15, 1860, from the H. V. Poor papers. These papers are in the writer's possession.

2. There is an excellent account of John Alfred Poor's work in promoting and building the Atlantic and St. Lawrence and other Maine railroads, in Edward C. Kirkland, *Men, Cities, and Transportation* (Cambridge: Harvard University Press, 1949), I, 206–222, 465–474. See also Laura Poor, *The First International Railway* (New York, 1890), pp. 25–76. Letters in the H. V. Poor collection show Henry's close connection with his brother's work before 1849.

3. The story of Poor's intellectual development is taken from the Poor papers

and is fully developed in chap. 1 of the writer's biography of H. V. Poor, a Harvard doctoral dissertation.

4. For Poor's views on the effect of the railroad and the machine on the economic growth of the country and the progress of the race, see *American Railroad Journal*, 22:136, 152 (March 3, 10, 1849); 23:520, 521, 694 (August 17, November 2, 1850); 24:8, 33–34 (January 4, 18, 1851). Hereafter the *American Railroad Journal* will be cited as *ARJ*.

5. *ARJ*, 25:785 (December 11, 1852).

6. Poor's work in serving the investor is briefly described in A. D. Chandler, Jr., "Henry Varnum Poor: Business Analyst," *Explorations of Entrepreneurial History*, 2:181–187 (May 15, 1950).

7. This phenomenal expansion is accurately described and excellently illustrated by maps in Frederick L. Paxson, "The Railways of the Old Northwest before the Civil War," *Transactions of the Wisconsin Academy of Sciences, Arts and Letters*, XVII, pt. 1 (1914), 243–274.

8. See Frank W. Stevens, *The Beginnings of the New York Central* (New York, 1926), pp. 350–387, and *ARJ*, 26:266–267 (April 23, 1853); George H. Burgess and Miles C. Kennedy, *Centennial History of the Pennsylvania Railroad Company, 1846–1946* (New York, 1949), pp. 176–178. For more complete details see *ARJ*, 29:315–317, 330–331, 360 (May 17, 24, June 7, 1856).

9. For joint operations see Robert L. Black, *The Little Miami Railroad* (Cleveland, 1940), pp. 101–102, 106, 108; Alvin F. Harlow, *The Road of the Century* (New York, 1947), pp. 361–363; *ARJ*, 27:412–422 (July 8, 1854); *ARJ*, 29:545–546 (August 30, 1856); *ARJ*, 30:225 (April 12, 1857); *ARJ*, 31:433 (July 10, 1858).

10. For good examples of and discussion about these early conventions, see *ARJ*, 27:538–539, 605, 664, 758–759, 810 (August 26, September 23, October 21, December 2, December 23, 1854); *ARJ*, 28:197–198, 249 (March 31, April 21, 1855).

11. These generalizations are made from data found chiefly in H. V. Poor, *History of the Railroads and the Canals of the United States* (New York, 1860); *Department of Interior, United States Census Office, Tenth Census, 1880, Report on the Agencies of Transportation*, especially p. 290; statistics in *ARJ* and in the *Railway Times* (Boston). Especially useful in *ARJ* are the share lists in the mid-fifties and a statistical chart prepared by George C. Schaeffer, the best statistical compilation on American railroads between Von Gerstner's work in 1840 and Poor's in the fifties, *ARJ*, 20:169 (March 17, 1847).

12. It is illuminating to compare the following operational statistics for the Western Railroad of Massachusetts running between Albany and Worcester, one of the very largest operating units in the country in 1850, and those of the Erie in 1855. Data on the Western (including the Albany and West Stockbridge)is from *Annual Reports of Railroad Corporations in the Commonwealth of Massachusetts, 1850* (Boston, 1851), pp. 240–241; for the Erie from *Annual Report of the Railroad Commissioners of the State of New York. . . 1855* (Albany, 1856), II, 195, 209.

	The Western, 1850	The Erie, 1855
Miles run, passengers	256,758	1,464,839
Miles run, freight	453,111	1,676,500
No. of passengers carried in cars	467,086	1,033,922
Ton of freight carried in cars	261,296	842,054
Expenses	$607,549	$2,625,744
Salaries and wages paid — nearest thousand (excluding pres., treas., and supt.)	$175,000	$ 795,000

13. *Reports of the President and the Superintendent of the New York and Erie Railroad Company to the Stockholders for the Year Ending September 30, 1855* (New York, n.d.), p. 34. Hereafter cited as *Erie Report, 1855.* Moreover, as Henry Poor pointed out, the work of an operative on a railroad was on the whole much more skilled and required much more responsibility than that of a mill hand, *ARJ*, 27:808 (December 23, 1854).

14. *ARJ*, 26:609–611, 826–827 (September 24, December 24, 1853); *ARJ* 27:147–148 (March 11, 1856); also *Report of the Directors of the New York and Erie Railroad Company to the Stockholders, November, 1853* (New York, 1853), pp. 47–48. Hereafter cited as *Erie Report, 1853.*

15. For comments on Massachusetts roads see *ARJ*, 28:721–723 (November 17, 1855). At this time the *Journal's* assistant editor for engineering, Zerah Colburn, turned his attention to urging the New England roads to adopt the latest technical developments. See especially his articles entitled "Concentration of Power as Applied to the Leading New England Roads," beginning with *ARJ*, 27:193, (February 18, 1854); and "The Economy of Railroads as Affected by the Adoption of Locomotive Power — Addressed to the Railroad Interests of New England," beginning with *ARJ*, 27:632 (October 7, 1854).

16. *ARJ*, 27:147–148 (March 11, 1854). See also *ARJ*, 29:264–265 (April 22, 1856).

17. *ARJ*, 17:548–549 (September 2, 1854); see also *ARJ*, 28:129–130 (March 3, 1855). McCallum's brilliant organizing ability was put to good use during the Civil War when he was commissioned "director and superintendent" of all the Union railroads necessary for the successful prosecution of the war. Before the end of the war he was operating with great efficiency over two thousand miles of line; Dumas Malone, ed., *Dictionary of American Biography* (New York, 1933), XI, 565–566.

18. *ARJ*, 27:548 (September 2, 1854); this editorial discusses fully McCallum's initial reforms.

19. See the *Erie Report, 1855,* pp. 45–51. For Poor's emphatic approval of this reform which he urged all roads to adopt, see, besides the editorial cited in note 18, *ARJ*, 29:40–41, 473, 712 (January 19, July 26, November 8, 1856). For other good comments on this improvement, see *Annual Report of the Railroad Commissioners of New York. . . 1855*, I, xxxii–xxxiv, xxxvii–xxxix.

20. *ARJ*, 27:548 (September 2, 1854).

21. This chart is described in *ARJ*, 29:280 (May 3, 1856). Poor noted that, "It was first suggested by McCallum for reference merely, but has been lithographed and is offered for sale at one dollar." McCallum's system of organization, communication, and information is fully described in the *Erie Report, 1855.* For Poor's comments on this report, see *ARJ*, 29:225–226 (April 12, 1856); see also *ARJ*, 28:568 (September 8, 1855). This outstanding report was highly praised by Captain Douglas Galton, head of the Railway Department of England's Board of Trade and one of the world's foremost railroad experts, who strongly recommended that British railroads adopt McCallum's management methods and his use of the telegraph; Captain Douglas Galton, *Report to the Lords of the Committee of Privy Council for Trade and Foreign Plantations on the Railways of the United States*, London, 1857), pp. 20–23, 27. McCallum's report also won approval in the popular press and periodicals; see, for example, *The Atlantic Monthly*, 2:642–644 (November, 1858).

22. *ARJ*, 29:184 (March 22, 1856). In this article Poor describes the careful and minute organization of the Susquehanna Repair Shop; see also *Colburn's Railroad Advocate* (New York), October 27, 1855, hereafter cited as the *Advocate.*

23. There was much controversy over the requirement to wear uniforms. Poor's

reply to an article in the *Railroad Record*, Cincinnati, disapproving of McCallum's uniform regulations gives a good picture of the requirements and the controversy; *ARJ*, 28:40 (September 1, 1855).

24. *Erie Report, 1855*, p. 40.

25. *Erie Report, 1855*, p. 51.

26. *ARJ*, 28:675 (October 27, 1855).

27. *Erie Report, 1855*, p. 52. McCallum's reporting system like the organization plan and the use of the telegraph had been initiated in part on the Erie before McCallum became General Superintendent (see *Erie Report, 1853*, pp. 46–53), but he greatly improved the initial plans and unified them so that they were all integral parts of one great operating scheme.

28. *Erie Report, 1855*, p. 53.

29. *ARJ*, 28:497–499, 817–818 (August 11, December 29, 1855); *ARJ*, 29:161–163, 263–265 (March 15, April 26, 1856); *ARJ*, 32:408 (June 25, 1859).

30. For comments on the value of engineering reports, see *ARJ*, 28:497–499, 547 (August 11, September 1, 1855); examples of such analyses are *ARJ*, 31:296–297 (May 8, 1858); *ARJ*, 32:534 (August 20, 1859). The *Advocate*, which claimed to speak for the engineers and other skilled operatives, favored monthly reports, stating that: "Although, perhaps, for a purely selfish purpose, the monthly reports acknowledge the full doings of each engineer, they still serve as an honorable stimulant to exertion." *Advocate*, November 24, 1855.

31. Besides the Erie, the New York Central, and the Pennsylvania, the Baltimore and Ohio, the Illinois Central, and the Cleveland and Pittsburgh had their monthly engine reports printed in the public press. See for examples and comment, *Advocate*, October 13, 20, November 17, December 15, 1855, January 13, 1856; such engine reports are scattered through *ARJ* from 1855 on.

32. For an excellent editorial on the essential need for understanding "the absolute and comparative cost of different kinds of traffic" as the only basis for rate-making, see *ARJ*, 28:817–818 (December 29, 1855); see also *ARJ*, 29:120, 161–163, 193–195, 225–226, 229 (February 23, March 15, 29, April 12, 1856); *ARJ*, 30:456–457 (July 18, 1857); *ARJ*, 32:680 (October 22, 1859), and *Erie Report, 1855*, pp. 78–80.

33. A brief discussion of the high fare — low fare controversy is in Kirkland, *Men, Cities, and Transportation*, I, 357–361. For Poor's remarks, see *ARJ*, 29:145–146, 161–162, 177–179, 193–195, 264–265; (March 7, 15, 22, 29, April 26, 1856); compare these articles with *Railway Times*, March 20, 1856; January 8, 1857; *Railroad Record* (hereafter cited as the *Record*) 5:365, 553–554 (July 30, October 22, 1857); see also *ARJ*, 28:721–722 (November 17, 1855); *ARJ*, 30:456 (July 18, 1857).

34. *ARJ*, 30:456 (July 18, 1857).

35. Ellet's best work is found in his *Report on the Tariff Toll for the Virginia Central Railroad* (Washington, 1858); for Jervis, see his *Railway Property: A Treatise on the Construction and Management of Railways* (New York, 1861), esp. pp. 203–220, 251–256, and 271–276. Colburn's views are scattered throughout *ARJ* in 1853 and 1854 and in his own journal, the *Advocate*, between 1854 and 1857; see also note 15. Except for McCallum, these men like their post-Civil War successors were primarily interested in bettering methods of rates, cost, and expense determination; in improving accounting and statistics; and in making the most efficient use of present equipment and in devising new and more efficient equipment. Unlike Poor they made few significant studies of the broad principles of management.

36. Alpheus T. Mason, *Brandeis, A Free Man's Life* (New York, 1946), ch. xx;

see also Frederick A. Cleveland and Fred W. Powell, *Railroad Finance* (New York, 1912), pp. 158–165.

37. Poor was in England from May until September 1858. While there he had long and fruitful discussions with such leading railroad men as Douglas Galton, Daniel Gooch, Sir Charles Fox, and Robert Stephenson; see letters Henry V. Poor to Mary Poor, May 29, June 10, 13, 20, 27, July 1, 18, August 2, 1858. For the importance of the last three of these men in railroad history see Leslie Stephens and Sidney Lee, *Dictionary of National Biography* (London, 1908), VII, 533–534; XI, 473–474; XVIII, 1075–1076. At the same time Poor discussed the more general aspects of railroading with James Wilson, editor of the *Economist*, J. L. Sampson, financial editor of the London *Times*, and with such important bankers as George Peabody, Robert Benson, Thomas Smith, and Curtis M. Lampson; see letters cited above and also those to Mary Poor dated July 5, 25, 29, 1858. Poor recorded his findings in a series of letters published in the *ARJ* in September and October 1858.

38. See the *Report of the President of the New York and Erie Railroad to the Stockholders for the Year Ending September 30, 1857* (New York, 1858), pp. 7–8; *ARJ*, 29:584, 641–642 (September 13, October 11, 1856); *Record*, 4:594 (November 13, 1856); 5:36 (March 12, 1857). For somewhat similar strikes on the Baltimore and Ohio, see *Record*, 5:169, 185 (May 7, 14, 1857).

39. The call for the meeting is given in full in the *Record*, 4:689 (December 25, 1856); see also *Record*, 4:722, 738 (January 8, 15, 1857); and *Advocate* (October 27, November 3, 24, December 8, 22, 1855, August 25, 1856).

40. *ARJ*, 29:341, 342 (October 11, 1856).

41. *ARJ*, 32:40–41 (January 15, 1859). For further significant comments on labor relations, see *ARJ*, 31:56–57 (January 23, 1858); *ARJ*, 32:72–73, 488 (January 29, July 30, 1859). The *Record* had the same views as the *Journal* on this matter (e.g. *Record*, 4:721–722, January 8, 1857), while the *Railway Times* strongly disagreed. The *Times* referring to the Erie strike of 1856 commented: "Reduce rational, immortal man, of aspiring genius to mere machines! Horrible! Intolerable! So they argued and spouted and got sympathy of a good many fools," *Times*, March 26, 1857; see also *Times*, November 20, 1856, January 1, November 14, 1857.

42. *ARJ*, 32:424 (July 2, 1859). See also *ARJ*, 32:370 (June 11, 1859).

43. *ARJ*, 31:577–578 (September 11, 1858). For other comments on bureaucratization of railroad management, see *ARJ*, 30:408–409 (June 27, 1857); *ARJ*, 31:152–153, 560–561 (March 6, September 4, 1858); *ARJ*, 32:40, 370 (January 15, June 11, 1859).

44. *ARJ*, 31:578 (September 11, 1858).

45. For comments on leadership and responsibility of top management, see *ARJ*, 27:745–747 (December 1, 1854); *ARJ*, 28:722 (November 17, 1855); *ARJ*, 31:88–89, 104–105, 136–137, 153, 520, 560–562, 593–594 (February 6, 13, 27, March 6, August 14, September 4, 18, 1858); *ARJ*, 32:40–41, 368–369 (January 15, June 11, 1859).

46. *ARJ*, 32:561–562 (September 4, 1858).

47. *ARJ*, 32:562 (September 4, 1858).

48. *ARJ*, 31:168 (March 13, 1858); see also *ARJ*, 26:808 (December 23, 1854); *ARJ*, 30:369–370, 408–409 (June 3, 27, 1857); *ARJ*, 31:98, 104, 136–137, 152–153, 168, 577–578 (February 13, 24, March 6, 13, Sept. 11, 1858); and an excellent letter from a British subscriber describing the same situation in England, *ARJ*, 32:643 (October 9, 1859).

49. *ARJ*, 31:593 (September 18, 1858). See also *ARJ*, 31:460–461 (September 4, 1858); *ARJ*, 32:370 (June 11, 1859).

50. Comments on the stockholder's position are scattered throughout *ARJ*; for some of the best articles see *ARJ*, 27:529, 537–538, 692, 745–747 (August 26, October 7, November 4, December 2, 1854); *ARJ*, 30:408–409, 530, 536, 568–569 (June 27, August 22, September 5, 1857); *ARJ*, 31:97–99, 152–153 (February 13, March 6, 1858); *ARJ*, 32:370 (June 11, 1859).

51. See citations from *ARJ* in note 53 and also *Record*, 4:258, 433 (June 1, September 4, 1856), and the *Railway Times*, December 22, 1857.

52. *ARJ*, 32:370 (June 11, 1859); also *ARJ*, 31:97 (February 13, 1858); for recognition of the same situation in England see *ARJ*, 32:641–643 (October 9, 1859).

53. *ARJ*, 30:584 (September 12, 1857); also *ARJ*, 26:808 (December 23, 1854); Jervis, *Railway Property*, pp. 59, 299.

54. *ARJ*, 31:562 (September 4, 1858).

55. Like his comments on stockholders Poor's discussion of the Board of Directors is found scattered throughout the *Journal*. His best editorials are: *ARJ*, 27:433–434, 529, 692, 745–747 (July 15, August 26, November 4, December 2, 1854); *ARJ*, 28:104 (February 17, 1855); *ARJ*, 29:264–265 (April 26, 1856); *ARJ*, 30:392, 536, 554–557 (June 27, August 22, 29, 1857); *ARJ*, 31:88–89, 104–105, 121–122, 152–153 (February 6, 13, 20, March 6, 1858); *ARJ*, 32:370 (June 11, 1859).

56. *ARJ*, 32:370 (June 11, 1859); also *ARJ*, 31:136–137 (February 27, 1858).

57. *ARJ*, 31:153 (March 6, 1858); also *ARJ*, 32:600 (September 17, 1859).

58. *ARJ*, 30:568 (September 5, 1857).

59. *ARJ*, 31:153 (March 6, 1858); also *ARJ*, 30:408–409 (June 27, 1857).

60. For example see *Railway Times*, June 13, March 14, April 11, 1850, September 14, 1854, October 12, 1854, July 14, 1855, December 12, 1857; *Record*, 5:413 August 20, 1858); *United States Railroad Register and Mining Gazette* (hereafter cited as the *Register*), 3:116, 148, 196 (September 5, October 3, November 14, 1857); 4:46 (February 12, 1858); *Hunt's Merchant's Magazine*, 34:622–623 (May, 1856); 39:750 (December, 1858).

61. The only other writer of the day to consider both the nature of the corporation and company management was John B. Jervis in his *Railway Property*. He did not, however, explicitly tie the two together as carefully as did Poor. Like Poor and others Jervis feared that lack of control by the stockholder over the directors made corporate investment unsafe for them, stating that: "It is a question of grave import whether our civilization had reached a degree that can permit reasonable confidence in this kind of property, especially to small proprietors." (*Railway Property*, p. 329.) An English writer had made the similar remark that a higher "state of civilization" was necessary if the corporation was to function properly, *ARJ*, 31:641–643 (October 9, 1858).

62. Emphasizing the differences between the effects of dishonest and incompetent directors, Poor wrote: "The speculations of the former are usually necessarily small in amount, while the mistakes of the latter may, and often do, involve the entire sum invested in the road," *ARJ*, 31:153 (March 6, 1858).

63. Besides these two major reforms Poor suggested many minor, more technical ones. These dealt primarily with improving the caliber and curbing the power of the Board of Directors — the weakest organ in the corporate form of business. See esp. *ARJ*, 27:785–786 (December 16, 1854); *ARJ*, 30:376–377, 408–409, 729 (June 13, 27, November 14, 1857); *ARJ*, 32:440 (July 9, 1859).

64. *ARJ*, 27:808–809 (December 23, 1854); for a full discussion of the contract or lease system see also *ARJ*, 27:692–693 (November 4, 1854); *ARJ*, 18:722 (November 17, 1855); see also citations under notes 70 and 71 and also *ARJ*, 32:408, 600 (June 25,

September 17, 1859). Poor seems to have been the first to suggest this reform in print. The *Railway Times* mentions such a plan first in its issue of August 2, 1855, calling it "new to most men and almost original. . . " James M. Whiton, *Railroads and Their Management* (Concord, N. H., 1856), p. 62, mentions it as a new idea in 1856, while a similar plan appeared in 1858; see *Hunt's Merchant's Magazine*, 39:753 (December, 1858). By the mid-fifties the premium system, especially for locomotive engineers, was coming into practice and being used with good results on the Erie, the Pennsylvania, the Reading, and the Boston, Concord and Montreal; *Advocate*, December 15, 1855, January 5, 1856. It later became standard practice on American roads; see Cleveland and Powell, *Railroad Finance*, pp. 158–159.

65. *ARJ*, 27:809 (December 23, 1854).

66. *ARJ*, 22:392 (June 23, 1849).

67. This is described in *Herapath's Railroad and Commercial Journal* (London), 16:564–565, 577, 582–583 (June 3, 10, 1854); see also the *Railway Times*, June 29, October 26, 1854; May 3, August 5, 1855.

68. Repair and maintenance by contract on the New York canals had been authorized by a law passed in 1854 which was put into effect at once; see *New York State, Canal Commissioners, Annual Report, 1854* (Albany, 1855), pp. 141–146. See also *Railway Times*, July 26, 1855, January 3, 10, 1856.

69. *ARJ*, 27:808 (December 23, 1854).

70. For the importance of the British trip on the development of Poor's views concerning the contract system, see *ARJ*, 31:561–562, 577–578, 593–594 (September 4, 11, 18, 1858).

71. *Twentieth Annual Report of the President and Directors of the Stockholders of the Philadelphia, Wilmington, and Baltimore Railroad Company for the year ending November 30, 1857* (Philadelphia, 1858), p. 17. Pages 17–18 of this report and page 15 of the *Nineteenth Annual Report* and pages 15–16 of the *Twenty-First Annual Report* give the best summary of the contract system in operation. For Poor's full comments on the working of this system on Felton's road, see *ARJ*, 32:488–489 (July 30, 1859); see also *ARJ*, 32:503, 504 (August 6, 1859).

72. *ARJ*, 32:353, 376–377 (June 4, July 2, 1859). For fuller details of the contract see New York *Tribune*, June 8, 1859.

73. *ARJ*, 32:456–457, 472, 513–514, 520, 580–581 (July 16, 23, August 13, September 10, 1859); see also New York *Times*, June 30, 1859; New York *Tribune*, August 11, 1859, and Edward H. Mott, *Between the Ocean and the Lakes, the Story of Erie* (New York, 1908), p. 129.

74. For example, *ARJ*, 22:502, 580–581 (August 11, September 15, 1849).

75. Examples of Poor's comments on publicity and the investor see *ARJ*, 25:785 (December 11, 1852); *ARJ*, 26:136, 170 (February 26, March 12, 1853).

76. *ARJ*, 32:600 (September 17, 1859).

77. *ARJ*, 30:568 (September 5, 1857). Poor's editorials and comments on the need for and the undoubted effectiveness of publicity to reform railroad administration and operation appear constantly in the *Journal*. For the best of his views see *ARJ*, 26:640–641 (October 8, 1853); *ARJ*, 27:637–638, 692, 777–778, 785–786, 817 (October 7, November 4, December 9, 16, 30, 1854); *ARJ*, 28:9, 105, 232–233 (January 6, February 17, April 14, 1855); *ARJ*, 29:264–265, 626 (April 26, October 4, 1856); *ARJ*, 30:136, 392, 408–409, 568, 593 (February 28, June 20, 27, September 5, 19, 1857). Publicity was advocated by other railroad commentators besides Poor. Nearly all the railroad periodicals supported it. Even railroad executives claimed to favor this reform; see, for example, the views of Charles Moran, President of Erie in

ARJ, 32:657–658, 690–692 (October 15, 29, 1859). But the whole emphasis of the writing and legislation on publicity in the 1850's was on protection of the investor and public. Few besides Poor saw publicity as a method to improve management.

78. *ARJ*, 31:99 (February 13, 1858).

79. *ARJ*, 31:137 (February 27, 1858).

80. *ARJ*, 31:153 (March 6, 1858).

81. *ARJ*, 30:392 (June 20, 1857).

82. *ARJ*, 31:424 (July 3, 1858); see also *ARJ*, 33:372 (March 31, 1860). Massachusetts first began publishing annual reports of railroads in 1837 but it was not until 1846 that full, detailed, and uniform regulations covering reports were set up and not until 1849 that abstracts and statistical summaries were made of these reports. The other New England states followed Massachusetts' example by passing special legislation in the early fifties requiring reports and publishing statistics from them. Poor considered the Vermont law the best of these. Pennsylvania passed similar legislation in 1859, but only after a long struggle in the legislature. Several of the western states including Ohio, Illinois, Iowa, and Michigan followed New York's example and made provision for reporting in their general railroad laws passed in the early 1850's, but unlike New York they made no effort to carry out these provisions. The southern states like Virginia, North Carolina, Tennessee, Missouri were able to get better returns because careful reporting was a prerequisite to state financial assistance.

83. *ARJ*, 26:640–641 (October 8, 1853); also *ARJ*, 26:153 (March 5, 1853). Poor expressed this same view when commenting on the British requirements for railroad reports and independent auditing; *ARJ*, 31:561 (September 4, 1858); see also *ARJ*, 31:642–643 (October 9, 1858).

84. See *ARJ*, 26:153, 640–641 (March 5, October 8, 1853); *ARJ*, 30:217, 536, 593 (April 25, August 22, September 19, 1857); *ARJ*, 32:658–659 (October 15, 1859). The southern roads included the Wilmington and Weldon, the South Carolina, the Georgia, the Georgia Central, and the Atlanta and LaGrange.

85. *ARJ*, 29:264–265 (April 26, 1856); *ARJ*, 31:97–98 (February 13, 1858); *ARJ*, 32:360 (June 4, 1859).

86. *ARJ*, 31:610 (September 25, 1858).

87. *ARJ*, 31:610.

88. *ARJ*, 31:98 (February 13, 1858). Poor's publicity plan was proposed and described in the February 13, 1858 issue of the *ARJ*, pp. 97–99, 104–105, and fully expounded in subsequent editorials of February 27, March 6, 13, 1858, pp. 136–137, 152–154, 161, 168. These editorials are the best Poor wrote on publicity as a major reform. The "Interrogatories" are given in installments from February 20 to March 13 inclusive. The questionnaire is basically an expansion and combination of the data required by Massachusetts and New York and an earlier questionnaire that Poor sent out to the railroads in 1854 (see Chandler, *Explorations in Entrepreneurial History*, 2:200–202 for a copy of the 1854 questionnaire). Many of the financial questions later went into the questionnaires that were used in making up Poor's *Manuals*. There was comparatively little comment on Poor's plan in the press; but for a strong criticism, see *Register*, 4:58, 66 (March 6, 20, 1858).

89. *ARJ*, 31:99 (February 13, 1858).

90. *ARJ*, 31:98, 104 (February 13, 1858).

91. *ARJ*, 32:584–585, 600, 657–658, 673–674 (September 10, 17, October 15, 22, 1859); *ARJ*, 33:766 (September 1, 1860); *ARJ*, 34:120–121 (February 9, 1861).

92. These statistical analyses ran weekly in *ARJ* from August 6 to October 5,

1859 inclusive. For a further analysis of these and other statistics, see *ARJ*, 32:408, 489, 534, 568, 680 (June 25, July 30, August 20, September 3, October 22, 1859).

93. Poor, *History of Railroads and Canals*, p. v.

94. H. V. Poor, *Manual of the Railroads of the United States, for 1871–1872* (New York, 1871), p. xxxi. *U. S. Congress. Senate, Select Committee on Interstate Commerce. . . . Regulation of Interstate Commerce by Congress* (Washington, D. C., 1886), II, 232.

95. For good examples of such warnings, see *ARJ*, 30:584, 712 (September 12, November 7, 1857); *ARJ*, 31:88, 153–154 (March 6, February 6, 1858).

96. For Poor's remarks on Moran as a prime example of the failure of the financier in management, see *ARJ*, 30:40–41, 72–73, 88, 353, 376–377, 424, 657–658 (January 15, 29, February 5, June 4, 11, July 2, October 15, 1858).

XI. The Business Elite in Business Bureaucracies

By William Miller

1. *Dictionary of American Biography*, essay on Baer.

2. As he described himself in *Who's Who in America*.

3. Alpheus T. Mason, *Brandeis* (New York: The Viking Press, 1946), p. 86.

4. Adolf A. Berle, Jr., "Modern Legal Profession," in *Encyclopedia of the Social Sciences*, IX, 341. See also John R. Dos Passos, *The American Lawyer* (New York: Banks Law Publishing Co., 1907); Robert T. Swaine, *The Cravath Firm* (3 vols.; New York: Privately printed. 1946, 1948); and J. Willard Hurst, *The Growth of American Law* (Boston: Little, Brown and Co., 1950), chap. xiii.

5. Swaine, *Cravath Firm*, II, 127.

6. H. H. Gerth and C. Wright Mills (trans. and eds.), *From Max Weber* (New York: Oxford University Press, 1946), p. 200.

7. Talcott Parsons (trans. and ed.), *Max Weber: The Theory of Social and Economic Organization* (New York: Oxford University Press, 1947), pp. 339, 340. This, of course, need not mean that those with wealth could not also acquire the requisite knowledge.

8. Gerth and Mills, *From Max Weber*, p. 226 (italics Weber's). On the extent to which big business in most recent times takes this "leveling of the governed" for granted, see "Is Anybody Listening?", *Fortune*, September 1950.

9. Parsons, *Max Weber*, p. 339. Weber also says in this connection: "Every bureaucracy seeks to increase the superiority of the professionally informed by keeping their knowledge and intentions secret. Bureaucratic administration always tends to be an administration of 'secret sessions': in so far as it can, it hides its knowledge and action from criticism." (Gerth and Mills, *From Max Weber*, p. 233.)

10. The persistence of "anti-trust" agitation as a political topic in the United States is one index of the need to conciliate the public. At the time of the passage of the Sherman Act in 1890, conservative Republican Senator Orville Platt said: "The conduct of the Senate . . . has not been in the line of honest preparation of a bill to prohibit and punish trusts . . . the whole effort has been to get some bill headed: 'A Bill to Punish Trusts' with which to go to the country." It was this Act of which Mr. Dooley said at the time of the formation of the United States Steel Corporation in 1901: "What looks like a stone-wall to a layman is a triumphal arch

to a corporation lawyer." On the Interstate Commerce Act of 1887, Senator Nelson W. Aldrich said: The act was "a delusion and a sham . . . an empty menace to great interests, made to answer the clamor of the ignorant and the unreasoning." (Quoted from Thomas C. Cochran and William Miller, *The Age of Enterprise*, New York: The MacMillan Co., 1942, pp. 171–172.) On more recent times see J. K. Galbraith, "Monopoly and Concentration of Economic Power," in Howard S. Ellis, ed., *A Survey of Contemporary Economics* (Philadelphia: The Blakiston Co., 1948), pp. 115–124.

11. See footnote, pp. 286–287, above.

12. Here and elsewhere, "peak" or "listed" position, company, or industry refers to the presidency, chairmanship, or partnership which, as indicated in the footnote on pp. 286–287, made men eligible for this study.

13. On the importance of businessmen's dynastic aspirations, see Joseph A. Schumpeter, *Capitalism, Socialism and Democracy* (New York: Harper & Brothers, 1942), pp. 156ff.

14. Since all the men studied were selected because of their *business* positions, the group of lawyers includes only those who actually were president or board chairman of business corporations in 1901–1910. No regular members of "law factories" are included. Thus the group is not representative in size or composition of the whole class of business or corporation lawyers. Since this is so and since even most of the lawyers included here had professional rather than distinctly business careers, little more will be said of them. See William Miller, "American Lawyers in Business and Politics," *Yale Law Journal*, Vol. LX, No. 1, January, 1951.

15. *Dictionary of American Biography*, essay on Mellen.

16. Eight of these men who themselves never started a business were part of a large panel of outstanding men in all fields who in 1902 were asked if they would advise "a young man of experience and ability, at a fair salary, to go into business for himself." One of the eight gave no answer. The remaining seven said "yes" even if it was "upon borrowed capital." (Nathaniel C. Fowler, Jr., *The Boy: How to Help Him Succeed*, Boston: Oakwood Publishing Co., 1902, pp. 167ff.)

17. Andrew Carnegie, *The Empire of Business* (New York: Doubleday, Page & Co., 1902), p. 190.

18. It may be true, as Robert K. Merton says in summarizing Weber's theory, that "bureaucracy maximizes vocational security." (Robert K. Merton, *Social Theory and Social Structure*, Glencoe, Ill.: The Free Press, 1949, p. 152). But in business at least this is relatively certain only in comparison to the "vocational security" of the ordinary worker. It has yet to be shown that the bureaucrat, even on the highest levels, is more secure than the great "captain of industry," for example, either in his hold on his status or in the psychological attributes of it. Even while the bureaucrat may be supposed, in Weber's terms, to be "set for a *'career'* . . . in which *tenure for life* is presupposed," Weber notes that "this is not recognized as the official's right to the possession of the office." (Gerth and Mills, *From Max Weber*, pp. 202, 203. Italics Weber's.) I am aware that this complicates the ideal bureaucratic picture with "patrimonial" factors; but it seems that in business at least the hierarchical nature of ascent may not be altogether divorced from the patrimonial aspects of tenure. Indeed, it may well be that the higher a bureaucrat goes the more dependent is his tenure on patrimonial factors.

19. Will C. Ferril (ed.), *Sketches of Colorado* (Denver: Western Press Bureau Co., 1911), p. 179.

20. *Independent*, 61:1491 (December 20, 1906).

21. *World Today*, 13:829 (August 1907).

22. Clarence W. Barron, *More They Told Barron* (New York: Harper & Brothers, 1931), pp. 153, 168.

23. "More Facts About Presidents," in *The Corporate Director* (November 1950). Virtually all of these presidents were of firms large enough to be listed on the New York Stock Exchange.

24. Carnegie, *Empire of Business*, p. 190.

25. The Burlington Archives, Newberry Library, Chicago, Ill. I am indebted for this to Professor Thomas C. Cochran, who has permitted me to see the material he has collected for his forthcoming book on the railroad executive in the nineteenth century.

26. See the discussion in Herbert N. Casson, *The Romance of Steel* (New York: A. S. Barnes & Co. 1907), pp. 145ff.

27. Barron, *More They Told Barron*, p. 218. The rumors about Schwab's heavy gambling are said to have speeded his departure from the Steel Corporation (*Barron*, p. 86). He was succeeded by Corey, one of whose "closest friends" is reported to have told *World's Work*, (6:4027, June 10, 1903) that "Corey's life is tempered to his business duties, simple, regular, such a life as others of the men who are doing great things persist in leading. Nor is there any danger of his 'going up in the air.'" Casson also wrote of Corey in 1907: "He has few interests, if any, outside of his office. Not only is he president of the biggest corporation in this world — he is part of the mechanism itself. . . He has sunk himself, his personal likes and dislikes, in the socialized steel business." (*Romance of Steel*, p. 160). Yet that very year Corey had left his wife for the musical comedy singer Mabelle Gilman, and was eventually involved in a sensational divorce.

Allan Nevins notes that Rockefeller's partner, Henry H. Rogers, "would have liked to head the Standard himself [when Rockefeller stepped down], though he knew that his gambling propensities, diversity of interests, and unhappy public reputation made any thought of his selection preposterous." (Nevins, *John D. Rockefeller*, 2 vols.; New York: Charles Scribner's Sons, 1940, p. 437.)

28. *Harper's Weekly*, 52:11 (June 20, 1908). For the era in which career men were hardly likely to get to the top even in railroading, see Edward C. Kirkland, *Men, Cities, and Transportation* (2 vols.; Cambridge: Harvard University Press, 1948), II, 452–454.

29. *St. Louis Post Dispatch*, February 1, 1912.

30. Louis D. Brandeis, *Business — A Profession* (Boston: Small, Maynard & Co., 1914), p.l. For Higginson's views, see Samuel A. Eliot, *Biographical History of Massachusetts* (Boston: Massachusetts Biography Society, 1911–1918), vol. IX (no pagination).

31. See Parsons, *Max Weber*, p. 331. For an illuminating account of the nature of this "war" in a man who eventually became president of the New Jersey Bell Telephone Company and one of the most enlightening writers on bureaucracy in business, see Chester I. Barnard, "Collectivism and Individualism in Industrial Management," an address delivered in 1934 at the Fourth Annual Economic Conference for Engineers at the Stevens Institute of Technology Engineering Camp, and printed by the Institute.

32. *Nation's Business* (October 1947), pp. 40ff.

33. *Business Week* (January 28, 1950), p. 21.

34. See Chester I. Barnard, *The Functions of the Executive* (Cambridge: Harvard University Press, 1938), pp. 224–225 and chap. xvii, esp. pp. 272, 278; Talcott Par-

sons, "The Professions and Social Structure," in Talcott Parsons, *Essays in Sociological Theory Pure and Applied* (Glencoe, Ill.: The Free Press, 1949), p. 198; and Schumpeter, *Capitalism, Socialism and Democracy, passim*.

35. Cambridge: Harvard University Press, 1914; see especially chap. xxi, 558–560. See also Frederick W. Taylor, "Shop Management," first published in 1903 and reprinted with other works of Taylor's in *Scientific Management* (New York: Harper & Brothers, 1947). See pp. 17, 18.

36. New York: Harper & Brothers, 1911. See especially chap. ii where the prevailing system of "initiative and incentive" is contrasted with Taylor's "scientific management." In the former, in the vernacular of our own time, management did not manage, but left the initiative and planning of production to the worker.

37. Edward C. Mack, *Peter Cooper* (New York: Duell, Sloan and Pearce, 1949), p. 109.

38. These quotations are from John T. Flynn, *God's Gold* (New York: Harcourt, Brace & Co., 1932), p. 336; Matthew Josephson, *The Robber Barons* (New York: Harcourt, Brace & Co., 1934), p. 338; Barron, *More They Told Barron*, p. 77; *Dictionary of American Biography*, essay on Rogers; John D. Rockefeller, *Random Reminiscences of Men and Events* (New York: Doubleday, Page & Co., 1909), p. 6.

39. Cf. note 27, above. Of Archbold, who succeeded Rockefeller when Rogers wanted that role for himself, Nevins writes: "Never as cautious as Rockefeller, he had learned from him that in a multitude of councillors there is wisdom; he believed in a large executive committee, and insisted that it hold daily meetings to present a variety of points of view. . . He reserved his judgment until the end, and usually based it upon a consensus of opinion." (Nevins, *Rockefeller*, II, 433.)

40. *Dictionary of American Biography*, essay on Rogers; Nevins, *Rockefeller*, II, 436. On Rogers generally, see Barron, *More They Told Barron*, pp. 76, 89.

41. *New York World*, March 27, 1898; and from an unidentified newsclip in the *New York Times* "morgue" but obviously from the same period and probably based on the same interview as that reported in the *World*. For the large holdings of the Matthiessen family, see Dewing, *Corporate Promotions*, chap. iv.

42. Kenneth Burke, *The Grammar of Motives* (New York: Prentice-Hall, Inc., 1945). This entire work is given to an elaboration of the interrelations of Burke's "pentad" — act, scene, agent, agency, purpose.

43. See N. R. Danielian, *A. T. & T.* (New York: The Vanguard Press, 1939), pp. 45, 70–71.

44. Chester I. Barnard, *Organization and Management* (Cambridge: Harvard University Press, 1949), p. 210.

45. Barnard, *Functions of the Executive*, p. 224.

46. Wheaton J. Lane, *Commodore Vanderbilt* (New York: Alfred A. Knopf, Inc., 1942), p. 330.

47. Fowler, *The Boy*, pp. 101–102.

48. "The Thirty Thousand Managers," *Fortune* (February 1940), p. 62.

49. David Riesman, "The Saving Remnant: A Study of Character," in John W. Chase, ed., *Years of the Modern* (New York: Longmans, Green and Co., 1949), p. 131.

50. Fowler, *The Boy*, p. 282.

51. *Dictionary of American Biography*, essay on Jeffery.

52. Quoted from C. Wright Mills, "The Contributions of Sociology to Studies of Industrial Relations," in *Proceedings of the First Annual Meeting*, Industrial Re-

lations Research Association (1949: Champaign, Ill.: by the Association), pp. 214–215.

53. *Dictionary of American Biography*, essay on Jeffery.

54. Barnard, *Functions of the Executive*, p. 148; Danielian, *A. T. & T.*, pp. 43–44.

55. Barron, *More They Told Barron*, pp. 83–84.

56. A discussion of this theme may be found in C. Wright Mills, *White Collar* (New York: Oxford University Press, 1951), pp. 182–188.

57. Charles A. and Mary R. Beard, *The Rise of American Civilization* (New York: The Macmillan Co., 1930, 2 vols. in 1), II, 196.

58. With the engineers included in the "managerial" class, the proportion of independent entrepreneurs in that class is 20 per cent, and in the "technical" class, 5 per cent.

59. Beard, *Rise of American Civilization*, II, 196.

60. Walter Bagehot, *Economic Studies* (New York: Longmans, Green and Co., 1902; first ed., 1879), p. 28.

61. Bagehot, p. 61.

62. One of the earliest systematic books on the administration of the office is J. William Schulze, *The American Office* (New York: Key Publishing Co., 1913). The importance of office work in successful management was emphasized as early as the 1850's by Henry V. Poor (See "Henry Varnum Poor," by Alfred D. Chandler, Jr., chap. X of this book). Frederick W. Taylor put good office administration at the core of business success. See "Shop Management" (1903) in *Scientific Management*, as cited, especially pp. 61ff., and 121f.

63. B. C. Forbes, *Men Who Are Making America* (New York: B. C. Forbes Publishing Co., 1917), p. 391.

64. President's Letters, Burlington Archives, the Newberry Library, Chicago, Ill.

65. Casson, *Romance of Steel*, p. 304.

66. Peter F. Drucker, *Concept of the Corporation* (New York: John Day Co., 1946), p. 65. See also Drucker, *The New Society* (New York: Harper & Brothers, 1950), pp. 222ff.

67. *Business Week*, December 10, 1949, p. 34.

68. Barnard, *Functions of the Executive*, pp. 121, 225.

69. Sidney W. Martin, *Florida's Flagler* (Athens: University of Georgia Press, 1949), is largely devoted to this. See also Nevins, *Rockefeller*, II, 435.

70. Letter of Mellen's in files of James T. White and Co., November 23, 1912.

71. "Is Anybody Listening?", *Fortune* (September 1950), p. 178.

XII. American Historians and the Business Elite

By William Miller

1. One reason for this may be that the traditional framework and the traditional assumptions of American history writing preclude serious questions about personal aspirations and the patterns of ascent. This framework is the "presidential synthesis," and one of the key assumptions is equality of opportunity. On this theme see Thomas C. Cochran, "The 'Presidential Synthesis' in American History," *American Historical Review*, LIII (1948), 748–59. See also N. W. Stephenson, "Roosevelt and the Stratification of Society," *Scripps College Papers*, No. 3 (1930), esp. pp. 71–72.

2. The role of such social factors and of others to be considered here, such as education, nationality, and faith, in the selection of men even for training for high executive posts in modern corporations is brilliantly set forth by the former president of the New Jersey Bell Telephone Company, Chester I. Barnard, in his book, *The Functions of the Executive* (Cambridge: Harvard University Press, 1938). See also "The Thirty Thousand Managers," *Fortune*, February 1940.

3. Sociologists (and a few others in special fields) were the first to adapt to the analysis of elite recruitment in social terms quantitative methods evolved by statisticians and used initially in elite studies by eugenists. For the early literature, see J. McKeen Cattell, *American Men of Science* (2d ed.; New York: The Science Press, 1910), p. 537.

4. The first was published in 1940 by Edwards Brothers, Inc., Ann Arbor, Michigan; the second in 1947 by Hafner Publishing Co., New York.

5. The problem of defining "entrepreneurial" functions in modern business and of locating the actual "entrepreneurs" in modern corporate bureaucracies has been occupying economists and business historians for some years. Probably the best book on the subject, one rich in bibliography, is Robert A. Gordon's *Business Leadership in the Large Corporation* (Washington: The Brookings Institution, 1945). Also suggestive are the papers read at the 1946 meeting of the Economic History Association and collected in THE TASKS OF ECONOMIC HISTORY (Supplemental Issue of THE JOURNAL OF ECONOMIC HISTORY), Vol. VI (1946), and the papers and discussion at the 1948 meeting of the American Economic Association, published in the *American Economic Review* (1949), XXXIX, 322–55.

6. For a provocative explanation of why Redlich himself has not synthesized his findings, see his preface to *The Molding of American Banking*.

7. These are the major statistical studies. A few others discuss certain limited groups of business leaders or only one or two factors in the lives of national samples of the business elite. Of the first, one of the best, on New England railroad men in the later nineteenth century, is in Edward C. Kirkland, *Men, Cities and Transportation: A Study in New England History 1820–1900* (Cambridge: Harvard University Press, 1948), II, 452–79. Two examples of the second type are J. R. Shannon and Maxine Shaw, "Education of Business and Professional Leaders," *American Sociological Review*, V (1940), 381–83; Scott Nearing, "The Younger Generation of American Genius," *Scientific Monthly*, II (1916), 48–61. There are useful tables in Pitirim Sorokin, *Social Mobility* (New York: Harper & Brothers, 1927). A few tables appear in such inspirational books as B. C. Forbes, *Men Who Are Making America* (New York: B. C. Forbes Publishing Co., 1917), and B. C. Forbes, ed., *America's Fifty Foremost Business Leaders* (New York: B. C. Forbes & Sons Publishing Co., 1948). Popular but informative is "The Thirty Thousand Managers," *Fortune*, February 1940. Not designed as a study of business leaders but actually concerned with them in a social capacity is Hubert P. Beck, *Men Who Control Our Universities* (New York: King's Crown Press, 1947). An interesting study of English business leaders is Simon Haxey, *England's Money Lords, Tory M.P.* (New York: Harrison-Hilton Books, 1939). Useful statistical studies of leaders in other fields include Cortez A. M. Ewing, *The Judges of the Supreme Court 1789–1937* (Minneapolis: University of Minnesota Press, 1938); E. Pendleton Herring, *Federal Commissioners: a Study of Their Careers and Qualifications* (Cambridge: Harvard University Press, 1936); George H. Haynes, *The Senate of the United States, Its History and Practice* (Boston: Houghton Mifflin Co., 1938); C. Wright Mills, *The New Men of Power: America's Labor Leaders* (New York: Harcourt, Brace & Co., 1948); and

Edwin L. Clarke, *American Men of Letters: Their Nature and Nurture* (New York: Columbia University Press, 1916).

8. *The Journal of Social Forces,* III (1925), 627–40.

9. The Tasks of Economic History (Supplemental Issue of The Journal of Economic History), VI (1946), 28–49.

10. The Tasks of Economic History (Supplemental Issue of The Journal of Economic History), V (1945), 20–44.

11. New York: The Macmillan Co., 1932.

12. In extenuation it should be said that Destler's list makes his study more interesting than it would have been had he taken seriously the instructions to participants in the "program on entrepreneurial leadership" for which he wrote his paper. In a note (p. 29) he says: "In a circular memorandum sent in advance . . . to the contributors to the program . . . the suggestion was made that each select the 'typical entrepreneur' of his epoch and then analyze his career in reference to his personal life. . . ." No suggestion appears to have been made as to how such a "typical entrepreneur" could be selected without *first* making a study such as the one Destler made. He continues: "A cursory examination of the personalities and careers of the so-called 'robber barons' revealed that there was no one figure who might be regarded as typical of the group. Instead of the study of an individual career, therefore, an analysis of a relatively large group of 'robber barons' seemed called for if significant results were to be attained."

13. Mills was aware of this but concluded that the *DAB* nevertheless "forms a convenient point of departure for an over-all view of the social characteristics of eminent American businessmen" (p. 20). On this no one yet really can gainsay him; by using the *DAB* he naturally lost a number of the topmost business leaders, but any more objectively composed list would also have lost some. In my list, for example (see pp. 313–319), neither John D. Archbold nor Thomas F. Ryan appears; to have stretched a point to include them would have meant to distort the objective criteria by which the others were named or to alter those criteria in such ways that others would have fallen out. Not until a good deal more is known about the whole universe of American business leaders (for which a dictionary of such leaders would be an excellent starting point) or about commensurable parts of that universe can anyone say with precision how good or how bad the *DAB* is as a source of a representative sample of the business elite; and not until we can make samples that we have confidence in — as market researchers have confidence in national samples based on national censuses — will we be able easily and scientifically to extend and deepen our knowledge of that universe.

14. *The Journal of Political Economy,* XLII (1934), 404–6.

15. Taussig and Joslyn used mail questionnaires to get information from about 7,000 businessmen, selected in a thoroughly objective fashion from Poor's 1928 national *Register of Directors,* on the following points: age, age on first entering business, most important position now held, age on assuming this position, size of company, occupation of father and grandfather, education, assistance from relatives and friends. Mills used the *DAB* for both his names and his information and sought the following data for 1,464 business leaders born between 1570 and 1879: date of birth, region of birth and of "success" (objectively defined by him), social class of family, education, father's occupation, political activity.

16. Destler, "Entrepreneurial Leadership," The Tasks of Economic History (Supplemental Issue of The Journal of Economic History), VI (1946), 28.

17. See John Moody, *The Truth About the Trusts* (New York: Moody Publishing Co., 1904), pp. 453–76.

18. For a study of business bureaucrats it seemed reasonable to select the leaders from among those who held the topmost *positions* in the largest business companies. This was done without regard to the problem of getting biographical information on the men who happened to hold these positions. As it turned out, most of the information sought (approximately thirty questions to be answered for each of these men were put on a schedule, the answers then being coded and punched on Hollerith cards) could be obtained for all but a few of these men. Only a part of this information is analyzed in this essay.

To describe in detail the sources used for information would use up far too much of the space available here. Besides obvious sources such as individual biographies (of which only eighteen of these business leaders have been subjects), the *DAB* (which has essays on only fifty-six of these men), the *National Cyclopedia of American Biography* (a much more useful source than the *DAB* and often more accurate), and other encyclopedias, state and local histories, and diverse *Who's Who*'s, I consulted magazine articles, newspaper files, folders of clippings in morgues of newspapers and magazines, and carried on an extensive correspondence with business companies, historical societies, and relatives of men discussed here.

19. Of the seventy-four nonfinancial corporations represented by the men studied here, fifty-eight (under original or other names) are among Berle and Means' two hundred. Forty-five are among the two hundred (as of 1937) listed in Monograph 29, "The Distribution of Ownership in the 200 Largest Nonfinancial Corporations," of the TNEC *Investigation of Concentration of Economic Power* (Government Printing Office, 1940). See pp. 346–47.

20. Those in the first three fields were taken from Part VI of Moody's *The Truth About the Trusts*, published in 1904. Financial companies are not listed in Moody's book, hence they were taken from Moody's *Manual*, 1903. The leading investment-banking houses were named not on the basis of size but largely on that of testimony before the Pujo Committee, of which the following is a pertinent example: Louis Untermeyer questioning George F. Baker: "Will you be good enough to name a single transaction in the last 10 years of over $10,000,000 in amount which had been financed without the participation of Messrs. *Morgan & Co.*, or the City Bank, or *Kuhn, Loeb & Co.*, or *Speyer & Co.*, or *Lee, Higginson & Co.*, or *Kidder, Peabody & Co.*, of Boston, and the First National Bank and the Illinois Trust and Savings Bank, of Chicago?" Mr. Baker could not name one. See United States Congress, Committee on Banking and Currency, *Money Trust Investigation* (Government Printing Office, 1913), II, 1540. Men from all the banks named here are included in this study; those italicized are the five investment banking houses from which nine partners were selected.

21. Among the leading studies in this field are those already cited, by Gordon, Barnard, and Berle and Means.

22. Selection of the 188 political leaders is discussed in detail in *Yale Law Journal*, January 1951, 68 f. It is sufficient to state here that this number includes *all* the presidents, vice-presidents, cabinet members, and United States Supreme Court judges in the decade 1901–1910, these being 44 men plus 67 United States senators and 77 representatives. Twenty-three of the senators and 31 of the representatives held *all* the chairmanships in the 57th through the 61st Congresses of "major" committees in their respective houses, the list of committees being adapted from that in George H. Haynes, *The Senate of the United States*, II, 1059, and that in DeAlva Stanwood

Alexander, *History and Procedure of the House of Representatives* (Boston: Houghton Mifflin Co. 1916) pp. 399–410. The remaining 44 senators and 46 representatives held all the chairmanships of certain other committees designated "minor" but sometimes of major importance in channeling legislation. Of the total of 144 senators and representatives, only 14 were not members of some "major" committee.

23. The only exception is Bruce H. Ismay, an Englishman, who was president of the International Mercantile Marine Company beginning in 1904 and who served in this capacity abroad.

24. This information is based on listings for 85 men in the *Directory of Directors, City of New York,* 1909–1910; for 58 men, in similar directories issued during the decade 1901–1910; for 31 men, on other sources. Two thousand seven hundred and twenty directorships is a conservative figure; were the maximum number ever held by each of these men available, the total would be appreciably higher.

25. P. 129.

26. II, 172–73.

27. II, 134.

28. *Growth of the American People,* p. 129.

29. P. 168.

30. *Rise of American Civilization,* II, 173.

31. "The Thirty Thousand Managers," *Fortune,* February 1940, p. 61.

32. In fairness to the Beards it should be pointed out that they were aware of changes in the recruitment of business leaders by the turn of the century. They write: "By the end of the century the government of American railways and staple industries, with exceptions of course, had been lost by the men who had grown up in the roundhouses and the mills through all the technical processes. On the whole, the high command in the empire of business was now in the hands of great banking corporations, and captains of industry were as a rule no longer evolved by natural selection; they were chosen by the dominant bankers who served as financial guardians." — *Rise of American Civilization,* II, 196–97. Two things must be said about this statement. (1) After making it, the Beards say nothing more about the leaders selected under the new conditions; they name no men and make no comparisons with the older group discussed earlier in such detail. (2) Much more important, they fail to focus upon the lasting change that took place in the period of which they write. They say the new men no longer were selected from the plants. But whence, then, did they come? The Beards do not even raise this question. They do not, in fact, even establish that the older business leaders did rise from long years in "the roundhouses and the mills," and indeed it is more likely that, except for some in railroads, the older leaders started their own enterprises at early ages and rose *with* not *in* those enterprises. But whatever may be said of the older men, the majority of the *new* business leaders, along with hundreds of thousands of others who never rose out of the "ruck," did spend many years in the plant, or, in more instances, in the offices of their industries — for the problems of administration had already become complex enough to take an entire career to master. Bankers and other directors at the turn of the century did place "outsiders" at the head of companies they financed — after all, many of these were newly organized or reorganized companies into which the introduction of outsiders early in their history probably was necessary and expedient. No one, to my knowledge, has studied the business backgrounds of these outsiders. I suggest that they were frequently experienced in the industries if not the companies into which they were placed. But the lasting change was not the importation of outsiders by the bankers; it was the tendency to select

top bureaucrats from the hierarchy below. And the question of lasting social import is not whom did the bankers select from the outside but whom did the top bureaucrats select from the whole eager army of aspirants *within* the hierarchies to develop for, and finally install at, the top? Virtually all the candidates have been, in recent decades, so to speak, in business, often in *the* business. What then were the factors that differentiated the more from the less successful? If this was not the key question earlier in our history when business bureaucracies, in the main, were nonexistent, since the turn of the century it has been a question the answer to which has been of increasing social moment — a question, nevertheless, that most historians have not yet asked.

33. *Rise of American Civilization*, II, 181. The adjective "Barnumesque" is Allan Nevins'; see his *John D. Rockefeller, the Heroic Age of American Enterprise* (New York: Charles Scribner's Sons, 1940), I, 15–16. See also I, 39–40, for Nevins' discussion of the role of the business background in Rockefeller's life. See, too, John D. Rockefeller, *Random Reminiscences of Men and Events* (New York: Doubleday, Page & Co., 1909), p. 33.

34. Henry B. Parkes, *Recent America* (New York: Thomas Y. Crowell Co., 1945), p. 55. Heinze's father was a German immigrant.

35. Andrew Carnegie, *The Empire of Business* (New York: Doubleday, Page & Co., 1902), pp. 107–11.

36. The last quotation in this paragraph is from Ida M. Tarbell, *The Life of Elbert H. Gary* (New York: D. Appleton & Co., 1925), p. 20. The other quotations are from the *DAB*.

37. The average age of the 190 business leaders in 1905 was 54 years; of the political leaders, 57 years.

38. In his study of 1,464 businessmen born between 1570 and 1879, Mills found that 18.6 per cent had been foreign-born. He divided his men, by birth dates, into seven generations starting in the following years (in parentheses after each date is the proportion of foreign-born businessmen in the generation starting at that date): 1570 (78.4%), 1700 (28.3%) 1730 (28.1%), 1760 (22.3%), 1790 (10.2%), 1820 (17.5%), 1850 (10.9%). Thus, in each of these generations, except that born between 1790 and 1819, there was a greater percentage of foreign-born businessmen than in Mills' last generation, which is nearest to the period of the present study and in the group used in this study. (Mills, "The American Business Elite," THE TASKS OF ECONOMIC HISTORY (Supplemental Issue of THE JOURNAL OF EOCONOMIC HISTORY), V (1945), 22).

39. Defining "colonial" families as those settled in America before 1776.

40. Forbes, *Men Who Are Making America*, p. 232.

41. Henry Lee Higginson, senior partner in Lee, Higginson & Co. early in this century, once said: "If there were just one thing I could tell the boys of this country it would be to tell them to be expert in whatever they set out to do. This country sorely needs experts. There is a scarcity of experts and a great opportunity for the boy who wants to be of the greatest service." — Quoted from Samuel A. Eliot, *Biographical History of Massachusetts* (Boston: Massachusetts Biography Society, 1911–1918), Vol. IX (no pagination). Since Higginson spoke, this scarcity of experts in some lines has been so fully overcome that big corporations sometimes seem to be choked by them. The early business bureaucrats studied here, however, as a rule had no formal business or professional training. Those who went to college found few courses in business subjects when they were in attendance. About 9 per cent of the whole group attended secretarial, bookkeeping, or technical schools; 10 per cent had

formal engineering training; 16 per cent had legal educations. Sixty-five per cent had no formal vocational, business, or professional education.

42. Based on 180 business leaders about whom all three kinds of data are known.

43. An estimate based on data about the presidents and partners studied here showing elapsed working time indicates that 61 per cent of the middle- and lower-class, noncollege, early starters (before 19 years of age) spent *more* than thirty years at work before acquiring the position that made them eligible for this study while 66 per cent of the upper-class, college, late starters (19 years of age or older) spent *less* than thirty years.

XIII. The Recruitment of the American Business Elite

By William Miller

1. New York: Macmillan Co., 1932.

2. Two books published since this article was originally written merit attention: W. L. Warner and James Abegglen, *Occupational Mobility in American Business and Industry, 1928–1952* (University of Minnesota Press, 1955); and Mabel Newcomer, *The Big Business Executive* (Columbia University Press, 1955).

3. See *Economic Journal*, XLIII (September 1933), pp. 502–505. See also the review by Professor William F. Ogburn in the *Journal of Political Economy*, XLII (June 1934), pp. 404–406; and that by Professor F. B. Garver in the *American Economic Review*, XXIII (June 1933), pp. 278–280.

4. The period covered by this paper is the decade 1901–1910. A similar study for an earlier period, that of the 1870's, projected along comparative lines, will be found in Chapter VII of this Torchbook edition.

5. William Miller, "American Historians and the Business Elite," *Journal of Economic History*, IX (November 1949), pp. 184–208, and reprinted in the Appendix to this Torchbook edition. This paper contains a detailed discussion of the statistical literature on the social origins and careers of American business leaders. See pp. 310–311.

6. These quotations, representative of others to be found in similar books, are from Samuel E. Morison and Henry S. Commager, *The Growth of the American Republic* (2 Volumes, New York: Oxford University Press, 1942), II, 134; and Arthur M. Schlesinger, *The Political and Social Growth of the American People* (New York: Macmillan Co., 1941), p. 129.

7. A full discussion of the method used in selecting these 190 business leaders and their companies appears on pp. 312–13 above. See pp. 313–319 for a list of the men and companies. Here it is sufficient to point out that each of these men was either president or chairman in the decade 1901–1910 of at least one of the largest American corporations in the following fields (the number in parentheses after each is the number of men selected from each field): manufacturing and mining (64), railroads (58), public utilities (31), and finance (commercial banking 19, and life insurance 9), or was a partner (9) in one of the five leading unincorporated investment banking houses. Except for these partners, all of these men were office holders; many of them never started a business of their own. On this account alone they may be described as America's first big business bureaucrats. That they were of great influence not only in their companies but in the business community generally is

suggested by the following statistics on their business directorships. The 174 men about whom this information is available held approximately 2,720 directorships; a few held more than 100 each; the average was about 16.

8. A collection of examples of leading businessmen of two generations who have resorted to the stereotypes and slogans of self help may be found in B. C. Forbes, *Men Who Are Making America* (New York: B. C. Forbes Publishing Co., 1917), and B. C. Forbes, ed., *America's Fifty Foremost Business Leaders* (New York: B. C. Forbes and Sons Publishing Co., 1948). For interesting comment on some of the motivations for such slogans and stereotypes, see Thomas C. Cochran, "Role and Sanction in American Entrepreneurial History," in *Change and the Entrepreneur* (Cambridge: Harvard University Press, 1949), pp. 167–168.

9. Harvey O'Connor, *The Guggenheims* (New York: Covici-Friede, 1937), p. 169. For more than thirty years, including the period of this essay, Daniel was the head of the Guggenheim family and of the family enterprises.

10. The most readily accessible statistics on this subject are in Warren S. Thompson and P. K. Whelpton, *Population Trends in the United States* (New York: McGraw-Hill Book Co., 1933). See especially table 28, pp. 96–98.

11. To have augmented this group appreciably, however, would have made it less representative of the topmost business leadership. If, for example, more men in my group had been taken from life insurance companies or from certain industrial lines, such men would have had to come from companies much smaller than those now used exclusively or from lower status jobs in the large firms. In either case, less highly influential men would have mingled with the national elite.

12. Only one of these Jews was an industrialist, the others were primarily private bankers and financiers.

13. It is interesting to note that five of these six Jews were also of German origin (the sixth was a Swiss). Including them, there are nineteen men of German origin among the business leaders studied here. Forty-seven per cent of these German-originated men (compared to only 14 per cent of the rest of these business leaders) attained their peak jobs in firms previously owned or managed by Germans. Excluding the German Jews, this figure becomes 21 per cent.

14. The writings of Chester I. Barnard, the former president of the New Jersey Bell Telephone Company, are very illuminating on this theme. In *The Functions of the Executive* (Cambridge: Harvard University Press, 1938) and in various papers collected in *Organization and Management* (Cambridge: Harvard University Press, 1948), he develops fully and with a high degree of abstractness the thesis of the apparent desirability (if not actual inevitability) of what may be termed social solidarity in bureaucratic management, or social uniformity in the managerial elite— and the role this plays in society in general. See especially "Functions and Pathology of Status Systems in Formal Organizations," in *Organization and Management* (pp. 210–211). See also Chapters IX and XV in *The Functions of the Executive*.

Highly pertinent to this theme is "The Thirty Thousand Managers," *Fortune,* February 1940, especially p. 62. See also Thurman W. Arnold, *The Folklore of Capitalism* (New Haven: Yale University Press, 1937), Chapter XIV.

15. It may be noted, furthermore, that the proportion of foreign-born in this segment of the general population was almost certainly even higher than this in those regions and especially in those cities in which most of the business elite originated. For regional and city-size distributions, see Tables III and IV, below.

16. The percentage for the business elite is based on fathers' birthplaces, but few, if any, with native-born fathers had foreign-born mothers. This is also true of the

population generally. Census data is from the *Twelfth Census of the United States, 1900,* Part II, vol. II, pp. xxxviii–xxxix.

Among 40-year-old white males in 1890, it may be noted, the foreign-born were 35 per cent, those with foreign or mixed parentage 45.3 per cent, almost identical with the proportions for the 50-year-olds in 1900. (See *Eleventh Census of the United States, 1890,* Part II, pp. 2–5.)

17. Seventy-two per cent of the business elite had American-born grandfathers or still more distant ancestors; 56 per cent, a far greater proportion than was possible for the population generally, traced the American settlement of their paternal lines to the seventeenth century. (See William Miller, "American Historians and the Business Elite," p. 323 above; cf. Edward C. Kirkland, *Men, Cities, and Transportation* (2 volumes, Cambridge: Harvard University Press, 1948), II, pp. 467–468.

18. These were computed for use in administering the "quota" immigration act of 1924. See Thompson and Whelpton, *op. cit.,* Chapter III; Roy L. Garis, *Immigration Restriction* (New York: Macmillan Co., 1927) *passim.*

19. Besides their general commercial and financial atmosphere, these sections, and especially the larger cities in them, afforded such added advantages as more and better schools, and proximity to the great and growing business bureaucracies themselves.

20. More than one-third of the elite born in rural areas, moreover, were sons of men who, if they farmed at all, were also in some other kind of business when these sons were born and raised.

21. Theoretically, of course, men from urban working class families would have had similar geographical backgrounds, but very few such men are found in the group being studied here. See Table 5.

22. Some fathers of these businessmen, of course, engaged in more than one occupation. Where this was true, the occupation counted appeared to have been the major one at the time the son was raised. In the few instances where this was ambiguous, a choice was made by which business (including higher managerial positions as well as ownership) took precedence over farming, and professional over both. This conforms roughly to the ascending order of status used in classifying occupations today. In no instance was there a problem in classifying the few fathers counted here as workers. (On the problems involved in such classifications, even where the original data are superior to those in the older censuses, see Dewey Anderson and Percey E. Davidson, *Occupational Trends in the United States* (Stanford University Press, 1940), pp. 40 ff.)

23. The problem of describing the class structure of the American population around the middle of the nineteenth century, when most of these business leaders were born and raised, is exceedingly complex. It is only less difficult to rank by class special groups in the population such as the fathers or families of these businessmen. This I undertook to do with care in my earlier paper (see "American Historians and the Business Elite," p. 326 above) where criteria for class allocations are fully described. Figures presented there show that 50 per cent of these business leaders were of upper class, 45 per cent of middle class, and only 5 per cent of lower class, origins. However class data on the whole population are arranged, they must surely present a picture quite the reverse of this. On the class structure of the population in the period under discussion, see especially Edgar W. Martin, *The Standard of Living in 1860* (Chicago: University of Chicago Press, 1942), and the bibliographical references there; Rufus S. Tucker, "The Distribution of Income Among Income Taxpayers in the United States, 1863–1895," *The Quarterly Journal of Economics,* LII (August

1938), pp. 547–587; and Lewis Corey, *The Decline of American Capitalism* (New York: Covici-Friede, 1934).

24. Thirty-five per cent of these men first went to work between the ages of 16 and 18; 45 per cent delayed their business start until they were 19 or older.

25. Cf. Edgar W. Martin, *op. cit.*, p. 297; Newton Edwards and Herman G. Richey, *The School in The American Social Order* (Boston: Houghton Mifflin Co., 1947), p. 423.

26. *Report of the Commissioner of Education for the Year 1872* (Washington, D. C., Government Printing Office, 1873), pp. 946–947; 964–965. Cf. Charles F. Thwing, *The American College: What It Is and What It May Become* (New York,' Platt and Peck Co., 1914), p. 283; and Charles F. Thwing, *College Training and the Business Man* (New York, D. Appleton and Co., 1904) *passim*.

ROCKMONT COLLEGE LIBRARY.